Studies in International Law of the Sea and Maritime Law
Internationales Seerecht und Seehandelsrecht

Herausgegeben von | Edited by

Prof. Dr. Doris König
Prof. Dr. Nele Matz-Lück
Prof. Dr. Alexander Proelß
Prof. Dr. Wolfgang Wurmnest

Band 20 | Volume 20

Nina Tavakkoli

Regulatory Challenges of Ship-Source Pollution

Where EU Legislation Meets International Law

Nomos

The Deutsche Nationalbibliothek lists this publication in the Deutsche Nationalbibliografie; detailed bibliographic data are available on the Internet at http://dnb.d-nb.de

a.t.: Hamburg, Univ., Diss., 2025

Original title: “Regulatory Challenges of Ship-Source Pollution: Where EU Legislation Meets International Law”

ISBN 978-3-7560-3294-5 (Print)
ISBN 978-3-7489-6070-6 (ePDF)

Onlineversion
Nomos eLibrary

1st Edition 2025

Acknowledgments

I am deeply grateful to my doctoral supervisor, Prof. Dr. Markus Kotzur, for believing in this project and granting me the chance to pursue it under his guidance. Prof. Kotzur's willingness to always make time for me, his attentive listening and his ability to offer precisely the right advice helped me refocus whenever needed. With his instructive feedback and sincere encouragement, he always left me better than he found me.

I also wish to express my gratitude to Prof. Dr. Alexander Proelss, who served as the second reviewer. I appreciate his feedback and insights upon reading my study. As a leading authority in maritime environmental law and the law of the sea, Prof. Proelss's commendation of my research and its contribution holds great personal and academic significance to me.

Finally, I am profoundly indebted to my family, who during this process had to do without me at times. To my parents, whose unwavering support and faith in me have been fundamental. This study would not have been possible without their encouragement and sacrifices. I am also grateful to my husband, whose continuous support, advice and trust in me and this endeavour have been invaluable. Above all, this is dedicated to my children. Thank you for the love, the laughter and the lessons.

Table of Contents

List of Abbreviations

Abbreviation	*Meaning*
AG	Advocate General
BC	Basel Convention on the Control of Transboundary Movements of Hazardous Wastes and their Disposal
CBDR	Common but differentiated responsibilities
CDEM	Construction, Design, Equipment or Manning
CIEL	Center for International Environmental Law
COP	Conference of Parties
CO_2	Carbon dioxide
DCS	Data Collection System for Fuel Oil Consumption of Ships
DWT	Deadweight tonnage
EC	European Community
ECJ	Court of Justice of the European Union
EEA	European Environment Agency
EEC	European Economic Community
EEDI	Energy Efficiency Design Index
EEOI	Energy Efficiency Operational Indicator
EESC	European Economic and Social Committee
EEXI	Energy Efficiency Existing Ship Index
EEZ	Exclusive Economic Zone
EGCS	Exhaust gas cleaning systems
EGCSA	Exhaust Gas Cleaning Systems Association
EMSA	European Maritime Safety Agency
ETS	Emission trading scheme
EP	European Parliament
EU	European Union
GAIRS	Generally accepted international rules and standards
GATT	General Agreement on Tariffs and Trade 1994
GATS	General Agreement on Trade in Services

GHG	Greenhouse gas(es)
GT	Gross tonnage
Gt	Gigatonnes
HELCOM	Baltic Marine Environment Protection Commission
HFO	Heavy fuel oil
HKC	The Hong Kong International Convention for the Safe and Environmentally Sound Recycling of Ships
ICAO	International Civil Aviation Organization
ICCT	The International Council on Clean Transportation
ICJ	International Court of Justice
IEA	International Energy Agency
IHM	Inventory of Hazardous Materials
ILC	International Law Commission
ILO	International Labour Organization
IMCO	Inter-Governmental Maritime Consultative Organization
IMO	International Maritime Organization
IPCC	Intergovernmental Panel on Climate Change
ITF	International Transport Forum
ITLOS	International Tribunal for the Law of the Sea
LDT	Light displacement tonnes
LNG	Liquefied natural gas
MARPOL	International Convention for the Prevention of Pollution from Ships, 1973, as modified by the Protocol of 1978
MBM	Market-based measure
MEPC	Marine Environment Protection Committee
MFN	Most-favoured-nation
MGO	Marine gas oil
MRV-Regulation	Regulation (EU) 2015/757 of the European Parliament and of the Council of 29 April 2015 on the monitoring, reporting and verification of carbon dioxide emissions from maritime transport, and amending Directive 2009/16/EC
MS	Member State
NGO	Non-governmental organisation
NMFT	No more favourable treatment

OCIMF	Oil Companies International Marine Forum
OECD	Organisation for Economic Co-operation and Development
PCIJ	Permanent Court of International Justice
PSC	Port State Control
Reg	Regulation
REIO	Regional Economic Integration Organization
RO	Recognized Organization
SBSTA	Subsidiary Body for Scientific and Technological Advice
SECA	Sulphur Emission Control Area
SEEMP	Ship Energy Efficiency Management Plan
SO_x	Sulphur oxides
SRR	Regulation (EU) No 1257/2013 of the European Parliament and of the Council of 20 November 2013 on Ship Recycling and Amending Regulation (EC) No 1013/2006 and Directive 2009/16/EC
TEC	Treaty establishing the European Community
TEU	Treaty on European Union
TFEU	Treaty on the Functioning of the European Union
UN	United Nations
UNEP	United Nation Environment Programme
UNCLOS	United Nations Convention on the Law of the Sea
UNCTAD	United Nations Conference on Trade and Development
UNFCCC	United Nations Framework Convention on Climate Change
UNGA	United Nation General Assembly
VCLT	Vienna Convention on the Law of Treaties
WSR	Regulation (EC) No 1013/2006 of the European Parliament and of the Council of 14 June 2006 on shipments of waste
WTO	World Trade Organization
% m/m	Mass percent

A. Introduction

Shipping is notorious for its environmental and climate impact. Its record of pollution is long: the use of heavy fuel oil (HFO)—the standard fuel in shipping[1]—is responsible for emissions in carbon dioxide (CO_2), nitrogen oxides, sulphur oxides, particulate matter[2] and volatile organic compounds. One of the latter, methane, has gained more significance in international shipping[3] recently due to the increased use of liquified natural gas (LNG) as an alternative ship fuel.[4] Additionally, there is potential pollution from

1 The International Maritime Organization's (IMO's) Fourth Greenhouse Gas Study 2020 finds HFO to still be 'the dominant fuel in international shipping (79% of total fuel consumption by energy content in 2018, by voyage-based allocation)', Jasper Faber and others, *Fourth IMO GHG Study 2020* (IMO 2020) <https://wwwcdn.imo.org/localresources/en/OurWork/Environment/Documents/Fourth%20IMO%20GHG%20Study%202020%20-%20Full%20report%20and%20annexes.pdf> accessed 6 February 2023, 91; The International Energy Agency (IEA) asserts that in 2019 HFO accounted for 180 of 221 million tonnes of fuel used by maritime shipping, see IEA, *Energy Technology Perspectives 2020* (Revised version February 2021) <https://iea.blob.core.windows.net/assets/7f8aed40-89af-4348-be19-c8a67df0b9ea/Energy_Technology_Perspectives_2020_PDF.pdf> accessed 31 March 2023, 271.

2 On the composition of particulate matter, see Kent Salo and others, 'Emissions to the Air' in Karin Andersson and others (eds), *Shipping and the Environment: Improving Environmental Performance in Marine Transportation* (Springer 2016) 169, 206; see also 202–03 for a quick overview on the distinctions between *black carbon, organic carbon, elemental carbon* and *soot.*

3 The IMO defines *International Shipping* as 'Shipping between ports of different countries, as opposed to *domestic shipping.* International shipping excludes military and fishing vessels. By this definition, the same ship may frequently be engaged in both international and domestic shipping operations', Øyvind Buhaug and others, *Second IMO GHG Study 2009* (IMO 2009) <https://wwwcdn.imo.org/localresources/en/OurWork/Environment/Documents/SecondIMOGHGStudy2009.pdf> accessed 6 February 2023, xiii.

4 Faber and others, *Fourth IMO GHG Study 2020* (n 1) 100. See also The International Council on Clean Transportation calling for the IMO to regulate shipping's methane emissions: ICCT, 'New IMO Study Highlights Sharp Rise in Short-Lived Climate Pollution' (Press Release, 4 August 2020) <https://theicct.org/news/fourth-imo-ghg-study-finalreport-pr-20200804> accessed 6 February 2023. On the trade-off between carbon dioxide reduction and methane increase through LNG, see Salo and others (n 2) 180: 'The lower carbon content of LNG compared with common marine fuels, such as HFO, MGO [marine gas oil] and MDO [marine diesel oil], leads to reduced carbon dioxide [...] emissions by 20–25%. However, possible spills and slippage of

discharge (accidental or not) or leakage of oil and chemicals (eg from cargo or hull paint), sewage[5] or grey water[6] as well as (household) waste. Noise pollution and the entry of alien species through ballast water can also affect the balance of ecosystems.[7] On top of that, once a ship is considered waste, its treatment brings with it its own problems.[8]

In this context, while the term *marine environmental protection* refers to the protection of the oceans regardless of its source, the term *maritime environmental protection* refers to the protection of the environment from the effects of ship-source pollution specifically.[9] Nonetheless, ship-source pollution will almost always, directly or indirectly, affect the marine environment as well.[10] While it is obvious that the discharge of oil or sewage causes direct pollution to the marine environment, pollution of the air with sulphur oxides or emissions of carbon dioxide indirectly affect the marine environment as well.[11]

---

methane (CH_4) during the handling and combustion of LNG could increase the shipping-related contributions of GHGs because CH_4 is a potent GHG [greenhouse gas] […] with a GWP [global warming potential] that is more than 20 times higher than that of CO_2.'

5 Defined by Reg 1.3 MARPOL Annex IV, sometimes (partly) referred to as black water. On MARPOL, see section I.2.

6 Defined by the IMO as 'drainage from dishwater, galley sink, shower, laundry, bath and washbasin drains', IMO, Res MEPC.227(64) 2012 adopted on 5 October 2012, MEPC 64/23/Add.1, Annex 22, para 2.7.

7 For a graphic overview of the *Environmental impacts of marine transportation during the use of a vessel*, see Karin Andersson and others, 'Shipping and the Environment' in Andersson and others (eds), *Shipping and the Environment: Improving Environmental Performance in Marine Transportation* (n 2) 3, 17.

8 Salo and others (n 2) 181 also mention halogenated hydrocarbons used as refrigerants as a shipping pollutant for its ozone-depleting effects; for a detailed discussion, see 213–18.

9 This is in line with the meaning of *marine* and *maritime* found in the Oxford English Dictionary. There, *marine* is defined as '[o]f, relating to or characteristic of the sea; existing, originating, or found in the sea', while *maritime* is defined as '[c]onnected, associated, or dealing with shipping, naval matters, navigation, seaborne trade, etc.', Oxford English Dictionary, 'marine, n & adj' (September 2023) <https://www.oed.com/search/dictionary/?q=marine> accessed 2 October 2023 and Oxford English Dictionary, 'maritime, adj & n' (September 2023) <https://www.oed.com/search/dictionary/?q=maritime> accessed 2 October 2023.

10 One exception that comes to mind is where end-of-life ships are disposed of in an environmentally sound manner, namely in a setting where materials or substances do not enter the marine environment.

11 Both cause acidification (see section D.I. for sulphur oxides) with carbon dioxide being the primary driver of ocean acidification, see United Nations, *The Second World Ocean Assessment, Volume I* <https://www.un.org/regularprocess/sites/www.

On the other hand, the significance of maritime shipping for international trade and the world economy, as well as our dependency on it, is undeniable.[12] International shipping carries over 80% of the world trade by volume—roughly 12 billion tons in 2022.[13] Thus, maritime transport is also called the 'life blood of world trade'.[14] This means that any measure to improve shipping's environmental impact will almost inevitably translate into higher costs for the industry and may affect the global market. At the same time, international shipping's capacity to move these vast amounts of goods, makes shipping—as often cited—the most carbon-efficient mode of transport available,[15] awarding it an unrivalled position. Maybe for that reason, too, some significant measures to protect the environment from the consequences of shipping were only implemented in the aftermaths of shipping accidents, such as the *Exxon Valdez*, *Erika* and *Prestige* oil-spills (in 1989, 1999 and 2002, respectively), that caused environmental disasters and drew public attention.[16]

---

un.org.regularprocess/files/2011859-e-woa-ii-vol-i.pdf> accessed 5 May 2023, 86, 118 (footnote 3). For better readability, hereafter, the term *environment* or *environmental* used in the general discussion implies the climate effects of ship-source pollution as well.

12 The IEA (n 1) 271 considers shipping to be the 'least energy-intensive way to carry goods'. The European Commission also points to shipping as a 'key sector for the EU economy', see Commission, 'Integrating maritime transport emissions in the EU's greenhouse gas reduction policy', COM (2013) 479 final, 3.

13 United Nations Conference on Trade and Development, *Review of Maritime Transport 2023* <https://unctad.org/system/files/official-document/rmt2023_en.pdf> accessed 27 October 2023, 3, 55.

14 World Trade Organization, 'Maritime Transport' <https://www.wto.org/english/tratop_e/serv_e/transport_e/transport_maritime_e.htm> accessed 27 March 2023.

15 See eg IEA, *Energy Technology Perspectives 2017: Catalysing Energy Technology Transformations* <https://iea.blob.core.windows.net/assets/a6587f9f-e56c-4b1d-96e4-5a4da78f12fa/Energy_Technology_Perspectives_2017-PDF.pdf> accessed 5 May 2023, 88. It is noteworthy that the Fourth IMO GHG Study (n 1) 125 finds a continuing general trend towards the total fleet becoming more energy efficient.

16 See also Wang Hui, 'The EU Marine Oil Pollution Prevention Regime – Recent Developments', (2004) 13 EELR 292, 293, referring to the *Amoco Cadiz* oil spill as one disaster that initiated action by the European Community (EC) in 1978. For details on the *Erika*, *Prestige* and *Tasman Spirit* oil spills, see Olagunju G Anthony, 'Criminalization of Seafarers for Accidental Discharge of Oil: Is there Justification in International Law for Criminal Sanction for Negligent or Accidental Pollution of the Sea?' (2006) 37 J Mar L & Com 219, 220–22. For a detailed account of the *Prestige* incident, see also Veronica Frank, 'Consequences of the Prestige Sinking for European and International Law' (2005) 20 Int'l J Marine & Coastal L 1, 2–3. The most significant improvement was the introduction of the double-hull design

While '[i]n the international community it has long been agreed that the maritime industry should be governed by uniform international laws and regulations'[17], the European Union (EU) has been one of the advocates for stricter regulation of ships and has not shied away from passing its own legislation where it deemed international processes too slow or standards too low. In this, it is ambitious, despite its own commercial interests[18] and the fact that in 2019 it represented only 36.4% of the world fleet[19]. Notably, it took extensive action in response to the abovementioned *Erika* and *Prestige* accidents and demonstrated its impatience with international decision-making.[20] The so-called Erika I and II (legislative) packages[21] for

---

requirement—for an elaborate account of the regulatory progress in the aftermaths of the *Exxon Valdez, Erika* and *Prestige*, see Alan Khee-Jin Tan, *Vessel-Source Marine Pollution: The Law and Politics of International Regulation* (Cambridge University Press 2006), 139–55. See also the European Commission pointing out that '[h]istorically, less attention was given to address maritime emissions sources compared to land-based sources', Commission, 'Proposal for a Directive of the European Parliament and of the Council amending Directive 1999/32/EC as regards the sulphur content of marine fuels', COM (2011) 439 final, 1.

17 Colin de la Rue, 'Pollution from Ships: EU Directive on Criminal Sanctions for Ship-source Pollution' in D Rhidian Thomas (ed) *Liability Regimes in Contemporary Maritime Law* (Informa Law from Routledge 2007) para 2.8.

18 In 2022, 3.5 billion tonnes of freight were handled in EU ports, see Eurostat, 'Maritime freight and vessel statistics' <https://ec.europa.eu/eurostat/statistics-explained/index.php?title=Maritime_freight_and_vessels_statistics> accessed 7 December 2023; in the same year, 74% of the goods traded between the EU and the rest of the world by volume were transported by sea, accounting for 48% by value, see EUROSTAT, 'International trade in goods by mode of transport' <https://ec.europa.eu/eurostat/statistics-explained/index.php?title=International_trade_in_goods_by_mode_of_transport> accessed 7 December 2023.

19 This is in terms of ownership, ie owners registered in EU Member States, and as a share of global deadweight tonnage (DWT, in simple terms usually referred to as a ship's weight carrying capacity), European Environment Agency/European Maritime Safety Agency, *European Maritime Transport Environmental Report 2021* (Publications Office of the European Union 2021) 27.

20 See Nengye Liu and Frank Maes, 'The European Union's Role in the Prevention of Vessel-Source Pollution and its Internal Influence' (2009) 15 JIML 411, 413, who attest to the EU's 'visible political shift [...] to be more proactive and responsible for the protection of the marine environment rather than waiting for consensus in international decision making by the IMO.'; see also Henrik Ringbom, *The EU Maritime Safety Policy and International Law* (Martinus Nijhoff Publishers 2008), 43–44 who asserts that 'following the *Erika* [incidence] there was, for the first time, an acceptance, and even an expectation, that the principle political response to the accident would be made at an EU level. Very strong demands were accordingly made by civil society, national parliaments and the EU's own institutions alike, for the EU to introduce stricter safety rules for oil tankers and these demands were perhaps

example, often cited in this context, sped up the phasing out of single hull tankers, strengthened Port State Control[22] and established the European Maritime Safety Agency (EMSA).[23]

This study focuses on what happens when a regional organisation as powerful as the EU regulates an area as inherently global as international shipping that has its own long-standing system of (regulatory) processes and relevant actors. By means of three case studies that represent three different constellations, this study explores how EU environmental regulation of international shipping affects the industry, international negotiations and treaty-making, acting as a catalyst and a disruptor at the same time. It also demonstrates that EU legislation in this field risks conflicts with international law if not carefully implemented. What is more, the EU itself is reluctant to take a firm stance on questions of compatibility with international law and, thereby, misses its chance to contribute to the evolution of international law. With this, it fails to claim its status as an actor on the international plane and in the context of international law and policy. Thus ironically, while it is attempting to be a normative power[24] in strengthening

---

unusually well-received by the Commission at that particular time.' See also André Nollkaemper and Ellen Hey, 'Implementation of the LOS Convention at Regional Level: European Community Competence in Regulating Safety and Environmental Aspects of Shipping' (1995) 10 Int'l J Marine & Coastal L 281, 282, who find: 'Community policy in the area of the safety and environmental aspects of shipping activities [...] seems to be moving from a policy aimed solely at strengthening the implementation of existing international regulations to one also aimed at the development of autonomous Community law on the subject.'

21 Based on Commission, 'Communication from the Commission to the European Parliament and the Council on the Safety of the Seaborne Oil Trade' COM (2000) 142 final and 'Communication from the Commission to the European Parliament and the Council on a Second Set of Community Measures on Maritime Safety Following the Sinking of the Oil Tanker ERIKA' COM (2000) 802 final.

22 On Port State Control, see section 3.b.

23 For an overview of measures, see Hui (n 16) 292ff.

24 The concept of the EU as a *normative power*, ie a *Normative Power Europe*, with the 'ability to shape conceptions of "normal" in international relations' was introduced in 2002 by Ian Manners, 'Normative Power Europe: A Contradiction in Terms?' (2002) 40 J Common Mkt Stud 235, 239. The term *normative power* is used here based on this understanding and notwithstanding the conceptual discussions surrounding this term that have taken place since. In short, '[t]he normative power concept neatly captures a prominent identity discourse at the EU level, but as an analytical concept it nonetheless suffers from a lack of clarity', Marika Lerch and Guido Schwellnus, 'Normative by Nature? The role of coherence in justifying the EU's external human rights policy' (2006) 13 J Eur Public Policy 304, 305. For an overview of discussions, see Tuomas Forsberg, 'Normative Power Europe, Once Again: A Conceptual Analysis

environmental protection from international shipping, it neglects its potential as a normative power in the field of international law. This in turn ultimately weakens its overall status as a normative power and global actor.

I. The System of International Shipping

This section sets the scene for the analysis in chapters two through four. It presents the necessary background information on the designated international organisation for matters of international shipping, namely the International Maritime Organization, and its work (I.1.), the single most important treaty for the protection of the environment from ship-source pollution (I.2.), as well as on the relevant actors involved in international shipping (I.3. and 4.).

1. The International Maritime Organization (IMO)

The International Maritime Organization (IMO) headquartered in London, UK, is the United Nations (UN) agency and regulatory body for the safety and security of shipping, as well as for the prevention of marine and atmospheric pollution from ships.[25] Its founding treaty was adopted in 1948[26], entered into force in 1958, and brought into being the Inter-Governmental Maritime Consultative Organization (IMCO). It was renamed to become the IMO in 1982.[27] The IMO consists of the Assembly and the

---

of an Ideal Type' (2011) 49 J Common Mkt Stud 1183, who finds: 'The idea of "Normative Power Europe" is popular, but also confusing. Its appeal must be balanced against the frequent criticisms of NPE [Normative Power Europe] as an analytically poor and politically loaded concept. A good deal of the problems stem from the multiple meanings for the key concepts of "normative" and "power"', 1198–99.

25 The IMO also serves as the secretariat for the treaties concluded under its auspices.

26 For more on the Geneva conference of 1948, see IMO, 'Convention on the International Maritime Organization' <https://www.imo.org/en/About/Conventions/Pages/Convention-on-the-International-Maritime-Organization.aspx> accessed 12 May 2023.

27 For an overview on its history and work, see the IMO's brochure 'IMO—What it is' <https://wwwcdn.imo.org/localresources/en/About/Documents/What%20it%20is%20Oct%202013_Web.pdf> accessed 12 May 2023. The Convention on the Intergovernmental Maritime Consultative Organization was accordingly re-named the Convention on the International Maritime Organization effective as of 22 May 1982, see also n 30.

Council, while the regulatory work takes places in the five main committees that are supported by several sub-committees on technical matters. The committee in charge of the prevention and control of pollution from ships is the Marine Environment Protection Committee (MEPC)[28] that convenes roughly every 18 months. At time of writing in 2023, the IMO has 175 State Members and 3 Associate Members, while 66 intergovernmental organisations hold observer status and 88 international non-governmental organisations (NGOs) enjoy a consultative status.[29] Art 5 of the IMO Convention[30] only allows States to become members of the IMO and does not provide for a so-called Regional Economic Integration Organization (REIO) clause that would allow the EU to become a member[31] (neither do

---

28 The other four main committees are the Maritime Safety Committee, the Legal Committee, the Technical Cooperation Committee, and the Facilitation Committee.

29 For more information, see IMO, 'Member States, IGOs and NGOs' <https://www.imo.org/en/About/Membership/Pages/Default.aspx> accessed 12 May 2023. IMO Assembly Res A.1168(32) adopted on 15 December 2021, A 32/Res.1168, formalised the relation between the IMO and intergovernmental organizations.

30 Convention of the International Maritime Organization (adopted 6 March 1948, entered into force 17 March 1958) 289 UNTS 3. The IMO Convention was subsequently subject to the following amendments: Amendments to article 17 and 18 of the Convention on the International Maritime Organization (adopted 15 September 1964, entered into force 6 October 1967) 607 UNTS 276; Amendment to article 28 of the Convention on the International Maritime Organization (adopted 28 September 1965, entered into force 3 November 1968) 649 UNTS 335; Amendments to articles 10, 16, 17, 18, 20, 28, 31 and 32 of the Convention on the International Maritime Organization (adopted 17 October 1974, entered into force on 1 April 1978) 1080 UNTS 375; Amendments to the title and substantive provisions of the Convention on the International Maritime Organization (adopted 14 November 1975 and 9 November 1977, entered into force 22 May 1982, except for the amendment to Article 51, which entered into force on 28 July 1982) 1276 UNTS 468 and 1285 UNTS 318; Amendments to the Convention on the International Maritime Organization relating to the institutionalization of the Committee on Technical Co-operation in the Convention (adopted 17 November 1977, entered into force 10 November 1984) 1380 UNTS 268; Amendments to articles 17, 18, 20 and 51 of the Convention on the International Maritime Organization (adopted 15 November 1979, entered into force 10 November 1984) 1380 UNTS 288; Amendments to the Convention on the International Maritime Organization (institutionalization of the Facilitation Committee) (adopted 7 November 1991, entered into force 7 December 2008); Amendments to the Convention on the International Maritime Organization (adopted 4 November 1993, entered into force 7 November 2002) 2199 UNTS 113; Amendments to the Convention on the International Maritime Organization (London, 8 December 2021), adopted by IMO Assembly Res A.1152 (32) of 8 December 2021 (not yet in force).

31 On the REIO clause and EU Membership in International Organisations in general, see Rachel Frid de Vries, 'European Union, Membership in International Organiza-

the vast the majority of IMO treaties, for that matter[32]). Thus, the EU holds no official status within the IMO. The European Commission (hereafter the Commission) has been representing the EU as an observer since 1974, being officially limited to providing information and advice with no right to vote.[33]

The influence the Commission exercises within the IMO through its Member States (MSs) should not be underestimated, however. In addition to the possibility of informal coordination of MSs' positions of negotiation, Art 218 (9) TFEU[34] is considered to pave the way for a joint position of the MSs 'to be adopted on the Union's behalf in a body set up by an agreement'. While there is no compelling case for that interpretation, the Court of Justice of the European Union (ECJ) deems Art 218 (9) TFEU to be applicable where the EU itself is not a member of that organisation.[35] What is more, it considers the provision applicable where the subject matter at hand lies within the area of shared competences and the EU has not exercised its competences internally. The Court claims that 'the existence of an external EU competence is not, in any event, dependent on the prior exercise, by the Union, of its internal legislative competence

---

tion or Institutions' (last updated July 2019) in Anne Peters and Rüdiger Wolfrum (eds), *The Max Planck Encyclopedia of Public International Law* (OUP 2008) <https://opil-1ouplaw-1com-100b98fpw031a.emedien3.sub.uni-hamburg.de/display/10.1093/law:epil/9780199231690/law-9780199231690-e627?rskey=tT9jfr&result=1&prd=OPIL> accessed 12 May 2023, para 8.

32 One exception is the Protocol of 2002 to the Athens Convention relating to the Carriage of Passengers and their Luggage by Sea, 1974 (adopted 1 November 2002, entered into force 23 April 2014) Registration No 24817, UNTS volume number determined 3283 (see its Art 19).

33 On EU membership in international institutions in general, see also Thomas Gehring, Sebastian Oberthur and Marc Muhleck, 'European Union Actorness in International Institutions: Why the EU Is Recognized as an Actor in Some International Institutions, but Not in Others' (2013) 51 J Common Mkt Stud 849, 851–52, who assert that 'EU participation will become attractive for third parties only if this actor can significantly contribute to the related co-operation project separately from its member states. Committing the EU to implementing institutionalized obligations promises to further the envisaged co-operation project. In contrast, there will be no substantive advantage of additional EU participation if the EU merely represents a coalition of its Member States.'

34 Consolidated version of the Treaty on the Functioning of the European Union [2012] OJ C326/47.

35 Case C-399/12 *Federal Republic of Germany v Council of the European Union* ECLI: EU:C:2014:2258, paras 49–50, 55.

in the area concerned'[36]. Being a member of the IMO, nonetheless, would clearly elevate the EU in its power and impact.[37] Occasional attempts by the Commission to initiate action towards membership at IMO have so far been unsuccessful.[38] For one, EU membership at IMO would require an amendment to the IMO Convention, which in itself is a major obstacle. At the same time, IMO Members with strong commercial interests and industry representatives presumably do not favour granting more power to the EU, which traditionally has been pushing for stricter (and more costly) environmental standards.[39] This is apart from any reservation that EU MSs themselves may have to further restrict their negotiation powers at IMO.

2. The International Convention for the Prevention of Pollution from Ships (MARPOL)

A significant amount of work that takes place in the MEPC revolves around the single most important and prominent treaty on ship-source pollution—the International Convention for the Prevention of Pollution from Ships (MARPOL—as it is usually abbreviated). MARPOL is a result of growing

36 Case C-600/14 *Federal Republic of Germany v Council of the European Union* ECLI: EU:C:2017:935, para 67.

37 For a brief discussion of EU membership within the IMO, see de Vries (n 31) paras 35–36.

38 See eg Commission, 'Recommendation from the Commission to the Council in order to open and conduct negotiations with the International Maritime Organization (IMO) on the condition and arrangements for accession by the European Community' SEC (2002) 381 final; as well as Commission, 'Communication to the Commission from the President in Agreement with Vice-President Ashton: Strategy for the progressive improvement of the EU status in international organisations and other for a in line with the objectives of the Treaty of Lisbon' C (2012) 9420 final, seeing 'a clear case for action' with regard to the IMO 'due to the strategic and economic interest [...] for the EU and/or their impact on policy areas where the EU has important competences.' Meanwhile, when in 2005 the Commission requested the matter of 'IMO and ICAO: Community participation in these two organisations' to be placed on the agenda of the Council Transport Meeting, the Council merely took note; see Council, '2671st meeting of the Council of the European Union (Transport/Telecommunications/Energy), held in Luxembourg on 27–28 July 2005', 10566/05, 12. See also Commission, 'Green paper on better ship dismantling' COM (2007) 269 final, 11, proposing to 'have a[n] "REIO clause" inserted in order for the Community to become a party to the [IMO] Ship Recycling Convention'.

39 On the disproportionate influence of industry organisations in IMO decision-making, see A.I.4.

awareness in the 1960s and 1970s for the environmental damages caused by shipping and added a new focus to the work of the IMO (then IMCO) that had mostly been dealing with matters of safety.[40] The 1972 United Nations Conference on the Human Environment in Stockholm became a landmark for this growing awareness. It endorsed cooperation within the IMO (then IMCO) and specifically with regard to the Marine Pollution Conference that was scheduled for the upcoming year.[41] Later that year, the Convention on the Prevention of Marine Pollution by Dumping of Wastes and Other Matter (the London Convention)[42] was adopted, as 'one of the first global conventions to protect the marine environment from human activities'[43]. It was updated in 1996 through the London Protocol.[44] Finally,

40 The *Torrey Canyon* oil spill of 1967 is often mentioned as a starting point of this development, see Jesper Jarl Fanø, *Enforcing International Maritime Legislation on Air Pollution through UNCLOS* (Hart 2019) 7, and IMO, 'MARPOL – 25 years' <https://wwwcdn.imo.org/localresources/en/KnowledgeCentre/ConferencesMeetings/FocusOnIMOArchives/Focus%20on%20IMO%20-%20MARPOL%20-%2025%20years%20(October%201998).pdf> accessed 12 May 2023, 4, that also refers to it as the 'biggest oil pollution incident ever recorded up to that time.' See also Safety4Sea calling it the 'The world's first major oil tanker disaster' <https://safety4sea.com/cm-torrey-canyon-the-worlds-first-major-oil-tanker-disaster/> accessed 12 May 2023.

41 Report of the United Nations Conference on the Human Environment, Stockholm, 5-16 June 1972, A/CONF.48/14/Rev.1, Recommendations 86 (e) and 92 (a), 22–23.

42 Convention on the Prevention of Marine Pollution by Dumping of Wastes and Other Matter (adopted 13 November 1972, entered into force 30 August 1975) 1046 UNTS 120; for the corresponding Final Act of the Intergovernmental Conference on the Convention on the Dumping of Wastes at Sea, see (1972) 11 ILM, 1291. For a consolidated text of the treaty, see <https://wwwcdn.imo.org/localresources/en/OurWork/Environment/Documents/LC1972.pdf> accessed 12 May 2023. The First Meeting of Contracting States designated the IMO (then IMCO) as treaty secretariat for the London Convention, see Res LDC.1(0) ('Designation of a Competent Organization to be Responsible for Secretariat Duties in Relation to the Convention') adopted on 18 December 1975, LDC (7) Rev 1.

43 See IMO, 'Convention on the Prevention of Marine Pollution by Dumping of Wastes and Other Matter' https://www.imo.org/en/OurWork/Environment/Pages/London-Convention-Protocol.aspx accessed 12 May 2023.

44 Protocol to the Convention on the Prevention of Marine Pollution by Dumping of Wastes and Other Matter, 1972 (adopted on 7 November 1996, entered into force 24 March 2006) (1997) 36 ILM 1. For further amendments to the London Convention and its Protocol, see IMO, 'Status of IMO Treaties: Comprehensive information on the status of multilateral Conventions and instruments in respect of which the International Maritime Organization or its Secretary-General performs depository or other functions' (last updated 20 November 2023), 564ff <https://wwwcdn.imo.org/localresources/en/About/Conventions/StatusOfConventions/Status%202023.pdf> accessed 8 December 2023. For a list of Resolutions concerning the London

as the highlight of the efforts of the international community and the momentum created by the Stockholm Conference, MARPOL was adopted on 2 November 1973 as the Final Act of the International Conference on Marine Pollution.[45] As a response to further accidents[46] MARPOL was amended by an additional Protocol in 1978[47] (inter alia improving the requirements for oil tankers) that incorporated the 1973 Convention.

At that time, MARPOL consisted of a treaty body and Annexes I–V pertaining to the Prevention of Pollution by Oil[48], Noxious Liquid Substances in Bulk, Harmful Substances Carried by Sea in Packaged Form, Sewage and Garbage, respectively. MARPOL allows States becoming party to the treaty, however, to opt out of the Annexes III through V[49], thereby, lowering the threshold for potential new Parties. MARPOL as a combined treaty[50] and together with its Annexes I and II entered into force on 2 October 1982.[51] The Protocol of 1997 added an (optional) Annex VI to MARPOL pertaining

Convention and its Protocol, see IMO, 'London Convention (LDC, LC) and London Protocol (LP)' <https://www.imo.org/en/KnowledgeCentre/IndexofIMOResolutions/Pages/LDC-LC-LP.aspx> accessed 12 May 2023. See for a graphic timeline of events surrounding and including the London Convention, IMO, 'Fifty years of ocean protection: Major milestones since adoption of the London Convention in 1972 regulating dumping at sea' <https://wwwcdn.imo.org/localresources/en/MediaCentre/HotTopics/Documents/London%20Convention%20timeline_FINAL_(16-9-22)_01.pdf> accessed 12 May 2023.

45 International Convention for the Prevention of Pollution from Ships (adopted 2 November 1973) (1973) 12 ILM 1319.

46 Eg the incidents involving the *Metula* in 1974 and the *Argo Merchant* in 1976.

47 Protocol of 1978 relating to the International Convention for the Prevention of Pollution from Ships, 1973, (adopted 17 February 1978, entered into force 2 October 1983) 1340 UNTS 61.

48 Which according to Art 9 (1) MARPOL supersedes the International Convention for the Prevention of Pollution of the Sea by Oil, 1954 (adopted 12 May 1954, entered into force 26 July 1958) 327 UNTS 3. For more details, see IMO, 'MARPOL – 25 years' (n 40) 5.

49 Art 14 (1), referring to Annexes III–V as Optional Annexes.

50 The combined treaty is sometimes referred to as the *International Convention for the Prevention of Pollution from Ships, 1973, as modified by the Protocol of 1978*, or *MARPOL 73/78* in short. For simplicity, this paper will refer to the combined instrument as MARPOL. For a more detailed account of the coming into being of MARPOL and its early evolution, see IMO, 'MARPOL – 25 years' (n 40).

51 Annex III entered into force on 1 July 1992, Annex IV on 27 September 2003 and Annex V on 31 December 1988, IMO, 'International Convention for the Prevention of Pollution from Ships (MARPOL)' <https://www.imo.org/en/About/Conventions/Pages/International-Convention-for-the-Prevention-of-Pollution-from-Ships-(MARPOL).aspx> accessed 12 May 2023.

to the Prevention of Air Pollution from Ships that entered into force on 19 May 2005.[52] Since its inception MARPOL and its Annexes have undergone extensive amendments and revisions.[53]

3. State Actors in International Shipping

States acting in the realm of MARPOL, international shipping and the law of the sea are awarded rights and obligations based on the role they find themselves in. In a given situation they can be a flag State, a port State or a coastal State—much depends on this distinction. This section provides an overview of these roles that serve as a basis for the discussions in the following chapters.

a. The Flag State

According to Art 91 of the United Convention on the Law of the Sea (UNCLOS)[54], '[s]hips have the nationality of the State whose flag they are entitled to fly' and '[t]here must exist a genuine link between the State and the ship.' Obligations of the flag State are eg the duty to ensure the safety of the ship through regular surveys (Art 94 (3) and (4) UNCLOS), to adopt laws and regulations for the 'prevention, reduction and control of pollution of the marine environment' pursuant Art 211 (2) UNCLOS and to ensure compliance of the ship with those provisions and 'applicable international rules and standards' (Art 217 (1) UNCLOS). Irrespective of the fact that a universal definition of what constitutes such a *genuine link* is not to be found,[55] the reality looks different. There famously exist a number of countries that offer their flag to vessels that have little or no link to the registering country. They are mostly thought of as exercising a

52 MARPOL Annex VI is comprehensively discussed in section D.II.

53 To list of all of them here would not be practical. Therefore, reference is made to IMO, 'Status of IMO Treaties' (n 44) 150ff. For a brief summary of MARPOL's Annexes I–VI, see Robin Churchill, Vaughan Lowe and Amy Sander, *The Law of the Sea* (4th ed, Manchester University Press 2022) 630ff.

54 United Nations Convention on the Law of the Sea (adopted 10 December 1982, entered into force 16 November 1994) 1833 UNTS 3.

55 Douglas Guilfoyle, 'Article 92: Status of ships' in Alexander Proelss and others (eds), *United Nations Convention on the Law of the Sea: A Commentary* (CH BECK, Hart, Nomos 2017) para 17.

lax regime when it comes to ensuring compliance and enforcement of standards. In exchange they present themselves as cheaper alternatives to other flags whose taxes and duties are higher. The flag States are called Open Registries or—more pointedly—Flags of Convenience.[56] The International Tribunal for the Law of the Sea (ITLOS) asserts that the purpose of the 'genuine link'-requirement of UNCLOS is one of 'effective implementation of the duties of the flag State'.[57] However, where the chosen flag State of a vessel proves unwilling or unable to exercise its control—and effectively its jurisdiction—over the vessel, the jurisdiction of the port State and the coastal State become even more significant.[58]

b. The Port State

The port State is the 'State in one of whose ports a particular vessel lies',[59] eg at berth. Port State jurisdiction in this context becomes particularly relevant for Art 218 UNCLOS, namely the enforcement of applicable international rules and standards where a discharge violation has occurred or is suspected to have occurred outside of the State's maritime zones. In this, Art 218 (1) is an extension of the port State's jurisdiction.[60]

The exercise of port State jurisdiction provided for in Art 218 UNCLOS is a reaction to a (possible) violation allowing for investigations and possible sanctions, and is, therefore, different from Port State Control (PSC)

---

56 See eg Doris König and Tim René Salomon, 'Flags of Convenience' (last updated February 2022) in Peters and Wolfrum (eds) *MPEPIL* (n 31) <https://opil-1ouplaw-1com-100b98fpw031a.emedien3.sub.uni-hamburg.de/display/10.1093/law:epil/9780199231690/law-9780199231690-e1167?rskey=tgUikl&result=1&prd=OPIL> accessed 12 May 2023, paras 1–2; or with a presentation of the current realities, see Alan Boyle and Catherine Redgwell, *Birnie, Boyle & Redgwell's International Law and the Environment* (4th ed, OUP 2021) 522–23.

57 ITLOS, *The M/V Saiga (No. 2) Case (Saint Vincent and the Grenadines v Guinea)*, Judgment of 1 July 1999, ITLOS Reports 1999, para 83.

58 It is noteworthy, however, that the IMO does have in place the IMO Instruments Implementation Code (III Code, see Assembly Res A.1070(2) adopted on 4 December 2013, A 28/Res.1070), based on which IMO Members are regularly audited, see for more information, IMO, 'Member State Audit Scheme' <https://www.imo.org/en/ourwork/msas/pages/default.aspx> accessed 11 April 2023.

59 Robin Churchill and Alan Lowe, *The Law of the Sea* (3rd ed, Manchester University Press 1999) 344.

60 This widening of jurisdictional scope 'aims at compensating the deficiencies of flag State jurisdiction', Doris König 'Article 218: Enforcement by port States' in Proelss and others (eds), *United Nations Convention on the Law of the Sea* (n 55) para 2.

measures.[61] PSC is the inspection regime of a port State targeted towards foreign-flagged ships 'to verify that the condition of the ship and its equipment comply with the requirements of international regulations and that the ship is manned and operated in compliance with these instruments and ensure maritime safety and security and prevent pollution'[62]. PSC regimes are based on regional agreements that allow for coordinated action and exchange of information to detect substandard ships.[63] PSC measures, therefore, primarily aim to prevent violations.[64]

c. The Coastal State

A coastal State has the authority over its maritime zones, namely its internal waters, territorial sea and exclusive economic zone (EEZ). Accordingly, in the context of shipping, the coastal State is the 'State in one of whose maritime zones a particular vessel lies'[65]. Being one of the elementary principles of UNCLOS, the coastal State has to grant the right of innocent passage through its territorial sea (Art 17 UNCLOS).[66] While having to

61 That is not to say, that PSC is not linked to port State jurisdiction in general, see König, 'Article 218' (n 60) para 2, seeing port State jurisdiction and PSC as 'closely related [...], but distinct'. See also Erik J Molenaar, 'Port State Jurisdiction' (last updated January 2021) in Peters and Wolfrum (eds) *MPEPIL* (n 31) <https://opil-1ouplaw-1com-100b98fpw031a.emedien3.sub.uni-hamburg.de/display/10.1093/law:epil/9780199231690/law-9780199231690-e2052?rskey=YdRpQs&result=1&prd=OPIL> accessed 12 May 2023, para 6, noting that '[t]he term "port State jurisdiction" is broader than the term "port State control"'.

62 IMO, 'Port State Control'<https://www.imo.org/en/OurWork/IIIS/Pages/Port%20State%20Control.aspx> accessed 12 May 2023.

63 There are currently nine such agreements covering different geographical areas, with the USA Coast Guard maintaining its own PSC regime, see IMO, 'Port State Control' (n 62). The principal measure of PSC when detecting a violation is the detention of the ship until the violation has been rectified.

64 See König, 'Article 218' (n 60) para 2. PSC is also considered the 'back up to flag State implementation and "second line of defence" against substandard shipping', see IMO, 'Port State Control' (n 62). See also Molenaar, 'Port State Jurisdiction' (n 61) para 6, who refers to the regional PSC regimes being a response 'to inadequate flag State performance and ports of convenience'.

65 Churchill and Lowe, *The Law of the Sea* (n 59) 344.

66 The liberal notion of free navigation through territorial seas can be traced as far back as the beginning of the 17th century, when Hugo Grotius in his *Mare Liberum* argued against proprietary claims to the sea, Andree Kirchner, 'Law of the Sea, History of', (last updated September 2007) in Peters and Wolfrum (eds) *MPEPIL* (n 31) <https://opil-1ouplaw-1com-100b98fld03b0.emedien3.sub.uni-hamburg.de/display/10.1093/la

allow innocent passage, the coastal State, however, also has an inherent interest in preventing pollution near its coastline.[67] Art 211 (4) and (5) UNCLOS accommodates this by allowing the coastal State to adopt provisions within their territorial sea and EEZ to prevent, reduce and control marine pollution from ships. Similarly, Art 220 UNCLOS provides for extensive enforcement rights of the coastal State where a violation of its laws and regulations or international rules and standards has occurred within its territorial sea or EEZ.[68]

4. Private Actors in International Shipping

The main private actors of the maritime business represented at the IMO are shipowners, the ship (parts/equipment) building and bunker industry, port authorities and classification societies, which provide technical services to flag States and shipping companies[69]. A number of environmental NGOs also hold consultative status at the IMO but are considerably outnumbered by industry representatives.[70] In fact, from the 88 organisations that currently hold consultative status at the IMO or those pending approval, only 10 have a clear environmental agenda.[71] In comparison, the group of shipowners alone is represented through eight different organisations, including some specialised on specific vessel types. Industry organisations have been criticised for their undue and disproportionate influence in IMO decision-making, pushing lower than necessary standards and

w:epil/9780199231690/law-9780199231690-e1187?rskey=RTBGY5&result=1&prd=MPIL> accessed 2 October 2023, para 11.

67 Art 19 (2) (h) UNCLOS only renders a passage non-innocent where there is an 'act of wilful and serious pollution contrary to this Convention'.

68 For a general overview of the role of flag, port and coastal States in the implementation and enforcement of pollution standards, see Churchill, Lowe and Sander, *The Law of the Sea* (n 53) 647–54.

69 For more information on the role of classification societies, see section C.IV.3.

70 A Transparency International report in 2018 analysed five recent IMO committee meetings and found almost five times as many trade associations represented than civil society organisations, Transparency International, 'Governance at the International Maritime Organisation: The Case for Reform' <https://images.transparencycdn.org/images/2018_IMO_Governance_Report_EN.pdf> accessed 12 May 2023, 2.

71 IMO, 'Non-Governmental International Organizations which have been granted consultative status with IMO' <https://www.imo.org/en/OurWork/ERO/Pages/NGOsInConsultativeStatus.aspx> accessed 12 May 2023.

hampering meaningful progress.[72] At the same time, the decision-making process at IMO itself has been criticised for its lack of transparency.[73]

II. The EU as a Regulator of Ship-Source Pollution

Having looked at the setting against which international shipping takes place—the system of the IMO, MARPOL and UNCLOS as the main relevant treaties, and the range of actors involved—it comes as no surprise that EU action interfering with that setting is potentially problematic. This study aims to shed light on the casualties of such EU action. EU legislation regulating international shipping risks the disruption of an existing system and adding to regulatory fragmentation—including the legal uncertainty and potential market and competitive distortions it brings. It can pose an affront to the credibility of the IMO as an institution and is possibly nothing less than 'an encroachment on international law's overall claim to normative validity'[74].

EU regulations on ship-source pollution can be and have been an effective means to incentivise more ambitious action at the IMO to re-establish a level playing field and more uniform standards. For that, the EU is widely recognised as a potent leader, catalyst and driving force—and therefore, in fact, a normative power[75]—that moves the needle in favour of more stringent environmental protection standards.[76] It even assigns itself

72 Eg Influence Map, 'Corporate Capture of the International Maritime Organization – How the Shipping Sector lobbies to stay out of the Paris Agreement' <https://influencemap.org/report/Corporate-capture-of-the-IMO-902bf81c05a0591c551f965020623fda> accessed 12 May 2023; Transparency International (n 70); Harilaos N Psaraftis and Christos A Kontovas 'Influence and Transparency at the IMO: The Name of the Game' (2020) 22 Maritime Economics & Logistics 151.

73 ibid.

74 Alexander Proelss, 'The "Erika III" Package: Progress or Breach of International Law?' in Hans-Joachim Koch and others (eds), *Climate Change and Environmental Hazards Related to Shipping: An International Legal Framework* (Martinus Nijhoff Publishers 2013) 129, 155 (albeit in the context of maritime safety regulations).

75 On the concept of *normative power*, see n 24.

76 Angela Carpenter, 'The EU and Marine Environmental Policy: A Leader in Protecting the Marine Environment' (2012) 8 JCER 248, 249; Judith van Leeuwen and Kristine Kern, 'The External Dimension of European Union Marine Governance: Institutional Interplay between the EU and the International Maritime Organization' (2013) 13 Global Environmental Politics 69, 70, 81; Frank, 'Consequences of the Prestige Sinking for European and International Law' (n 16) 4, 64; Linda Finska and Henrik Ringbom, *Regulation of GHGs from Ships: On the Available Discretion*

a leadership role.[77] On the other hand, the shipping industry having to ultimately implement those stricter (ie more expensive) and sometimes fragmented regulatory requirements naturally holds an unfavourable view of single-handed EU initiatives.[78] At the same time, the IMO sees its authority as the designated UN body undermined.[79] Thus, the EU's currency is effectively unilateral action or the threat to resort to it.[80] EU legislative ac-

---

for Regulatory Solutions in a European and Finnish Perspective <https://www.centrumbalticum.org/files/5185/Regulation_of_GHGs_from_ships_final.pdf> accessed 3 April 2023, 24 (referring to the EU specifically in the context of GHG reduction as 'an important catalyst' and 'force behind many of the actions at IMO to date'); see also Joanne Scott and Lavanya Rajamani, 'EU Climate Change Unilateralism' (2012) 23 EJIL 2012, 469, 472–73, considering that '[t]he EU may be thought to be acting as a "norm entrepreneur", using (the threat of) unilateral action to stimulate climate action elsewhere'; Daniel Bodansky, 'What's So Bad about Unilateral Action to Protect the Environment?' (2000) 11 EJIL 339, 345 and 342, assigning 'a form of leadership' to States that do not accept the outcome of multilateral agreements as the least common denominator that merely represents the position of one or a few States rather than being 'an "authentic" decision of the international community.'

77 See Commission, 'Strategic Goals and Recommendations for the EU's Maritime Transport Policy until 2018' COM(2009) 8 final, 10, suggesting that '[i]f IMO negotiations should fail, however, then the EU should take the lead in implementing measures on matters that are of particular importance for the EU, as a first step'; see also 'European Parliament resolution on improving safety at sea (2003/2235 (INI)) (adopted on 21 April 2004) P5_TA(2004)0350, para 36.

78 See eg 'BIMCO Position Statement on "Keep Shipping Regulation Global"' <https://www.bimco.org/about-us-and-our-members/bimco-statements/01-keep-regulation-global> accessed 18 May 2023.

79 See eg the 'Address of the Secretary-General at the Opening of the Ninety-Fourth session of the Maritime Safety Committee (17 to 21 November 2014)' <https://www.imo.org/en/MediaCentre/SecretaryGeneral/Pages/MSC-94-opening.aspx> accessed 18 May 2023, stressing 'the importance of the IMO system of global co-operation involving flag, port and coastal States, the shipping industry and other maritime industry partners, which is excellent for sharing responsibilities for effective implementation of IMO Conventions and this is also in the interests of sustainable shipping. [...] Regional maritime community may use a local or regional approach with a specific test bed but shipping must meet the standards of each of [the] regional standards. Shipping needs harmonized approach based on global measures to be adopted at IMO.'

80 It has been argued that an approach is 'not truly unilateral because it supports the interests of specific other states or the international community in general', Erik Jaap Molenaar, 'Port State Jurisdiction: Towards Comprehensive, Mandatory and Global Coverage' (2007) 38 Ocean Dev Int Law 225, 243. See also Alan Boyle, 'EU Unilateralism and the Law of the Sea' (2006) 21 Int'l J Marine and Coastal L 15, who seems to regard the EU entering into force agreed standards ahead of the IMO timeline as a weaker type of unilateralism, albeit unilateral action, nonetheless. Here, the concept of unilateralism is referred to in its traditional understanding as an 'individualistic

tion to tackle environmental pollution from international shipping, therefore, is a trade-off. The acceleration and/or re-enforcement of international processes comes at a cost. If the costs of the EU's approach were to be considered prohibitively high, there may be a case for regulating international shipping exclusively internationally, as UNCLOS may suggest.[81] This analysis contributes to determining these costs of unilateral EU action that are invariably needed for a final and informed cost-benefit analysis. To this end, this analysis uses three indicators to measure the toll EU unilateral legislation takes on the international policy of ship-source pollution and international law: 1. (potential) conflicts of EU norms with international law; 2. transparency as to how EU institutions have considered arising questions of international law; 3. the implications for and disruptions of existing systems and dynamics, in particular the obstacles being created for the actors traditionally involved.

With these indicators in mind, three specific legislative acts addressing ship recycling, carbon dioxide and sulphur oxide emissions are analysed in-depth in three case-studies. All three case studies follow the same pattern. First, they describe the problem at hand, what the IMO has done to tackle the problem and how the EU has decided to regulate this area. The case studies then explore which (potential) conflicts these pieces of

---

approach to foreign affairs' in which States 'pursue their international aims individually, apart from other States', André Nollkaemper, 'Unilateralism/Multilateralism' (last updated March 2011) in Peters and Wolfrum (eds) *MPEPIL* (n 31) <https://opil-1ouplaw-1com-100b98fpw031a.emedien3.sub.uni-hamburg.de/display/10.1093/law:epil/9780199231690/law-9780199231690-e1682?rskey=cndLTN&result=1&prd=OPIL> accessed 12 May 2023, para 1. Therefore, when referring to EU unilateral action, what is meant here are the specific legislative initiatives that are not (fully) in line with the overall (lack of) consensus within the IMO or existing treaty instruments. Apart from its legislative action, the EU nonetheless intensely engages within the IMO and generally seeks multilateral solutions. It is accepted conceptually, that unilateralism and multilateralism do not stand in 'binary opposition' and a State can engage in both at the same time, Nollkaemper, 'Unilateralism/Multilateralism' (n 80) para 8.

81 While a number of UNCLOS' provisions refer to regional cooperation or regional rules and standards in one way or another—eg Arts 61 (2) and (5), 118, 197, 207 (4), 208 (5), 210 (4), 212 (3) and 268(e)—Art 211 that specifically addresses pollution from vessels, remains silent on any regional activity, while not ruling it out either. It, therefore, has been observed that there 'seems to emerge an implicit assessment that a regional approach is particularly appropriate as regards pollution from land-based sources, while it is much less appropriate as regards vessel-source pollution', Tullio Treves, 'Regional Approaches to the Protection of the Marine Environment' in Myron H Nordquist, John Norton Moore and Said Mahmoudi (eds) *The Stockholm Declaration and Law of the Marine Environment* (Martinus Nijhoff Publishers 2003) 137, 138.

EU legislation have brought about and how the legislative act places itself in the context of existing international law. Each case study represents a special setting as to the relationship between that piece of EU legislation and the corresponding treaty law on that subject matter. In the first case study, the treaty on ship recycling preceded the EU Regulation that was intended to accelerate acceptance for the treaty and bring it into effect. In the second case study, the EU Regulation on carbon dioxide reduction was thought of as a blueprint for an agreement at IMO level and took effect while deliberations at the IMO were still ongoing. Finally, in the third case study the provisions on sulphur oxide reduction anticipated agreed-on international provisions that had not yet taken effect while tightening the scope and even adding one measure that had no international precedence. Additionally, the measures in these legislative acts differ in their nature, eg their type of requirement and the maritime zones they affect, and, thereby, create very different (legal) challenges.

The case studies are arranged to allow for more basic concepts and notions to be addressed early in the analysis and the possibility to refer to these in the later more intricate discussions. To this end, the analysis begins with the study on ship recycling for which the international decision-making process was less lengthy and contentious than in the second and third case studies. The second case study on carbon dioxide emissions, on the other hand, contains more technical data to allow for better context, while the third case study on sulphur emissions analyses the adoption by the EU of multiple measures within one instrument. Also, due to their more contentious nature, the EU's legislation on carbon dioxide and sulphur emission reduction has found more attention, and literature on these specific topics is more readily available.

This analysis demonstrates that EU legislation often finds itself touching upon the boundaries of international law, while the EU institutions choose either not to address these (potential) conflicts or in a less than satisfactory way. This study looks at how the relevant bodies of the EU comment on the relevant EU legislation, as well as how they justify it or place it in the context of international law and policy. It finds that there is a strong impression that the EU avoids relevant questions of international law in favour of implementing its agenda. In this manner, the EU creates regulatory frameworks that impose additional burden on eg shipowners and MSs and significantly contribute to a patchwork of requirements. With this, the EU fails to seize the opportunity to strengthen its role as an actor on the international stage, as a relevant subject within the system of international law that has the potential to shape and evolve it. What is more, the EU risks its reputation considering the 'the conventional presentation and widespread understanding of the EU as an actor maintaining a distinctive commitment to international law and institutions.'[82]

One thing needs to be borne in mind throughout the analysis: the EU, just like the IMO, is an association of MSs. The discussion may make it seem at times that the EU is an abstract entity that places burden on its MSs without consideration for their individual national situation or international obligations. In the course of the analysis, it is sometimes easy to forget that the decision-making processes involve the Council that represents the national governments' positions. Why the questions discussed here were either not taken into account, ignored or accepted during the legislative procedures is beyond the scope of this study. Suffice it to say, it would do injustice to the system of the EU to view it as an overpowering institution, acting at will, while the MSs remain at its mercy. Similarly, it is understood that the EU is the sum of its organs—the most important in this context being the Commission and the European Parliament (EP) as legislative organs, and the ECJ as the main body that interprets that law. The actions and omissions of the individual institutions are attributed to the EU as an abstract entity and reflect on it, to shape the image of the EU to the outside world, ie to other States and organisations it interacts with or even the general public. The overall conclusions from the individual actions or omissions of the organs of the EU must, therefore, be drawn and understood, to be the position of the EU within the international community and reflecting on its overall image and reputation.

82 Gráinne de Búrca, 'The European Court of Justice and the International Legal Order after *Kadi*' (2010) 51 Harv Int'l LJ 1, 2.
See also Sebastian Oberthur & Lisanne Groen, 'The Effectiveness Dimension of the EU's Performance in International Institutions: Toward a More Comprehensive Assessment Framework' (2015) 53 J Common Mkt Stud 1319, 1321, who find that '"effective multilateralism" has been one of the main cornerstones of the EU's international strategy since at least the early 2000s, with a commitment to the United Nations and multilateral institutions enshrined in the Lisbon treaty'.

B. Case Study I: Disposing of Ships as Waste

This chapter constitutes the first of three case studies. It discusses the problem of ship recycling (I.) and the attempts of the international community and the EU to tackle the consequences of inadequate processes of ship dismantling. Focusing primarily on the current state of play, this chapter first assesses the applicability of previously existing legal instruments to regulate the environmental aspects of ship dismantling, namely the Basel Convention on the Control and of Transboundary Movements of Hazardous Waste and their Disposal[83] (BC) and the EU's Waste Shipment Regulation[84] (WSR; II.). It then assesses and compares the specifically developed legal instruments, namely the Hong Kong International Convention for the Safe and Environmentally Sound Recycling of Ships (HKC) and the EU's Ship Recycling Regulation[85] (SRR; III. and IV.). It also specifically sheds some light on the contentious relationship between the SRR and the BC and the more recent attempt to address this. Furthermore, the last section of this chapter investigates the financial instrument envisaged in the SRR and designed to prevent circumvention of its provisions (V.). It analyses the studies that have been conducted so far to find an effective and practical financial mechanism that is nonetheless compatible with international law. It shows that the studies contain misconceptions and lack a firm stance on the questions of international law, specifically the question of potential impermissible trade restrictions. The possibility of trade restrictions is discussed including possible applicable exceptions. The discussions surrounding a financial mechanism as part of the SRR prove just how complex the endeavour is and that there is good reason why—at time of writing in 2023, almost 10 years after its entry into force—such a financial mechanism, while crucial for securing compliance with the SRR, is still not in place.

---

83 Basel Convention on the Control of Transboundary Movements of Hazardous Wastes and their Disposal (adopted 22 March 1989, entered into force 5 May 1992) 1673 UNTS 57.

84 Regulation (EC) No 1013/2006 of the European Parliament and of the Council of 14 June 2006 on shipments of waste [2006] OJ L190/1.

85 Regulation (EU) No 1257/2013 of the European Parliament and of the Council of 20 November 2013 on Ship Recycling and Amending Regulation (EC) No 1013/2006 and Directive 2009/16/EC [2013] OJ L330/1.

I. Disposing of End-of-Life Ships

At the end of their life, when ships have 'outlived their economic utility'[86], they must be taken apart. Terms such as *Breaking*, *Scrapping*, *Dismantling*, *Demolition*, *Disposal* or *Recycling* all usually try to describe the same process and are most often used interchangeably. Which term to use can also be considered a matter of perspective.[87] This chapter will use the term *dismantling* to mean the process of taking apart a ship, the term *disposal* where the ship is treated as waste, and the term *recycling* where the ship is disposed of in an environmentally sound manner. *Beaching*, on the other hand, describes one specific method of breaking down a ship. It is a process

86 Tony George Puthucherril, *From Shipbreaking to Sustainable Ship Recycling: Evolution of a Legal Regime* (Martinus Nijhoff Publishers 2010) 1.

87 J Fredrik Lindgren, Karin Andersson and Hanna Landquist, 'Infrastructure, Marine Spatial Planning and Shipwrecks' in *Shipping and the Environment: Improving the Environmental Performance in Marine Transportation* (n 2) 237, 245. For a brief attempt to distinguish these terms, see Amy E Moen, 'Breaking Basel: The Elements of the Basel Convention and its Application to Toxic Ships' (2008) 32 Mar Policy 1053. For an overview on existing vocabulary and the stakeholders that use them: Nikos Mikelis, 'The IMO Ship Recycling Regulations: A perspective' (Cambridge Academy of Transport, July 2009) <https://wwwcdn.imo.org/localresources/en/KnowledgeCentre/Documents/The%20IMO%20ship%20recycling%20regulations%20-%20N.%20 Mikelis.pdf> accessed 10 February 2023, 2; Michael Galley, *Shipbreaking: Hazards and Liabilities* (Springer 2014), xi. See also Commission, 'Oil tanker phase out and the Ship Scrapping Industry: A Study on the Implications of the Accelerated Phase out Scheme of Single Hull Tankers proposed by the EU for the World Ship Scrapping and Recycling Industry' (2004), which for the purpose of its study defines the terms *Demolition* and *Ship breaking* to include the process of beaching while the term *Dismantle* does not, the term *Recycling* to refer to a process 'when procedures with respect for the environment and workers health and safety are applied' and the term *Scrapping* to be a neutral term used without regard to the procedure applied; to the knowledge of the author, this document is not publicly accessible anymore at time of finalization of this study, but can be viewed here: <https://dokumen.tips/documents/2004-06-scrapping-study-en.html?page=1> accessed 18 May 2023; a digital copy of the document can also be made available upon request. See also Bio Intelligence Service 'The Feasibility of a List of "Green and Safe" Ship Dismantling Facilities and of a List of Ships likely to go for Dismantling' (2010) <https://circabc.europa.eu/ui/group/636f928d-2669-41d3-83db-093e90ca93a2/library/f7fee 643-cdeb-42ae-89fd-fc40933fdb76/details?download=trueaccessed> 18 May 2023, 193, that for the purpose of the study defines the term *Dismantling* as not including the beaching method and considers *Scrapping* and *Breaking* to be terms 'usually employed within the ship dismantling industry in a more technical or economic context'.

that takes place on sandy beaches in so-called developing countries[88], mainly in the absence of a facility, and usually in the absence of proper (safety) equipment. To paint a more dramatic picture:

> Ships are driven as close as possible to a beach during high tide, and normally get stranded on the mudflats near the beach in the intertidal area. They are cut apart vertically into very big parts with no other help than that of blow torches and gravity - parts then crashing onto the mudflats. Workers are put at great risk, both acute and chronic, proper containment of hazardous materials is impossible, and the part of hazardous materials that is taken out separately is not treated adequately.[89]

Moreover, '[e]nd-of-life ships are rarely pre-cleaned before their arrival on the shores of South Asia. Instead, one of the traditional "cleaning" methods is the drilling of holes into the beached ship through which sea water can wash out oil-contaminated tanks at high tide.'[90] In fact, in 2015 78% of the overall broken down shipping tonnage was beached.[91] Asbestos, lead, heavy metals and ozone-depleting substances are some of the toxic materials that require special handlings as well as eg any cargo and oil residues such as fuel oil lubricants or oil residues contained in bilge water.[92] The problem of inadequate processes in ship dismantling not only affects the environment but is also a question of human health and occupational safety. To summarise the problem:

> The ship recycling business is considered one of the world's most dangerous occupations. Most accidents are caused by the falling of large heavy metal plates and by gas explosions. Furthermore, the workers typically use little or no protective equipment, directly exposing them to

88 Lindgren and others (n 87) 247. The two categories of so-called 'developing' and 'developed' countries/States are used here and have been left in the original in numerous citations for easier readability. It is understood, however, that these categories have been criticised for not sufficiently reflecting the range of the very different economic realities of so-called developing countries and being generally outdated.

89 European Parliament, Committee on the Environment, Public Health and Food Safety 'Report on the proposal for a regulation of the European Parliament and of the Council on ship recycling, (28 March 2013) A7-0132/2013, 69.

90 Commission Staff Working Document, 'Impact Assessment for an EU Strategy for Better Ship Dismantling' SEC (2008) 2846, 14.

91 Commission, 'Ship recycling: reducing human and environmental impacts' <https://circabc.europa.eu/ui/group/636f928d-2669-41d3-83db-093e90ca93a2/library/2a971118-bfe1-4e4e-b6c9-53a8e6490a0e/details?download=true> accessed 18 May 2023, 3.

92 Lindgren and others (n 87) 246–47.

> toxic substances and fumes. In addition, no or very few facilities exist for receiving and handling hazardous waste and toxic chemicals. Thousands of people are estimated to have died in the ship scrapping business in the last 20 years. [...] Waste and treatment reception facilities and barriers to contain or prevent oil or other liquids from entering the marine environment are often lacking or exist in low quantities at the ship scrapping sites in Asia, leading to a large threat to the marine environment in the vicinity of ship scrapping sites. [...] In addition, material that cannot be recycled, e.g. cable coatings of PVC, are often burned or dumped at the scrapping site.[93]

Ship recycling facilities buy ships from ship owners or so-called cash buyers[94] to dismantle them and extract their valuable materials, such as steel.[95]

---

93 ibid 247. For a table of 'Common hazards that are likely to cause work-related injuries and death, ill health, diseases and incidents among shipbreakers', see ILO, 'Safety and health in shipbreaking: Guidelines for Asian countries and Turkey' <http://www.ilo.org/wcmsp5/groups/public/---ed_protect/---protrav/---safework/documents/normativeinstrument/wcms_107689.pdf> accessed 10 February 2023, 8–9. For a table of dismantling activities and workers' exposure to hazardous substances, see Aage Bjørn Andersen, 'Worker safety in the ship breaking industries' (International Labour Office, 2001) <http://www.ilo.org/wcmsp5/groups/public/---ed_protect/---protrav/---safework/documents/publication/wcms_110357.pdf> accessed 10 February 2023, 34–35; for a table on 'Hazardous compounds to be identified at ships, classification of properties and their concentration limits in waste to be classified as hazardous' (including the classification according to the Basel Convention), see EMSA, 'Study on the certification of ship recycling facilities' <https://www.emsa.europa.eu/damage-stability-study/download/1015/602/23.html> accessed 10 February 2023, 41.

94 'Cash buyers are companies that specialise in the trade of end-of-life vessels, and most - if not all - sales of end-of-life ships to beaching yards in South Asia are conducted with the help of these scrap-dealers. [...] cash buyers first pay ship owners up-front before the ship reaches its final destination to be dismantled, and then re-sell the ship to the breaker that can offer the highest price, thereby making a profit with the price difference', NGO Shipbreaking Platform, 'Cash Buyers' <https://shipbreakingplatform.org/our-work/the-problem/cash-buyers/> accessed 16 October 2023.

95 For a rough overview on the 'Key drivers for the supply and demand of vessels to the shipbreaking industry', see Galley (n 87) 9. For an overview on the economics of ship dismantling, see Commission, 'Oil tanker phase out and the Ship Scrapping Industry' (n 87) 41ff; Commission, 'Green paper on ship dismantling' (n 38) 5; see also Urs Daniel Engels, *European Ship Recycling Regulation: Entry-Into-Force Implications of the Hong Kong Convention* (Springer 2013) 65ff. For the additional costs of environmentally sound ship dismantling, see Ecorys, 'The Ship Recycling Fund: Financing Environmentally Sound Scrapping and Recycling of Sea-Going Ships' (2005) <https://www.shipbreakingplatform.org/wp-content/uploads/2019/01/ECORYS-survey-on-a-ship-recyc-ling-fund.pdf> accessed 3 October 2017, 19–22. To the knowledge of the

The lower the standards on environmental protection and worker's health, the more the ship recycling facility will pay—hence, the lack of financial incentive for shipowners or cash buyers to select a facility that will take appropriate precautions to avoid these dangers. The five countries that dominate the market for ship dismantling are Bangladesh, China, India, Pakistan and Turkey; between 2012 and 2021, they handled 98% of the world's annual ship recycling volume on average.[96]

The topic of inadequate recycling of ships called for the work of multiple intergovernmental organisations. The International Labour Organization (ILO) addresses matters of occupational health in its 2004 Guidelines on Safety and Health in Shipbreaking.[97] The Secretariat of the BC published its Technical Guidelines for the Environmentally Sound Management of the Full and Partial Dismantling of Ships in 2003[98], in the understanding, however, that applying the provisions of the BC to the process of ship recycling poses difficulties and 'Basel controls may often be circumvented'[99]. The IMO has also been dealing with the question of environmentally sustainable ship recycling since 2000 and adopted its first Guidelines on Ship Recycling in 2003.[100] In the absence of a comprehensive regulatory framework and aware, that isolated work of these three organisations may not do justice to the complexity of the matter at hand, the ILO, the Conference of Parties (COP) of the BC and the IMO decided to seek a coordinated approach and establish a joint working group.[101] The three meetings of the

---

author, this document is not publicly accessible anymore at time of finalization of this study. A digital copy of the document can, however, be made available upon request.

96 IMO MEPC, 'Calculation of recycling capacity for meeting the entry-into-force conditions of the Hong Kong Convention' (20 September 2022) MEPC 79/INF.3, Annex, 3 (Table 3). For annual lists of dismantled ships from 2012 onwards, see NGO Shipbreaking Platform, 'Annual Lists of Scrapped Ships' <https://shipbreakingplatform.org/annual-lists/> accessed 18 May 2023.

97 ILO, 'Safety and health in shipbreaking: Guidelines for Asian countries and Turkey' (n 93).

98 <http://www.basel.int/Portals/4/Basel%20Convention/docs/meetings/sbc/workdoc/techgships-e.pdf> accessed 18 May 2023.

99 Secretariat of the Basel Convention, 'Ship Dismantling' <http://www.basel.int/Implementation/ShipDismantling/Overview/tabid/2762/Default.aspx> accessed 18 May 2023.

100 IMO Assembly Res A.962(23) adopted on 5 December 2003, A 23/Res.962, amended by Assembly Res A.980(24) adopted on 1 December 2005, A 24/Res.980.

101 See IMO, MEPC, 'Report of the Marine Environment Protection Committee on its Fifty-First Session' (22 April 2004) MEPC 51/22, para 3.18; BC, 'Report of the Conference of the Parties to the Basel Convention on the Control of Trans-

Joint ILO/IMO/BC Working Group on Ship Scrapping were held in 2005 and 2008.[102]

II. Applying Provisions on Waste Shipment to End-of-Life Ships

The initial instinct in the first attempts to counter the environmental damages resulting from inadequate ship dismantling has been to qualify end-of-life ships as waste under existing instruments. This section investigates how ships defined and treated as waste fare under the BC, as well as the EU's WSR. It shows that inadequacies of these instruments made specific provisions on ship recycling necessary.

1. The Basel Convention and the Element of Intent

The BC as its name suggests provides a framework for the cross-border shipping of hazardous waste. At its heart are a number of export restrictions (found eg in Art 4 BC) and a prior to export written notification and consent procedure (Art 6 BC). In 1995, the COP to the BC additionally agreed on the so-called Ban Amendment[103] prohibiting all transboundary movements of hazardous wastes from a Party to the Organisation for Economic Co-operation and Development (OECD), an EU MS or Liechtenstein (listed in Annex VII BC) to a third country for the purpose of disposal or further operations (as laid down in Annex IV BC). The BC's Ban Amendment did, however, not enter into force until 2019.

One of the initial questions in the discussions on ship recycling was whether the BC is applicable to end-of-life ships. This is the case where an end-of-life ship can be considered waste in accordance with Arts 1

boundary Movements of Hazardous Wastes and their Disposal' (25 January 2005) UNEP/CHW.7/33, para VII/25; ILO, 'Minutes of the 291st session' (November 2004) GB.291/PV, 36.

102 For more information (including links to the three reports of the Joint Working Group), see IMO, 'Joint ILO/IMO/BC Working Group on Ship Scrapping', see <https://www.imo.org/en/OurWork/Environment/Pages/JointILOIMOBCWorkingGroupOnShipScrapping.aspx> accessed 18 May 2023.

103 Amendment to the Basel Convention on the Control of Transboundary Movements of Hazardous Wastes and their Disposal (adopted on 22 September 1995, entered into force 5 December 2019) Registration No 28911 (no UNTS volume number determined yet). The Ban Amendment was inserted into the treaty as preambular para 7bis, Art 4a and Annex VII.

and 2 (1) BC. Art 2 (1) qualifies waste as inter alia 'substances or objects which are disposed of or are intended to be disposed of'. In that sense, a ship on its last voyage could easily be considered waste, however, only if prior to its last voyage the decision to dispose of the ship has already been taken by the shipowner—thus, the intention to dispose of the ship existed before the ship departed on its last journey. All other cases are neither easy nor clear. It is eg suggested that

> a vessel should be considered waste even if it will call at different ports with cargo, before it reaches the location for scrapping. But if the decision has been taken to scrap the vessel in some distant future, and it meanwhile will be used as a ship, the vessel should not be regarded as waste already from the time of the decision. It may be difficult to establish how close connection should be required between the decision and the actual scrapping, to consider the vessel to have become waste.[104]

This wider interpretation may lead to more equitable results as it not only strictly takes into account the mere existence of an intent to dispose of a ship, but also how immediate the disposal of the ship is, ie the realisation of the intent. However, it also demonstrates that a clear distinction is impossible, especially since this approach adds more vagueness to the already difficult task of establishing a subjective intent. It may, therefore, be easier to stick to a narrow definition of waste here, and to only qualify a ship as waste that is sailing to another country with the sole purpose of being dismantled there.[105] Regardless of which definition is applied, qualifying a ship as waste and, consequently, applying the provisions of the BC to it, may interfere with the ship's freedom of navigation as stipulated in Art 90 UNCLOS. This right is granted regardless of the ships' specific purpose of voyage and is expressly protected by Art 4 (12) BC.[106] To add to the unclarity, Art 2 (3) BC defines *transboundary movement* as

---

104 Geir Ulfstein, 'Legal aspects of Scrapping of Vessels', Annex I to UNEP, 'Legal Aspects of the Full and Partial Dismantling of Ships' (4 December 2001) UNEP/CHW/LWG/4/4, 8; this document served as a basis for the discussions on Agenda Item 6 of the Fourth Session of the Legal Working Group of the Basel Convention (18–19 January 2002).

105 Rüdiger Wolfrum and Nele Matz, *Conflicts in International Environmental Law* (Springer 2003) 115, who find that 'it might be better to favor the view' specified here. For a further linguistic analysis on the definitions of *Disposal* and *Waste*, assessing a shipowner's intent to dispose of and on the applicability of the MARPOL: see Engels (n 95) 125ff.

106 Wolfrum and Matz (n 105) 115.

> any movement of hazardous wastes or other wastes from an area under the national jurisdiction of one State to or through an area under the national jurisdiction of another State or to or through an area not under the national jurisdiction of any State, provided at least two States are involved in the movement [...].

Consequentially, a *transboundary movement* can be avoided where the decision to scrap the vessel is taken on the high seas, in the territorial waters of the State where the dismantling is to take place or in one of its other maritime zones.[107]

Another question that causes significant practical problems is which State would be responsible for ensuring compliance with the provisions of the BC. For a ship, its flag State is the main authority. Therefore, generally speaking:

> A ship which is proceeding on an international voyage to the ship breaking State would need to comply with all of the applicable international rules and standards. The responsibility to ensure compliance by the ship with such rules and standards rests mainly with the flag State (articles 94, 216 and 217). However, coastal and port States are also granted enforcement rights under UNCLOS. A port State has the right to take administrative measures to prevent a ship from sailing, which does not meet the international rules and standards governing seaworthiness and thereby threatens damage to the marine environment (article 219).[108]

This assessment does not seem to take into consideration, however, the peculiarity of the BC—that is, the existing responsibilities of the *State of Export* pursuant Art 2 (10) BC, namely the 'Party from which a transboundary movement of hazardous wastes or other wastes is planned to be initiated or is initiated'. Where it is assumed that the BC is applicable to ships being exported for dismantling, the flag State administration's established role of primary authority would come into conflict with the waste exporting State's responsibilities under the BC. This means:

> When a vessel has become waste, it is the state from which it departs which, in conformity with other waste, must be considered the exporting state. Accordingly, in the absence of any express provision, the flag state

107 Ulfstein (n 104) 16.

108 UNEP, 'Legal Aspects of the Full and Partial Dismantling of Ships' (22 April 2002) UNEP/CHW/LWG/5/4, para 4, see also para 18.

as such has no obligation under the Convention to ensure the existence of a consent from the importing state.[109]

Consequently, where a ship is in a foreign port, 'the port state should be responsible for ensuring that the requirements for export are fulfilled.'[110] However, in light of Art 4 (12) BC and the status of ships under UNCLOS, it can be concluded that the port State, as the exporting State under the BC, has no jurisdiction to exercise powers over a ship that is not flying its flag but is leaving its port to be dismantled in the country of destination.[111] This lack of adequate possibilities of control and enforcement poses a major obstacle to the application of the BC to end-of-life ships. The difficulties in applying the BC to ships strongly support the notion that 'the deliberations of the Basel Convention originally did not actually consider ships themselves as wastes'.[112] It was not even until the Fourth Revised Draft of the treaty that the definition of *Wastes* was extended to mean *substances or objects* rather than just merely *materials*.[113] Also, upon conclusion of the BC, notes were given with regard to coastal and flag State's rights and duties 'in relation to prevention and accident response in the case of ships carrying cargoes of hazardous wastes while crossing territorial waters of coastal third States.'[114] Conversely, it can be assumed that the option of ships themselves becoming waste was not being considered, as that, too, would have called for clarification as to the respective flag State's role. Lastly, the text of the BC assumes that wastes that fall within its scope are *generated*, the *generator* meaning 'any person whose activity produces hazardous wastes or other wastes or, if that person is not known, the person who is in possession and/or control of those wastes' (Art 2 (18) BC). The idea that waste in the meaning of the BC is produced through action stands in contrast to a ship becoming waste through a simple shift of intention in the mind of the shipowner. The secondary liability of the person in possession of the waste, on the other hand, is only triggered where the *generator* is unknown. In this case, however, a generator would simply not

109 Ulfstein (n 104) 13.

110 ibid 13.

111 ibid 14, 16.

112 Wolfrum/Matz (n 105) 114.

113 UNEP, 'Fourth Revised Draft Convention on the Control of Transboundary Movements of Hazardous Wastes' (14 September 1988) UNEP/WG.189/L.2Rev. 1, 4.

114 UNEP, 'Note by the Executive Director on some Points of the Hazardous Wastes Convention which were not resolves at the Fourth Session of the Ad Hoc Working Group' (10 February 1989), UNEP/WG.191/2, 2.

exist. At the same time, considering the ship builder retrospectively to be the one who has generated the ship as waste neither matches the logic of the BC nor leads to equitable results.

The parties to the BC in 2004 did, however, note that 'a ship *may* become waste as defined in Art 2 of the Basel Convention, and that at the same time, it may be defined as a ship under other international rules'.[115] They also invited

> the International Maritime Organization to continue to consider the establishment in its regulations of mandatory requirements, including a reporting system for ships destined for dismantling, that ensure an equivalent level of control as established under the Basel Convention and to continue work aimed at the establishment of mandatory requirements to ensure the environmentally sound management of ship dismantling, which might include pre-decontamination within its scope.[116]

It is understood that 'given the global nature of the shipping industry and the practices associated with sending end-of-life ships for recycling, there has been difficulty in applying the provisions of the Basel Convention to ship recycling.'[117]

2. The EU Waste Shipment Regulation and the 'Implementation Gap'

The WSR in 2006 implemented into EU law the BC—stricter in some aspects and including export restrictions that reflect the BC's Ban Amendment (Arts 34 and 36 WSR) long before its entry into force—and the OECD decision on the transboundary movements of wastes destined for recovery operations.[118] The WSR applies to shipments of waste to, from, through or between MSs (Art 1 (2)). It also reiterates the understanding that a ship can be considered waste under the BC, while it can still be con-

---

115 BC, 'Report of the Conference of the Parties to the Basel Convention on the Control of Transboundary Movements of Hazardous Wastes and their Disposal' (25 January 2005) UNEP/CHW.7/33, Recital 6 of Decision VII/26.

116 BC, Decision VII/26 (n 115) para. 5.

117 Secretariat of the Basel Convention, 'Legal Aspects' <http://www.basel.int/Implementation/ShipDismantling/LegalAspects/Overview/tabid/2766/Default.aspx> accessed 3 March 2023.

118 OECD, 'Decision of the Council Concerning the Revision of Decision C(92)39/Final on the Control of Transboundary Movements of Wastes destined for Recovery Operations' (15 March 2004) C(2001)107/Final.

sidered a ship with regard to other rules of international law (Recital 35), assuming a dual role.

The WSR, however, is bound to face the same difficulties when it comes to its application to end-of-life ships. Art 2 (1) WSR borrows its definition of *waste* from Art 1 (1) (a) of the repealed Waste Shipment Directive 2006/12/EC[119], defining *waste* to mean 'any substance or object [...] which the holder discards or intends or is required to discard'. Therefore, the definition of a ship as waste, here too, crucially depends on whether the ship is disposed of or intended to be disposed of. The Waste Shipment Directive was repealed by Directive 2008/98/EC[120], which contains the same definition in its Art 3 (1). The discussion surrounding the element of intent in the BC, therefore, applies here, too. Hence, the WSR does not apply where the ship has left EU territory, and the intention to dismantle the ship is formed afterwards.[121]

The Commission understands the problem of implementation[122] and the problem of proving the shipowner's intent to dispose of his ship when applying the WSR.[123] Closing the 'implementation gap'[124] appeared even more urgent in light of the then upcoming phasing-out of single-hull tankers. The Commission expected that an additional 1300 single-hull tankers would have to go for dismantling by 2015, with a peak number in 2010 in which 800 of them would have to be taken out of service.[125] The Commission considers this legal gap in its Green Paper on better Ship Dismantling. It acknowledges the IMO's then beginning work on a ship recycling treaty and pledges that

> the objective is not to artificially bring back ship recycling business volumes to the EU, thus depriving countries in South Asia of a major source of revenue. On the contrary, while acknowledging the structural comparative cost advantage of such countries, the ultimate aim of the

119 Directive 2006/12/EC of the European Parliament and of the Council of 5 April 2006 on Waste [2006] OJ L114/9.

120 Directive 2008/98/EC of the European Parliament and of the Council of 19 November 2008 on Waste and repealing certain Directives [2008] OJ L312/3.

121 Commission Staff Working Document, 'Impact Assessment for an EU Strategy for Better Ship Dismantling' (n 90) 8.

122 Commission, 'Green paper on better ship dismantling' (n 38) 3; see also Commission, 'EU strategy on better ship dismantling' COM (2008) 767 final, para 2.2.

123 Commission, 'Oil tanker phase out and the Ship Scrapping Industry' (n 87) 35.

124 See Commission, 'Green paper on better ship dismantling' (n 38) 9.

125 ibid 2, 7.

EU is to ensure that minimum environmental and health and safety standards are observed worldwide.[126]

III. The Hong Kong Convention—A Treaty to Address End-of-Life Ships

With existing international regulations on waste clearly being difficult to apply to ship recycling, the 53rd session of the IMO's MEPC agreed to develop a new instrument on ship recycling.[127] In 2005, the IMO Assembly accordingly adopted Resolution A.981 (24) and requested the MEPC to draft a legally binding instrument on ship recycling, taking into account aspects of inter alia design, construction, operation and preparation of ships, operation of ship recycling facilities and an appropriate enforcement mechanism.[128] A diplomatic conference in 2009 adopted the text for the HKC.[129]

Art 2 (10) HKC defines *Ship Recycling* as

> the activity of complete or partial dismantling of a ship at a Ship Recycling Facility in order to recover components and materials for reprocessing and re-use, whilst taking care of hazardous and other materials, and includes associated operations such as storage and treatment of components and materials on site, but not their further processing or disposal in separate facilities.

In this sense, the term *Ship Recycling* implies the adequate handling and storage of materials and coins the term as the legally permissible and correct way of dismantling a ship. At the same time, it is noteworthy that the HKC does not address the matter of adequate handling of materials and substances where they take place outside of a ship recycling facility. The disposal of hazardous materials outside of the facility is only briefly ad-

126 ibid 3–4.

127 IMO, MEPC, 'Report of the Marine Environment Protection Committee on its Fifty-Third session' (25 July 2005) MEPC 53/24, paras 3.67.1. and .5.

128 IMO Assembly Res A.981 (24) adopted 1 December 2005, A 24/Res.981, para 1.

129 IMO, 'International Conference on the Safe and Environmentally Sound Recycling of Ships, Adoption of the Final Act and any Instruments, Recommendations and Resolutions resulting from the Work of the Conference, Hong Kong International Convention on the Safe and Environmentally Sound Recycling of Ships, 2009,' (19 May 2009) SR/CONF/45.

dressed in one of the non-binding guidelines that supplement the HKC.[130] Additionally, the HKC does not prescribe a specific method for the process of ship recycling, nor does it apply to ships of less than 500 gross tonnage[131] (GT) or ships that only operate in waters under the sovereignty or jurisdiction of their flag state (Art 3 (3) HKC).

Strongly simplified, the core of the Convention is a combination of construction requirements (Reg 4 Annex, Appendix 1), responsibilities of the shipowner to maintain a record of hazardous materials on board—the Inventory of Hazardous Materials (IHM, Reg 5 Annex)—and a certification requirement for ships (Reg 15 ff Annex). More specifically, the HKC bans or restricts the installation of asbestos, ozone-depleting substances, polychlorinated biphenyls and anti-fouling compounds and systems in new ships (Reg 4 in conjunction with Appendix 1). Furthermore, to ensure that the IHM is accurate, surveys are conducted at the beginning, middle and end of the operating life of a ship (Reg 10 Annex). Finally, the recycling of a specific ship is to be reported to the competent authorities and the envisaged process of dismantling it must be laid out in a ship-specific Ship Recycling Plan (Reg 9 Annex) subject to approval. While the HKC does not apply to ships owned or operated by a State party and used only on government non-commercial service, it still (and rather unusually for an IMO treaty) obliges State parties to strive for the recycling of such ships in conformity with the Convention (Art 3 (2)). Art 1 (2) explicitly allows for provisions stricter than those of the HKC. Furthermore, the HKC provides for the *no more favourable treatment* (NMFT) of non-Party ships (Art 3 (4), ie obliging Parties to apply the requirements of the HKC to ships flying the flag of non-Parties). The NMFT principle is found in IMO treaties to prevent ships from simply re-flagging to a non-Party State to evade treaty standards. It ensures that every ship is under obligation to fulfil requirements of that treaty upon entry into the port of a State Party. In practice this means, 'port States enforcing applicable standards in

130 IMO, Res MEPC.210(63) adopted on 2 March 2012, MEPC 63/23, Annex 4, paras 3.2.6. and 3.4.2.6.

131 The gross tonnage of a ship is a measure of the internal volume of the ship calculated according to Annex I of the International Convention on Tonnage Measurement of Ships, 1969 (adopted 23 June 1969, entered into force 18 July 1982) 1291 UNTS 3. As such, IMO Conventions usually reference the International Convention on Tonnage Measurement of Ships to define the GT in the context of a particular treaty, eg Art 2 (8) HKC.

a uniform manner to all ships in their ports, regardless of flag.'[132] With this, the NMFT principle is an expression of territorial jurisdiction and the right of the port State to exercise it.[133]

The provisions of the HKC are supplemented by six non-binding guidelines adopted to facilitate the application and implementation of the HKC by the administrative authorities and private sector stakeholders.[134] Art 17 (1) HKC provides for the entry into force of the treaty 24 months after the following three conditions have been met: 15 States must have become party to the treaty, their combined merchant fleet representing not less than 40% of the GT of the world's merchant fleet, and their combined maximum annual ship recycling volume over the past 10 years not being less than 3% of the GT of the combined merchant shipping of these states. This third entry-into-force criteria is specific to the HKC, and unusual compared to other IMO conventions. It serves an important purpose: it not only ensures that compliant ship recycling facilities actually exist when the treaty enters into force, but also that ship recycling business will not become focused on one recycling State only.

In 2021, 3% of 40% of the GT of the world fleet amounted to 17,764,212 GT. At the same time, while the five biggest ship recycling States—Bangladesh, China, India, Pakistan and Turkey— recycled a combined maximum annual volume of 37,509,862 GT between 2012 and 2021, the combined maximum annual ship recycling volume of the rest of the world during the same years amounted to a mere 1,418,668 GT.[135] It meant that two to three of the top five ship recycling countries had to become party to the treaty to reach the required recycling volume.[136] While, understandably,

132 Buhaug and others (n 3) para 2.32.

133 Fanø, *Enforcing International Maritime Legislation on Air Pollution through UNCLOS* (n 40) 74; see also at 75–76, where the author argues that the NMFT principle can be considered a principle of customary international law.

134 '2011 Guidelines for the Development of the Ship Recycling Plan' adopted by MEPC.196(62); '2012 Guidelines for Safe and Environmentally Sound Ship Recycling' adopted by MEPC.210(63); '2012 Guidelines for the Authorization of the Ship Recycling Facilities' adopted by MEPC.211(63); '2012 Guidelines for the survey and certification of ships under the Hong Kong Convention' adopted by MEPC.222(64); '2012 Guidelines for the inspection of ships under the Hong Kong Convention' adopted by MEPC.223(64); '2015 Guidelines for the development of the Inventory of the Hazardous Materials' adopted by MEPC.269(68).

135 IMO, MEPC, 'Calculation of Recycling Capacity for meeting the Entry-into-Force Conditions of the Hong Kong Convention' (n 96) 3.

136 At time of writing in 2023 an overall of 19 States have joined the treaty. For the number of contracting States and the world merchant shipping tonnage achieved,

it was initially thought that 'the fulfilment of its entry-into-force criteria will amount to a rather interminable process'[137], Turkey and India becoming party in 2019 gave confidence that Bangladesh, China or Pakistan becoming party to the HKC could soon bring it into effect. Finally, when Bangladesh became Party to the HKC on 26 June 2023, it triggered the treaty's entry into force by 26 June 2025.[138]

The EU from the outset did what it could to support the coming into force of the HKC. Not being able to become party to the HKC (see Art 16 (2)), the EU was only left with authorizing its MSs to become party to the HKC 'for the parts falling under the exclusive competence of the Union'[139].

IV. An EU Ship Recycling Regulation to Support the Hong Kong Convention

The initial expectation that the drafted HKC would not enter into force any time soon—after all, it will have been more than 16 years since its adoption when the HKC enters into force in 2025—together with the inadequacy of existing provisions on waste shipments to address the problems of ship dismantling, brought the Commission to contemplate its own measure. The initial EU Strategy for Better Ship Dismantling of 2008 claims that the objective 'is to ensure that ships with a strong link to the EU in terms of flag or ownership are dismantled only in safe and environmentally sound facilities worldwide, in line with the draft Ship Recycling Convention.'[140] A study initiated by the Commission speaks of the heightened responsibility

see IMO, 'Status of Treaties' <https://wwwcdn.imo.org/localresources/en/About/Conventions/StatusOfConventions/Status%20of%20IMO%20Treaties.pdf> accessed 18 May 2023.

137 Engels (n 95) 86; see also at 86–88 for a comprehensive assessment of the incentives and disincentives of states to ratify the HKC.

138 IMO, 'Hong Kong ship recycling Convention set to enter into force: Bangladesh and Liberia trigger entry into force of Convention for the Safe and Environmentally Sound Recycling of Ship' <https://www.imo.org/en/MediaCentre/PressBriefings/pages/Hong-Kong-Convention-set-to-enter-into-force-.aspx> accessed 8 December 2023.

139 Council of the European Union, 'Council Decision of 14 April 2014 concerning the ratification of, or the accession to, the Hong Kong International Convention for the Safe and Environmentally Sound Recycling of Ships, 2009, by the Member States in the interest of the Union', 2014/241/EU [2014] OJ L128/45.

140 Commission, 'EU Strategy on better ship dismantling' (n 122) 5.

of the EU[141] and encourages EU action on the basis of the HKC from a practical and moral standpoint:

> Early transposition of the Convention's key elements is crucial if it is to be ensured that the EU's role in taking action in the interests of environmental protection with respect to these tankers is not frustrated by failure to ensure the establishment of legal requirements for their safe and environmentally sound dismantling. [...] It is in fact considered that a firm commitment by the EU will foster an increased support for the international ship dismantling rules and will act as an incentive for other States to ratify the Ship Recycling Convention. The EU will reinforce its role as a driving force for implementation of global standards.[142]

The study also emphasises that the entry into force of the HKC will only be promoted if EU MSs become party to the HKC simultaneously, and if an EU measure fully implements the Convention rather than implementing it selectively, thereby creating inconsistent standards at EU and international level.[143] An impact assessment found that 'that the most appropriate option is that of an integrated policy approach combining legislative measures to implement and complement the draft Convention at EU level, and non-legislative measures to promote voluntary action by industry.'[144] Following up on this, the EU adopted the SRR in 2013. However, the provisions of the Regulation were only to apply '6 months after the date that the combined maximum annual ship recycling output of the ship recycling facilities included in the European List [ie approved by the Commission] constitutes not less than 2[.]5 million light displacement tonnes'[145], but latest as of 31 December 2018 (Art 32 (1) SRR). In that, the SRR attempted

---

141 Milieu Ltd & COWI, 'Study in relation to options for new initiatives regarding dismantling of ships: Note on pros and cons of early transposition of the Ship Recycling Convention' (2009) <https://ec.europa.eu/environment/pdf/waste/ships/early_transposition_note.pdf> accessed 18 May 2023, 8.

142 Milieu Ltd & COWI, 'Note on pros and cons of early transposition of the Ship Recycling Convention' (n 141) 11.

143 ibid (n 133) 22.

144 See Commission, 'Public consultation on the options for new initiative regarding dismantling of ships' <http://ec.europa.eu/environment/waste/ships/pdf/Consultation_ship_dismantling.pdf> accessed 18 May 2023, 1; that also refers to Commission Staff Working Document, 'Impact Assessment for an EU Strategy for Better Ship Dismantling' (n 90).

145 With *light displacement tonnes* defined in the SRR in accordance with common understanding as 'the weight of a ship in tonnes without cargo, fuel, lubricating oil in storage tanks, ballast water, fresh water, feedwater, consumable stores, passenger

to cater to the concern of non-availability of adequate ship recycling facilities, albeit with limited patience. The SRR primarily addresses EU-flagged ships (Art 2 (1)), while imposing documentation requirements on non-EU-flagged ships that enter an EU port (Art 12). The SRR entered into force on the 30 December 2013[146], has so far undergone one amendment[147] and has been supplemented by six Implementing Decisions.[148] This chapter first sheds some light on the relationship between the BC and the SRR, specifically whether the EU breached its obligations under the BC when it adopted the SRR (1.). The second part of this chapter then gives an overview of the provisions of the SRR, also in comparison to the HKC (2.).

---

and crew and their effects and […] the sum of the weight of the hull, structure, machinery, equipment and fittings of the ship' (Art 3 (23)).

146 For more information and an overview of documents, see Commission, 'Ships: EU rules on ship recycling aim to make it greener and safer, and to reduce the negative environmental and social impacts of ship recycling' <http://ec.europa.eu/environment/waste/ships/eu_policy.htm> accessed 18 May 2023.

147 Decision (EU) 2018/853 of the European Parliament and of the Council of 30 May 2018 amending Regulation (EU) No 1257/2013 and Directives 94/63/EC and 2009/31/EC of the European Parliament and of the Council and Council Directives 86/278/EEC and 87/217/EEC as regards Procedural Rules in the Field of Environmental Reporting and repealing Council Directive 91/692/EEC [2018] OJ L150/155.

148 Commission Implementing Decision (EU) 2015/2398 of 17 December 2015 on Information and Documentation related to an Application for a Facility located in a Third Country for inclusion in the European List of Ship Recycling Facilities [2015] OJ L 332/145; Commission Implementing Decision (EU) 2016/2321 of 19 December 2016 on the Format of the Ready for Recycling Certificate issued in accordance with Regulation (EU) No 1257/2013 of the European Parliament and of the Council on Ship Recycling [2016] OJ L 345/112; Commission Implementing Decision (EU) 2016/2322 of 19 December 2016 on the Format of the Statement of Completion of Ship Recycling required under Regulation (EU) No 1257/2013 of the European Parliament and of the Council on Ship Recycling [2016] OJ L 345/117; Commission Implementing Decision (EU) 2016/2323 of 19 December 2016 establishing the European List of Ship Recycling Facilities pursuant to Regulation (EU) No 1257/2013 of the European Parliament and of the Council on Ship Recycling [2016] OJ L 345/119 (amended through Commission Implementing Decision 10 times since); Commission Implementing Decision (EU) 2016/2324 of 19 December 2016 on the Format of the Report of Planned Start of Ship Recycling required under Regulation (EU) No 1257/2013 of the European Parliament and of the Council on Ship Recycling [2016] OJ L 345/129; Commission Implementing Decision (EU) 2016/2325 of 19 December 2016 on the Format of the Certification on the Inventory of Hazardous Materials issued in accordance with Regulation (EU) No 1257/2013 of the European Parliament and of the Council on Ship Recycling [2016] OJ L 345/131.

1. Reconciling the EU Ship Recycling Regulation and the Basel Convention

In the wake of the SRR, there was one claim that deserves special attention—the claim that the EU, as a Party to the BC, has violated its obligations under international law by passing the SRR. The basis for this claim is mainly that the BC does not explicitly exclude ships from its regulatory scope.[149]. It is claimed, therefore, that lacking any legal possibility in the BC itself to derogate from its provisions, the EU as Party to the BC would violate its international obligations if it introduced secondary legislation in contradiction to the BC.[150] In particular, Art 11 BC is considered to be inapplicable. Art 11 (1) BC provides that

> Parties may enter into bilateral, multilateral, or regional agreements or arrangements regarding transboundary movement of hazardous wastes or other wastes with Parties or non-Parties provided that such agreements or arrangements do not derogate from the environmentally sound management of hazardous wastes and other wastes as required by this Convention. These agreements or arrangements shall stipulate provisions which are not less environmentally sound than those provided for by this Convention in particular taking into account the interests of developing countries.

It is arguable whether an EU Regulation constitutes a *bilateral, multilateral or regional agreement or arrangement* considering the fact that the EU is Party to the BC as an entity in its own right and, therefore, any measure taken by the EU as one party could be considered unilateral.[151] In this case, the EU would not have Art 11 (1) BC to resort to for deviating from BC provisions. Assuming for the sake of argumentation, however, that Art 11 (1) BC could be relevant, the crucial test would be whether the EU Regulation at hand is 'not less environmentally sound' than those of the BC itself. With

149 Ludwig Krämer, 'The Commission proposal for a Regulation on ship recycling, the Basel Convention and the protection of the environment' (2012) <https://www.shipbreakingplatform.org/wp-content/uploads/2018/11/Legal-Analysis-of-EC-proposal_Ludwig-Kramer_FINAL-1.pdf> accessed 18 May 2023, para 7.

150 ibid para 11ff.

151 See ibid para 18, who pointedly asserts that '[t]he proposal for an EU Regulation on ship recycling does not constitute a "bilateral, multilateral, or regional agreement or arrangement". Rather it is a unilateral measure by a Contracting Party [...] to organize its internal legislation.'

regard to the provisions of the HKC itself a position paper of 2012 by the Center for International Environmental Law (CIEL) finds:

> While the implementation of the Hong Kong Convention - especially some of its measures such as the comprehensive inventory of hazardous materials on board ships - could contribute to improving the environmental, health, and human rights performance of shipbreaking, on the other hand, the Hong Kong Convention's scope is severely limited. Examples of these limitations include excluding whole categories of ships from the application of the legal regime (e.g., government owned non-commercial ships and warships as well as ships under 500GT) and thus not covering all hazardous waste aboard ships. Furthermore, although the Hong Kong Convention covers recycling of ships, it fails to monitor the hazardous waste processing facilities further downstream. [...] Overall, the Basel Convention's goal is to reduce transboundary movement of hazardous waste. The Hong Kong Convention, however, does not contemplate that goal. In addition, the Hong Kong Convention's enforcement mechanisms are much weaker than those of the Basel Convention's. The Hong Kong Convention does not include the actual waste treatment downstream of the dismantling yard, and does not provide for inspections of the recycling yards. Furthermore, in contrast to the Basel Convention, the Hong Kong Convention does not call for ex-ante authorization of recycling yards, and does not impose a duty on states to re-import illegally transferred waste. Equally important, the Hong Kong Convention does not criminalize the act of illegally transferring waste.[152]

152 Center for International Environmental Law, 'Legality of the EU Commission Proposal on Ship Recycling' <https://www.shipbreakingplatform.org/wp-content/uploads/2018/11/CIEL-legal-opinion-on-EU-Ships-Propos-ed-Regulation-12-Dec-2012.pdf> accessed 10 March 2023, 8–9. With regard to the exclusion of ships below 500 GT and warships it should be kept in mind that '[s]hips below 500GT will include many small vessels such a fishing boats and other non-ocean going ships; although their percentage of overall GT may only amount to 1%, collectively they account for some 36% in numbers of vessels that are scrapped each year' and that 'warships—even with their relatively high proportion of more valuable metals—can represent a challenge for even the most conscientious of breakers that goes beyond that associated with merchant ships. These ships, with their extensive compartmentalisation plus wide array of inbuilt equipment, can present a plethora of hazardous materials in both the insulating and electrical gear. In addition, the relatively long life of many naval vessels in comparison to the mercantile fleet can result in a much higher presence of hazardous materials within their structures.', Galley (n 87) 182–83. For a more detailed comparison of the BC and the HKC, *see* Center for International Environmental Law, 'Shipbreaking and the Basel Convention: Analysis

It, therefore, concludes that

> the Hong Kong Convention lacks certain elements of what would constitute an environmentally sound management of waste as envisaged by Article 11 of the Basel Convention. Similarly, the Proposed Regulation itself cannot be considered an Article 11 agreement as it implements the provisions of the Hong Kong Convention [...].[153]

Consequently, it considers the 'attempt to unilaterally exempt a certain category of hazardous waste covered by the Basel Convention [...] from the control mechanisms of the Convention [...] illegal under international law and EU law.'[154]

This argumentation, however, disregards one important aspect, namely that parts of the international community decided to draft the HKC as a stand-alone treaty dealing exclusively with the disposal of ships. In fact, the IMO, the ILO and the BC Secretariat had been cooperating within a Joint Working Group to inter alia feed into the process of drafting a new legally binding agreement on ship recycling.[155] The international community represented in these organisations decided that it is desirable that ships as waste be treated differently than waste is treated under the provisions of the BC. While the Joint Working Group's requests—eg to have the instrument of prior informed consent as existing within the BC be introduced in the HKC[156] or the HKC to 'enhance enforcement of standards'[157]—did not prevail, the Joint Working Group still worked together in the common understanding that an IMO treaty on ship recycling was in process. This strong dynamic within the international community and the organisations involved clearly express the intention to prospectively exclude ships from the realm of the BC.

In the case of the HKC—a treaty drafted under the auspices of the IMO—the result of this understanding is a treaty that reflects the peculiarities that are common in IMO treaties, such as limited applicability to smaller ships or non-commercial government-owned ships. The COP of the BC

of the Level of Control established under the Hong Kong Convention' <https://www.ciel.org/Publications/Shipbreaking_22Apr11.pdf> accessed 10 March 2023.

153 CIEL, 'Legality of the EU Commission Proposal on Ship Recycling' (n 152) 9.

154 Krämer (n 149) 11.

155 See Joint ILO/IMO/BC Group on Ship Scrapping (2nd session), 'Report of the Joint Working Group' (14 December 2005) ILO/IMO/BC WG 2/11, paras 1.7, 1.11, 4.12, 10.2.6.

156 ibid para 8.13.

157 ibid para 4.12.

itself has acknowledged that parties to the BC have different views on the equivalency of the HKC and the BC. Nonetheless, the COP '[e]ncourages parties to ratify the Hong Kong Convention to enable its early entry into force',[158] and, thereby, accept and respect it as a treaty meant to prevail when it comes to the treatment of end-of-life ships.

The EU has claimed in the context of the BC that 'taking a life cycle perspective [...] the Hong Kong Convention appears to provide a level of control and enforcement at least equivalent to that one provided by the Basel Convention for ships which are waste under the Basel convention'.[159] Also, the Legal Service of the Council of the EU in a Legal Opinion in 2012 referred to Art 31 Vienna Convention on the Law of Treaties[160] (VCLT) and the requirement of good faith interpretation of treaties enshrined therein. It held that

> [w]hilst the absence of an unequivocal view from the COP means the issue of equivalence is not entirely solved, the Legal Service nevertheless considers the fact that the COP encourages the Parties to ratify the Hong Kong Convention as reasonable justification for taking the view that the '*preliminary assessment*' of the EU and its Member States amounts to a good faith interpretation of the Basel Convention.[161]

The Council's Legal Service concludes

> that the Hong Kong Convention, and EU legislation giving effect thereto, would be likely to satisfy the requirements of Article 11 of the Basel Convention in its current form, as regards States which are Parties to the

---

158 BC, 'Report of the Conference of the Parties to the Basel Convention on the Control of Transboundary Movements of Hazardous Wastes and Their Disposal on its tenth meeting' (1 November 2011) UNEP/CHW.10/28, Decision BC-10/17, para 2.

159 See BC, 'Conference of the Parties to the Basel Convention on the Control of Transboundary Movements of Hazardous Wastes and Their Disposal on its tenth meeting' (11 August 2011), 'Compilation of the completed tables and submissions received pursuant to decision OEWG-VII/12', UNEP/CHW.10/INF/18, Annex II ('Submissions from Parties, Signatories and other relevant Stakeholders'), 39. Annex I of the document also provides a comprehensive table comparing the provisions of the BC and HKC.

160 Vienna Convention on the Law of Treaties (adopted 23 May 1969, entered into force 27 January 1980), 1155 UNTS 331.

161 Council, Opinion of the Legal Service, 'Proposal for a Regulation of the European Parliament and of the Council on ship recycling – relationship between Regulation 1013/2006 on waste shipments, the Basel Convention, and the Hong Kong Convention' (28 November 2012) 16995/12, para 21.

Hong Kong Convention, or which (pending the entry into force of the latter Convention) host recycling facilities authorised in accordance with the proposed regulation.[162]

Considering that the HKC is the outcome of a coordinated approach of the international community involving three international organisations, the interpretation of the Council Legal Service's conclusion that the EU in passing the SRR is acting in good faith in the sense of Art 31 (1) VCLT is at the very least defensible. The Legal Service's opinion also addresses the Ban Amendment (not yet in force then), however. It finds that removing end-of-life ships from the scope of the WSR raises 'legal concerns [...] with regard to compliance with the obligation in international law not to defeat the purpose and object of a Treaty'[163] (essentially Art 18 VCLT). It admits that the 'the most obvious difficulty' in the context of the Ban Amendment would be arguing that the recycling of ships under the SRR is *not less environmentally sound* than the application of the Ban Amendment, as '[c]onceptually, a prohibition appears on the face of it to be more protective of the environment than a regime of managed exports of hazardous waste.'[164] Therefore, the controversy around the SRR and its compatibility with the BC gained new momentum upon the entry into force of the BC's Ban Amendment in 2019. The CIEL offered an updated analysis on the relationship between the SRR and the BC. In this, it repeats its criticism that the EU through adoption of the SRR has taken EU-flagged end-of-life ships out of the scope of its WSR. Additionally, concerning the Ban Amendment now in force, it stresses that 'the inclusion of ship recycling facilities located in developing countries on the European List and the eventual export of EU-flagged ships to such facilities would be illegal under both EU and international law', or to put it more bluntly, '[t]here remains no legal means for the EU to export end of life ships for disposal to developing countries'.[165]

Eventually, in an attempt to reconcile the BC, the WSR and the SRR the Commission in 2021 tabled a proposal for a new WSR and amendments to the SRR, which at time of writing in 2023 is still undergoing the legislative

162 ibid 10.

163 ibid 13.

164 ibid 11.

165 CIEL, 'Legality of EU Proposals on Ship Recycling: Updated Legal Opinion of the Center for International Environmental Law (CIEL)' <https://www.shipbreakingplatform.org/wp-content/uploads/2020/09/CIEL-Legality-EU-Proposals-on-Ship-Recycling-2020.pdf> accessed 18 May 2023, 5.

process.[166] Emphasising its commitment to international law and referencing the entry into force of the BC's Ban Amendment, the Commission essentially proposes inter alia an export ban on ships to non-OECD countries that become waste while under the national jurisdiction of an EU MS (Recital 14, Art 2 (2) (h), Art 78 (amending Art 6 (2) of the SRR) of the proposal). With that, provisions of the SRR would be left to only apply to ships that become waste outside the EU, ie under the national jurisdiction of a third State or on the high seas. The new WSR could effectively set a precedence for the BC to be regarded as the primary instrument to address ships that become waste while under national jurisdiction and for the HKC to fill the gap where the ship becomes waste on the high seas. Even then, the question remains how this understanding could be brought into agreement with the wording of the HKC and the intention of its drafters and its contracting Parties.

2. The EU Ship Recycling Regulation

The overall structure of the SRR, being modelled after the HKC, is almost identical to the system established under the HKC. However, a few aspects are noteworthy. For one, similar to the HKC, the SRR also restricts and prohibits the use of certain material (see Art 4 and Annex I SRR). Annex I lists these prohibited or restricted materials. Unlike the HKC, which allows for the use of hydrochlorofluorocarbons in new installations until 1 January 2020 (Appendix 1), the SRR prohibits all ozone-depleting substances without exception and, in that, is stricter than the HKC. Similarly, the SRR additionally provides that Brominated Flame Retardants must be documented as hazardous materials. These two instances of stricter standards in the SRR do not appear problematic since the HKC explicitly allows for stricter standards (Art 1 (2) HKC).

The EU in its SRR tried to stay close to the structure of the HKC. It expressly refers to the IMO Guidelines to the HKC or the HKC itself for the purposes of interpretation of the SRR's provisions (Recital 12), the development of the Ship Recycling Plan (Recital 16, Art 7 (2) (a)), the standards applicable to the Ship Recycling Facility Plan (Art 15 (2) (g)), the conduct of surveys (Art 8) and inspections (Art 11 (2)), the establishment/maintenance

166 Commission, 'Proposal for a Regulation of the European Parliament and of the Council on Shipments of Waste and amending Regulations (EU) No 1257/2013 and (EU) No 2020/1056' COM (2021) 709 final.

(Art 5 (3),(4) and (7), Art 12 (3)) and validity (Art 10 (2) (a)) of the IHM, the certification (Art 9 (1) subpara 3 and (9) subpara 2) and the requirements for ship recycling facilities (Art 13 (1)). The two main certificates, namely the Ready for Recycling Certificate and the Inventory Certificate, seem to owe their names to their HKC counterparts, even though the latter is not an identical adoption of vocabulary. Furthermore, the SRR envisages adjustments to the Regulation to take into account development of the HKC (Recital 20, Arts 5 (8) and 30 (2)).

On the other hand, some important distinctions apply that can be deemed a result of the SRR's regional nature. Third states have to carry on board a statement of compliance issued by their flag States, verifying their documentation on hazardous materials. This statement may be modelled after the HKC's International Certificate on Inventory of Hazardous Materials (IHM, Art 12 (6)). The SRR, thereby, ensures that upon entry into force of the HKC, no additional burden is placed upon a ship flying the flag of a third country. This facilitates coexistence of the SRR and the HKC. Also, while the HKC tasks national administrations with authorizing ship recycling facilities, the SRR only allows ships to be recycled in ship recycling facilities contained in the European List (Art 6 (2) (a)). As an EU ship recycling yard, national authorisation is a necessary but not sufficient condition to be included (Art 13 (1) (a)). For EU ship recycling facilities, the Commission will include the facility based on the notification of MSs (Art 16 (1) (a)), while facilities located in third countries have to apply to the Commission to be included in the European List (Arts 15, 16 (1) (b)). It was not until 6 December 2018, however—shortly before the SRR became fully applicable—that the Commission published its Implementing Decision including a fourth update of the European List, which finally also contained ship recycling facilities located outside of the EU (two located in Turkey, one located in the United States).[167]

167 See Commission Implementing Decision (EU) 2018/1906 of 30 November 2018 amending Implementing Decision (EU) 2016/2323 to update the European List of ship recycling facilities established pursuant to Regulation (EU) No 1257/2013 of the European Parliament and of the Council [2018] OJ L310/29. Commission Implementing Decision (EU) 2016/2323 has so for been amended an overall of nine times, the most recent European List of ship recycling facilities can be found in the Annex of Commission Implementing Decision (EU) 2022/2462 of 14 December 2022 amending Commission Implementing Decision (EU) 2016/2323 establishing the European List of Ship Recycling Facilities pursuant to Regulation (EU) No 1257/2013 of the European Parliament and of the Council, [2022] OJ L321/42.

One deviation from the HKC, celebrated as a success, was the banning of beaching practices by the SRR. While *beaching* is not expressly addressed anywhere in the regulation, it is difficult to conceive how a facility that dismantles ships through *beaching* would ever be able to fulfil the conditions set out in Art 13 (1) SRR, especially its subpara (c) ('operates from built structures').[168]. It is, however, argued that the requirement for a ship recycling yard to demonstrate *control of any leakage, in particular in intertidal zones*, implies the prohibition of beaching practices.[169] Also, the legislator's intent is clear.[170]

The most problematic deviation from the HKC, however, is the envisaged introduction of a financial instrument as a compliance mechanism of the Regulation (Recital 19, Art 29). This financial instrument is a central piece for the effectiveness of this regulation. It is the instrument that is supposed to prevent the re-flagging of EU ships to avoid having to comply with the SRR's provisions, since the SRR (with the exception of Art 12) applies to EU-flagged ships only (Art 2 (1)). A financial mechanism to achieve just that may have seemed easy at first sight. This short Art 29 and Recital 19 in the preamble, however, pose the biggest challenge to the implementation of the SRR.

V. The Quest for a Financial Instrument to Complement the EU Regulation

This section takes a closer look at the options for a financial mechanism that have been proposed over time. While being effective (ie encouraging compliance with the requirements of the SRR) a financial mechanism would ideally be proportionate, easy to implement and create only a low administrative burden for shipowners. Furthermore, and most importantly, it would not affect market forces and be compatible with international law. The latter aspect for its sheer significance is the focus of this analysis. This section demonstrates that the real risk of breaching international law is the reason why—at time of writing in 2023, almost 10 years after its entry into

168 See Galley (n 87) 201 (footnote 41): in this context the claim that 'carrying out work within the hull of a vessel being demolished might actually constitute working within a built structure' seems to be at odds with the provision.

169 ibid 201.

170 See the statement of the Rapporteur of the Committee on the Environment, Public Health and Food Safety of the European Parliament, Carl Schlyter, during the final vote: <http://www.europarl.europa.eu/sides/getDoc.do?pubRef=-//EP//TEXT+CRE+20131022+ITEM-008-01+DOC+XML+V0//EN> accessed 18 May 2023.

force—the SRR still has no financial mechanism in place. To this end, it examines the suggestions for a financial instrument as part of the SRR.

The underlying notion of all propositions is that a suitable financial regime embedded in an appropriate set of regulations must close the shipowner's revenue gap or, in one case, the facility owner's revenue gap. This revenue gap is the financial loss of the shipowner or facility owner due to higher recycling costs of the ship recycling facility and the therefore reduced price paid to the shipowner when recycling in a compliant manner. All proposals are also based on the idea, that the means to close this gap have to somehow be collected from the shipowner in advance, and that the shipowner forgoes his right to remuneration if he chooses a sub-standard recycling facility for eventual ship disposal.

So far, over the course of more than a decade a range of quite different possible financial mechanisms have been proposed in an overall of four studies and a final report. The following section outlines proposals that have been presented, focusing on the incoming part of the mechanism, namely how the funds to close the cost gap would be generated. The question of how accumulated funds are to be released and disbursed has also been subject to discussion but proves to be much less difficult to answer. The disbursement side of a potential financial mechanism will only be addressed in the one case where it raises doubts in terms of its legitimacy. Discriminatory disbursement of funds was only suggested during the EU's legislative procedure of the SRR, introducing the notion that only the recycling of EU-flagged ships should be subsidised, while all ships entering an EU port would feed the corresponding funds.[171] This suggestion, however, did not prevail.

1. The General Notion of a Global Ship Recycling Fund

First suggestions for a Ship Recycling Fund date back to 2005 when the environmental NGO Greenpeace initiated a study carried out by the consultancy Ecorys. Proposed as a revolving fund, it was envisaged to be operated through levies charged at construction of the ship or during the lifetime of a ship, the latter affecting existing ships as well.[172] A Scrapping Life Insurance

171 See EP, 'Report on the proposal for a regulation of the European Parliament and of the Council on ship recycling, Committee on the Environment (n 89) 72 (para 6 ad a) of the Explanatory Statement).

172 Ecorys (n 95) 27 and 30.

was introduced as an alternative.[173] At this point, the focus was on a global ship recycling fund, preferably under the auspices of the IMO.[174] In 2007, the Commission still considered a mandatory ship dismantling fund linked with international regulations on ship dismantling, while emphasizing that '[i]f an IMO-based fund is not achievable, a regional system could be considered.'[175] However, when the idea of a Ship Recycling Fund did not sufficiently resonate in the IMO, it became clear that the discussions on such a fund would have to be held with a future EU legislative initiative in mind. The focus then shifted to a financing mechanism that would supplement the prospective EU legislation. It was thought of as an instrument that would first exist on a regional level but would be designed to allow for it to be adjusted to apply globally if it generated enough of a spill-over effect.

2. Introducing the Concept of EU Responsibility

The Commission initiated its own study to investigate the options for such a Ship Recycling Fund.[176] The study in 2009 presented three options: an environmental charge for newly built vessels, a recurrent tax on the shipping industry and a charge on ships calling at EU ports. The charge on newly built ships would not affect existing ships, thereby not complying with the Polluter-Pays Principle.[177] But more importantly, the study establishes that the first two options would, in principle, distort competition between the EU shipping industry and non-EU flag States. Nonetheless, it dismisses the possibility of a factual distortion of competition because of the rather negligible additional costs that these mechanisms would impose compared to total costs of ship construction or operation.[178] Even though this de minimis argument may overcome the self-imposed criteria that any measure should not distort international competition,[179] it may prove to be a slippery slope where a range of measures creating seemingly negligible

173 ibid 30.
174 ibid 32.
175 Commission, 'Green paper on ship dismantling' (n 38) 15.
176 Milieu Ltd & COWI, 'Study in relation to options for new initiatives regarding dismantling of ships: Note on the ship dismantling fund: Pros and cons of the three options' (2009) <http://ec.europa.eu/environment/waste/ships/pdf/fund_note.pdf> accessed 18 May 2023.
177 ibid 10.
178 ibid 10–11.
179 ibid 8.

market distortions add up. What is more, since the measures would directly affect EU-flagged ships, the possibility that EU-flagged ships may re-flag to avoid these charges is another obvious weakness of these two options and a very realistic outcome.

The solution to this very essential problem is presented in the form of a third option for a financial mechanism, namely the introduction of charges for ships calling at EU ports. Elaborating on this port levy, the study first dismisses as impractical the previously published declaration of the Commission that

> [t]he general objective of an EU strategy on ship dismantling is to ensure that ships with a strong link to the EU in terms of flag or ownership are dismantled only in safe and environmentally sound facilities worldwide, in line with the draft Ship Recycling Convention.[180]

Instead, it finds that 'because of the global nature of the shipping industry, where evasion of regulation is possible through re-flagging of ships, it might be appropriate to operate with an alternative and more pragmatic definition of *EU responsibility*'.[181] This statement introduces the notion that a fund may address ships that are not EU-flagged or EU-owned and uses the vague term of *EU responsibility* as a guiding principle and seemingly moral justification for broadening the scope of EU action to ships that actually have no link with the EU. The fragility of this construction becomes visible where the attempt is made to create an artificial link between the EU and non-EU-flagged or -owned ships to justify a financial measure that addresses the latter:

> Not considering ownership of vessels or flag state, the EU responsibility could be connected solely to the EU's share of *worldwide shipping services*. The *world wide shipping services* could be accounted for in various ways. The most consistent approach would be to count the shipping transport volume measured in tons/km worldwide. Another approach, and a good proxy to the method above, would be to count the number of ships calling at ports worldwide and in the EU.[182]

In light of the considerations of the EU as a worldwide provider of shipping services, it would 'technically [be] a service charge on "shipping services"

180 Commission, 'EU strategy for better ship dismantling' (n 122) 5.

181 Milieu Ltd & COWI, 'Note on the ship dismantling fund: Pros and cons of the three options' (n 176) 7.

182 ibid 7.

to be paid by the shipping companies and eventually consumers.'[183] Distortions of competition are considered unlikely due to the lack of viable alternatives to EU ports where goods are delivered to the EU.[184] Therefore, it is established that '[t]he major disadvantage of this financing mechanism is the fact that it may not be suitable in the long-term for the global fund because a tax collection system is not efficient in all countries (globally).'[185] The study concludes that the choice of measure should reflect the notion of such an *EU responsibility*,[186] and it establishes that 'an EU revolving fund based on recurrent charges on ships calling at ports would probably be the most feasible option, until the entry into force of the Ship Recycling Convention.'[187]

3. First Thoughts on Jurisdiction and Compliance with WTO Law

The next study on this subject was commissioned by the NGO Shipbreaking Platform and presented by the company Profundo in 2013, the year the SRR was adopted. It takes into account the draft provisions of the SRR as they were presented to the EP.[188] It analyses the options for a Ship Recycling Fund and a Ship Recycling Insurance, but concludes that a Ship Recycling Account in combination with a Transitional Fund would be the preferable option.[189] The Ship Recycling Account, unlike the Ship Recycling Fund, would be a savings account assigned to a ship and administered by a financial institution. It would be supplemented by a Transitional Fund for the recycling of older ships that would consist of a 'temporary surcharge on the deposits of all ships'.[190]

However, the question what measure would be appropriate and effective takes a back seat in this study while the search for a legal basis for a unilateral financial measure to be applied to all ships entering an EU port and the

183 ibid 11.
184 ibid 11.
185 ibid 12, see criteria established at 8.
186 ibid 17.
187 ibid 19.
188 Profundo, 'Financial mechanism to ensure responsible ship recycling: A research paper prepared for the NGO Shipbreaking Platform' (2013) <https://www.shipbreakingplatform.org/wp-content/uploads/2018/11/Financial-mechanisms-for-resonsible-ship-recycling-22_01_2013-FINAL.pdf> accessed 19 May 2023, 6.
189 ibid iii.
190 ibid 30–33.

discussion on compliance with international law are most noteworthy. The authors of the study pick up and support the notion that a measure should not merely be based on EU-ownership or flag.[191] They advocate the entry and exit of EU ports as a 'legal ground' upon which to introduce a measure. On a general note, they conclude:

> The legal analysis suggests that there will not be any strong legal objections to any of the three options, as long as they respect the non-discrimination principle as laid down in the WTO/GATT agreements. Placing European Court [sic] financial obligations on non-EU companies is not contrary to principles of customary international law, as each State has complete and exclusive sovereignty over its territory.[192]

This concluding summary addresses two aspects that require further consideration in this context. Firstly, the question of whether a fee imposed by a port State violates international law of the sea. Secondly, whether such a fee would be contrary to the agreements of the World Trade Organization (WTO)—hereafter referred to as WTO law. While the former question is dealt with simply and the point on a State's sovereign right to regulate within its territory may seem legitimate, the question of a possible violation of WTO law remains somewhat unanswered. Both assertions need further analysis.

a. The EU's Jurisdiction as a Coastal and Port State

While the brief conclusion cited above on the States' sovereign rights to pass regulation in their territory appears over-simplified, the authors of this study further elaborate on the question of coastal/port State authority and in that demonstrate a crucial error in reasoning. They assert:

> Following the Articles 56 and 73 of UNCLOS coastal states have jurisdiction in the Exclusive Economic Zone over ships and on ship[s] calling at ports. Harbour states can impose measures and legislation upon ships when these sail in the Exclusive Economic Zone or enter a harbour. A good example of legislation based on the harbour state principle is Council Directive 2009/16/EC of the European Parliament and of the Council of 23 April 209 on port State control. It establishes the obligation

191 ibid i.
192 ibid ii.

> for Member States of the European Union to enforce and control several European and international measures and laws.[193]

This paragraph contains quite a few misconceptions. Both, Arts 56 and 73 UNCLOS refer to the coastal States' rights in the EEZ which is not territory of the coastal State, but by definition of Art 55 UNCLOS 'an area beyond and adjacent to the territorial sea'. Furthermore,

> the scope of the coastal State's jurisdiction with regard to [...] the protection and preservation of the marine environment is not governed by Art. 56 (1) itself, but rather depends on the scope of other provisions codified in the Convention where the respective subject matter is further developed.[194]

The scope of the coastal State's jurisdiction concerning the protection and preservation of the marine environment can be found in Part XII of UNCLOS. With regard to the relevant Articles of Part XII, however, two important distinctions have to be made and have been fully disregarded in the argumentation of the study. That is, firstly, the distinction between the authority to put in place a prescriptive regulation and the authority to enforce it. Secondly, the related distinction between the coastal and the port State as established categories of UNCLOS. Amidst the confusion on the relevant provisions and the authority of coastal and port State, it is helpful to take a step back and look at a potential financial mechanism imposed on all ships upon their entry into a port of an EU member state and its compliance with UNCLOS step by step.

Art 211 UNCLOS addresses the law-making powers of States to prevent, reduce and control the pollution of the marine environment from vessels. Art 211 (4) to (6) UNCLOS addresses the coastal State's powers. Art 211 (3) UNCLOS allows for the establishment of port-entry requirements for foreign vessels. In this context, the coastal State is also the port State. Therefore, the question whether para 3 addresses the port State or the coastal State is rather theoretical here.[195] This is especially so, because the prescriptive authority of the port State seems to be considered a specific form of

193 ibid 12.

194 Alexander Proelss, 'Article 56: Rights, jurisdiction and duties of the coastal State in the exclusive economic zone' in Proelss and others (eds), *United Nations Convention on the Law of the Sea* (n 55) para 1.

195 See Kristin Bartenstein, 'Article 211: Pollution from vessels' in Proelss and others (eds), *United Nations Convention on the Law of the Sea* (n 55) paras 21–22, who points out that '[s]ome authors assert however, that port States have no prescriptive,

coastal jurisdiction resulting from the very idea of sovereignty of a State over its territorial waters.[196] In this, it is argued that Art 211 (3) UNCLOS does nothing less than pre-suppose an (almost) unlimited authority of a port State to introduce port-entry requirements.

> In the legal literature it is widely accepted that UNCLOS provides port States with extensive prescriptive jurisdiction over foreign ships, despite the absence of any very explicit provisions to this effect. Or, more accurately, the absence of particular provisions to the contrary, in combination with the implied acceptance of such jurisdiction in the articles quoted above [Arts 25 (2), 38 (2) and 211 (3) UNCLOS], is generally treated as evidence that this matter is regulated by general international law, rather than by UNCLOS. General international law, as noted above, includes few *a priori* limitations to this effect.[197]

To phrase it in a more figurative way: 'what has occurred is an assertion of the legal principle, that, within a port, the host state has absolute jurisdiction over visiting vessels in the same manner as if the visiting vessel were a foreign citizen vacationing or doing business in the host country.'[198]

On the other hand, Art 211 (4) UNCLOS confirms the coastal State's right to exercise its sovereignty within its territorial waters to adopt provisions to prevent, reduce and control marine pollution from foreign vessels. Art 211 (4) UNCLOS, however, only defines the scope of the coastal state's authority and, therefore, must be read against the backdrop of the general provisions of UNCLOS, especially concerning the right of foreign ships to innocent passage.[199] It is Art 21 UNCLOS that allows the coastal State to 'adopt laws and regulations [...] relating to innocent passage through the territorial sea' relating to inter alia 'the preservation of the environment of the coastal state and the prevention, reduction and control of pollution

---

but only enforcement authority as set forth in Art. 218, and that any prescription with regard to internal waters and ports is based on coastal State jurisdiction.'

196 See ibid para 22, who also asserts that '[t]he legal basis of port States' prescriptive authority is not to be found in Art. 211 (3), but indirectly in other provisions of the Convention, such as Arts. 2, 8 and 25, and in customary law.'; see also Ringbom, *The EU Maritime Safety Policy and International Law* (n 20) 212.

197 Ringbom, *The EU Maritime Safety Policy and International Law* (n 20) 214–15.

198 Ted L McDorman, 'Port State Control: A comment on the Tokyo MoU and issues of international law' (1997) 7 Asian Yearbook of International Law 229, 231; see to the same effect Fanø, *Enforcing International Maritime Legislation on Air Pollution through UNCLOS* (n 40) 74.

199 See Bartenstein (n 195) paras 22 and 27.

thereof' (para 1 (f)). The wording of this provision reveals one crucial aspect that the authors of the report did not have to address when mistakenly referring to Arts 56 and 73 UNCLOS. Art 21 (1) (f) UNCLOS explicitly refers to the protection of the coastal State's environment. It is in the inherent interest of the coastal state to protect its own environment that justifies the restriction of innocent passage through its territory.[200] Coastal State action on behalf of the environment as some kind of a common value deserving of protection is not provided for in this context.

The predominant part of all dismantled ships is being beached, ie potentially harm the marine environment in a way that could indeed negatively affect the coastal areas of EU MSs. Nonetheless, a thorough examination and consideration of a financial instrument as suggested here, should have included an extensive analysis of the UNCLOS provisions the EU as a party is bound to. The study should have addressed to what extent sub-standard ship recycling practices in Asian countries result in pollution of the EU's coastal environment. The EU's right to regulate its coasts to prevent harm from sub-standard ship recycling taking place in remote countries is not a given. The SRR itself refers to 'the environment' that it means to protect as exemplified in the first sentence of Art 1: 'The purpose of this Regulation is to prevent, reduce, minimise and, to the extent practicable, eliminate accidents, injuries and other adverse effects on human health and the environment caused by ship recycling.' The second sentence almost casually creates the link to coastal State rights granted by UNCLOS and is the only reference of this kind to be found in the SRR: 'The purpose of this

200 See also: Richard A Barnes, 'Article 21: Laws and regulations of the coastal State relating to innocent passage' in Proelss and others (eds), *United Nations Convention on the Law of the Sea* (n 55) para 1: 'Art. 21 seeks to balance coastal State interests with collective interests in maritime navigation.' More clearly: Bartenstein (n 195) para 2: 'Coastal States' interest in extensive authority over vessel-source pollution, in order to protect the marine environment contiguous to their coasts, stands in opposition to the needs of merchant fleets'; referring to land and coastal pollution, Barnes, 'Article 21', para 17: 'It may be observed that Art. 21 (1) (f) refers to the environment of the coastal State, so is not limited to mere pollution of the marine environment. This provides the basis for controls on atmospheric pollution and measures to prevent, control or deal with land and coastal pollution resulting from activities in marine spaces'; Veronica Frank, *The European Community and Marine Environmental Protection in the International Law of the Sea: Implementing Global Obligations at the Regional Level* (Martinus Nijhoff Publishers 2007) 196: 'the LOSC extends the capacity of coastal States to control dangerous traffic and defend their marine environment'.

Regulation is to enhance safety, the protection of human health and of the Union marine environment throughout a ship's life-cycle'.

In conclusion, it can be argued that the EU has prescriptive authority as a port State and as a coastal State to introduce a financial mechanism that imposes charges upon entry into a port of one of its MSs. However, a more thorough argument for this, as well as the demonstration of awareness for the fact that UNCLOS is the vital instrument of international law to be observed and followed, would have been desirable.

To complete the picture on coastal and port State's right in this context, it has to be pointed out that Art 218 UNCLOS and the enforcement powers of the port State cannot serve as a legal basis for such an instrument. However, this is what the authors seem to argue when they refer to the 'harbour state principle' and the EU's PSC Directive[201] that allows the 'European Union to enforce and control several European and international measures and laws'.[202] Once again, different concepts are confused. While it is true that Art 218 UNCLOS grants enforcement rights to the port State, the enforcement of provisions by a port State by virtue of its port State jurisdiction must be distinguished from the concept of PSC:

> While port State control measures are primarily proactive *viz.* preventive aiming at ensuring better compliance with internationally agreed maritime safety and pollution prevention rules and standards, port State jurisdiction in the sense of Art. 218 is reactive, focusing on the detection and punishment of discharge violations.[203]

This said, a financial mechanism as part of the SRR cannot be considered an enforcement measure, since its purpose would not be to punish an existing violation. Rather, it is thought of as an in-built regulatory mechanism to prevent circumvention of the SRR obligations. Moreover, as a measure, its nature would not match the PSC regime that is mainly based on the control of certification and documents carried on board. What would potentially qualify for a PSC inspection, however, would be the requirement to carry on-board a Statement of Compliance, issued to prove that any contributions to a financial instrument have been made. However, this is not subject of the discussion in question.

---

201 Directive 2009/16/EC of the European Parliament and of the Council of 23 April 2009 on Port State Control [2009] OJ L131/57.

202 Profundo (n 188) 12.

203 König, 'Article 218' (n 60) para 2.

b. Possible Conflicts with WTO law and the Principle of Non-Discrimination

The Profundo study also refers to a possible violation of WTO law and establishes that '[i]f a financial mechanism for responsible ship recycling does not discriminate between ships from different flag States or owners, non-compliance with the principle of non-discrimination can be avoided.'[204] While this statement is far from actually confirming that compliance with WTO law can be established if the instrument is applied equally to all ships, this study commenced the general discussion of WTO law compliance of a financial mechanism.

The study continues: 'The levying of a fee by the harbour authorities in Member states of the European Union should be feasible without discrimination and independent of the flag state of a ship or the country where the owner of a ship is established.'[205] Unfortunately, the authors of the study do not state the definite criteria according to which the mechanism would have to be created to ensure non-discrimination and compliance with WTO law. Actual WTO law provisions are neither cited nor assessed. This analysis leaves ample room for interpretation and is in line with the conclusion cited above that there will be no 'strong objection' to any measures that respect the principle of non-discrimination.[206] Instead, it refers to ECJ Case 366/10,[207] which the authors believe

> does not seem to consider as illegal, from a point of view of customary international law, the imposing of a financial participation to non-EU based companies. [...] the European Court ruled on prejudicial questions regarding the obligation of non-EU aviation companies to pay for the emission of greenhouse [...] via the inclusion of aviation activities in the scheme for greenhouse gas emission allowance trading.
> Following the European Court of Justice, this type of financial obligation laid upon non-EU companies are not contrary to principles of customary international law as the principle that each state has complete and exclusive sovereignty over its airspace, the principle that no state may validly

204 Profundo (n 188) 21.

205 ibid 22.

206 ibid 22.

207 Case C-366/10 *Air Transport Association of America and Others v Secretary of State for Energy and Climate Change* ECLI:EU:C:2011:864. This decision is discussed further in sections C.IV.4.c.–d. as to the Court's elaborations on the EU's jurisdiction to install an emission trading scheme for the aviation sector.

purport to subject any part of the high seas to its sovereignty, and the principle which guarantees freedom to fly over the high seas. Following this case law, it is not to be expected that (levying a fee for) a Ship Recycling Fund would be contrary to customary international law.'[208]

Needless to say, the ECJ is not the authority on the existence or interpretation of international customary law. Its findings can only be considered one legal opinion and are merely indicative.[209] Also, in its judgment, the ECJ assesses the three principles of customary international law it mentions with regard to Directive 2008/101/EC[210] that subjects aviation to an emission trading scheme and applies 'to those parts of flights which take place outside the airspace of Member States, including to flights by aircraft registered in third states'.[211] A Ship Recycling levy, however, would not take into account parts of a journey undertaken outside of the territory of the EU, since the calculation of the levy would not depend on distances travelled but on a ship's call in EU ports. As a result, the payment would not be based on an event that has occurred outside of EU territory. A quasi-appropriation of the high seas or foreign territory is, therefore, not even in question here. Reference to this judgment is justified at most with regard to the Court's finding that aircraft physically present in the territory of an EU MS 'are thus subject on that basis to the unlimited jurisdiction of the European Union'[212]. This statement represents the equivalent to the almost unlimited jurisdiction of the port State supported by UNCLOS, as discussed in the previous section. Therefore, the reference to case C-366/10 provides no new insights, much less seems to solve the question of compliance with WTO law.

Examining the Profundo study shows how complex the discussion on a financial mechanism for the SRR is and how important it is in that context to carefully distinguish existing concepts and appraise them comprehen-

208 Profundo (n 188) 22. The same argument is repeated at 28 and 34 for the other two suggested measures.

209 As such, the ECJ's opinion can be considered by the International Court of Justice in its deliberations (Art 38 (1) lit d of the Statute of the International Court of Justice, XV UNIO 355; the UNIO volumes can be found at <https://digitallibrary.un.org/record/1300969> accessed 11 December 2023).

210 Directive 2008/101/EC of the European Parliament and of the Council of 19 November 2008 amending Directive 2003/87/EC so as to include aviation activities in the scheme for greenhouse gas emission allowance trading within the Community [2009] OJ L8/3.

211 *Air Transport Association of America* (n 207) para 112.

212 ibid para 125.

sively. The question of compliance with WTO law—as is shown below—is the most important aspect to consider. A Final Report published by the Commission of 2014 discusses it more extensively (see B.V.5.). However, the Profundo study of January 2013 was first followed by another study initiated by the EP.

4. The Amount of a Levy and the Discriminatory Disbursement of Funds

In the month after the Profundo study, the fourth study on the implementation of a financial instrument as part of the SRR was presented by the EP as an Impact Assessment.[213] The paper was a reaction to the proposals for amendment of the SRR brought forward by the EP's Committee on the Environment, Public Health and Food Safety during the legislative process. The Committee's draft report contained a proposal to include in the SRR a new Art 5a that would impose a levy of EUR 0.03 per GT on EU and non-EU ships calling at a port or anchorage within the territory of a MS.[214] A Recycling Fund was thought to then 'provide a premium for ship recycling facilities on the European list for the recycling of EU ships that have been flying the flag of a Member State for at least two years prior to the approval of the ship recycling plan.'[215] The idea of a premium being paid to recycling facilities was a new approach which, however, does not raise serious concerns. On the other hand, paying such a premium only for the recycling of EU ships, does seem problematic. The disbursement of funds to facilities for the recycling of EU ships only is supposed to offer a privilege for EU ships and create an incentive for ships to remain under EU flag.[216] The premium to be paid to the recycling facility was proposed to

213 EP, 'Financing the environmentally sound recycling and treatment of ships: Impact Assessment of a substantive amendment to the Proposal for a Regulation on ship recycling' (2013) <https://www.europarl.europa.eu/document/activities/cont/201303/20130305ATT62130/20130305ATT62130EN.pdf> accessed 19 May 2023. This study was conducted by Milieu Ltd who also co-authored the Commission's 2009 study.

214 EP, Committee on the Environment, Public Health and Food Safety, 'Draft Report on the proposal for a regulation of the European Parliament and of the Council on ship recycling' (20 November 2012) 2012/0055(COD) 30ff.

215 ibid 31.

216 ibid 32, 82.

be EUR 30 per LDT.[217] It was conceded that as an initial proposal it would need further refinement.[218]

EP's Impact Assessment uses this proposal as a starting point to further analyse possible financial instruments. The criteria for assessment are: 'effective as quickly as possible', 'require as little administrative burden as possible', 'avoid distortion of competition between EU and non-EU ships' and 'be adaptable to fluctuating market conditions'.[219] Possible market distortions between EU ports and non-EU ports are not assessed, while possible distortions of competition within the EU are assessed. It further adds to the discussion the notion that a possible levy could be complemented by the possibility to provide a financial guarantee from a financial institution as an alternative to an actual payment.[220] The Impact Assessment generally seems to favour a levy system, while pointing out that it would have to provide for a mechanism to not disadvantage ships that frequently enter EU ports.[221] The study attempts to find an amount that is appropriate for a potential levy. Proclaimed uncertainties that play into such a calculation are fluctuating volumes of ships to be recycled, number and tonnage calling at EU ports, domestic prices for scrap steel, business cycles, domestic inflation and international exchange rates.[222] Ultimately, depending on the scenario, a levy of between EUR 0.006 and 0.04 or between EUR 0.01 and 0.025 per GT is considered appropriate.[223]

The Impact Assessment closes with an Annex that briefly points to questions of international law the analysis of which apparently was not part of the terms of reference. The authors point to the extensive rights port States enjoy under UNCLOS but also touch upon the fact that non-EU flag States could challenge a potential levy or fee based on the notion that a ship, while on the high seas, is only subject to the jurisdiction of its flag State.[224] That seems to address the problem of subjecting high seas to EU jurisdiction discussed in the previous sub-chapter. In terms of WTO law, the authors believe that a system of collecting contributions from all ships calling an

217 ibid 31.
218 ibid 32.
219 EP, 'Financing the environmentally sound recycling and treatment of ships (n 213) 22.
220 ibid 15.
221 ibid 58.
222 ibid 40.
223 ibid 58, 59.
224 ibid 60.

EU port, while disbursing funds for the recycling of EU-flagged ships only, could be considered discriminatory.[225]

Based on these findings, an alternative version of Art 5a to the SRR was proposed in the Final Report of the Committee on the Environment, Public Health and Food Safety of March 2013.[226] It provided for a levy per port call of EUR 0.05 per GT or, alternatively, for an annual levy of 20 payments to be paid, each corresponding to EUR 50 per LDT. The disbursement premium that was now to be paid for both, the recycling of EU ships and the recycling of non-EU ships, was set at EUR 35 per LDT. It, furthermore, provided for the possibility to review and adapt the amounts for the levy and the premium. A new proposed Art 5b provided for the possibility of depositing a financial guarantee instead of making an actual payment. Despite having taken into consideration all the recommendations of the Impact Assessment, the proposal to introduce a concrete financial instrument into the SRR was ultimately voted down by the EP by a narrow margin[227].

During further deliberations, Art 5a, at one point, read:

> Article 5a
> Incentive-based system
> In view of the current situation of ship recycling, characterised by an extreme externalisation of costs and unacceptable conditions involved in the dismantling of ships, the Commission shall, before the end of 2015, submit a legislative proposal for an incentive-based system that would facilitate safe and sound ship recycling.[228]

The final text of Art 29 SRR requires (or, in fact, required) the Commission to submit a report on the feasibility of a financial instrument by 31 December 2016. Its Recital 19 also makes clear that a financial instrument is to be applied to all ships calling at an EU port to generate the means

225 ibid 60, 61.

226 EP, 'Report on the proposal for a regulation of the European Parliament and of the Council on ship recycling' (n 89) 23ff.

227 See Ecorys, DNV GL and Erasmus School of Law, 'Financial Instrument to Facilitate Safe and Sound Ship Recycling: Final Report (Commission 2016) <https://op.europa.eu/de/publication-detail/-/publication/68d273df-433c-11e6-9c64-01aa75ed71a1> accessed 19 May 2023, 27, which mentions insufficient elaboration, unclarity as to the implementation of the levy and possible negative impacts on the competitiveness of EU ports as main arguments against the proposal, 30.

228 As adopted at the EP's first reading: EP, 'Amendments adopted by the European Parliament on 18 April 2013 on the proposal for a regulation of the European Parliament and of the Council on ship recycling' (18 April 2013) P7_TA(2013)0182.

to facilitate environmentally sound ship recycling, while not incentivising ships to flag-out.

5. Exploring a Ship Recycling Licence and Possible Conflicts with WTO law

In June 2016, the Commission published a Final Report 'Financial Instrument to Facilitate Safe and Sound Ship Recycling'.[229] It is a comprehensive document summarizing all proposals that had been made so far and elaborating further on aspects of the proposed levy and questions of compatibility with WTO law.

a. The Levy is Really a Tax—The Alternative of a Ship Recycling Licence

In it, the Commission adds a new dimension to the introduction of a port levy when it logically and in line with the general understanding of the nature of taxes[230] finds: 'if the port levy is essentially a forced payment to the government and the government does not provide any direct, individual performance to the shipowner in return, the port levy must be considered a (general) tax.'[231] The report continues to imply that the EU is lacking the necessary legislative competence to install such a tax, and even then, a unanimous Council decision would be required. The report cites Arts 113, 115 TFEU, however omits as a potentially applicable norm Art 192 (2) (a) TFEU, which refers to 'provisions primarily of a fiscal measure' and also requires a unanimous Council decision. As an alternative to the levy, which would effectively be a tax, the authors propose a new instrument, namely a Ship Recycling Licence. This licence would require all ships calling at EU ports to obtain a licence prior to entry. The fee for this licence would then be composed of an administrative fee and a contribution to the Ship Recycling Fund.[232] Since the fee for this licence would be 'earmarked' and

229 Ecorys, DNV GL and Erasmus School of Law, 'Financial Instrument to Facilitate Safe and Sound Ship Recycling' (n 227).

230 The OECD eg defines a tax as a 'compulsory, unrequited payment to general government', OECD, 'Tax' <https://www.oecd-ilibrary.org/taxation/tax/indicator-group/english_76e12892-en> accessed 15 December 2023.

231 ibid 48.

232 ibid 50.

result in an immediate entitlement for a future reimbursement, the one-sidedness of the payment that characterises a tax would be removed.[233] The study also considers combining this licencing scheme with a Ship Recycling Escrow Account, previously introduced in the Profundo study of 2013 as a Ship Recycling Account administered by a private financial institution.[234] However, the study concludes in the context of a Ship Recycling Insurance that 'there appeared to be no appetite on the part of the insurance market and the P&I [Protection & Indemnity] club to take an active role in developing the initial concept into a workable insurance product'.[235] It, therefore, raises the question whether private financial institutions would be willing to participate in developing a system for and executing a Ship Recycling Account.

The study suggests that the licensing scheme would have to be administered by an existing or newly established EU agency and eventually integrated into the PSC system.[236] It does not have an answer as to what would happen to funds that are forfeited by shipowners due to non-compliance and asks for this to be explored further.[237] One of the advantages stated in favour of the Ship Recycling Licence is that

> [a]lthough the present recommendations are not specifically geared towards smaller sized ships currently excluded from the scope of SRR, it is believed that the proposed ship recycling licence is neutral towards possible future inclusion of also these smaller ships in the scope of the SRR. Neutral, because if the ship recycling licence were to become applicable to smaller sized ships as well, this would not lead to disproportional financial consequences. [...] the capital amount to be accumulated would be relative to the ship's size and revenue gap.[238]

It is unclear whether the authors of the study are innocently pointing out a potential future advantage or are basing this statement on the understanding that the Commission is intending, at a later stage, to extend the applicability of the SRR to smaller ships—and, thereby, un-align the SRR with the HKC. It becomes clear here that the financial instrument to be

233 ibid 51.
234 ibid 52, 31; Profundo (n 188) 30ff.
235 Ecorys, DNV GL and Erasmus School of Law, 'Financial Instrument to Facilitate Safe and Sound Ship Recycling' (n 227) 47.
236 ibid 103, 105.
237 ibid 104.
238 ibid 105.

introduced as part of the SRR at this point is understood to be more than a mere 'additional *interim measure* to make early transposition effective'[239], since the authors of the study consider exporting this proposal to the IMO for 'the adoption of a similar instrument with global effect'.[240] In fact, it would be naive to believe that the Commission would settle for the SRR as a mere accelerator and then do away with it. The Commission would more likely than not use the pressure of an existing regional regulation in the future to push for even stricter standards once the HKC is in force.

With the option of a Ship Recycling Licence established as the official recommendation of the study[241], the Final Report dedicates the Annex B of the Report to the question of WTO law compliance in a comparatively comprehensive manner. It assesses an instrument applicable to all ships calling to EU ports against the principles of 'Freedom of Transit' and 'Non-discrimination' contained in the General Agreement on Tariffs and Trade 1994[242] (GATT), as well as its exceptions for the protection of public morals, human health and the environment.

b. Internal Charges and Freedom of Transit—Articles III and V GATT

Art V:1 GATT defines a vessel to be 'in transit across the territory of a contracting party when the passage across such territory, [...] is only a portion of a complete journey beginning and terminating beyond the frontier of the contracting party across whose territory the traffic passes.' Art V:3 GATT provides that

> except in cases of failure to comply with applicable customs laws and regulations, such traffic coming from or going to the territory of other

239 See Milieu Ltd & COWI, 'Note on the ship dismantling fund: Pros and cons of the three options' (n 176) 23, and similar assumptions at 6, 8, 10 and 19.

240 Ecorys, DNV GL and Erasmus School of Law, 'Financial Instrument to Facilitate Safe and Sound Ship Recycling' (n 227) 105.

241 See also ibid 81 for details on the 'Economic impacts', such as costs of licences, accumulated revenues, potential coverage and resulting incentives, and 101–06 for the 'Detailed design of preferred option and roadmap'.

242 General Agreement on Tariffs and Trade 1994, Annex 1A to the Marrakesh Agreement establishing the World Trade Organization (concluded 15 April 1994, entered into force 1 January 1995) 1867 UNTS 190. The provisions cited refer to the provisions of the General Agreement on Tariffs and Trade 1947 (concluded 30 October 1947, provisionally entered into force 1 January 1948) 55 UNTS 187, as incorporated into GATT 1994.

> contracting parties shall not be subject to any unnecessary delays or restrictions and shall be exempt from customs duties and from all transit duties or other charges imposed in respect of transit, except charges for transportation or those commensurate with administrative expenses entailed by transit or with the cost of services rendered.

The crucial question, therefore, is whether or not, eg a licencing fee imposed on ships entering an EU port, is a charge raised for a service provided. It is highly questionable whether setting up an involuntary savings account for a ship that will financially support the dismantling of that ship at a later stage (ie up to 25 years later) can be considered a service. Moreover, while a part of the licencing fee is designated to cover administrative costs, those can hardly be considered 'administrative expenses entailed by transit', ie costs as a direct result of the ship being in transit. Even in the absence of case-law,[243] it is quite clear that the wording presumes that those costs and charges have a reciprocal dimension.

The authors of the Commission's Final Study point to the financial entitlements that are acquired through payment of a licence fee, but they do acknowledge that the crux of the matter is that any entitlements are forfeited where the shipowner decides to send the ship for dismantling to a facility not included in the European list: 'The possibility that accrued rights are forfeited as a penalty remains a problematic feature of the financial instrument vis-à-vis Article V:3.'[244] Facing a possible violation of Art V:3 GATT, the authors of the study try to find a way out:

> Arguably, a proposed financial instrument may violate Article V:3 if it is deemed to constitute an unnecessary restriction to traffic in transit. However, it could equally be argued that this restriction on traffic in transit is necessary, because without it the EU cannot effectively implement its public policies on safe and sound ship recycling practices and the 'polluter pays principle'. As discussed [...], other possible measures are not effective in this regard because of the possibility of flagging out and the common practice that the ownership in a ship is transferred several times during the ship's life span. Some support for this approach might be found in Article III:4, 2nd sentence GATT 1994, which permits 'the application of differential internal transportation charges based exclusively

243 Ecorys, DNV GL and Erasmus School of Law, 'Financial Instrument to Facilitate Safe and Sound Ship Recycling' (n 227) 118.

244 ibid 118.

> on the economic operation of the means of transport (...)'. If so, the EU regime would appear consistent with Article V:3.[245]

This paragraph, however, contains an array of misconceptions. Therefore, the argument has to be analysed carefully and on multiple levels.

To start with, the reader is kept in the dark about the source of an apparently claimed right of the EU to pass restrictions in contradiction to the wording of Art V:3 GATT, where it is essential for the EU to effectively implement its self-imposed (environmental) policies. Secondly, the cited Art III:4 2nd sentence GATT is unfit to provide any assistance here for the simple reason that, by virtue of its wording, it is not applicable to Art V:3 GATT. Art III:4 GATT reads in full:

> The products of the territory of any contracting party imported into the territory of any other contracting party shall be accorded treatment no less favourable than that accorded to like products of national origin in respect of all laws, regulations and requirements affecting their internal sale, offering for sale, purchase, transportation, distribution or use. The provisions of this paragraph shall not prevent the application of differential internal transportation charges which are based exclusively on the economic operation of the means of transport and not on the nationality of the product.

Looking at Arts V:3 and III:4 GATT side by side, it becomes rather clear how the selective citation in the Final Report is misleading. Unlike what is suggested through the partial citation, the test of Art III:4 2nd sentence GATT is not whether any transportation charges are based on the economic operation of that mode of transport or not. The test is whether the transportation charge is based on the economic operation of the means of transport or (by contrast) on the nationality of the product. Only the latter interpretation affords this second sentence the logical meaning it has in the context of differential treatment of imported and domestic goods.

There is also no indication that Art III:4 2nd sentence GATT (placed under the title of *National Treatment on Internal Taxation and Regulation*) embodies some sort of underlying principle that could apply to Art V GATT (*Freedom of Transit)* mutatis mutandis. Rather, the WTO Appellate body has held in one particular case that Art III:4 and Art XX (b) 'are distinct and independent provisions of the GATT 1994 each to be interpreted

245 ibid 118.

on its own.'[246] It, thereby, declared that a health risk assessment to examine the *likeness* of products as given in Art V:3 1st sentence GATT has to be carried out independently of the risk assessment in Art XX (b) GATT. In that, the Panel establishes that the risk assessment of the very same product can yield different results when carried out in the context of two different provisions:

> The scope and meaning of Article III:4 should not be broadened or restricted beyond what is required by the normal customary international law rules of treaty interpretation, simply because Article XX(b) exists and may be available to justify measures inconsistent with Article III:4. The fact that an interpretation of Article III:4, under those rules, implies a less frequent recourse to Article XX(b) does not deprive the exception in Article XX(b) of effet utile. [...] Evaluating evidence relating to the health risks arising from the physical properties of a product does not prevent a measure which is inconsistent with Article III:4 from being justified under Article XX(b). We note, in this regard, that, different inquiries occur under these two very different Articles. Under Article III:4, evidence relating to health risks may be relevant in assessing the competitive relationship in the marketplace between allegedly 'like' products. The same, or similar, evidence serves a different purpose under Article XX(b), namely, that of assessing whether a Member has a sufficient basis for 'adopting or enforcing' a WTO-inconsistent measure on the grounds of human health.[247]

With such a strong case in favour of giving independent meaning to GATT provisions, it remains inconceivable how an argument can be constructed that would allow the exception of Art III:4 2nd sentence to apply to a measure that would otherwise possibly be in violation of Art V:3. It is further noteworthy that for Art III:4 GATT to apply to the proposed concept of a Ship Recycling Licence, the transportation charge imposed in EU ports would also have to qualify as an *internal charge* in the sense of the provision. In the deliberations for the text of the Havana Charter, however, the drafting committee 'inserted the word "internal" to make clear that the phrase "differential transportation charges" does not refer to

246 WTO, *European Communities: Measures Affecting Asbestos and Asbestos-Containing Products—Report of the Appellate Body* (12 March 2001) WT/DS135/AB/R, para 115.
247 *EC: Asbestos*, WT/DS135/AB/R (n 246) para 115.

international shipping'.[248] Art III:4, therefore, needs to be understood to apply to domestic transportation charges. In conclusion, Art III:4 is not available as justification for the introduction of a licence fee, neither as an exception to Art V GATT in general nor as a measure to impose charges on international shipping specifically.

c. Principles of Non-Discrimination in GATT and GATS

In a second step, the authors of the Final Report assess the potential financial instrument against the principles of non-discrimination established by WTO law. In this context, the reference to Art I and III GATT may seem a little far-fetched since both provisions pertain to the trade in goods. Art I contains the Most-favoured-nation (MFN) Treatment obligation, requiring equal treatment of *like* products regardless of origin and destination 'to ensure all WTO Members equality of opportunity to export to, or import from, other WTO Members.'[249] Art III contains the National Treatment obligation, requiring no less favourable treatment of goods compared to *like* domestic ones.[250] Moreover, the authors point to the Panel's finding that a ship, in general, can qualify as a product that is being imported.[251] The overwhelming majority of ships arriving at an EU port and becoming subject to a potential fee, however, are not being imported but are transporting goods and are, therefore, vessels in transit. Much more relevant and offering a fresh perspective on the matter is the Final Report's assessment of a possible violation of the MFN Treatment obligation and the National Treatment obligation with regard to trade in services provided for

248 United Nations Conference on Trade and Employment held at Havana, Cuba from 21 November 1947 to 24 March 1948, 'Reports of Committees and Principal Sub-Committees'<https://www.wto.org/gatt_docs/English/SULPDF/90180096.pdf> accessed 27 March 2023, 64 (para 50 of the 'Report of Sub-Committee A of the Third Committee on Articles 16, 17, 18 and 19').

249 Peter Van den Bossche and Denise Prévost, *Essentials of WTO Law* (2nd edn, Cambridge University Press 2021) 55.

250 See for a concise discussion on the likeness of products, Van den Bossche and Prévost (n 249) 58.

251 Ecorys, DNV GL and Erasmus School of Law, 'Financial Instrument to Facilitate Safe and Sound Ship Recycling' (n 227) 120; see WTO, *European Communities: Measures Affecting Trade in Commercial Vessels—Report of the Panel* (22 April 2005) WT/DS301/R, para 7.63.

in Art II:1 and XVII:1 of the General Agreement on Trade in Services[252] (GATS). Article II:1 and XVII:1 GATS provide for the above-mentioned MFN Treatment obligation and National Treatment obligation with regards to services, respectively.

Art I:1 GATS defines the scope and requires that the measure in question constitute a trade in services, with services including any service in any sector except 'services supplied in the exercise of governmental authority' (Art I:3 (b)). The relevant mode of service supply here would be Art I:2 (b) GATS as the service is supplied *in the territory of one Member*, ie the country in which the ship recycling facility is located, *to the service consumer of any other Member*, ie the shipowners. This represents a situation where the consumption of services happens outside of the Member's territory, ensuring 'the freedom for the member's residents to purchase services in the territory of another member'.[253] The MFN treatment obligation of Art II:1 GATS regarding trade in services 'is to ensure all WTO Members equality of opportunity to supply services, regardless of the origin or destination of the services or the nationality of the service suppliers.'[254] Art II GATS, however, does not apply here as negotiations on Maritime Transport Services have been suspended. Art II will accordingly enter into force 'for international shipping, auxiliary services and access to and use of port facilities at the same time as the conclusion of negotiations'.[255]

Art XVII:1 GATS, on the other hand, requires a specific commitment[256] by the WTO Member to grant National Treatment, ie 'treatment no less favourable than that it accords to its own like services and service suppliers'. In the sector of Maritime Transport Services—that includes service in sub-sectors such as *Maintenance and Repair of Vessels* and *Supporting Ser-*

252 General Agreement on Trade in Services, Annex 1B to the Marrakesh Agreement establishing the World Trade Organization (concluded 15 April 1994, entered into force 1 January 1995) 1869 UNTS 183.

253 WTO, 'Guide to reading the GATS Schedules of Specific Commitments and the List of Article II (MFN) Exemptions' <https://www.wto.org/english/tratop_e/serv_e/guide1_e.htm> accessed 28 March 2023.

254 Van den Bossche and Prévost (n 249) 60.

255 WTO, 'Decision on Maritime Transport Services: Adopted by the Council for Trade in Services on 28 June 1996, S/L/24 (3 July 1996) paras 1 and 4.
See also WTO Analytical Index GATS - Article II (Practice) <https://www.wto.org/english/res_e/publications_e/ai17_e/gats_art2_oth.pdf> accessed 19 May 2023, para 1.3.3.

256 Known as the *Schedule of Specific Commitments* (Art XX GATS) or *Services Schedule.*

vices for Maritime Transport—some EU MSs have committed themselves to National Treatment as provided for in Art XVII:1 GATS (inter alia for 'Consumption abroad' constellations).[257] Assuming, therefore, that XVII:1 GATS is applicable to at least some EU MSs, the financial measure in question can be put to the test applying the following criteria:

1. the services or service suppliers in question must be 'like services and service suppliers';
2. that foreign services and service suppliers are granted treatment no less favourable than domestic services or service suppliers.[258]

On No.1: the *likeness* criteria, as is the case with the term *like products* under GATT, is not a clear-cut term. On the *likeness* of services and service suppliers, the WTO Appellate Body has held that: 'the concept of "likeness" of services and service suppliers under Article II:1 and XVII:1 of the GATS is concerned with the competitive relationship of services and service suppliers.'[259] There, it refers to and reiterates its previous finding that '[i]f there is – or could be – *no* competitive relationship between products, a Member cannot intervene, through internal taxation or regulation, to protect domestic production.'[260] It adds:

> Further, in the context of trade in goods, the Appellate Body noted that there is a spectrum of degrees of 'competitiveness' or 'substitutability' of products in the marketplace. The assessment of such a competitive relationship requires a market-based analysis. The Appellate Body also stated that not all products that are in some competitive relationship are

257 Schedules of commitments can be found in the following database: WTO Members' GATS commitments, MFN exemptions, and preferences under the LDC Services Waiver as notified by Members <http://i-tip.wto.org/services/Search.aspx> accessed 27 March 2023. The recent Schedule of Specific Commitments of the EU is also published as document GATS/SC/157 (7 May 2019). One could also consider ship recycling services to be part the Environmental Services sector and its sub-sector Refuse Disposal Services. This, however, would not do justice to the specific characteristics of the maritime industry that is clearly given its own sector category and including services related to the maritime transport sector. Either way, the outcome would be the same as almost all EU MSs have also committed themselves to National Treatment within the Refuse Disposal Services sector for 'Consumption abroad'.

258 For a step-by-step test, see Van den Bossche and Prévost (n 249) 61.

259 WTO, *Argentina: Measures Relating to Trade in Goods and Services—Report of the Appellate Body* (14 April 2016) WT/DS453/AB/R, para 6.25.

260 *EC: Asbestos*, WT/DS135/AB/R (n 246) para 117; *Argentina: Trade in Goods and Services* (n 259) para 6.25.

'like products', and that it is difficult, if not impossible, in the abstract, to indicate precisely where on this spectrum the word 'like' falls. In our view, the same is true with respect to 'like services and service suppliers', and, thus, the likeness of services and service suppliers can only be determined on a case-by-case basis, taking into account the specific circumstances of the particular case.[261]

On No. 2: the *less favourable treatment* is specified through Art XVII:3 GATS in that '[f]ormally identical or formally different treatment shall be considered to be less favourable if it modifies the conditions of competition in favour of services or service suppliers of the Member compared to like services or service suppliers of any other Member.' With this, the provision prohibits de jure, as well as de facto discriminatory measures.[262] In this case, a de facto discrimination could result from the fact that the EU's own ship recycling facilities or some WTO Members' are more equipped than other Members' facilities to meet the requirements needed to enter the European list. At the same time, recycling in a yard on the European list would be a precondition for a shipowner to claim back its contributions from the envisaged licencing scheme.

The Final Report, therefore, correctly points out that the proposed financial instrument could benefit EU-law compliant ship recycling facilities to the disadvantage of ship recycling services providers that are not eligible to be included in the EU list, specifically facilities located in South Asia. The Report also correctly concludes that more data on the market is needed to more specifically assess whether and, if so, how the proposed financial measure would affect competition among ship recycling facilities worldwide. The Report does not mention that the SRR provisions and its financial scheme are actually intended to affect market conditions among ship recycling facilities in favour of more environmentally friendly practices, ie incentivizing higher environmental protection and occupational health standards in currently low-standard facilities. Rather casually, however, it concludes its remarks on these provisions by pointing out that the 'proposed financial instrument is to be understood only as [a] measure

261 *Argentina: Trade in Goods and Services* (n 259) para. 6.26.

262 ibid para 6.105.; *European Communities: Regime for the Importation, Sale and Distribution of Bananas—Report of the Appellate Body* (9 September 1997) WT/DS27/AB/R, para 233.

designed to make the SRR more effective.'[263] Unfortunately, the authors fail to further elaborate on why and how a financial measure that is embedded in an EU regulation to enable better enforcement is exempt from having to conform with WTO law. Finally, as an alternative argument, the report also claims that 'it is arguable, by juxtaposing environmentally sound ship recycling and environmentally unsound ship recycling, that the two kinds of services are in reality not „like services" at all.'[264] Where the term environmentally sound is considered to be the standard as set out in the SRR, this is a mere circular argument. The likeness of services cannot simply be based on criteria defined by the very regulation that contains the financial measure under scrutiny. As seen above, the question whether services or service suppliers are *(a)like* requires an assessment of their competitive relationship. Also, 'the term "like" must be interpreted in the light of its context and the object and purpose of the agreement in which the relevant provision appears.'[265]

d. The Exceptions of Article XX GATT and Article XIV GATS

Eventually the Final Report takes recourse to General Exceptions of Art XX GATT and Art XIV GATS, respectively, for justification of a possible violation of GATT or GATS provisions. The Final Report specifically invokes Art XX (a), (b) and (g) GATT, namely the protection of public morals, the protection of human, animal or plant life or health, and the conservation of exhaustible natural resources, respectively, as possible grounds to remedy an otherwise GATT-infringing financial measure. The first two grounds of justification can be also found in Art XIV (a) and (b) GATS.[266] Thus, the analysis of Art XX (a) and (b) GATT is valid for Arts XIV (a) and (b) GATS as well.[267] As the grounds for exceptions in these two provisions become more specific toward the bottom of the list, it makes sense to examine them in reverse order.

---

263 Ecorys, DNV GL and Erasmus School of Law, 'Financial Instrument to Facilitate Safe and Sound Ship Recycling' (n 227) 128.

264 ibid 126.

265 *Argentina: Trade in Goods and Services* (n 259) para 6.31, referring to WTO, *Japan: Taxes on Alcoholic Beverages—Report of the Appellate Body* (4 October 1996) WT/DS8/AB/R, WT/DS10/AB/R, WT/DS11/AB/R.

266 Art XIV (a) GATS contains an additional reference to the necessity to 'maintain public order'.

267 See n 312.

aa. Conserving Exhaustible Natural Resources

Art XX (g) GATT stipulates an exemption for measures 'relating to the conservation of exhaustible natural resources if such measures are made effective in conjunction with restrictions on domestic production or consumption'.

On the term *exhaustible natural resources*, it has been held:

> Textually, Article XX(g) is not limited to the conservation of 'mineral' or 'non-living' natural resources. [...] One lesson that modern biological sciences teach us is that living species, though in principle, capable of reproduction and, in that sense, 'renewable', are in certain circumstances indeed susceptible of depletion, exhaustion and extinction, frequently because of human activities. Living resources are just as 'finite' as petroleum, iron ore and other non-living resources.
> [...] The words of Article XX(g), 'exhaustible natural resources', were actually crafted more than 50 years ago. They must be read by a treaty interpreter in the light of contemporary concerns of the community of nations about the protection and conservation of the environment.[268]

The Appellate Body then refers inter alia to the preamble of the WTO Agreement, Art 56 UNCLOS and the principle of the International Court of Justice (ICJ) that treaty concepts are 'by definition, evolutionary'[269], and concludes:

> it is too late in the day to suppose that Article XX(g) of the GATT 1994 may be read as referring only to the conservation of exhaustible mineral or other non-living natural resources. [...] We hold that, in line with the principle of effectiveness in treaty interpretation, measures to conserve exhaustible natural resources, whether *living* or *non-living*, may fall within Article XX(g).[270]

268 See WTO, *United States: Import Prohibition of Certain Shrimp and Shrimp Products—Report of the Appellate Body* (12 October 1998) WT/DS58/AB/R, paras 128–29.

269 *US: Shrimp* (n 268) para 130, referring to ICJ, *Legal Consequences for States of the Continued Presence of South Africa in Namibia (South West Africa) Notwithstanding Security Council Resolution 276 (1970)* (Advisory Opinion) 1971 <https://www.icj-cij.org/sites/default/files/case-related/53/053-19710621-ADV-01-00-EN.pdf> accessed 19 May 2023, para 53.

270 See *US: Shrimp* (n 268) para 131.

Unfortunately, the Appellate Body subsequently passes on the chance to comment on a possible 'implied jurisdictional limitation' of Art XX (g) that would restrict a country's claim to the resources it has jurisdiction over, or on 'the nature or extent of that limitation.'[271] Instead, the Appellate Body held that the sea turtle species in question occur in waters over which the Appellant has jurisdiction. While 'it is not claimed that *all* populations of these species migrate to, or traverse, at one time or another, waters subject to United States jurisdiction',[272] the Appellate Body, nonetheless, found 'that in the specific circumstances of the case [...], there is a sufficient nexus between the migratory and endangered marine populations involved and the United States for purposes of Article XX(g).'[273] Since the Appellate Body refers to the specific case before it only, it is unclear whether it intended to make a general statement applicable to any other case. Therefore, it is arguable whether the Appellate Body, thereby, established a standard of protection beyond a State's own territory, ie reaching into other States and the high seas.[274]

Furthermore, as the wording goes, the measure in question has to *relate* to the conservation of exhaustible natural resources. That is the case where the measure 'is primarily aimed'[275] at the conservation of exhaustible natural resources, requiring 'a close and genuine relationship of ends and means'[276] It is safe to say here that the financial tool is primarily directed towards ensuring compliance with SRR provisions, which in turn will reduce instances of sub-standard ship dismantling and hence environmental damage. Finally, for successfully invoking Art XX (g) GATT, the measure has to be *made effective in conjunction with restrictions on domestic production or consumption.* This is understood to mean that restrictions on

271 ibid para 133.

272 ibid.

273 ibid.

274 See to that effect, Frederik M Abbott, Christine Breining-Kaufmann and Thomas Cottier, *International Trade and Human Rights: Foundations and Conceptual Issues* (The University of Michigan Press, 2006), 54.

275 WTO, *United States: Standards for Reformulated and Conventional Gasoline—Report of the Appellate Body* (29 April 1996) WT/DS2/AB, 19.

276 WTO, *China: Measures Related to the Exportation of Rare Earths, Tungsten, and Molybdenum—Report of the Appellate Body* (7 August 2014) WT/DS431/AB/R, WT/DS432/AB/R, WT/DS433/AB/R, para 5.90; WTO, *China: Measures Related to the Exportation of Various Raw Materials—Report of the Appellate Body* (30 January 2012) WT/DS394/AB/R, WT/DS395/AB/R, WT/DS398/AB/R, 355; *US: Shrimp* (n 268) para 136.

imports should come with restrictions on domestic products resulting in an '*even-handedness* in the impositions of restrictions'.[277] For this, 'the trade restriction must operate jointly with the restrictions on domestic production or consumption.'[278] The measure in question does cause a trade restriction through the imposition of a fee on a third-party ship upon entry into an EU port that serves to ensure compliance with the requirements of the SRR. This measure, however, is not operating as a complementary measure to a domestic production or consumption restriction. The term *consumption* must be read here to mean consumption in products rather than services covered by GATS. The underlying notion of this requirement is that the '"burden" of measures taken to preserve exhaustible natural resources may not only weigh on imported products but must be spread over imported and domestic products.'[279]

bb. Securing Compliance with Laws or Regulations

Art XX (d) GATT offers an exception where it is 'necessary to secure compliance with laws or regulations which are not inconsistent with the provisions of this Agreement'. It does not refer specifically to products and seems in this context to be a more appropriate provision to justify a financial instrument that, viewed on its own, is a measure not designed as an enforcement measure, but a measure to prevent circumvention of the SRR provisions.

Firstly, there is no indication that the provisions of the SRR themselves are in violation of the non-discrimination principles of GATT. Secondly, the term *laws or regulations* is understood in a broad way, meaning 'rules that form part of the domestic legal system of a WTO Member',[280] regardless of whether they are adopted by a legislative or executive power.[281] It is also understood that the instances mentioned in the Art XX (d) GATT—'relating to customs enforcement, the enforcement of monopolies operated

277 *China: Rare Earths* (n 276) paras 5.93.–5.94.; *US: Gasoline* (n 275) 21.
278 *China: Raw Materials* (n 276) para 356.
279 Van den Bossche and Prévost (n 249) 116.
280 WTO, *Mexico: Tax Measures on Soft Drinks and Other Beverages—Report of the Appellate Body* (6 March 2006) WT/DS308/AB/R, para 75.
281 WTO, *India: Certain Measures Relating to Solar Cells and Solar Products—Report of the Appellate Body* (16 September 2016) WT/DS456/AB/R, para 5.108; *Mexico: Beverages* (n 280) para 69.

under paragraph 4 of Article II and article XVII, the protection of patents, trade marks and copyrights, and the prevention of deceptive practices'—are exemplary and not exhaustive.[282] The Appellate Body elaborated on that and broadened the scope even further when it held that '"laws or regulations" refer to rules of conduct and principles governing behaviour or practice that form part of the domestic legal system of a Member.'[283] The concrete requirement that prima facie fulfils all of the formal criteria to qualify as a *law* or *regulation*[284] can be found in Art 6 (2) (a) SRR that stipulates:

> [...]
>
> 2. Ship owners shall ensure that ships destined to be recycled:
> (a) are only recycled at ship recycling facilities that are included in the European List;
>
> [...]

This obligation, however, applies to EU-flagged ships (Art 2 (1) SRR) 'a criterion that can easily be circumvented through timely re-flagging to a non-EU flag' which is the very reason a financial incentive is sought.[285] It is worth keeping in mind that, therefore, the financial mechanisms, as they are discussed in the reports presented here[286], are meant to extend this obligation to non-EU flagged ships beyond the actual scope of the current SRR. This said, a possible future extension of the Art 6 (2) (a) SRR requirement to third country ships will likely be introduced in the SRR itself.

With such an accompanying amendment to the SRR, it would be easy to qualify the financial measure at hand as also *securing compliance* with this rule in that the prospect of foregoing the repayment of their monetary contributions will serve as an incentive for non-EU shipowners to seek the

282 *Mexico: Beverages* (n 280) para 70 (footnote 150).

283 *India: Solar Cells* (n 281) para 5.106, with reference to *Mexico: Beverages* (n 280) para 70.

284 For more on the interpretation of the term 'laws or regulations', see *India: Solar Cells* (n 281) para 5.109, 5.111 and 6.6; assessment of the SRR or Art 6 (2) (a) against these criteria would reach beyond the scope of this chapter and this study. Suffice it to say at this point that prima facie there is no indication that would suggest that the provisions of the SRR or the requirement of Art 6 (2) (a) SRR could possibly not qualify as a *law* or *regulation* in the sense of Art XX (d) GATT.

285 *See* Ecorys, DNV GL and Erasmus School of Law, 'Financial Instrument to Facilitate Safe and Sound Ship Recycling' (n 227) 10, 27.

286 Section B.V.

services of an EU listed ship recycling yard. While there is no certainty that it will in all cases lead to SRR-compliant disposal of an end-of-life ship, absolute certainty is not what is required:

> The Appellate Body explained that absolute certainty in the achievement of a measure's stated goal, as well as the use of coercion, are not necessary components of a measure designed 'to secure compliance' within the meaning of Article XX(d). Instead, a measure can be said 'to secure compliance' with 'laws or regulations' when it seeks to secure observance of specific rules, even if the measure cannot be guaranteed to achieve such result with absolute certainty.[287]

It is noteworthy that the Appellate Body makes the important and necessary distinction between an enforcement measure (imposed after a violation has taken place) and a measure to secure that the relevant provision is abided by.

Finally, for exception of Art XX (d) GATT to apply, the measure has to be *necessary*. In short, the term *necessary* in the context of Art XX

> involves in every case a process of weighing and balancing a series of factors which prominently include the contribution made by the compliance measure to the enforcement of the law or regulation at issue, the importance of the common interests or values protected by that law or regulation, and the accompanying impact of the law or regulation on imports or exports."[288]

However, '[t]he greater the contribution, the more easily a measure might be considered to be "necessary".'[289] Additionally, where

> the complaining party identifies an alternative measure that, in its view, the responding party should have taken, the responding party will be required to demonstrate why its challenged measure nevertheless remains

287 *India: Solar Cells* (n 281) para 5.108; WTO, *Colombia: Measures relating to the Importation of Textiles, Apparel and Footwear—Report of the Appellate Body* (7 June 2016) WT/DS461/AB/R, paras 5.69, 5.126 and 5.131 and *Argentina: Trade in Goods and Services* (n 259) para 6.203.

288 WTO, *Korea: Measures Affecting Imports of Fresh, Chilled and Frozen Beef—Report of the Appellate Body* (11 December 2000) WT/DS161/AB/R, WT/DS169/AB/R, para 164; WTO, *China: Measures Affecting Trading Rights and Distribution Services for Certain Publications and Audiovisual Entertainment Products*—Report of the Appellate Body (21 December 2009) WT/DS363/AB/R, para 251.

289 *Korea: Beef* (n 288) para 163; *China: Entertainment Products—AB* (n 288) para 251.

> 'necessary' in the light of that alternative or, in other words, why the proposed alternative is not a genuine alternative or is not 'reasonably available'. If a responding party demonstrates that the alternative is not 'reasonably available', in the light of the interests or values being pursued and the party's desired level of protection, it follows that the challenged measure must be 'necessary'.[290]

Hence, while the burden of proof concerning the *necessity* of the measure lies with the responding party, 'a responding party need not identify the universe of less trade-restrictive alternative measures and then show that none of those measures achieves the desired objective.'[291] Assessing the 'necessity'-criteria in the context of the Ship Recycling Licence in full length would certainly be beyond the scope of this research. A comprehensive assessment is also not possible without knowing the full extent of its real life effects. On the other hand, the long-term struggle for a financial instrument to ensure compliance with SRR provisions has demonstrated that a potential claimant in a WTO law dispute would equally struggle to argue in favour of an alternative but equally effective measure.

cc. Protecting Life or Health and Public Morals

The application of Art XX (b) GATT offering an exception for measures 'to protect human, animal or plant life or health' faces a difficulty that has already been touched upon in the context of Art XX (g) GATT, namely the question of extraterritorial application.

---

290 *China: Entertainment Products—AB* (n 288) para 319 with reference to WTO, *United States: Measures Affecting the Cross-Border Supply of Gambling and Betting Services—Report of the Appellate Body* (7 April 2005) WT/DS285/AB/R, paras 309–11; both decisions deal with the definition of 'necessity' within the context of Art XIV GATS. However, in *US: Gambling—AB*, para 2.91, the Appellate Body found 'previous decisions under Article XX of the GATT 1994 relevant for [the Panel's] analysis under Article XIV of the GATS' based on the similar wording of Art XX GATT and Art XIV GATS, especially with regard to the term *necessary*—this must also apply vice versa.

291 *US: Gambling—AB* (n 290) para 309; for a concise summary of WTO jurisdiction on assessment of Art XX (a) GATT see also WTO, *European Communities: Measure Prohibiting the Importation and Marketing of Seal Products—Report of the Appellate Body* (22 May 2014) WT/DS400/AB/R, WT/DS401/AB/R, para 5.169.

> The Appellate Body has yet to rule on whether measures that aim to protect one of the listed societal values or interests *outside* the territorial jurisdiction of the Member taking the measure can be justified under Article XX of the GATT 1994. There is no explicit jurisdictional limitation in Article XX, but it is an open question whether such a jurisdictional limitation can be implied.[292]

The authors of the Final Report themselves recognise the difficulty associated with Art XX (b) GATT, namely that extraterritorial effects would have to be argued first.[293] The question of extraterritorial application of the norm, however, appears more of an obstacle with Art XX (b) GATT than with Art XX (a) GATT that very generally refers to the protection of 'public morals'. In invoking Art XX (a), the authors of the Final Report argue that the protection of public morals is called for where poor work conditions in sub-standard recycling yards threaten the health of adults and children and violate their basic human rights.[294] To determine whether or not their respective public morals are affected, the Panel grants WTO Members some discretion. It has been held that the concept of *public morals* 'denotes standards of right and wrong conduct maintained by or on behalf of a community or nation.'[295] It follows that 'the content of these concepts for Members can vary in time and space, depending upon a range of factors, including prevailing social, cultural, ethical and religious values'[296] and 'Members should be given some scope to define and apply for themselves the concepts of „public morals" [...] in their respective territories, according to their own systems and scales of values.'[297] Judicial review seems to be limited as the Appellate Body has held that in an analysis of Art XX (a) GATT the Panel does not necessarily have to 'identify the exact content of the public morals standard at issue.'[298]

---

292 Van den Bossche and Prévost (n 249) 108.

293 Ecorys, DNV GL and Erasmus School of Law, 'Financial Instrument to Facilitate Safe and Sound Ship Recycling' (n 227) 123.

294 ibid.

295 WTO, *United States: Measures Affecting the Cross-Border Supply of Gambling and Betting Services—Report of the Panel* (10 November 2004) WT/DS285/R, para 6.465.

296 *US: Gambling* (n 295) para 6.461.

297 ibid; WTO, *China: Measures Affecting Trading Rights and Distribution Services for Certain Publications and Audiovisual Entertainment Products—Report of the Panel* (12 August 2009) WT/DS363/R, para 7.759.

298 *EC: Seal Products* (n 291) para 5.199.

Art XX (a) GATT further requires that the measure in question be designed and necessary to achieve its objective, namely the protection of public morals. The measure is considered *designed to protect public morals* if it is 'not incapable' of protecting public morals.[299] This involves an assessment of its 'content, structure, and expected operation.'[300] While the assessment of the *design* criteria is not considered a 'particularly demanding step'[301], the examination of whether the measure at hand is *necessary* is slightly more complex as seen above. Therefore, here again, a thorough and complete assessment would only be possible with an actual concrete measure in place that would also allow an assessment of its real-life effects.

dd. Arbitrary and Unjustifiable Discrimination

The two-tier test generally applied by the Appellate Body requires that a measure falling within the purview of at least one of the Art XX GATT exceptions is then, in a second step, assessed with regards to the requirements of the chapeau of Article XX.[302] The chapeau allows recourse to the exceptions of Art XX only if the measure in question is 'not applied in a manner which would constitute a means of arbitrary or unjustifiable discrimination between countries where the same conditions prevail, or a disguised restriction on international trade'. The terms *arbitrary discrimination, unjustifiable discrimination* and *disguised restriction* are to be read 'side-by-side', while the term *disguised restriction* also encompasses 'arbitrary and unjustifiable discrimination'.[303] Furthermore, '[t]he provisions of the chapeau cannot logically refer to the same standard(s) by which a violation of a substantive rule has been determined to have occurred'[304], meaning that the notion of discrimination in the chapeau is distinctly

299 See *Colombia: Textiles* (n 287) para 5.68; WTO, *Brazil: Certain Measures Concerning Taxation and Charges—Report of the Panel* (30 August 2017) WT/DS472/R, WT/DS497/R, para 7.570.

300 *Colombia: Textiles* (n 287) para 5.69.

301 Report of the Appellate Body, *Colombia: Textiles* (n 287); *Brazil: Taxation and Charges* (n 299) para 7.570.

302 WTO, *Indonesia: Importation of Horticultural Products, Animals and Animal* Products—*Report of the Appellate Body* (9 November 2017) WT/DS477/AB/R, WT/DS478/AB/R, para 5.96.

303 *US: Gasoline* (n 275) 25.

304 *EC: Seal Products* (n 291) para. 5.298, citing *US: Gasoline* (n 275) 23 and referring to *US: Shrimp* (n 268) para 150.

different than that provided for in the provisions the violation of which Art XX is supposed to remedy. In the absence of a clear-cut definition for the discrimination criteria, it is understood that the discriminatory nature can 'most often be discerned from the design, the architecture, and the revealing structure of a measure.'[305] Also,

> discrimination will be arbitrary or unjustifiable when the reasons given for the discrimination 'bear no rational connection to the objective' or 'would go against that objective'. Thus '[o]ne of the most important factors' in the assessment of arbitrary or unjustifiable discrimination is the question of whether the discrimination can be reconciled with, or is rationally related to, the policy objective with respect to which the measure has been provisionally justified under one of the subparagraphs of Article XX. This factor is 'particularly relevant in assessing the merits of the explanations provided by the respondent as to the cause of the discrimination'.[306]

In sum, '[t]he chapeau of Article XX is, in fact, but one expression of the principle of good faith.'[307] Translating this to the measure at hand, the EU as a potential defendant in a WTO dispute would have to demonstrate that the requirements of the chapeau apply to the Ship Recycling Licensing Scheme.[308] The most pressing question to answer would be why a measure that is introduced explicitly and specifically to prevent EU-flagged ships from circumventing the provisions and objectives of the EU SRR through last-minute re-flagging will eventually affect all third-state-flagged ships that enter an EU port at one point in their life span. To give a glimpse

---

305 *Japan: Alcoholic beverages* (n 265) 29; *EC: Seal Products* (n 291) para 5.302.

306 WTO, *United States: Measures Concerning the Importation, Marketing and Sale of Tuna and Tuna Products: Recourse to Article 21.5 of the DSU by Mexico—Report of the Appellate Body* (20 November 2015) WT/DS381/AB/RW para 7.316, with references to WTO, *Brazil: Measures Affecting Imports of Retreaded Tyres—Report of the Appellate Body* (3 December 2007) WT/DS332/AB/R, para 227 and *EC: Seal Products* (n 291) para 5.306. See also WTO, *United States: Measures Concerning the Importation, Marketing and Sale of Tuna and Tuna Products: Recourse to Article 21.5 of the DSU by the United States/Second Recourse to Article 21.5 of the DSU by Mexico* (14 December 2014) WT/DS381/AB/RW/USA, WT/DS381/AB/RW2, paras 6.278, 6.288, 7.12.

307 *US: Shrimp* (n 268) para 158.

308 WTO, *European Communities: Conditions for the Granting of Tariff Preferences to Developing Countries— Report of the Panel* (1 December 2003) WT/DS246/R, para 7.228: 'Bearing in mind the well-established rule that it is for the party invoking Article XX to demonstrate the consistency of its measure with the chapeau'.

of the proportions: in the first quarter of 2023 15,074 ships amounting to 232.64 million GT were flying an EU MS flag compared to 102,981 ships representing an overall of 1,987.82 million GT flagged elsewhere in the world.[309] These numbers give a rough idea of the imbalance between the objective of disincentivising re-flagging of EU-flagged ships and addressing the rest of the world's fleet with a financial measure to achieve that. In case of a dispute, the EU would possibly be called out on this incongruity.[310]

Concluding the assessment on WTO compliance, it does appear possible that the EU could rely on the exemption of Art XX (a) GATT if the envisaged financial instrument was deemed to violate GATT provisions. The bigger challenge would be to argue compliance with the requirements of the chapeau, however, where the Licensing scheme would generously include all third-flagged ships above 500 GT that at any time during their lifetime enter an EU port, and that are actually not the primary target of the scheme. It has to be borne in mind that last-minute re-flagging to avoid sound ship recycling according to the SRR is, by itself, not even illegal, but merely considered 'against the spirit of the regulation'[311]. This said, a full and comprehensive examination of the proposed Ship Recycling License Scheme is not within the scope of this research. It is also not possible due to missing information on the details of the prospective instrument, as well as the exact mode of operation or the ultimate real impact on trade. The same must hold true for applicability of the exception provided for in Art XIV (a) and (b) GATS. The wording of these two provisions is very similar, and it has been held that where similar language is used findings on Art XX GATT can be applied in an analysis of Art XIV GATS.[312]

VI. Conclusion

The EU's ambition was that the SRR expedite the coming into force of the HKC by 'facilitating early ratification [...] both within the Union and

309 This includes all ships with an IMO number and above 100 GT. EMSA, 'The EU Maritime Profile—the maritime cluster in the EU' <https://emsa.europa.eu/eumaritimeprofile/section-2-the-eu-maritime-cluster.html> accessed 15 December 2023.

310 On a side note: this also makes it difficult to argue that the Ship Recycling License is actually a measure that observes the principle of proportionality as laid down in Recital 5 of the SRR itself.

311 Ecorys, DNV GL and Erasmus School of Law, 'Financial Instrument to Facilitate Safe and Sound Ship Recycling' (n 227) 44.

312 *US: Gambling—AB* (n 290) para 291.

in third countries' (Recital 5). Almost 10 years after the entry into force of the SRR, the HKC currently counts 22 Contracting States. Bangladesh only very recently in June 2023 joined the treaty and triggered its entry into force in June 2025. Currently, only 11 of the 22 parties to the treaty are EU MSs. Therefore, the presumed expectation of the EU that with an SRR in place EU MSs might feel they may as well become party to the HKC was not fulfilled.[313] The EU's objective may have materialised with enough pressure created through a financial instrument. It would have rendered the SRR a regulation that affects all ships that call at an EU port, a regulation that factually could not be ignored. The analysis has shown the multitude of difficulties that pose themselves when contemplating an effective and low-burden financial mechanism that is compatible with international law. The fact that the studies conducted display one or the other blind spot and/or misconception shows just how complex this endeavour is legally, politically and practically. It does not come as a surprise that at time of writing in 2023, the Commission has not been able to table a concrete proposal for a financial instrument within the framework of the SRR and is not expected to do so anymore. While it is commendable that the EU has not ignored legal concerns in favour of ambition, the SRR remains an unfinished business. EU-flagged ships can easily avoid the SRR by re-flagging shortly before the recycling process, while foreign ships calling at an EU port may have to present the paperwork required by the SRR with no incentive for their owners to eventually resort to safe and sound recycling of those ships. The fact that no compliance can be secured leaves the SRR toothless and the EU on that matter in an impasse.

At the same time, the emergence of the SRR brought about the question as to where the SRR belongs in the dynamic of the BC and the EU's WSR, and especially with regard to the BC's Ban Amendment that has come into force. The EU is attempting to clarify the relationship between the SRR and the Ban Amendment, through a proposal that would give precedence to the stricter Ban Amendment where the ship becomes waste within EU MSs' national jurisdiction. This still leaves the underlying question unanswered, namely how the BC and its Ban Amendment relate to the HKC. This also begs the question on how the dynamic between these instruments will change and how their scopes need to be (re)framed or redefined once the HKC is in force. The interference of the SRR with existing waste regulation,

313 One reason for the reservation of EU MSs to become party to the HKC may have been the slight, but inconvenient deviations in structure and wording of the instruments. The additional burden in the legislative process may have been a deterrent.

therefore, has raised questions of compatibility and reconcilability while falling short of its proclaimed goal of expediting the coming into effect of the HKC or substantial contribution to effectively regulating environmentally sound recycling of ships. More effect can be attributed to the EU's legislation on data collection of carbon dioxide emissions that is discussed in the following case study. It represents the reverse situation, namely regulation that was passed in anticipation of IMO action and to serve as an example for an IMO measure. Also, compared to the SRR, the EU could be deemed to regulate conduct out of EU territory which further complicates the dynamic and adds the question of the limits of EU jurisdiction to the discussion.

C. Case Study II: Regulating Carbon Dioxide Emissions

The second example this study uses to analyse the EU's unilateral environmental policy in the field of international shipping is Regulation (EU) 2015/757 installing a monitoring, reporting and verification system for carbon dioxide emissions from maritime transport[314] (MRV-Regulation). While the SRR's objective was to increase acceptance among the international community and to accelerate the entry into force of the existent draft Ship Recycling treaty, the EU adopted the MRV-Regulation to expedite the long ongoing negotiations on carbon dioxide reduction measures within the IMO. The MRV-Regulation was drafted as a model for a potential future international instrument, while in the case of the SRR, conversely, the draft HKC served as a blueprint for EU regulation. The MRV-Regulation even explicitly allows for the possibility of a review and alignment of its provisions in the light of a future international agreement (Art 22 (3) MRV-Regulation). Since this regulation awards a fair amount of discretion to the Commission, however, there was and is a very real danger that the EU and the international provisions end up being two different—possibly conflicting—standards that ship operators would have to abide by.

This chapter investigates the different challenges posed by the MRV-Regulation. To this end, this chapter first outlines the problem of carbon dioxide emissions in international shipping (I.), as well as the failed attempt of the international community to address this problem within the United Nations Framework Convention on Climate Change[315] (UNFCCC; II.), where some would argue this topic belongs. It then looks at the lengthy process within the IMO to effectively reduce carbon dioxide emissions, as well as the obstacles to an agreement for an actual market-based measure (MBM), including suggestions for how they could be overcome (III.). The final section of this chapter is dedicated to the EU's response to these developments, namely the MRV-Regulation itself (IV.). It shows how, with

314 Regulation (EU) 2015/757 of the European Parliament and of the Council of 29 April 2015 on the monitoring, reporting and verification of carbon dioxide emissions from maritime transport, and amending Directive 2009/16/EC [2015] OJ L123/55.

315 United Nations Framework Convention on Climate Change (adopted 9 May 1992, entered into force 21 March 1994) 1771 UNTS 107.

regard to the publication of data and the process of data verification, the MRV-Regulation disrupts established dynamics of international shipping. Most importantly, it also explores the question of the jurisdictional basis for the requirement of the MRV-Regulation to submit data that also pertains to shipping activities outside of its territory. It shows that the EU avoids a unified stand on the legal grounds of its jurisdiction and that recourse to the right to impose port-entry requirements is a less-than-optimal resort. It also demonstrates that there is a good case for invoking more overarching principles in this context, such as the *Effects Doctrine* or the *Common Concern of Humankind.* Finally, it shows that the absence of a discriminatory element in the MRV-Regulation significantly reduces concerns of WTO law violations whereas these played a major role in the discussion surrounding a financial mechanism for the SRR.

I. International Shipping's Contribution to Global CO_2 Emissions

The Fourth IMO Greenhouse Gas Study 2020 found that total shipping in 2018—the last year for which it generated results—accounted for 2.89% of global CO_2 emissions or 1,056 million tonnes of CO_2,[316] with overall shipping emissions projected to increase by up to 50% to 1,500 million tonnes CO_2 in 2050.[317] Of that, applying a vessel-based approach, international shipping in 2018 accounted for 919 million tonnes and 2.51% of global carbon dioxide emissions.[318] This amounts to an 8.4% increase compared to 2012.[319] Applying a voyage-based approach that neglects merely domestic voyages, 740 million tonnes of CO_2 and a 2.02% global share can be allocated to international shipping for 2018.[320] Similarly, the EU

316 Faber and others (n 1) 112.

317 ibid 26, 236.

318 ibid 112. It is noteworthy that in the context of international shipping the terms *carbon dioxide emissions* and *greenhouse gas emissions* are often used interchangeably. For coherency purposes, the terms are replicated as used by the actors themselves. In reality, there has not been any serious or substantial discussion on the reduction of a greenhouse gas resulting from international shipping other than carbon dioxide.

319 Jasper Faber and others, *Fourth IMO GHG Study 2020: Executive Summary* (IMO 2020) <https://wwwcdn.imo.org/localresources/en/OurWork/Environment/Documents/Fourth%20IMO%20GHG%20Study%202020%20Executive-Summary.pdf> accessed 31 March 2023, 1.

320 Faber and others (n 1), 112; see also IMO, 'Fourth Greenhouse Gas Study 2020: Key findings from the Fourth IMO GHG Study 2020 <https://www.imo.org/en/OurWo

estimates international shipping's carbon dioxide emissions for the year 2021 at 699,722 million tonnes with a global share of 1.8%. With that it places international shipping almost on par with South Korea, the seventh highest CO_2-emitting country.[321]

Measures to reduce carbon dioxide emissions from shipping roughly fall within one of three categories: technical, operational or market-based. Technical measures include eg improvements on ship design, main engine retrofits, the installation of waste heat recovery systems and the use of low- or zero-carbon fuels, such as LNG. Operational measures include eg slow steaming (ie speed reduction/speed optimization), weather routing and optimised voyage planning.[322] The areas of logistics, maintenance and speed are those, however, that have the largest impact on the carbon dioxide efficiency.[323] MBMs are mostly self-explanatory, the more common and known of which are the fuel tax and the emission trading scheme (ETS).[324] 'In theory, taxes and charges have broadly the same effects, the difference being that a tax provides certainty on the price but not on the environmental

---

rk/Environment/Pages/Fourth-IMO-Greenhouse-Gas-Study-2020.aspx> accessed 31 March 2023.

321 Monica Crippa and others, *CO_2 Emissions of all World Countries* (Publications Office of the European Union 2022) <https://edgar.jrc.ec.europa.eu/booklet/CO2_emissions_of_all_world_countries_2022_report.pdf> accessed 20 March 2023, 12 and 33.

322 For more examples of operational and technical measures, see Tim Bäuerle and others, *Integration of Marine Transport into the European Emissions Trading System: Environmental, Economic and Legal Analysis of Different Options* (Umweltbundesamt 2010) <https://www.umweltbundesamt.de/sites/default/files/medien/461/publikationen/3942.pdf> accessed 27 October 2023, 27–28 (albeit presented in categories of *engine-related, fuel-related, hull and design-related, operational* and *long-term innovative* measures). For another overview including a brief discussion on the reduction potential of international shipping (even assuming that a decarbonisation of the sector before 2050 is theoretically possible), see Aki Kachi, Silke Mooldijk, Carsten Warnecke, 'Carbon pricing options for international maritime emissions' (NewClimate — Institute for Climate Policy and Global Sustainability gGmbH 2019) <https://newclimate.org/sites/default/files/2019/04/Carbon-pricing-options-for-international-maritime-emissions.pdf> accessed 19 May 2023, 5–7.

323 'All three aspects are determined by the fuel price and the fleet size, and by the overall transport demand', Jasper Faber et al, 'Technical Support for European Action to Reducing Greenhouse Gas Emissions from International Transport' (CE Delft 2009) <https://cedelft.eu/wp-content/uploads/sites/2/2021/04/7731_finalreportJF.pdf> accessed 30 March 2023, 104; see also at 90 for a schematic overview of factors contributing to maritime CO_2 emissions.

324 Discussing an offsetting scheme, an ETS and a climate levy as possible MBMs for international maritime emissions, see Kachi, Mooldijk and Warnecke (n 322) 19ff.

effect, whereas emissions trading provides certainty on the environmental effect, but not on the price.'[325]

In the context of shipping, the IMO asserts,

> MBMs place a price on GHG emissions and serve two main purposes:
>
> .1 providing an economic incentive for the maritime industry to reduce its fuel consumption by investing in more fuel efficient ships and technologies and to operate ships in a more energy efficient-manner (in-sector reductions); and
>
> .2 offsetting in other sectors of growing ship emissions (out-of-sector reductions).[326]

II. Addressing Shipping's CO_2 Emissions within UNFCCC

Carbon dioxide emissions from shipping have traditionally been excluded from the efforts that take place under the umbrella of the UNFCCC. Most notably the Kyoto Protocol to the UNFCCC of 1997[327] in its Art 2 (2) provided that:

> [t]he Parties included in Annex I [of the UNFCCC] shall pursue limitation or reduction of emissions of greenhouse gases not controlled by the Montreal Protocol from aviation and marine bunker fuels, working through the International Civil Aviation Organization and the International Maritime Organization, respectively.[328]

325 Faber and others, 'Technical Support for European Action to Reducing Greenhouse Gas Emissions from International Transport' (n 323) 104.

326 IMO, 'Market-Based Measures' <https://www.imo.org/en/OurWork/Environment/Pages/Market-Based-Measures.aspx> accessed 19 May 2023.

327 Kyoto Protocol to the United Nations Framework Convention on Climate Change (adopted 11 December 1997, entered into force 16 February 2005) 2303 UNTS 162.

328 The question of whether Art 2 (2) Kyoto Protocol merely repeated the precedence of the IMO and the International Civil Aviation Organization (ICAO) or whether it actually mandated these organisations and, thereby, established an otherwise lacking authority, may appear like a mere academic question. The response to this, however, is pivotal in the context of the applicability of the principle of *Common But Differentiated Responsibilities* to measures negotiated within the IMO, which is discussed below in section C.III.5.

The 2015 Paris Agreement[329] followed suit and has even left the shipping sector completely unaddressed, and therefore, excluded from its scope—and this does make sense. It is only intuitive that shipping has remained outside of the UNFCCC's purview for the simple reason that emissions from international shipping cannot reasonably be attributed to one particular State. The randomness of a ship's flag—manifested in the reality of flags of convenience[330]—does not allow for a sensible allocation of a ship's (carbon dioxide) emissions to its flag State.[331] This is demonstrated by the decade-long endeavour of the UNFCCC to allocate international marine bunker fuel emissions to one Party. The COP in its very first session agreed to charge two of its Subsidiary Bodies 'to address the issue of the allocation and control of emissions from international bunker fuels'[332]. International bunker fuel is defined as 'fuel sold to any air or marine vessel engaged in international transport [that] is reported separately from other sectors in national emissions inventories.'[333]

The Subsidiary Body for Scientific and Technological Advice (SBSTA), on the other hand, in 1995 'with a view to overcoming inconsistencies in the

329 Paris Agreement (adopted 12 December 2015, entered into force 4 November 2016) 3156 UNTS 79.

330 See section A.I.3.a.

331 For a comparison of carbon dioxide emissions by flags of registration vs economies of ownership, see UNCTAD, *Review of Maritime Transport 2023* (n 13) 58–60. It is noteworthy that the top three open registries Liberia, Panama and the Marshall Islands, accounting for over one-third of CO_2 emissions in 2022, do not even appear on the list of the top 29 economies of ownership.

332 UN, Framework Convention on Climate Change, 'Report of the Conference of the Parties on its First Session, held at Berlin from 28 March to 7 April 1995' (6 June 1995) FCCC/CP1995/7/Add.1, Decision 4/CP.1, para 1 (f). *International bunker fuels* mean marine bunker fuels as well as bunker fuels for aviation. They are often discussed together in the context of UNFCCC.

333 UNFCCC, Subsidiary Body for Scientific and Technological Advice (SBSTA), 'Communications from Parties included in Annex I to the Conventions: Guidelines, schedule and process for consideration, Possible revisions to the guidelines for the preparation of national communications by Parties included in Annex I to the Convention, Addendum: Methodological Issues' (24 October 1996) FCCC/SBSTA/1996/9/Add.1, para 21. See also in contrast the definition of the Intergovernmental Panel on climate change (IPCC) that defines '[e]missions from international marine bunkers' as 'emissions from fuels burned by sea-going ships of all flags that are engaged in international transport', IPCC, *Revised 1996 IPCC Guidelines for National Greenhouse Gas Inventories*, 1.5 <https://www.ipcc-nggip.iges.or.jp/public/gl/invs4.html> accessed 19 May 2023.

presentation of data on inventories'[334] called on the UNFCCC Secretariat to provide allocation options to be discussed at SBSTA[335]. The Secretariat followed SBSTA's request and, subsequently, presented to it for consideration the following eight options for allocating international shipping's emissions to a country, ie to a specific Party's carbon dioxide inventory:[336]

1. No allocation;
2. Allocation to Parties in proportion to their national emissions;
3. Allocation to Parties according to the country where the bunker fuel is sold;
4. Allocation to Parties according to the nationality of the transporting company or to the country where the vessel is registered, or to the country of the operator;
5. Allocation to parties according to the country of departure or destination of a vessel. Alternatively the emissions related to the journey of a vessel could be shared between the country of departure and the country of arrival;
6. Allocation to Parties according to the country of departure or destination of passenger or cargo. Alternatively, the emissions related to the journey of a passenger or cargo could be shared by the country of departure and the country of arrival;
7. Allocation to Parties according to the country [...] that owns the cargo or [of] origin of the passenger;
8. Allocation to the Party of emissions generated in its national space.[337]

The factors that were taken into account when developing these options were the 'characteristics of the shipping industry', as well as 'data required to implement different options', 'the need for methodologies' and 'the relationship of the options to possible policies and measures, such as taxes,

334 UNFCCC, 'Report of the Subsidiary Body for Scientific and Technological Advice on the Work of its Second Session, held at Geneva from 27 February to 4 March 1996' (25 April 1996) FCCC/SBSTA/1996/8, para 62.

335 UNFCCC, 'Report of the Subsidiary Body for Scientific and Technological Advice on the Work of its First Session held at Geneva from 28 August to 1 September 1995' (5 October 1995) FCCC/SBSTA/1995/3, para 37.

336 The formatting of the proposal titles has been slightly altered here for better readability.

337 UNFCCC, SBSTA, 'Communications from Parties included in Annex I to the Conventions: Guidelines, schedule and process for consideration, Addendum: Detailed Information on Electricity Trade and International Bunker Fuels' (26 June 1996) FCCC/SBSTA/1996/9/Add.2, paras 66–79.

standards and voluntary agreements.'[338] From the outset, proposals five to eight were 'considered to be less practical because of data requirements or inadequate global coverage.'[339] Nonetheless, SBSTA decided to only exclude options two, seven and eight from further consideration and based its further work on options one and three through six.[340]

> The three discarded options have several important disadvantages. To name a few: option 2 would not be equitable and would lead to practical problems, such as assigning maritime emissions to land locked countries that have no control over them; option 7 would suffer from heavy data requirements; and option 8 would leave emissions on and over the high seas outside the responsibility of any party.[341]

After the Kyoto Protocol excluded the limitation and reduction of GHG from marine bunker fuels from its purview, the COP made a point to further push the efforts to include international marine bunker fuel emissions into the Parties' national inventory. In December 1997, it recalled

> that, under the Revised 1996 Guidelines for National Greenhouse Gas Inventories of the Intergovernmental Panel on Climate Change, emissions based upon fuel sold to ships or aircraft engaged in international transport should not be included in national totals, but reported separately; and urges the Subsidiary Body for Scientific and Technological Advice to further elaborate on the inclusion of these emissions in the overall greenhouse gas inventories of Parties; [...].[342]

---

338 SBSTA, 'Detailed Information on Electricity Trade and International Bunker Fuels' (n 337) para 66.

339 SBSTA, 'Detailed Information on Electricity Trade and International Bunker Fuels' (n 337) page 28, see asterisks added to the title of the options and corresponding footnote.

340 SBSTA, 'Report of the Subsidiary Body for Scientific and Technological Advice on the Work of its Fourth Session, Geneva, 16–18 December 1996' (27 January 1997) FCCC/SBSTA/1996/20, para 55.

341 Jasper Faber and other, 'Aviation and Maritime Transport in a post 2012 Climate Policy Regime' (CE Delft 2006) <https://cedelft.eu/wp-content/uploads/sites/2/2021/03/06_7153_59.pdf> accessed 30 March 2023, 59.

342 UNFCCC, 'Report of the Conference of the Parties on its Third session, held at Kyoto from 1 to 11 December 1997, Addendum: Part Two: Action taken by the Conference of the Parties at its Third session (25 March 1998) FCCC/CP/1997/7/Add.1, Decision 2/CP.3, para 4.

This is how the question of actual allocation that would have brought those emissions under Party's commitment[343] became a general discussion on emission reporting modalities. Perhaps for good reason,

> allocation is discussed in isolation from policies and measures, which are discussed in IMO and ICAO. If a decision were to be taken on allocation, Parties would be faced with responsibilities without an existing framework for mitigative policies and measures, which, to be effective, require to a large extent international coordination. Countries may be expected to be reluctant to take on responsibilities without a clear prospect of how to meet potential obligations.[344]

From here, therefore, discussions under the auspices of the UNFCCC continued with a focus on the estimation and reporting of emissions. Instead, reporting of the IMO on its progress became a regular and main agenda item.[345]

In the negotiations for a follow-up treaty to the Kyoto Protocol post-2012, the discussion on international bunker fuels seemed to gain momentum.[346] However, none of the seven text proposals to address reduction and limitation of GHG from international shipping (six of which aimed for a sectoral agreement and/or multilateral collaboration) ultimately prevailed.[347] Now that the 2015 Paris Agreement remains fully silent on the reduction and limitation of GHG emissions from shipping or aviation, it is asserted:

---

343 See Faber and others, 'Aviation and Maritime Transport in a post 2012 Climate Policy Regime' (n 341) 69.

344 ibid 51; for 'the most logical combinations of policies and measures on the one hand and allocation options on the other hand', see also at 61.

345 For a chronological overview of SBSTA's work on international bunkers, see UNFCCC <https://unfccc.int/sites/default/files/resource/Chronological%20development%20bunkers%20under%20the%20SBSTA.pdf> accessed 19 May 2023; for a history of the discussions on bunker fuels in the context of UNFCCC, see Beatriz Martinez Romera, 'The Paris Agreement and the Regulation of International Bunker Fuels' (2016) 25 Rev Eur Comp & Int'l Envtl L 215, 216–18, 219–20.

346 See also the Council, 'EU position for the Copenhagen Climate Conference (7-18 December 2009)' (21 October 2009) 14790/09, Recital 19, calling for a 'global emission reduction target [...] for [...] maritime transport', 'consistent with a global reduction path towards meeting the 2°C objective'.

347 UNFCCC, 'Report of the Ad Hoc working Group on Long-term Cooperative Action under the Convention on its Seventh Session, held in Bangkok from 28 September to 9 October, and Barcelona from 2to 6 November 2009' (20 November 2009) FCCC/AWGLCA/2009/14, 101–02.

> The omission of IBFs [international bunker fuels] from the Paris Agreement has tipped the balance in favour of regulation of IBFs outside the UN climate regime [...] In this scenario, unilateral action seems to be the only remaining trigger for ICAO and IMO to pursue meaningful measures. [...] the omission also means that the case for unilateral/regional action, if inaction at the multilateral level continues, has been reinvigorated, since regional measures could help to break an impasse.[348]

With a clear signal that CO_2 emissions were not going to be seriously addressed by the UNFCCC system, the following section examines how the IMO handled this more or less explicit assignment. It looks at how much action or inaction there has been at the IMO to reduce and/or limit carbon dioxide emissions from international shipping.

III. IMO's Efforts to Reduce/Limit International Shipping's CO_2 Emission

In 1997, the COP to MARPOL adopted a Protocol to add to the treaty its Annex VI ('Regulations for the Prevention of Air Pollution from Ships') to address nitrogen oxides, sulphur oxides and ozone depleting substances. The conference also adopted Resolution 8 on CO_2 emissions of ships that invited the IMO to initiate a study to estimate shipping's CO_2 emissions and examine how they relate to global CO_2 emissions and their future projections[349]—this became the basis for the IMO's regular GHG Studies. The conference also invited the IMO's MEPC 'to consider what CO_2 reduction strategies may be feasible in light of the relationship between CO_2 and other atmospheric and marine pollutants'.[350] With reference to the outcome of this conference, the Kyoto Protocol and the First IMO Study on GHG emissions published in 2000, the IMO's Assembly in 2003 urged the MEPC

---

348 Romera (n 345) 225, 227; the author also calls unilateral action 'the sole effective threat for climate action on IBFs at ICAO and IMO', 226.

349 IMO, Conference of Parties to the International Convention for the Prevention of Pollution from Ships, 1973, as modified by the Protocol of 1978 relating thereto, 'Text of Conference Resolutions 1 to 8 and the Technical Code on Control of Emission of Nitrogen Oxides from Marine Diesel Engines' (22 October 1997) MP/CONF.3/35, Annex, Conference Resolution 8 ('CO_2 Emissions from Ships'). To the knowledge of the author, this document is not publicly available in full. The complete document was provided by the UN's Dag Hammarskjöld Library. A digital copy can be made available upon request.

350 ibid.

'to identify and develop the mechanism or mechanisms needed to achieve the limitation or reduction of GHG emissions from international shipping'. To this end, MEPC was supposed to establish inter alia a GHG emissions baseline and a GHG emission index to reflect the GHG efficiency of ships as well as evaluate technical, operational and market-based solutions as a matter of priority.[351]

1. The Struggle for a Market-Based Measure

In 2006, MEPC 55 agreed to 'follow-up [on] all the action items to the Assembly resolution and [that] IMO should maintain its leading position to avoid unilateral action either on a global, regional or national level.'[352] To this end, it adopted a work plan as requested by the Assembly, including a timetable for its future work to be concluded at its 59th session in 2009. With this, the MEPC embarked on a tough and arduous journey to find mechanisms to reduce international shipping's GHG emissions. Extensive discussions followed, based on a wide array of proposals and submissions and a course that was not always straightforward. The following paragraphs will, therefore, give only a brief account of the developments at the subsequent MEPC sessions and focus on the important landmarks.

In 2009, at the MEPC's 59th session

> [t]he Committee considered a large number of views and contributions on the subject, and agreed by overwhelming majority that a market-based measure was needed as part of a comprehensive package of measures for GHG emissions from international shipping. A few delegations [only] recommended IMO to concentrate its work on the elaboration of technical and operational measures.[353]

To this end, the Committee agreed on a new work plan that inter alia requested further submissions on possible MBMs and planned feasibility studies and impact assessments. Based on these inputs, it was going to determine which MBMs it would continue to include in its deliberations.

351 IMO Assembly Res A.963 (23) adopted on 5 December 2003, A 23/Res. 963, 2–3.

352 IMO, MEPC, 'Report of the Marine Environment Protection Committee on its Fifty-Fifth Session' (16 October 2006) MEPC 55/23, para 4.25.

353 IMO, MEPC, 'Report of the Marine Environment Protection Committee on its Fifty-Ninth Session' (27 July 2009) MEPC.59/24, para 4.106.

Further steps would then be presented to MEPC 62.[354] Despite this apparent firm commitment in favour of an MBM, the Committee never fully honoured its pledge. At time of writing in 2023—well over 10 years later—there is no MBM in place. Rather, the Committee's deliberations took a detour via discussions on 'Further Technical and Operational Measures for Enhancing the Energy Efficiency of International Shipping' which by MEPC 67 (in mid-2018) became the established go-to agenda item for discussing GHG emission reductions, named after the Correspondence Group that was tasked by MEPC 66 to 'consider the development of a data collection system for fuel consumption of ships'[355]. It more or less replaced the initial agenda items 'Prevention of Air Pollution from Ships' that later became the agenda item 'Reduction of GHG Emissions from Ships'.

According to the work plan agreed to at MEPC 59, an Expert Group went about to assess the large number of proposals that had so far been submitted to the Committee for consideration. The results of the Expert Group were presented to MEPC 61. The Expert Group investigated the proposed measures, amongst others, with regard to their effectiveness, practical feasibility and compatibility with the existing IMO framework. They also evaluated the measures as to their compatibility with customary international law 'as depicted in UNCLOS' and with regard to other treaties, such as UNFCCC, the Kyoto Protocol and WTO agreements.[356] The Expert Group assessed 10 proposals, suggesting, among other things, an ETS, a port levy, two proposals calling for mandatory energy efficiency standards, and an international GHG fund involving a reduction target and an offsetting mechanism.[357] 'However, many of the issues considered by the Group were complicated by the fact that none of the proposals have final legal text from which to evaluate the administrative and legal criteria

354 IMO, MEPC, 'Report of the Marine Environment Protection Committee on its Fifty-Ninth Session' (28 July 2009) MEPC.59/24/Add.1, Annex 16.

355 IMO, MEPC, 'Report of the Marine Environment Protection Committee on its Sixty-Sixth Session' (25 April 2014) MEPC 66/21, para 4.1.6.

356 IMO, MEPC, 'Full Report of the work undertaken by the Expert Group on Feasibility Study and Impact Assessment of possible Market-based Measures' (13 August 2010) MEPC 61/INF.2, para 1.2.6.

357 For a brief overview of those 10 proposals with a table on the 'Evaluation of the cost of additional burden to crew associated with operations and maintenance', see Andreas Chrysostomou and Eivind S. Vågslid, 'Climate Change: A challenge for IMO too' in Regina Asariotis and Hassiba Benamara (eds) *Maritime Transport and the Climate Change Challenge* (Routledge 2012) 97–102.

given by the MEPC.'[358] Therefore, '[t]he proposed measures would require further elaboration and development to enable a full assessment of all possible impacts in a comparable analysis.'[359] The Expert Group presented its Report to the 61st session of MEPC. The Committee, however, was not able to agree which proposal for an MBM it should continue to work on. Also, not for the first time, some countries strongly voiced their demand that any proposal take into account the UNFCCC's principle of *Common But Differentiated Responsibilities* (CBDR) rather than the NMFT principle to be found in IMO treaties (eg in Art 5 (4) MARPOL) that extends the requirements of the treaty to ships of non-Parties.[360] The MEPC agreed to task an Intersessional Working Group to further investigate the options for an MBM. Remarkably, retreating from its already agreed position on the necessity of an MBM, the Committee also tasked the Working Group to 'examine and provide the Groups' opinion on the compelling need and purpose of Market-based Measures [...] as a possible mechanism to reduce greenhouse gas emissions from international shipping'.[361] The Working Group mainly found that there was no agreement as to the 'compelling need for an MBM' and acknowledged the need for 'further study of the direct and indirect impacts on developing countries due to the introduction of an MBM for international shipping.'[362] The latter call to investigate the effects on so-called developing countries, notably, appears to have been an attempt to take into account the repeated calls of some States for consideration of the CBDR principle, now that the very need of an MBM had also been called into question.

358 MEPC, 'Full report of the work undertaken by the Expert Group on Feasibility Study and Impact Assessment of possible Market-based Measure' (n 356) para 1.6.

359 IMO, MEPC, 'Report of the Marine Environment Protection Committee on its Sixty-First Session' (6 October 2010) MEPC 61/24, para 5.76.4.

360 IMO, MEPC, 'Report of the Marine Environment Protection Committee on its Sixty-First Session' (n 359) Annex 3 ('Statements by Delegations on Matters of Principle or Policy Concerning Reduction of GHG Emissions from Ships), 1–11. Art 5 (4) MARPOL reads: 'With respect to the ships of non-Parties to the Convention, Parties shall apply the requirements of the present Convention as may be necessary to ensure that no more favourable treatment is given to such ships.'

361 IMO, 'Report of the Marine Environment Protection Committee on its Sixty-First Session' (n 359) Annex 7 ('Terms of Reference for the Third Intersessional Meeting of the Working Group on GHG emissions from Ships (GHG-WG 3)'), para 1.

362 IMO, MEPC, 'Report of the third Intersessional Meeting of the working group on greenhouse gas emissions from ships' (8 April 2011) MEPC 62/5/1, paras 2.22–2.25.12, 6.2; paras 3.71, 4.4, 6.6.

The discussion on an impact assessment was postponed until the 65th session in 2013, where 'the Committee agreed to suspend discussions on Market-Based Measures and related issues to a future session except [...] the following three items [...]:

.1 Update of the GHG emission estimate for international shipping;
.2 WTO-related matters; and
.3 UNFCCC matters.'[363]

2. Adopting the Data Collection System for Fuel Oil Consumption of Ships

At the same time, the discussions around *Further measures to improve the energy efficiency of ships* gained momentum following an invitation of the 63rd session for submission of proposals on an 'IMO performance standard for fuel consumption measurement for ships'[364]. Most notably, one submission proposed a three-phased approach to a mandatory efficiency standard, involving a data collection phase which would lead up to a pilot phase and a full implementation phase.[365] Seven sessions later, the Committee adopted amendments to MARPOL Annex VI introducing a Data Collection System for Fuel Oil Consumption of Ships (DCS)[366] which entered into force on 1 March 2018 to be 'the first step in a three-step approach, the second step being data analysis and the third step being decision making on what further measure, if any, are required.'[367]

The structure of the DCS is rather simple. It requires each ship of 5000 GT and above to collect data on its fuel consumption by fuel type, its distance travelled and its hours underway (initially adopted as Reg 22A.1, now Reg 27.1 MARPOL Annex VI). At the end of each year, the data is aggregated and reported to its flag State administration (initially adopted as Reg 22A.3, now Reg 27.3). The flag State verifies the data and issues a Statement of Compliance certificate which becomes part of the necessary

363 IMO, MEPC, 'Report of the Marine Environment Protection Committee on its Sixty-Fifth Session' (24 May 2013) MEPC 65/22, para. 5.1.

364 IMO, MEPC, 'Report of the Marine Environment Protection Committee on its Sixty-Third Session' (14 March 2012) MEPC 63/23, para. 5.59.

365 IMO, MEPC, 'Proposal of the United States to enhance energy efficiency in international shipping: Submitted by the United States' (8 March 2013) MEPC 65/4/19.

366 IMO Res MEPC.278(70) adopted on 28 October 2016, MEPC 70/18/Add.1, Annex 3.

367 See IMO, MEPC, 'Report of the Marine Environment Protection Committee on its Sixty-Ninth Session' (13 May 2016) MEPC 69/21, para 6.8.

documentation on board (Reg 6.6.4), ie the certificate is to be presented as part of the inspection of PSC officers. The flag State transfers the data on fuel consumption, along with personalised information of the ship, including its technical specifications, to the IMO (initially adopted as Reg 22A.9, now Reg 27.9). The IMO then produces an annual report and feeds the data into its Ship Fuel Oil Consumption Database; the data therein is made available to the Parties in an anonymised form (initially adopted as Reg 22A.10 and .11, now Reg 27.10 and .12). Five additional documents offer further specifications, such as the verification of data, the development of the database or reporting formats.[368] It is noteworthy that the flag State can outsource its role to 'any organization duly authorized by it'. In the language of the IMO this means that the flag State can resort to a Recognized Organization (RO) in the meaning of IMO's so-called RO-Code.[369] In practice, those entities that fulfil all of the criteria of the RO-Code and are assessed and approved by flag States as ROs are classification societies.[370] The role of classification societies will be further discussed below.[371]

Parallel to the deliberations and adoption of the DCS, a broadly supported initiative called for international shipping to determine and contribute its 'fair share' to the reduction of GHG and the efforts to stop the rise in global average temperature.[372] This initiative, which used the momentum created by the UNFCCC's Paris Agreement, effectively asked nothing less

368 See IMO Res MEPC.346(78) ('2022 Guidelines for the Development of a Ship Energy Efficiency Management Plan (SEEMP))' adopted on 10 June 2022 MEPC 78/17/Add.1; Res MEPC.348(78) ('2022 Guidelines for Administration Verification of Ship Fuel Oil Consumption Data and Operational Carbon Intensity') adopted on 10 June 2022, MEPC 78/17/Add.1; IMO Res MEPC.349(78) ('2022 Guidelines for the Development and Management of the IMO Ship Fuel Oil Consumption Database') adopted on 10 June 2022, MEPC 78/17/Add.1; IMO, MEPC Circular 'Guidance for Submission of Data to the IMO Data Collection System of Fuel Oil Consumption of Ships from a State Not Party to MARPOL Annex VI' (24 June 2022), MEPC.1/Circ.871/Rev. 1; IMO, MEPC Circular 'Sample Format for the Confirmation of Compliance, Early Submission of the SEEMP Part II on the Ship Fuel Oil Consumption Data Collection Plan and its Timely Verification Pursuant to Regulation 5.4.5 of MARPOL Annex VI' (16 April 2018), MEPC.1/Circ. 876.

369 IMO Res MEPC.237 (65) adopted on 17 May 2013, MEPC 65/22/Add.2.

370 For more detailed information on Classification Societies, see the information paper of the International Association of Classification Societies, 'Classification societies – what, why and how?' <https://iacs.org.uk/media/8871/classification-what-why-how.pdf> accessed 19 May 2023.

371 See section C.IV.3.

372 See MEPC, 'Report of the Marine Environment Protection Committee on its Sixty-Ninth Session' (n 367) paras 7.4–7.7.

than for IMO to set itself a carbon dioxide reduction target. It resulted in the adoption of a 'Roadmap for developing a comprehensive IMO strategy on reduction of GHG emissions from ships' meant to join and align all of IMO's strategies concerning the reduction of GHG.[373] At its heart was the adoption of an Initial IMO Strategy by early 2018, including possible short-, mid- and long-term future measures with an update scheduled for early 2023.

3. The IMO's GHG Reduction Strategies—An IMO Paris Agreement?

The IMO adopted its 'Initial Strategy on Reduction of GHG Emissions from Ships' in April of 2018. Its goal was 'to reduce CO_2 emissions per transport work [ie improving energy efficiency], as an average across international shipping, by at least 40% by 2030, pursuing efforts towards 70% by 2050, compared to 2008' and 'to peak GHG emissions from international shipping as soon as possible and to reduce the total annual GHG emissions by at least 50% by 2050 compared to 2008 whilst pursuing efforts towards phasing them out [...] as a point on a pathway of CO_2 emissions reduction consistent with the Paris Agreement temperature goals.'[374] The IMO's Initial GHG Strategy was called the 'first global climate framework for shipping'[375] or even 'IMO's 2018 climate agreement'[376]. Even more enthusiastically, it was called the 'Paris Agreement for Shipping'.[377] Ironically, the initial self-imposed minimum reduction target of '50% by 2050 compared to 2008' was actually not consistent with the targets of the Paris Agreement. The Paris Agreement's minimum target is '[h]olding the increase in the global

373 IMO, MEPC, 'Report of the Marine Environment Protection Committee on its Seventieth Session (11 November 2016) MEPC 70/18, paras 7.8–7.19 and MEPC 70/18/Add.1, Annex 11.

374 IMO, Res MEPC.304 (72) adopted on 13 April 2018, 'MEPC 72/17/Add.1, Annex 11, para 3.1.

375 ICCT, 'The International Maritime Organization's initial greenhouse gas strategy' (2018) <https://theicct.org/wp-content/uploads/2021/06/IMO_GHG_StrategyFInal PolicyUpdate042318.pdf> accessed 17 April 2023.

376 Tristan Smith, 'The IMO's 2018 climate agreement explained' <https://gmn.imo.org /wp-content/uploads/2018/05/IMOs-2018-climate-agreement-explained-a-UCL-do cument.pdf> accessed 30 March 2023.

377 International Chamber of Shipping, 'Reducing CO_2 Emissions to Zero: The "Paris Agreement for Shipping"' (Marisec Publication 2018) <https://www.ics-shipping.or g/wp-content/uploads/2020/08/reducing-co2-emissions-to-zero-the-paris-agreeme nt-for-shipping.pdf> accessed 30 March 2023.

average temperature to well-below 2°C above pre-industrial levels', striving for a limitation of a maximum increase of 1.5°C (Art 2 (1) (a)). In 2018, the world had at its disposal an overall *remaining carbon budget*[378] of 800 gigatonnes (Gt) of CO_2[379] it was not allowed to exceed to have a 67% chance to hold the temperature increase right between 1.5°C and 2°C. Of that, international shipping, based on its global share in CO_2 emissions, would be allocated a budget of ca. 17 Gt CO_2[380]. However, between a best-case scenario where international shipping fully decarbonised by 2050 and the worst case-scenario of the minimum 50% reduction in absolute emissions by 2050 with decarbonisation by 2100, international shipping would still be emitting an overall of 28 to 43 Gt CO_2 between 2015 and 2100.[381] One reason for this, especially compromising the efficiency goal, is the choice to make 2008 the reference year—2008 being the year with the highest carbon dioxide emissions in recent history[382], before ships more readily employed

378 *Remaining carbon budget* being defined as the '[e]stimated cumulative net global anthropogenic CO_2 emissions from the start of 2018 to the time that anthropogenic CO_2 emissions reach net zero that would result, at some probability, in limiting global warming to a given level, accounting for the impact of other anthropogenic emission', with *Net zero CO_2 emissions* being *carbon neutrality* where 'anthropogenic CO_2 emissions are balanced globally by anthropogenic CO_2 removals over a specific period', see IPCC, *Global warming of 1.5°: An IPCC Special Report on the impacts of global warming of 1.5°C above pre-industrial levels and related global greenhouse gas emission pathways, in the context of strengthening the global response to the threat of climate change, sustainable development, and efforts to eradicate poverty*, Annex I, 557 and 555, respectively <https://www.ipcc.ch/site/assets/uploads/sites/2/2022/06/SR15_Full_Report_HR.pdf> accessed 30 March 2023.

379 See IPCC, *Global warming of 1.5°C* (n 378) 108 (Table 2.2).

380 ICCT, 'The International Maritime Organization's Initial Greenhouse Gas Strategy' (n 375) 5.

381 ibid 5. The author wishes to thank Dr Bryan Comer, Senior Researcher at the ICCT's Marine Program and Lead Author of Annex A and B of the Fourth IMO GHG Study 2020 (n 1) for his invaluable insights used here and correspondence based on his analysis. For a direct comparison of the IMO's ambition of the Initial GHG Strategy with the goals of the Paris Agreement, see also Bryan Comer, 'Zero-Emission Shipping and the Paris Agreement: Why the IMO Needs to Pick a Zero Date and Set Interim Targets in its Revised Strategy' (8 September 2021) <https://theicct.org/zero-emission-shipping-and-the-paris-agreement-why-the-imo-needs-to-pick-a-zero-date-and-set-interim-targets-in-its-revised-ghg-strategy/> accessed 6 April 2023.

382 See Tristan Smith and others, *Third IMO Greenhouse Gas Study 2014: Executive Summary and Final Report* (IMO 2015) <https://wwwcdn.imo.org/localresources/en/OurWork/Environment/Documents/Third%20Green house%20-Gas%20Study/GHG3%20Executive%20Summary%20and%20Report.pdf> accessed 19 May 2023, 1 (Table 1a).

easily available measures, such as slow steaming, as a reaction to rising fuel prices during the global financial crisis.

To meet its objectives, the Initial GHG Strategy contained a list of candidate short-, mid- and long-term measures to be considered.[383] They strongly focused on the improvement of operational and technical energy efficiency—especially the long existing Energy Efficiency Design Index—intended to further investigate low- and zero-carbon fuels and made a careful commitment to explore 'new/innovative emission reduction mechanism(s), possibly including Market-based Measures [...], to incentivize GHG emission reduction'.[384] With this, MEPC basically followed the recommendations of OECD[385] and the IEA—who was actually involved in negotiating and writing the GHG Strategy[386]—but in one important point. While the IEA accepts the benefits of efficiency improvements,[387] it deems it indispensable that efficiency measures and the reduction of carbon content in fuel are accompanied by a carbon pricing mechanism.[388]

383 With short-term measures to be agreed and finalised between 2018–2023, mid-term measures between 2023–2030 and long-term measures beyond 2030. For a timeline for the period of 2018–2023, see IMO MEPC, 'Report of the Marine Environment Protection Committee on its Seventy-Third session (5 December 2018) MEPC 73/19/Add.1, Annex 9.

384 IMO, Res MEPC.304 (72) (n 374) paras 3.1.1, 4.7–4.9; for a detailed timeline of activities, see 'Programme of follow-up actions of the initial IMO strategy on reduction of GHG emissions up to 2023'in IMO, 'Report of the Marine Environment Protection Committee on its Seventy-Third session (5 December 2018) MEPC 73/19/Add.1, Annex 9.

385 IMO, Intersessional Meeting of the Working Group on Reduction of GHG Emissions from Ships, 'GHG emissions scenario to reach a temperature target of 1.75°C and candidate short-, mid- and long-term measures: Submitted by OECD' (22 September 2017) ISWG-GHG 2/2/14.

386 See IEA, 'International Maritime Organization agreed to first long-term plan to curb emissions' <https://www.iea.org/commentaries/international-maritime-organization-agrees-to-first-long-term-plan-to-curb-emissions> accessed 19 May 2023.

387 The IEA recognises that '[i]mproved efficiency (including wind assistance) accounts for the largest share of GHG abatement' in the Beyond 2°C Scenario (giving it a 50% chance to keep the increase of average global temperature to 1.75°C); ISWG, 'GHG emissions scenario to reach a temperature target of 1.75°C and candidate short-, mid- and long-term measures' (n 385) paras 4, 12.

388 ibid paras 7, 17.3, 18.4; see also IEA (n 15) 60, 84, 88–89. Carbon pricing is one type of a market-based measure, the most widely known being an ETS—for an overview of different carbon pricing mechanisms, see Carbon Pricing Leadership Coalition, 'What is Carbon Pricing' <https://www.carbonpricingleadership.org/what/> accessed 31 March 2023.

In July 2023, the IMO revised its Initial GHG Strategy and replaced it with its 2023 IMO Strategy on Reduction of GHG Emissions from Ships[389]. This put the IMO on the path towards the goals of the Paris Agreement.[390] While the 2023 Strategy retains its goal of a 40% reduction by 2030 compared to 2008, it tightens its ambitions on decarbonisation, namely to 'reach net-zero GHG emissions by or around, i.e. close to, 2050'.[391] As an interim goal, its ambition is to ensure the 'uptake of zero or near-zero GHG emission technologies, fuels and/or energy sources to represent at least 5%, striving for 10%, of the energy used by international shipping by 2030'.[392] These levels of ambition are accompanied by two indicative checkpoints 'to reduce the total annual GHG emissions from international shipping by at least 20%, striving for 30%, by 2030' and 'at least 70%, striving for 80%, by 2040', with 2008 remaining the baseline.[393] If these levels of ambition are achieved, 'international shipping will exceed its current share of the world's 1.5°C carbon budget by approximately 2032 but will not exceed the well below 2°C carbon budget'.[394] With that, the IMO can claim its 2023 Strategy to indeed be in line with the Paris Agreement temperature goals.

To achieve its objectives, the timeline of the 2023 Strategy leading up to the adoption of a 2028 Strategy provides for the adoption and entry into force of mid-term measures by 2025 and 2027, respectively.[395] For this, a 'basket of measures' is to be finalised by early 2024, including one measure with a 'technical element, namely a goal-based marine fuel standard regulating the phased reduction of the marine fuel's GHG intensity', as well as one with 'an economic element, on the basis of a maritime GHG emissions pricing mechanism'.[396] In terms of immediate action, however, the 2023 Strategy names one single short-term measure, namely the review of two

389 IMO, Res MEPC.377(80) adopted on 7 July 2023, MEPC 80/17/Add.1, Annex 15. The '2023 IMO Strategy on Reduction of GHG Emissions from Ships' is found in the Annex to the resolution.

390 It is noteworthy that preambular paragraph 7 of the resolution expressly refers to the Paris Agreement.

391 IMO, Res MEPC.377 (80) (n 389) para 3.3.4.

392 ibid 3.3.3.

393 ibid 3.4.

394 Bryan Comer and Francielle Carvalho, 'IMO's Newly Revised GHG Strategy: What it means for Shipping and the Paris Agreement' <https://theicct.org/marine-imo-updated-ghg-strategy-jul23/> accessed 15 December 2023.

395 ibid para 6.2.

396 ibid 4.5.

measures of MARPOL Annex VI to be completed by 2025.[397] The measures addressed are the Energy Efficiency Existing Ship Index (EEXI) and the Carbon Intensity Indicator (CII), the former being a design/technical measure and the latter being an operational measure. They join the Energy Efficiency Design Index (EEDI) as a measure into which much hope was placed, even as recently as the 2018 Initial GHG strategy. It has played an important role in the IMO's GHG policy for a long time. All three instruments, however, are efficiency measures directed towards individual ships and, therefore, cannot ensure an absolute emission reduction in the sector. They have, nonetheless, been placed in the context of the general IMO strategy to advance the shipping sector's emissions reductions, and even reach decarbonisation. The following section, therefore, discusses the EEDI as the instrument the IMO has been counting on so heavily and also addresses the more recent EEXI and CII to further its reduction goals.

4. Mobilising Technical and Operational Measures to Reach Reduction Goals

Until its inclusion in the 2018 Initial GHG Strategy, the debates and developments around the Energy Efficiency Design Index (EEDI) mostly took place rather independently from the discussions on MBMs or reduction targets. The discussions on MBMs and the discussions on Further Technical and Operational Measures after the idea of an MBM had failed, were held in the full understanding that measures in addition to the EEDI were necessary—hence the reference to *further* measures, meaning technical measures beyond the EEDI and operational measures beyond the closely linked Ship Energy Efficiency Management Plan (SEEMP) and Energy Efficiency Operational Indicator (EEOI).

The regulations on the EEDI, previously a voluntary measure, were adopted in July 2011 and entered into force 1 January 2013, together with the regulations on the SEEMP, as part of a package to improve technical (ie design) and operational ship efficiency. They were added to MARPOL's Annex VI as a new Chapter Four—*Regulations on Energy Efficiency for Ships*—thereby introducing the concept of energy efficiency and the underlying notion of carbon dioxide reduction as a permanent theme to MAR-

397 ibid 4.3.

POL.[398] While expanding the scope of Annex VI was deemed legitimate by IMO's Legal Office, it remained a point of contention for some Parties.[399] Such was the level of controversy on this and the closely linked question of the applicability of the CBDR principle that the provisions of the EEDI were only passed by the unusual procedure of a vote, opposed to the common practice of decision-making by consent.[400] It can safely be assumed that the proponents of applying the CBDR principle in the IMO context (predominantly so-called developing countries) feared the precedence that the EEDI as a carbon dioxide mitigation measure would set for the future if it were enshrined in MARPOL. With the EEDI eventually established in MARPOL Annex VI, the IMO takes pride in addressing 85% of the carbon dioxide emissions from international shipping,[401] and has complimented itself for passing the 'first global mandatory GHG-reduction regime for an international industry sector.'[402]

---

398 IMO, Res MEPC.203(62) adopted on 15 July 2011, MEPC 62/24/Add.1, Annex 19.

399 IMO, MEPC, 'Report of the Marine Environment Protection Committee on its Sixtieth Session' (12 April 2010) MEPC 60/22, paras 4.29, 4.33–4.36.

400 For more details, see IMO, MEPC, 'Report of the Marine Environment Protection Committee on its Sixty-Second session' (26 July 2011) MEPC 62/24, paras 6.108–6.111. The IMO stresses the wide representation of the affirmative votes: 'From the outcome of the vote it may be worth noting that the yes-voting countries represent some 79% of the world's merchant shipping tonnage, be that tonnage flagged in developing or developed countries. Moreover, in illustration of the universality of the regulatory measures now introduced into MARPOL Annex VI, the yes-voting countries represent all regions of the world – both exporters and importers, as well as the largest flag States, most of the large ship building nations and many of the countries that are most likely to suffer first from the effects of climate change. Perhaps most importantly, the yes-voting countries represent about 75% of CO_2 emissions from international shipping which, therefore, augurs well for the environmental effectiveness of the new IMO treaty obligations', IMO, 'Note by the International Maritime Organization to the thirty-fifth session of the Subsidiary Body of Scientific and Technical Advice (SBSTA 15)' <https://seors.unfccc.int/applications/seors/attachments/get_attachment?code=BK9JQY56QGYRELGCZJJR3XDTED1J4OUS> accessed 15 December 2023, para 15. See also statements by some delegations that voted against adoption, MEPC, 'Report of the Marine Environment Protection Committee on its Sixty-Second Session', MEPC 62/24/Add.1, Annex 20.

401 See IMO, Intersessional Meeting of the Working Group on Reduction of GHG Emissions, 'Existing IMO activity related to reducing GHG emissions in the shipping sector' (21 February 2017) ISWG-GHG 1/2, paras 22, 32; see also Foreword by the Secretary-General Mr Koji Sekimizu to the *Third IMO Greenhouse Gas Study* (n 382).

402 ISWG, 'Existing IMO activity related to reducing GHG emissions in the shipping sector' (n 401) para 19.

In very simple terms, the EEDI sets reference lines (ie baselines) for different ship types based on the average design efficiency of new ships between 1998 and 2010 (depending on ship type[403]). It then requires new ships of 400 GT and above, or those regarded as new due to major conversions, to continually improve their design efficiency (defined as CO_2 emission/capacity*speed) in line with predetermined reduction factors. It provides for a gradual increase in reduction factors in four phases—starting from 0% in 2013 and moving up to 30% in gradual increases becoming applicable in 2015, 2020 and 2025. It grants the industry the freedom to choose the design improvements that help achieve those efficiency targets. The details of its implementation which are anything but straightforward are laid down in Guidelines that have continuously been under review.[404] The introduction of the EEDI was complemented by the mandatory regulations for all ships to keep on board an SEEMP, a tool to help monitor and improve ship operational efficiency.[405] The application of the EEOI, a monitoring tool, in this context remains voluntary.[406]

An initial study on the reduction potential of the EEDI and SEEMP in 2011 estimated an average annual reduction in CO_2 of 13% by 2020 and 23% by 2030, compared to the business-as-usual scenario. The same study also found, however, that 'none of the scenarios modelled will achieve a reduction in total CO_2-level relative to year 2010'.[407] This points to an

403 The scope of the EEDI was gradually extended to include ship types previously unaddressed, such as LNG carrier and cruise passenger ships. For the complete table of ship types and their reduction factors, see Reg 21 MARPOL Annex VI as contained in IMO, Res MEPC.324(75) adopted on 20 November 2020, MEPC 75/18/Add.1.

404 See the IMO, 'Index of MEPC Resolution and Guidelines related to MARPOL Annex VI: Guidelines related to Energy Efficiency of Ships <https://www.imo.org/en/OurWork/Environment/Pages/Index-of-MEPC-Resolutions-and-Guidelines-related-to-MARPOL-Annex-VI.aspx> accessed 19 May 2023.

405 See also the '2016 Guidelines for the Development of a Ship Energy Efficiency Management Plan (SEEMP)', IMO, Res MEPC.282 (70) adopted on 28 October 2016, MEPC 70/18/Add.1, Annex 10, later revoked by the '2022 Guidelines for the Development of a Ship Energy Efficiency Management Plan', IMO, Res MEPC.346(78) adopted on 10 June 2022, MEPC 78/17/Add.1, Annex 8.

406 See IMO, 'Guidelines for Voluntary use of the Ship Energy Efficiency Operational Indicator (EEOI)' (17 August 2009), MEPC.1/Circ.684.

407 Zabi Bazari and Tore Longva, 'Assessment of IMO Mandated Energy Efficiency Measures for International Shipping', IMO, MEPC, 'Estimated CO_2 emissions reduction from the introduction of mandatory technical and operational energy efficiency measures for ships: Executive summary: Note by the Secretariat' (31 October 2011) MEPC 63/4/1, Annex 1, paras 10.3, 11.

important characteristic of the EEDI: while it may be technically correct to call the EEDI a *reduction regime for an entire sector*, it leaves space for misinterpretation in that the EEDI sets reduction targets for individual ships only. In other words, while each ship is supposed to reduce its carbon dioxide output by a specific predetermined amount, there is no mandatory overall reduction target for the entire sector. In fact, the EEDI has been criticised for its lax reduction targets. A study conducted in 2017 (excluding inter alia ro-ro cargo and ro-ro passenger ships) estimated that at least 20% of new ships were over-complying with the EEDI reduction requirements—ie already meeting the reduction requirements of 2020 onwards—with efficiency improvements worsening in 2016 compared to 2015 and having come to a halt in 2016.[408]

To account for future developments, the EEDI system from its outset provided for two reviews:

> At the beginning of Phase 1 and at the midpoint of Phase 2, the Organization shall review the status of technological developments and, if proven necessary, amend the time periods, the EEDI reference line parameters for relevant ship types and reduction rates set out in this regulation.' (Reg 21.6 MARPOL Annex VI)

In 2016 and 2017 respectively, the MEPC decided to 'retain the current reduction rates, time periods and EEDI reference line parameters in the phase 2 requirements for ship types other than ro-ro cargo and ro-ro passenger ships.'[409]. However, it adjusted the parameter for determining the reference line to loosen reduction requirements for those ro-ro cargo and ro-ro passenger ships[410]. The second EEDI review was more fruitful in that the MEPC in 2019 agreed to move the third phase forward from 2025 to 2022 for a number of ships[411] and to raise the phase three reduction rate

408 Jasper Faber, 'Estimated Index Values of Ships 2009-2016: Analysis of the Design Efficiency of Ships that have Entered the Fleet since 2009' (2017) <https://cedelft.eu/wp-content/uploads/sites/2/2021/04/2017_07_CE_Delft_7L97_Estimated_Index_Values_of_Ships_2009-2016_def_2017.pdf> accessed 19 May 2023, 4.

409 MEPC, Report of the Marine Environment Protection Committee on its Seventieth Session' (n 373) para 5.31.

410 IMO, MEPC, 'Report of the Marine Environment Protection Committee on its Seventy-First Session' (24 July 2017) MEPC 71/17/Add.1, Annex 15; IMO, MEPC, 'Report of the Marine Environment Protection Committee on its Seventy-Second Session' (3 May 2018) MEPC 72/17, para 3.50 and MEPC 72/17/Add.1, Annex 6.

411 Gas carriers of 15,000 DWT and above, container ships, general cargo ships, LNG carriers and cruise passenger ships.

for containerships based on their carrying capacity from 30% up to 50% for container ships of 200,000 DWT and above.[412] It ended up adopting a more differentiated approach for container ships based on their DWT (now Reg 24.2 MARPOL Annex VI).[413] At the same time, however, the MEPC set out to consider a new phase for the EEDI to fulfil the IMO's Initial GHG Strategy.[414]

As the IMO sees it, the EEDI and SEEMP as '[g]oal-based and technology-neutral regulations have incentivised the use of energy-efficient technology such as hull air lubrication, wind assisted propulsion, waste heat recovery, etc.'[415]. However, the time gap between adoption and entry into force and the first two-year phase (2013–2015) with a zero-reduction requirement delayed the taking into effect of the EEDI regulations. Additionally, with the regulations targeting new ships and a usually assumed life span of a ship of between 25 and 30 years, the EEDI was always designed to be more of a long-term measure.[416] Therefore, in its plan to tap the potential of the EEDI system to further its GHG emission goals, the IMO adopted new instruments on the basis of the EEDI and SEEMP as short-term measures as part of its 2018 Initial GHG Strategy. Chapter Four of Annex VI was retitled *Regulations on the Carbon Intensity of International Shipping* with its goal 'to reduce the carbon intensity of international shipping, working towards the levels of ambition set out in the *Initial IMO Strategy on reduction of GHG emissions from ships*' stated in its Reg 20. It now contains regulations on the design/technical efficiency of existing ships similar to those of the EEDI, based on an EEXI. This is matched with the CII, a measurement for the operational efficiency, that is monitored (based on an amended SEEMP and DCS data) for each ship to achieve a gradually increasing

412 IMO, MEPC, 'Report of the Marine Environment Protection Committee on its Seventy-Fourth Session' (9 June 2019) MEPC 74/18, paras 5.82–5.87, 5.91.

413 Adopted by IMO Res MEPC.328(76), MEPC 76/15/Add.1 (24 August 2021).

414 IMEPC, 'Report of the Marine Environment Protection Committee on its Seventy-Fourth session (n 412) para 5.103.

415 IMO, 'Improving the Energy Efficiency of Ships' <https://www.imo.org/en/OurWork/Environment/Pages/Improving%20the%20energy%20efficiency%20of%20ships.aspx> accessed 31 March 2023.

416 See Bazari and Longva (n 407) para 11. It is noteworthy that the fear that Administrations would make extensive use of their right to waive the EEDI requirements for individual ships under their flag (Reg 19.4 MARPOL Annex VI) did not materialise. At time of writing in 2023, an overall of 10 waivers were notified by five Parties. These notifications according to Reg 19.6 MARPOL Annex VI are registered at IMO, GISIS: Annex VI <https://gisis.imo.org/Public/MARPOL6/Notifications.aspx?Reg=19.6> accessed 19 May 2023.

reduction factor of between 5–11% from 2023 to 2026 relative to 2019[417].[418] Where a ship is in poor performance, it has to take corrective measures, ie make sure to improve its efficiency. Both measures came into effect as of 1 January 2023. They have so far been the only concrete measures implemented within the framework of the 2018 Initial GHG Strategy. The review of the EEXI and CII as short-term measures is also more or less the only concrete measure mentioned in the 2023 IMO GHG Strategy.

5. *Common but Differentiated Responsibilities* as the Roadblock to Progress

Examining the causes for the failure of MBM ambitions so far and the initial difficulties of adopting the EEDI reveals one major culprit: The CBDR principle—a major controversial point in both processes. The IMO's 2018 GHG reduction strategy might not have been adopted, had it not determined its first guiding principles to be:

> 1. the need to be cognizant of the principles enshrined in instruments already developed, such as:
>
> .1 the principle of non-discrimination and the principle of no more favourable treatment, enshrined in MARPOL and other IMO conventions; and
> .2 the principle of common but differentiated responsibilities and respective capabilities, in the light of different national circumstances, enshrined in UNFCCC, its Kyoto Protocol and the Paris Agreement;[419]

The identical wording is found in the IMO's 2023 strategy.[420] How the NMFT principle that MARPOL requirements apply to non-Party ships is to be reconciled with the principle that some are exempted from obligations under the CBDR principle, however, is not addressed. One possible way the IMO seems to be exploring is that of technical cooperation. However, it has no mandatory measure for it in place.[421] The question of the applicability

---

417 See IMO Res MEPC.338(76) adopted on 17 June 2021, MEPC 76/15/Add.2, para 4.1.

418 The EEXI and the CII are supplemented by a number of Guidelines, see IMO, 'Index of MEPC Resolutions and Guidelines related to MARPOL Annex VI' (n 404).

419 IMO, Res MEPC.304 (72) (n 374) para 3.2.1.

420 IMO, Res MEPC.377 (80) (n 389) para 3.5.1.

421 See eg IMO, Res MEPC.323 (74) adopted on 17 May 2019, MEPC 74/18/Add.1, Annex 19 explicitly adopted in the context of the Initial GHG Strategy; see also IMO, 'Integrated Technical Cooperation Programme (ITCP)' <https://www.imo.o

of the CBDR principle in the context of IMO policy has proven to be a highly disruptive factor in debates around the reduction of CO_2 emissions from international shipping. One former MEPC chairperson (2003-2013) has asserted:

> In fact, it can be safely claimed that the wording of Article 2.2 [of the Kyoto Protocol] has been the main reason why the IMO has not yet been able to enact a GHG regime for international shipping in a timely and comprehensive manner.[422]

Therefore, the principle of CBDR and the challenges it has brought to the MEPC discussions, deserve a closer look.

The principle of CBDR is found in Art 3 (1) UNFCCC that requests Parties to 'protect the climate system [...] on the basis of equity and in accordance with their common but differentiated responsibilities and respective capabilities', therefore often referred to as *CBDR-RC* including the reference to the *respective capabilities.* It is also referred to in Principle 7 of the 1992 Rio Declaration on Environment and Development[423] and is repeated in the chapeau of Art 10 of the Kyoto Protocol[424].

> The concept of common but differentiated responsibilities in international environmental law entails that while pursuing a common goal, States take on different obligations, depending on their socio-economic situation and their historical contribution to the environmental problem at stake.[425]

---

rg/en/OurWork/TechnicalCooperation/Pages/ITCP.aspx> accessed 19 May 2023, that addresses climate change amongst other topics.

422 Chrysostomou and Vågslid (n 357) 81.

423 'States shall cooperate in a spirit of global partnership to conserve, protect and restore the health and integrity of the Earth's ecosystem. In view of the different contributions to global environmental degradation, States have common but differentiated responsibilities. The developed countries acknowledge the responsibility that they bear in the international pursuit of sustainable development in view of the pressures their societies place on the global environment and of the technologies and financial resources they command.'

424 Introducing Parties' obligations with a reference to them 'taking into account their common but differentiated responsibilities and their specific national and regional development priorities, objectives and circumstances'.

425 Ellen Hey and Sophia Paulini, 'Common but Differentiated Responsibilities' (last updated October 2021) in Peters and Wolfrum (eds) *MPEPIL* (n 31) <https://opil-1ouplaw-1com-100b98fdz01e3.emedien3.sub.uni-hamburg.de/display/10.1093/law:epil/9780199231690/law-9780199231690-e1568?rskey=nmstZ2&result=1&prd=MPIL> accessed 19 May 2023, para 1. It is noteworthy that the notion that underlies

Ultimately, this translates into different responsibilities for so-called developed and developing countries, which in the context of UNFCCC and the Kyoto Protocol are also called Annex I and non-Annex I countries, respectively—whereas only Parties of Annex I are addressed by the commitments of the Kyoto Protocol. When it comes to whether the CBDR principle is applicable within the IMO context, everything depends on how Art 2 (2) Kyoto Protocol is interpreted. Art 2 (2) Kyoto Protocol is clear in that it explicitly and specifically addressed and obliged Annex I Parties to pursue the reduction or limitation of GHG emissions from marine bunker fuels, acting through the IMO. The crucial legal question is whether this Art 2 (2) confirmed or established IMO's authority to regulate reductions and limitations of GHG emissions from marine bunker fuels. If the IMO was acting on a mandate of UNFCCC, it would make sense, that it would have to take into account its principles. On the other hand, if the IMO was an organisation acting in its own right, then naturally its own established principles would apply.[426]

Early on in 2008, the IMO's legal service attempted to resolve the disagreements surrounding the CBDR principle. In a note to the Committee, it established that Art 2 (2) Kyoto Protocol is only the acknowledgement of IMO's original authority rooted in the IMO Convention and UNCLOS, and that 'provisions regulating GHG emissions from combustion of marine

the CBDR principle is neither new nor an invention of international environmental law, see there, paras 2 and 3, where the authors trace first expressions of the concept as far back as the Versailles Peace Treaty of 1919.

426 This is, unless CBDR were widely regarded as a general principle of customary international law, which it is not, see eg Tuula Honkonen, 'The principle of Common But Differentiated Responsibility in Post-2012 Climate Negotiations' (2009) 18 Rev Eur Comp & Int'l Envtl L 257, 258; Christopher D. Stone, 'Common but Differentiated Responsibilities in International Law' (2004) 98 Am J Int'l L 276, 281 with further references; Anita M Halvorssen, 'Common but Differentiated Commitments in the Future Climate Change Regime—Amending the Kyoto Protocol to Include Annex C and the Annex C Mitigation Fund' (2007) 18 Colo J Int'l Envtl L & Pol'y 247, 254 (asserting that 'the CBDR principle is not considered binding international law'); see also Lavanya Rajamani, 'The Principle of Common but Differentiated Responsibility and the Balance of Commitments under the Climate Regime' (2000) 9 Rev Eur Comp & Int'l Envtl L 120, 124 giving a brief account of the efforts of the delegation of the USA to avoid the appearance of laying down customary international law or opinion juris during the negotiations around Art 3 UNFCCC, prompting the author to suggest that '[p]erhaps therefore the notion of common but differentiated responsibility within the FCCC cannot technically be termed a "principle"'.

bunker fuels is a task which is properly within the purview of IMO'.[427] Indeed, the very structure of the shipping business defies a strict distinction of States similar to the Kyoto Protocol's Annex I and non-Annex I States to determine the application of regulatory obligations. A ship flying the flag of a so-called developing country does not require the same protection as the so-called developing country itself from compliance with reduction measures. In fact, in most cases, the owner of the ship will be located in a so-called developed country and is seeking that flag State for economic purposes only or, if not already registered in a so-called developing country, could easily change its flag.[428] Consequently, the allocation of emissions to either country would not be justified:

> a ship belonging to a shipowner incorporated in a developed country, but registered or flagged in a developing country, cannot presumptively be considered as a source of emission coming either from the developing

---

427 IMO, MEPC, 'Legal aspects of the Organization's Work on Greenhouse Gas Emissions in the Context of the Kyoto Protocol: Note by the Secretariat' (1 August 2008) MEPC 58/4/20, paras 4.3, 4.6; see similar assessments by Romera (n 345) 225: 'Neither ICAO nor IMO's mandate could come directly from Kyoto, since there is no hierarchical relationship between them. The mandate for ICAO and the IMO must come from the will of their own members, established in their constituent documents, that is, the Chicago Convention and the IMO Convention, and/or expressed in other legal instruments related to the organizations.' Md. Saiful Karim and Shawkat Alam, 'Climate Change and Reduction of Emissions of Greenhouse Gases from Ships: An Appraisal' (2011) 1 AsianJIL 131, 147: 'The IMO's competence to propose and initiate a global instrument for the reduction of ship-generated GHG emissions does not derive from the Kyoto Protocol. The IMO's competence basically comes from UNCLOS and the IMO Convention.' The authors cite Art 211 (1) and 212 (3) UNCLOS—pointing out that only Art 207 UNCLOS considers 'the economic capacity of developing States'—as well as Art 59 IMO Convention. They basically call the wording of Art 2 (2) Kyoto Protocol a mishap, since 'the drafters of this article failed to foresee the complexity of implementing the CBDR principle in the maritime sector.' and 'Article 2 (2) of the Kyoto Protocol totally failed to consider the issue of flags of convenience', 134 and 138; see also there at 143, 144 for a brief account of the attempts of the Parties to rectify this.

428 See Jodie Moffat, 'Arranging Deckchairs on the Titanic: Climate Change, Greenhouse Gas Emissions and International Shipping' (2010) 24 Austl & NZ Mar LJ 104, 124; for a table that shows that almost all flags of convenience are also UNFCCC non-Annex I, ie so-called developing States, with a lot of them being so-called Least Developed Countries or Small Island Developing States. In an interesting twist, flags of convenience countries are 'also nations which are likely to be disproportionately affected by climate change, and which have been active in lobbying UNFCCC for more stringent measures to be taken to address climate change', there at 109.

> or developed country. It is simply a ship navigating across national boundaries and on the high seas.[429]

In other words, the free combination of registry/flag and location/nationality of the shipowner renders CBDR in the sense of a selective application of GHG reduction obligations, a concept not fitting the dynamics of international shipping. Rather, the international character of shipping warrants equal treatment as expressed in the NMFT principle according to which a Party shall apply MARPOL obligations regardless of whether the flag State of a particular ship is actually party to the treaty.[430] Therefore, applying the CBDR principle to GHG reduction measures agreed to at the IMO, where States would be obliged to reduce their GHG and some would not, does not appear sensible. Applying the CBDR in this manner, would also mean that a large share of ships would not be addressed:

> [...] about three quarters of the world tonnage, by dead weight, of all merchant vessels engaged in international trade is registered in developing countries [...] hence making it a large portion of the world fleet; it would be ineffective for any regulatory regime to act only on the remaining portion, namely one quarter of the world fleet.[431]

Consequently,

> IMO shipping regulations are, as a matter of principle, and must be, as a practical matter, global in nature and applicable to all commercial ships, with appropriate differences, if any, to be based on factors such as their type, structure, manning and operational features, irrespective of the flag they are flying or the degree of industrial development of the flag State or the State of nationality of the owner or the operator.[432]

These premises, however, are not universally accepted. Some IMO Members continuously and strongly oppose regulatory measures that are envis-

---

429 MEPC, 'Legal aspects of the Organization's Work on Greenhouse Gas Emissions in the Context of the Kyoto Protocol' (n 427) para 4.7.

430 See Art 5 (4) MARPOL: 'With respect to the ships of non-Parties to the Convention, Parties shall apply the requirements of the present Convention as may be necessary to ensure that no more favourable treatment is given to such ships.'

431 Buhaug and others (n 3) para 2.45.

432 MEPC, 'Legal aspects of the Organization's Work on Greenhouse Gas Emissions in the Context of the Kyoto Protocol' (n 427) para 4.8.

aged to address all ships indiscriminately.[433] Citing UNFCCC as the primary political platform for negotiations in GHG reductions, opposition has gone as far as denying the IMO the political, legal and economic competence to regulate the reduction of GHG emissions from ships, reducing the IMO's role to the technical aspects of it.[434] Hence, the impasse at the MEPC when it comes to agreeing on an MBM or reduction target. One reason for this is that Parties invoking the CBDR principle in IMO negotiations, mainly aim at establishing different regulatory obligations for so-called developed and developing States. This would, indeed, be irreconcilable with the NMFT principle. However, a broader and more flexible approach to the CBDR principle, which takes into account so-called developing States' weaker economic situation through other ways of differentiated treatment, is possible. As described in Art 3 (1) UNFCCC, there are *common responsibilities* and *differentiated responsibilities*. So-called developing countries can be awarded differential treatment without compromising their overall responsibility of protecting the environment.[435] Such an understanding and application of the CBDR principle in a broader sense could reconcile the notion of *differentiated responsibilities* with the equal treatment in line with the NMFT principle.[436] Suggestions for establishing differentiated responsi-

433 Eg IMO, MEPC, 'Report of the Marine Environment Protection Committee on its Fifty-Seventh Session' (7 April 2008) MEPC 57/21, paras. 4.74, 4,78 (Statement by the delegation of China) and 4.79 (Statement by the delegation of India); IMO, MEPC 'Report of the Marine Environment Protection Committee on its Fifty-Eighth Session' (16 October 2008) MEPC 58/23, para 4.27 and the statements of the delegations of China, Brazil, Saudi Arabia, India, Argentina and others in Annex 9; IMO, MEPC, 'Report of the Marine Environment Protection Committee on its Sixty-First Session' (n 359) para 5.3, and the statements by a similar group of States in Annex 3. It is noteworthy, that at one point early in the process, the MEPC had indeed agreed 'that the draft Assembly resolution on IMO Policies and Practices related to reduction of greenhouse gas emission from ships should be based on a common policy applicable to all ships, rather than based on the provisions of Kyoto Protocol which states that the reduction of greenhouse gas emissions is under the responsibility of the Annex I countries of the Protocol.', IMO, MEPC, 'Report of the Marine Environment Protection Committee on its Forty-Ninth Session' (8 August 2003) MEPC 49/22, para 4.9.

434 Statement by the Delegation of China on GHG issues, MEPC, 'Report of the Marine Environment Protection Committee on its Fifty-Ninth Session' (n 354) Annex 13, 2.

435 Karim and Alam (n 427) 136.

436 The notion that both principles need to be reconciled is also supported by the UNFCCC Secretariat itself: 'We have to commit ourselves to work on a solution which respects both principles, and allows each treaty regime to retain the integrity of its principles and practices', Intervention by the UNFCCC Secretariat, MEPC,

bilities without touching upon the universal responsibility to protect the environment have included:

- preferential treatment of goods that are transported from least developed countries;[437]
- differential treatment based on the destination of goods;[438]
- exemptions for routes to and from least developed countries and differentiated allocation of revenue;[439]
- the (re)distribution of revenues generated from an MBM;[440]
- a rebate mechanism for developing countries to compensate their costs of an MBM;[441]
- in the scenario of a global charge on fuels, developing countries keeping their tax revenues and possible additional compensation for the economic burdens of these charges.[442]

'Report of the Marine Environment Protection Committee on its Sixty-First Session' (n 359) Annex 6, 2.

437 Karim and Alam (n 427) 146.

438 Statement by World Wide Fund Nature (WWF), MEPC 'Report of the Marine Environment Protection Committee on its Fifty-Eighth Session' (n 433) Annex 9, 26.

439 European Federation for Transport and Environment, 'Bunker Fuels and the Kyoto Protocol: How ICAO and the IMO Failed the Climate Change Test' (2009) <https://www.transportenvironment.org/wp-content/uploads/2021/05/2009_06_aviation_shipping_icao_imo_history.pdf> accessed 19 May 2023.

440 Annela Anger and others, 'International Shipping and Market Based Instruments 2009: Final Report' (2009) MEPC 60/INF.21 (15 January 2010), Annex, paras 1.6, 1.33, 5.27; Honkonen (n 426) 257–258, who identifies the redistribution of resources through financial assistance or transfer of technology as one of two main forms of CBDR. It is noteworthy that in 2009 '[t]he Committee noted that there was a general preference for the greater part of any funds generated by a market-based measure under the auspices of IMO, to be used for climate change purposes in developing countries through existing or new funding mechanisms under the UNFCCC or other international organizations', MEPC, 'Report of the Marine Environment Protection Committee on its Fifty-Ninth Session' (n 353) para 4.129. See also suggesting redistribution of funds with regard to an ETS or a climate levy, Kachi, Mooldijk and Warnecke (n 322) 25, 27.

441 IMO, MEPC, 'A rebate mechanism for a market-based instrument for international shipping: Submitted by International Union for Conservation of Nature (IUCN)' (29 January 2010) MEPC 60/4/55, para 17; see also IMO, MEPC, 'Ensuring no net incidence on developing countries from a global maritime Market-Based Mechanism: Submitted by World Wide Fund for Nature (WWF)' (22 December 2011) MEPC 63/5/6, that further elaborates on background and applicability of a rebate mechanism to different types of MBMs.

442 Michael Keen, Ian Parry and Jon Strand, 'Market-Based Instruments for International Aviation and Shipping as a Source of Climate Finance' (World Bank 2012)

Unfortunately, none of the suggestions for embracing the CBDR principle in the IMO context have so far prevailed or helped overcome the debate. In fact, even the 2015 Paris Agreement, the successor treaty to the Kyoto Protocol, which does not refer to shipping anymore and has done away with the distinction between Annex I and non-Annex I countries, has not ended the debate. It would have been expected that the two elements that make up the very basis of the controversy missing in the Paris Agreement would render the discussion a matter of the past.[443] However, the discussion seems to live on, even with its basis being revoked. It remains to be seen whether and, if so, how, the measures based on the Initial GHG Strategy will solve this impasse; as the GHG Strategy requires that any measure take into account both principles, CBDR and NMFT.

IV. The EU's intervention—The MRV-Regulation

While the IMO was struggling to find a way to further address international shipping's carbon dioxide emissions and long before the adoption of its Initial GHG Strategy or the introduction of the EEXI, the EU decided to spearhead the movement towards an MBM. In 2015, it put into place the MRV-Regulation, its own system to collect data on international shipping's carbon dioxide. As early as 2009, the Council and the European Parliament had committed the Commission to take action should the IMO fail to agree on a reduction target:

> In the event that no international agreement which includes international maritime emissions in its reduction targets through the International Maritime Organisation has been approved by the Member States or no such agreement through the UNFCCC has been approved by the Community by 31 December 2011, the Commission should make a proposal to include international maritime emissions in the Community reduction commitment with the aim of the proposed act entering into force by 2013.[444]

<http://documents1.worldbank.org/curated/en/678661468155734989/pdf/WPS5950.pdf> accessed 19 May 2023, 1 (Abstract), para 118.

443 Similarly Romera (n 345) 224.

444 Decision No. 406/2009/EC of the European Parliament and of the Council of 23 April 2009 on the effort of Member States to reduce their greenhouse gas emissions to meet the Community's greenhouse gas emissions reduction commitments up to 2020 [2009] OJ L140/136, Recital 2; repeated in a slightly amended

In 2011, the Commission declared the need for the EU to reduce its carbon dioxide emissions from maritime transport by 40% or, if possible, 50% by 2050 compared to 2005.[445] Following a public consultation that tested the ideas of a compensation fund, a maritime ETS, a fuel or carbon tax and a mandatory emission reduction target for individual ships,[446] the Commission presented its three-step strategy in 2013. The three steps to include maritime GHG emissions in the EU's policy include a Monitoring, Reporting and Verification scheme, the definition of reduction targets for the maritime transport sector and, ultimately, the application of an MBM.

1. Paving the Way for a Market-Based Measure

The first step of this approach materialised when the MRV-Regulation was adopted in April 2015—amended by Delegated Regulation (EU) 2016/2071[447] and complemented by Delegated Regulation (EU) 2016/2072[448] and Implementing Regulations 2016/1927[449] and 2016/1928.[450]

way in Directive 2009/29/EC of the European Parliament and of the Council of 23 April 2009 amending Directive 2003/87/EC so as to improve and extend the greenhouse gas emissions allowance trading scheme of the Community [2009] OJ L140/63, Recital 3.

445 Commission, 'White Paper: Roadmap to a Single European Transport Area – Towards a competitive and resource efficient transport system', COM (2011) 144 final, para 29.

446 To view the contributions received, see the public consultation on 'Including maritime transport emissions in the EU's greenhouse gas reduction commitment' <https://climate.ec.europa.eu/news-your-voice/consultations/including-maritime-transport-emissions-eus-greenhouse-gas-reduction-commitment_en> accessed 3 April 2023.

447 Commission Delegated Regulation (EU) 2016/2071 of 22 September 2016 amending Regulation (EU) 2015/757 of the European Parliament and of the Council as regards the methods for monitoring carbon dioxide emissions and the rules for monitoring other relevant information [2016] OJ L320/1.

448 Commission Delegated Regulation (EU) 2016/2072 of 22 September 2016 on the verification activities and accreditation of verifiers pursuant to Regulation (EU) 2015/757 of the European Parliament and of the Council on the monitoring, reporting and verification of carbon dioxide emissions from maritime transport [2016] OJ L320/5.

449 Commission Implementing Regulation (EU) 2016/1927 of 4 November 2016 on templates for monitoring plans, emissions reports and documents of compliance pursuant Regulation (EU) 2015/757 of the European Parliament and of the Council on monitoring, reporting and verification of carbon dioxide emissions from maritime transport [2016] OJ L299/1.

In a nutshell, the MRV-Regulation requires shipowners or responsible operators (hereafter referred to as *company* in line with the terminology of the MRV-Regulation) to annually report to the Commission the CO_2 emissions of their ships on a per-voyage and annual basis, along with supplementing information. Its Art 2 (1) initially stipulated that the MRV-Regulation

> applies to ships above 5 000 gross tonnage in respect of CO_2 emissions released during their voyages from their last port of call to a port of call under the jurisdiction of a Member State and from a port of call under the jurisdiction of a Member State to their next port of call, as well as within ports of call under the jurisdiction of a Member State.

The parameters to be monitored and reported include information on CO_2 emitted, distance travelled, transport work and cargo carried (Arts 9, 10). The data is to be monitored according to a pre-verified monitoring plan that determines which monitoring methods are applied (Arts 6, 13). This is particularly relevant for determining the annual CO_2 emitted. The MRV-Regulation allows for four methods of CO_2 monitoring, all of which are calculation methods, three of them based on fuel consumption and the fourth based on actual measured CO_2 emission flows in exhaust gas stacks.[451] The required information is to be submitted to the Commission by 30 April each year for the previous calendar year as an emissions report approved by an independent verifier (Art 11). Upon submitting a satisfying emissions report to the verifier, the verifier then issues a document of compliance that is to be carried on board (Arts 17, 18).[452] The Commission is then required to make public the information on emissions reported by individual ships as well as publish an annual report (Art 21 (1), (2) and (4)).

450 Commission Implementing Regulation (EU) 2016/1928 of 4 November 2016 on determination of cargo carried for categories of ships other than passenger, ro-ro and container ships pursuant Regulation (EU) 2015/757 of the European Parliament and of the Council on monitoring, reporting and verification of carbon dioxide emissions from maritime transport [2016] OJ L299/22.

451 For a brief explanation of the four monitoring methods, see Dagmar Nelissen and Jasper Faber, Economic impacts of MRV of fuel and emissions in maritime transport' (CE Delft 2014) <https://cedelft.eu/wp-content/uploads/sites/2/2021/04/CE_Delft_7B83_Economic_impacts_of_MRV_FINAL_1389349788.pdf> accessed 19 May 2023, 8–9.

452 For a simplified diagram of the processes, see Commission, 'Proposal for a regulation of the European Parliament and of the Council on the monitoring, reporting and verification of carbon dioxide emissions from maritime transport and amending Regulation (EU) No 525/2013' COM (2013) 480 final, 7.

Recital 8 MRV-Regulation gives the reason for the EU's unilateral approach. It specifically refers to the IMO's EEDI and SEEMP

> which will bring improvement in terms of reducing the expected increase in greenhouse gas emissions, but alone cannot lead to the necessary absolute reductions of greenhouse gas emissions from international shipping to keep efforts in line with the global objective of limiting increase in global temperatures to 2°C.

Nonetheless, throughout the evolution of the MRV-Regulation, the Commission never grew tired of emphasising in one way or the other its preference for a global solution and commitment to international cooperation while continually establishing the role of the MRV as a catalyst for the international process.[453] It seems that it preferred a global solution so much so that it hoped that the MRV-Regulation would make an impression on the IMO and prompt the international community to intervene. This could be an explanation as to why the MRV-Regulation entered into force on

453 See eg Commission, 'Roadmap to a Single European Transport Area' (n 445) para 29: 'The EU should strive – in cooperation with IMO and other international organisations – for the universal application and enforcement of high standards of [...] environmental protection [...]'; Commission, 'Integrating maritime transport emissions in the EU's greenhouse gas reduction policies' (n 12) 4: 'The EU has a strong preference for a global approach led by the IMO, as the most appropriate international forum to regulate emissions from shipping. [...] the EU will continue to engage in the international developments to reduce GHG emissions from ships'; there also at 5: 'The EU's approach is designed to actively contribute to an agreement on global measures to reduce GHG emissions from ships in the IMO [...] The implementation of a global MRV system should be a priority in IMO negotiations'; there also at 6: 'The current Commission proposal is for a fuel consumption based MRV scheme to be started at regional level, with the aim of serving as an example for a global scheme [...]. The proposed EU's MRV system feeds into the discussions at the IMO, with the aim of speeding up the IMO process.' Commission, 'Proposal for a regulation of the European Parliament and of the Council on the monitoring, reporting and verification of carbon dioxide emissions from maritime transport' (n 452) 3: 'Given the Commission's clear preference for measures taken at global level, the EU MRV should serve as example for the implementation of a global MRV with the aim to speed up the international discussions'; see also Recital 34 of the MRV-Regulation itself: 'The Union MRV system should serve as a model for the implementation of a global MRV system. A global MRV system is preferable as it could be regarded as more effective due to its broader scope.' See also, the Commissioner for Transport Violeta Bulc at the Transport, Telecommunications and Energy Council on 8 June 2017 elaborating on a possible IMO emission reduction objective and the upcoming MEPC session declaring that 'shipping is a global business that needs global solutions' <https://video.consilium.europa.eu/event/en/22678?start_time=0> starting at 09:20:44, accessed 26 May 2023.

1 July 2015 (Art 26), but the first year for data monitoring and reporting was not going to be until 2018, with the monitoring plan to be verified by 31 August 2017 (Arts 6, 8). Also, to keep a backdoor open, Art 22 (3) MRV-Regulation allows for its adjustment to an international instrument:

> In the event that an international agreement on a global monitoring, reporting and verification system for greenhouse gas emissions or on global measures to reduce greenhouse gas emissions from maritime transport is reached, the Commission shall review this Regulation and shall, if appropriate, propose amendments to this Regulation in order to ensure alignment with that international agreement.

The Commission first made use of the option to revise the MRV-Regulation when it passed Delegated Regulation (EU) 2016/2071 of 22 September 2016, just shortly before the IMO DCS was adopted by MEPC in October 2016. This might have been an attempt to send a signal of good will and that it was possible to reconcile these two systems in order to accommodate concerns that could have jeopardised the adoption of the DCS. The first revision, however, merely addressed modalities of reporting, eg stipulating the default emissions factors for standard fuels—a parameter used to translate fuel use into CO_2 emitted—to be the same that the IMO uses in the EEDI context. From the outset, a full adjustment of the MRV-Regulation to the IMO's DCS seemed unlikely, not least because the IMO's DCS does not seem to fulfil the same standards as the MRV-Regulation:

> Notwithstanding key common principles such as the 5,000 GT threshold, the document of compliance, the required monitoring method, or the annual report, the IMO's DCS and the EU's MRV are diametrically opposed in their respective design, scope of application, policy objectives and stepwise approach. The EU MRV is a relatively exhaustive carbon inventory process, while the IMO DCS is a simplified data collection and reporting procedure on fuel consumption. [...] If the purpose of the EU MRV is to accurately measure annual CO_2 emissions and fuel consumption and to monitor and report different parameters in order to implement reduction targets and market-based measures in the medium-run, the provisions proposed by the IMO mainly aim to analyse energy efficiency without a clear agenda for a market-based measure.[454]

454 Laurent Fedi, 'The Monitoring, Reporting and Verification of Ships' Carbon Dioxide Emissions: A European Substantial Policy Measure towards Accurate and Transparent Carbon Dioxide Quantification' (2017) 31 Ocean YB 381, 399.

Accordingly, the proposal for amendments of the MRV-Regulation tabled by the Commission in 2019 did not contain any substantive alignments of the MRV-Regulation with the DCS.[455] It effectively proposed to align definitions, as well as monitoring and reporting modalities, to ease administrative burden. The proposal explicitly retained its most contentious features discussed in the next sections, namely, its scope of governance (inter alia addressing non-EU ships and parts of their voyages outside of EU territory), its verification scheme and its transparency (ie publication) of data. These were considered critical to the objectives of the MRV-Regulation.[456] With this, it seemed clear that the promise of a full alignment Art 22 (3) MRV-Regulation carried would most likely not materialise.[457] In

455 See Commission, 'Proposal for a Regulation of the European Parliament and of the Council amending Regulation (EU) 2015/757 in order to take appropriate account of the global data collection system for ship fuel oil consumption data' COM (2019) 38 final. The proposal was presented as part of the EU's *Fit for 55* legislative package to meet its GHG reduction targets. In this, it was accompanied by two legislative proposals to address ship fuel and ship energy: the first is now Regulation (EU) 2023/1805 of the European Parliament and of the Council of 13 September 2023 on the use of renewable and low-carbon fuels in maritime transport, and amending Directive 2009/16/EC [2023] OJ L234/48; the second is 'Proposal for a Council Directive restructuring the Union framework for the taxation of energy products and electricity (recast)' COM (2021) 563, which is currently undergoing the legislative process.

456 Commission, 'Proposal for a Regulation amending Regulation (EU) 2015/757 in order to take appropriate account of the global data collection system for ship fuel oil consumption data' (n 455) 5, 6; see also Recital 10, there at 11: 'The impact assessment indicated that a partial alignment of the two monitoring, reporting and verification systems could contribute to reduc[ing] the administrative burden for shipping companies, while preserving the key objectives of the EU MRV Regulation. Such a partial alignment should however not modify the governance, scope, verification, transparency or CO_2 reporting requirements of the EU MRV Regulation as it would severely undermine its objectives and affect its capacity to inform future policy-making decisions and to incentivise the uptake of energy efficiency measures and behaviours in shipping. Any amendments to the EU MRV Regulation should therefore limit the alignment with the global IMO DCS in relation to definitions, monitoring parameters, monitoring plans and templates.'

457 This was criticised by the European Economic and Social Committee, see EESC, 'Opinion of the European Economic and Social Committee on "Proposal for a Regulation of the European Parliament and of the Council amending Regulation (EU) 2015/757 in order to take appropriate account of the global data collection system for ship fuel oil consumption data"' [2019] C240/41, paras 1.5, 2.2, 2.5. The EP Committee on the Environment, Public Health and Food Safety in its Amendment 16 also suggested for Recital 7 of the Commission's proposal to clarify that '[i]t is important that, irrespective of any global measures, the Union remains able to be

its first reading, the EP adopted substantial amendments to the proposal. Pointing inter alia to the 'slow and insufficient progress made by IMO' (Amendment 5), it proposed obliging the Commission to adopt a delegated act to extend the scope of the MRV-Regulation to methane emissions (Amendment 41), a labelling system for the environmental performance of ships (Amendment 54) and subjecting maritime transport to an ETS (Amendment 60).[458]

With the discussions to extend the scope of the EU ETS to include shipping gaining momentum, the Commission in 2021 tabled a new combined proposal to establish an ETS for maritime transport and amend the MRV-Regulation[459]—it meant to complement the previously proposed amendments to the MRV-Regulation[460] even though the elements of the first proposal did not materialise. The additional amendments to the MRV-Regulation mainly addressed verification and reporting of data at company level and the role of the national authority accounting for the operation of the ETS for maritime transport (hereafter Shipping ETS).[461] Amendments to the MRV-Regulation were finally adopted in May 2023 as Regulation (EU) 2023/957[462], and brought two important changes apart from changes

---

ambitious and demonstrates climate leadership by maintaining or adopting more stringent measures within the Union', EP, 'Report on the proposal for a regulation of the European Parliament and of the Council amending Regulation (EU) 2015/757 in order to take appropriate account of the global data collection system for ship fuel oil consumption data'(n 455) 17.

458 EP, Committee on the Environment, Public Health and Food Safety, 'Report on the proposal for a regulation of the European Parliament and of the Council amending Regulation (EU) 2015/757 in order to take appropriate account of the global data collection system for ship fuel oil consumption data' (29 July 2020) A9-0144/2020, 9, 31–32, 38 and 42–47. The EP also acknowledged its own role as a catalyst: 'The IMO has promised for more than 20 years that it will tackle shipping emissions and has only introduced its Data Collection System after the EU has implemented the MRV Regulation', there at 48.

459 Commission, 'Proposal for a Directive of the European Parliament and of the Council amending Directive 2003/87/EC establishing a system for greenhouse gas emission allowance trading within the Union, Decision (EU) 2015/1814 concerning the establishment and operation of a market stability reserve for the Union greenhouse gas emission trading scheme and Regulation (EU) 2015/757' COM (2021) 551 final.

460 ibid 2.

461 Directive (EU) 2023/959 that was adopted alongside the amendments to the MRV-Regulation and established the EU's Shipping ETS will be further discussed below (C.IV.4.).

462 Regulation (EU) 2023/957 of the European Parliament and of the Council of 10 May 2023 amending Regulation (EU) 2015/757 in order to provide for the

in the reporting and verification modalities. The MRV-Regulation will apply to ships between 400 and 5000 GT and off-shore ships above 5000 GT as of 1 January 2025 (Art 2 (1a) and (1b)). Furthermore, as of 2024 the MRV-Regulation will additionally apply to ships' methane and nitrous oxide emissions (Art 2 (1c)), with the Commission tasked with adopting delegated acts by 1 October 2023 accordingly (Art 6 (8) subpara 2 and Art 11 (4)). Both these regulatory measures will become relevant to the Shipping ETS at a later time.[463] At time of writing in 2023, however, these measures do not provide necessary information for the implementation of the Shipping ETS.

With that, some problems remain, not only with regard to the compatibility of the MRV-Regulation and the IMO DCS, but also with regard to the MRV-Regulation disrupting the shipping industry, as is often claimed by industry representatives. The truly simplest of all inconsistencies is the logical problem that the company may not always know months or even a year beforehand whether its ship(s) is/are going to have a voyage to or from an EU port in the next year. Sometimes, a ship that has departed on a voyage may not even know that it will be calling at an EU port until it is already well under way. Therefore, in the most unfortunate cases, monitoring plans will have to be developed in vain and emissions will have to be monitored that will never be reported. This is somewhat alleviated by Art 6 (2) MRV-Regulation that allows ships to whom the provisions apply for the first time after 31 August 2017 to submit their monitoring plan after its first call to a port of a MS. Either way, the MRV-Regulation is still posing larger challenges. The following sections, therefore, explore how the publication of collected data (2.) and the system of data verification in the MRV-Regulation (3.) disrupt the shipping industry. Also, with regard to the compatibility with international law, the jurisdictional basis of the MRV-Regulation is discussed (4.) and compatibility of the obligations imposed through the MRV-Regulation with WTO law are briefly touched upon (5.).

---

inclusion of maritime transport activities in the EU Emission Trading System and for the monitoring, reporting and verification of emissions of additional greenhouse gases and emissions from additional ship types [2023] OJ L130/105.

463 See section C.IV.4. below.

2. Public Access to Individual Ships' Data—'Name-and-Shame'

One major point of contention with regard to the MRV-Regulation is the public access to non-aggregated data pursuant to its Art 21 (1)[464]. Making what amounts to commercially sensitive data publicly available has a clear intention that the MRV-Regulation lays out in its Recitals 10 and 11:

> Public access to the emissions data will contribute to removing market barriers that prevent the uptake of many cost-negative measures which would reduce greenhouse gas emissions from maritime transport. [...] The adoption of measures to reduce greenhouse gas emissions and fuel consumption is hampered by the existence of market barriers such as a lack of reliable information on the fuel efficiency of ships or of technologies available for retrofitting ships, a lack of access to finance for investments in ship efficiency, and split incentives, as shipowners would not benefit from their investments in ship efficiency when fuel bills are paid by operators.

The Commission's proposal for a second review reiterates this notion that the 'publication of individual ships' data [...] help[s] remove market barriers'[465]. As a reminder, the so-called split incentive addressed in the Recital refers to the dilemma that a shipowner investing in more fuel-efficient technology will not reap the benefits of that investment; it is the ship operator that charters the ship that will ultimately save fuel costs. The shipowner, therefore, has no inherent reason to care for its fleet to be more fuel-efficient.[466] If the fuel-efficiency of individual ships becomes public knowledge, however, ship operators can make an informed decision as to whether or not they prefer to charter more fuel-efficient ships to save in operation costs. With that, the argument goes, the barrier of split incentive would be removed. Moreover, there also seems to be an assumption that this would indirectly create better financial opportunities for shipowners

464 The data is published at EMSA, THETIS-MRV <https://mrv.emsa.europa.eu/#public/emission-report> accessed 26 May 2023.

465 Commission, 'Proposal for a Regulation amending Regulation (EU) 2015/757 in order to take appropriate account of the global data collection system for ship fuel oil consumption data' (n 455) 8.

466 For a technical analysis of the split incentive, esp with regard to the different types of charter contracts and including a table on the *Cost allocation between shipowner and charterer in the different types of contracts*, see Nishatabbas Rehmatulla and Tristan Smith, 'The Impact of Split Incentives on Energy Efficiency Technology Investments in Maritime Transport' (2020) 147 Energy Policy 111721, 2.

willing to invest in the fuel-efficiency of their fleet, as well as increasing shipowners' understanding of available technologies to invest in.[467] Industry representatives, on the other hand, have voiced strong concerns as to what was often perceived to be nothing more than a 'name-and-shame' system, meant to disincentivise charterers from resorting to ships displayed as inefficient due to the oversimplification of complex technical processes.[468] In fact, even before its adoption, it was predicted that the MRV-Regulation

> will neither reduce the split incentive between ship owners and charterers, nor provide ship owners with sufficient additional insight into their fuel consumption pattern to take any further action. This is the case because the proposed regulation does not require the accurate measurement of fuel consumption or the reporting of indicators that are specific

---

467 Recitals 10 and 11 of the MRV-Regulation appear rather toned down compared to the initial reasoning in Commission, 'Integrating maritime transport emissions in the EU's greenhouse gas reduction policies' (n 12) 5, 7: 'Lack of awareness about costs, benefits and return on investment regarding already available technologies seem to hinder the introduction of such technologies on a larger scale. This kind of information could provide useful insights into the performance of individual ships, their associated operational costs and potential resale value for the benefit of ship-owners, who would be better equipped to take decisions on major investments and to obtain the corresponding finance. [...] An MRV could also increase the pressure for the removal of other market barriers, such as split incentive between ship owners and operators, by providing clarity on energy efficiency, emissions sources and abatement potential. [...] An MBM can effectively remove the market barriers, especially the split of incentives, e.g. by implementing the polluter-pays principle. A[n] MBM has the potential to overcom[e] market barriers relating to the access to finance provided that potential revenues generated are channelled to ensure the support of private finance to the sector.' One should consider that members of the shipping industry may not like to be told by outsiders that they are unaware of ships' existing or available technology, the dynamics of their market or potentials to operate ships more efficiently, when fuel costs make up a major part of their operating costs. In other words, they may not like to be told by outsiders that they do not know their business.

468 See eg European Community Shipowners' Association, 'Proposal for a Regulation of the European Parliament and of the Council on the monitoring, reporting and verification of carbon dioxide emission from maritime transport and amending Regulation (EU) No 525/2013: ECSA Position Paper (11 October 2013)' <https://www.ecsa.eu/sites/default/files/publications/EU%20MRV%20Regulation%20proposal_ECSA%20Position%20paper_Final_11.10.2013.pdf> accessed 26 May 2023, 2; International Chamber of Shipping, 'Brief for EU Member States and Members of the European Parliament: Preliminary ICS Comments on Draft EU Regulation on MRV' (10 October 2013) <https://www.ics-shipping.org/wp-content/uploads/2020/11/ICS-Preliminary-Comments-on-EU-MRV-Proposal-No-525-2013.pdf> accessed 26 May 2023, 8.

enough for charterers to use in their evaluation of ships. What would e.g. constitute more useful information for charterers are ship specific speed-fuel consumption curves set up for different conditions and updated on regular basis.[469]

3. Verification of Data through Independent Verifiers

Another aspect of the MRV-Regulation that has disrupted the dynamics of the shipping industry is the requirement that monitoring plans and emissions reports for submission to the Commission have to be reviewed by a verifier (Art 13 (1) and (2)), who is also responsible for issuing a document of compliance which has to be kept on board and must be part of a PSC inspection by a MS (Arts 17, 18 and 19 (2)). The verifier needs to be accredited for these activities by a national accreditation body in line with Regulation (EC) No 765/2008 (Art 16 (2)). Details on the accreditation of verifiers and the work of the verifiers are laid down in Delegated Regulation (EU) 2016/2072.

The requirement to hire such an independent verifier, however, is completely foreign to the system of international shipping.[470] For this kind of task, the shipping industry, the IMO and flag States usually rely on classification societies. It is the traditional task of classifying ships that lends its name to these independent organisations:

> The purpose of a Classification Society is to provide classification and statutory services and assistance to the maritime industry and regulatory bodies as regards maritime safety and pollution prevention, based on the accumulation of maritime knowledge and technology. The objective of ship classification is to verify the structural strength and integrity of essential parts of the ship's hull and its appendages, and the reliability and function of the propulsion and steering systems, power generation and those other features and auxiliary systems which have been built

469 Nelissen and Faber, 'Economic Impacts of MRV of fuel and emissions in maritime transport' (n 451) 36.

470 Hence, the International Chamber of Shipping's objections that 'the verification and certification method that has been developed by the EU will be overly complex. It seems that EU climate officials wish to ignore the tried and tested processes for statutory certification used in international shipping, and instead propose an additional administrative burden for ship operators', ICS, 'Reducing CO_2 Emissions to Zero' (n 377) 14.

> into the ship in order to maintain essential services on board. Classification Societies aim to achieve this objective through the development and application of their own Rules and by verifying compliance with international and/or national statutory regulations on behalf of flag Administrations.[471]

Classification societies, therefore, often act as the extended arm of the Flag State Administration. Flag State Administrations choose to authorise classification societies because of their concentrated technical expertise, their workforce and their global representation. Flag State Administrations, however, can only delegate their responsibilities, such as carrying out inspections and surveys, or issuing documents, if the respective treaty permits them to. Customarily, treaties concluded under the auspices of the IMO allow for this possibility. In the case of the DCS, as seen above, the Flag State Administration is allowed to delegate its tasks of receiving the data, verifying the data and issuing the Statement of Compliance to 'any organization duly authorized by it' (Reg 6.6.4 and 27.3–.5 Annex VI MARPOL). As mentioned above, in reality, these organisations are classification societies that are approved by flag States in accordance with the IMO's RO-Code and are then entrusted with those tasks. In fact, it is hard to imagine that any other existing entity would be able to fulfil the entire catalogue of requirements specified by the RO-Code. Hence, classification societies are an indispensable service provider for the maritime industry and Flag State Administrations, acting as a one-stop shop.

The EU-MRV disrupts this established system by introducing an additional actor, namely the independent verifier that is accredited by the respective national accreditation body in accordance with the requirements of the EU-MRV, Commission Delegated Regulation (EU) 2016/2072 and Regulation (EC) No 765/2008[472]. The ensuing constellation seems to weak-

---

471 International Association of Classification Societies, 'Classification societies – their key role' <https://iacs.org.uk/media/8875/classification-societies-key-role.pdf> accessed 26 May 2023, 3. It is noteworthy that eg the classification society DNV GL, a merger of Germanischer Lloyd and Det Norske Veritas, both of which were created to support the maritime industry and reach as far back as the 19th century, today is involved in other industry sectors such as Food and Beverage or Healthcare as well.

472 Regulation (EC) No 765/2008 of the European Parliament and of the Council of 9 July 2008 setting out the requirements for accreditation and market surveillance relating to the marketing of products and repealing Regulation (EEC) No 339/93 [2008] OJ L218/30.

en the status of the classification companies by creating competition, a development by and all appreciated by smaller verifiers. However, effectively, the monopoly of classification societies is further manifested. This is because classification societies should have no difficulty gaining national accreditation, thereby being able to offer flag States/shipowners both services for fulfilment of the IMO DCS requirements and of those of the EU-MRV, albeit in different roles. They can, therefore, continue to offer a one-stop shop solution. Other companies, however, wishing to offer both service packages need accreditation in accordance with EU rules and, additionally, the recognition of Flag State Administrations in accordance with the RO-Code. The latter, in principle, is possible as the RO-Code provides for the possibility of a partial recognition (see para 2.5 RO-Code[473]). In that, a company can be recognised as a RO for a limited range of services as long as the general requirements regarding eg qualifications or quality management are met. Within the EU, however, recognition of a company as an RO is the prerogative of the Commission only. This is because, the EU Regulation on ship inspection and survey organisations[474] establishes that 'organisations entrusted with the inspection, survey and certification of ships for compliance with the international conventions on safety at sea and prevention of marine pollution' become recognised by the Commission upon request of a MS (Arts 1, 3 (1) and 4 (1)). Even with a generous interpretation that would include the activities of the verifier under the EU-MRV to be part of an 'inspection, survey or certification' activity, this Regulation does not provide for a partial recognition for specific services.

Consequently, the situation as it presents itself at time of writing in 2023 is as follows: Classification societies can easily obtain accreditation for MRV-verification through an EU national accreditation body. On the other hand, independent verifiers, cannot realistically obtain RO-status within the EU even though a partial recognition would, by and all, be possible under the IMO's RO-Code. As a result, an EU Flag State Administration

473 'ROs subject to this Code need not offer all types of statutory certification and services and may have a limited scope of recognition, provided that the requirements of this Code are applied in a manner that is compatible with the limited scope of recognition. Where any requirement of this Code cannot be applied due to the scope of services delivered by an RO, this shall be clearly identified by the flag State and recorded in the RO's quality management system.'

474 Regulation (EC) No 391/2009 of the European Parliament and of the Council of 23 April 2009 on common rules and standards for ship inspection and survey organisations [2009] OJ L131/11.

wishing to delegate tasks for fulfilment of the DCS requirements will always have to resort to a classification society that is recognised by the Commission in line with EU norms, even though other independent verifiers that are already involved in the MRV-system may be able to provide the same services just as well. As a result, the flag State may be inclined to outsource services related to both instruments to one EU-recognised RO for convenience. A shipping company, on the other hand, is free to opt for any accredited verifier (that may be, but is not necessarily, a classification society) to support in fulfilling MRV-Regulation requirements. One could argue that the services outsourced in the context of the IMO DCS are basically services for the flag State, while the services outsourced to verifiers in the context of the MRV-Regulation are basically services for the shipowner. However, if the combined provision of services was not lucrative and desirable for independent verifiers, they would not actively seek dual recognition (ie for the provision of MRV and DCS services) with non-EU flag States.[475] Therefore, where the misalignment could have been a disruption in a positive sense, breaking up established market mechanisms, it ends up being a disruption that creates market inconsistencies.

4. EU Jurisdiction to Adopt the MRV-Regulation

While the questions of publication and verification of data relate to its technical implementation, the MRV-Regulation also prompts an important question of international law. A discussion on the MRV-Regulation that links consequences to the activity of a foreign ship outside of EU territory, necessarily brings up the question of jurisdiction. The question of jurisdiction is discussed with regard to the MRV-Regulation as the stand-alone measure that it initially was and partly still is. Despite it now being embedded in an ETS as far as CO_2 emissions are concerned,[476] the MRV-Regulation will be a stand-alone instrument for methane and nitrous oxide

475 See eg Verifavia Shipping, 'Verifavia inks as IMO DCS verifier for Liberian vessels' <https://www.verifavia-shipping.com/shipping-carbon-emissions-verification/press-media-verifavia-inks-as-imo-dcs-verifier-for-liberian-vessels-273.php> accessed 3 April 2023.

476 Directive 2003/87/EC of the European Parliament and of the Council of 13 October 2003 establishing a system for greenhouse gas emission allowance trading within the Union and amending Council Directive 96/61/EC [2003] OJ L275/32, Arts 3gd and 3ge.

emissions coming within its scope as of 2024; that is, until 1 January 2026 when methane and nitrous oxide emissions, too, will come under the scope of the EU's ETS.[477] The same holds true for ships between 400 and 5000 GT and offshore ships larger than 400 GT to which the MRV-Regulation will apply as of 1 January 2025 (Art 2 (1a) and (b)). Here, too, the MRV-Regulation will be a stand-alone instrument, with only the option that ships and offshore ships between 400 and 5000 GT may be placed within the scope of the Shipping ETS upon the Commission presenting a feasibility report to the EP and the Council by latest 31 December 2026.[478] Despite focusing on the MRV-Regulation as a stand-alone instrument, it can be instructive at times to contrast it with the Shipping ETS. Therefore, a brief account of the EU Shipping ETS[479] is given here.

The EU's ETS for maritime transport addresses emissions of intra-EU voyages and voyages to and from third countries. With regard to the latter, ie for voyages that begin at an EU port and end in a port of a third country or begin at the port of a third country and end in an EU port the ETS effectively only applies to 50% of emissions.[480] This is to enable third countries 'to decide on the appropriate action in respect of the other share

477 Directive 2003/87/EC establishing a system for greenhouse gas emission allowance trading within the Union (n 476) Annex I.

478 ibid Art 3gg (5).

479 Maritime transport was brought under the existing EU ETS through Directive (EU) 2023/959 of the European Parliament and of the Council of 10 May 2023 amending Directive 2003/87/EC establishing a system for greenhouse gas emission allowance trading within the Union and Decision (EU) 2015/1814 concerning the establishment and operation of a market stability reserve for the Union greenhouse gas emission trading system [2023] OJ L130/134. Here again, there is strong reference to the inaction of the IMO and the EU's role as a forerunner and catalyst: 'while recently there has been progress in the IMO, this has so far not been sufficient to achieve the objectives of the Paris Agreement [...] it is important that the Member States and the Union within their respective competences work with third countries to step up diplomatic efforts to strengthen global measures and make progress on the development of a global market-based measure at IMO level', Recital 19 of Directive (EU) 2023/959. Directive 2003/87/EC (n 476) was further complemented by Commission Implementing Regulation (EU) 2023/2599 of 22 November 2023 laying down rules for the application of directive 2003/87/EC of the European Parliament and of the Council as regards the administration of shipping companies by administering authorities in respect of a shipping company [2023] OJ L 2023/2599, 23.11.2023.

480 Directive 2003/87/EC establishing a system for greenhouse gas emission allowance trading within the Union (n 476), Art 3ga.

of emissions.'[481] Also, this concession is considered 'a practical way to solve the issue of common but differentiated responsibilities and capabilities'[482] and 'limiting the risk of evasive port calls and the risk of delocalisation of transhipment activities outside the Union.'[483] Apparently to further increase acceptance, it provides for a phase-in period from 2024–2026 for which allowances would have to be surrendered for initially 40% of verified emissions with a gradual increase to 100% for 2026.[484] It also contains a review clause in case the IMO adopts an MBM and in case the IMO does not adopt an MBM by 2028.[485]

With a Shipping ETS in place, it becomes clear that the question on EU jurisdiction discussed in this section has become practically relevant outside of the MRV-Regulation as well. Simply subjecting half of the emissions of a ships' voyage to the ETS can be nothing more than a rough estimate and no accurate calculation to ensure that absolutely no part of a voyage outside of EU territory is subjected to the ETS. Thus, it has to be assumed that parts of ships' voyages that have occurred outside of EU waters are still taken into account. Therefore, the following discussion on available jurisdiction also considers the specifications of this ETS alongside the MRV-Regulation, where it helps to contrast and highlight relevant aspects. A fully exhaustive debate, however, is beyond the scope of this study. It must suffice in this context to create a rough picture of the multi-layered legal problems and the different vantage points.

To put the upcoming discussion into context, it also has to be borne in mind that the discussion surrounding the MRV-Regulation and an ETS for the maritime sector in general differ from the discussions on a financial mechanism in the context of the SRR in one crucial point: the financial mechanisms proposed for the SRR were conceived as including obligations that were triggered upon entry into port and did not prescribe a certain conduct other than, in effect, a payment due upon entry. The MRV-Regulation, however, requires specific conduct of a ship while outside of EU territory (the collection of specific data) prior to the entry into port, including for parts of each journey that take place outside of EU territory.

481 Directive 2023/959 amending Directive 2003/87/EC establishing a system for greenhouse gas emission allowance trading (n 479) Recital 20.

482 ibid Recital 20 para 2.

483 ibid.

484 Directive 2003/87/EC establishing a system for greenhouse gas emission allowance trading within the Union (n 476), Art 3gb.

485 Directive 2003/87/EC establishing a system for greenhouse gas emission allowance trading within the Union (n 476), Art 3gg (1) subparas 1 and 2.

The relevant discussions revolving around the permissibility of extraterritorial prescriptive measures can be summarised in the following two questions: 1. How is *extraterritorial* defined, ie when is a measure extraterritorial in nature?[486] 2. Under what special circumstances may a measure that qualifies as an extraterritorial measure be permissible?[487] It must be kept in mind that discussions around this topic do not always follow the same logic. Thus, the concepts presented here should be considered somewhat fluid, sometimes (seemingly) overlapping and surely subject to controversy.[488] However, before these two questions on the definition and possible permissibility of an extraterritorial measures can be approached, the concept of extraterritoriality needs to be specified in the context of international law in general.

a. Extraterritorial Jurisdiction in International Law

As part of the following discussion, it is important to note the rather contentious finding of the Permanent Court of International Justice (PCIJ) in its *Lotus* case on the question of the permissibility of extraterritorial jurisdiction. In 1927, it held—6:6 (decided by the president's vote)—with three judges[489] expressly dissenting in the very point of the permissibility of extraterritorial jurisdiction:

> Now the first and foremost restriction imposed by international law upon a State is that—failing the existence of a permissive rule to the contrary—it may not exercise its power in any form in the territory of an-

486 The importance of this criteria is addressed by Cedric Ryngaert and Henrik Ringbom, 'Introduction: Port State Jurisdiction: Challenges and Potential' (2016) 31 Int'l J Marine & Coastal L 379, 380: 'whether a jurisdictional assertion is territorial is an important threshold question which in the traditional international law of jurisdiction yields its presumptive lawfulness'.

487 For the *Consequences of the invalid assertion of extraterritorial jurisdiction*, see UNGA, 'Report of the International Law Commission: Fifty-eighth session' (2006) A/61/10, Annex E ('Extraterritorial jurisdiction'), para 28 with further references.

488 In fact, the concept of jurisdiction itself is not clear-cut; see Cedric Ryngaert, *Jurisdiction in International Law*, (2nd edn, OUP 2015) 5, who expresses the insecurities surrounding the term in unequivocal words: 'While international lawyers often employ the term "jurisdiction", and most of them have an inkling of what it means, defining jurisdiction is hardly self-evident. What is certain is that jurisdiction somehow relates to sovereignty'.

489 B Loder, D Nyholm and R Altamira.

> other State. In this sense jurisdiction is certainly territorial; it cannot be exercised by a State outside its territory except by virtue of a permissive rule derived from international custom or from a convention.[490]

While the International Law Commission (ILC) has found that 'the *Lotus* case may be regarded as the starting point for the consideration of the rules of international law governing the extraterritorial exercise of jurisdiction by a State', it inter alia has named the emergence of the 'effects-principle', which is discussed later, as an important development since.[491] It is noteworthy, however, that the Court continued its deliberations as follows:

> It does not, however, follow that international law prohibits a State from exercising jurisdiction in its own territory, in respect of any case which relates to acts which have taken place abroad, and in which it cannot rely on some permissive rule of international law. Such a view would only be tenable if international law contained a general prohibition to States to extend the application of their laws and the jurisdiction of their courts to persons, property and acts outside their territory, and if, as an exception to this general prohibition, it allowed States to do so in certain specific cases. But this is certainly not the case under international law as it stands at present. Far from laying down a general prohibition to the effect that States may not extend the application of their laws and the jurisdiction of their courts to persons, property and acts outside their territory, it leaves them in this respect a wide measure of discretion which is only limited in certain cases by prohibitive rules; as regards other cases, every State remains free to adopt the principles which it regards as best and most suitable.[492]

The Court, thereby, further clarified its position that it does distinguish between a State's exercise of jurisdiction outside of its territory and merely extending the coverage of its law to acts that take place outside of its territory.

> Thus, under *Lotus*, States could set rules for persons, property and acts outside their territory in the absence of a prohibitive rule, provided that

---

490 PCIJ, *The Case of the S.S. "Lotus" (France v Turkey)*, Series A No 10 <https://icj-cij.org/sites/default/files/permanent-court-of-international-justice/serie_A/A_10/30_Lotus_Arret.pdf> accessed 7 June 2023, 18–19.

491 UNGA, 'Report of the International Law Commission: Fifty-eighth session' (n 487) Annex E, paras 9–10.

492 PCIJ, *Lotus Case* (n 490) 19.

> they enforced those rules territorially (in keeping with the ban on extraterritorial enforcement jurisdiction). [...] Territorial sovereignty would relate to enforcement jurisdiction, but not to prescriptive jurisdiction.[493]

The Court's overall reasoning has generated considerable criticism.[494] While strongly debated, the underlying premise is, nevertheless, considered to be the root of the scholarly disagreement on the permissibility of extraterritorial jurisdiction.

> There is no convergence of views in legal literature as to whether port States may impose requirements relating to extraterritorial conduct. The difference of opinion appears to originate in the question as to whether the prescriptive jurisdiction regime of the law of the sea represents an *exhaustive* set of rules, or whether States' prescriptive rights may be assumed to be unconstrained unless specific limitation are identified.[495]

b. What is Extraterritorial and What is Not

Before continuing to evaluate the legal bases of extraterritorial jurisdiction, it is important to take a closer look at the term *extraterritorial*

493 Ryngaert (n 488) 32; see to the same effect Boyle and Redgwell (n 56) 525.

494 See Sophia Kopela, 'Port-State Jurisdiction, Extraterritoriality, and the Protection of the Global Commons' (2016) 47 Ocean Dev Int'l L 89, 91; Hugh Handeyside, 'The Lotus Principle in ICJ Jurisprudence: Was the Ship ever Afloat?' (2007) 29 Mich J Int'l L 71; see Christopher Staker, 'Jurisdiction' in Malcolm D Evans (ed), *International Law* (5th edn, OUP 2018) 294, pointing out that the case has given rise to 'a tiresome and oddly persistent fallacy' and with a particular view on the reversal of the burden of proof if the reasoning of the court was taken at face value; see also Ryngaert (n 488) 34, asserting that '[t]he basic norm is not the *Lotus*-like jurisdictional merry-go-round with States doing whatever they like, but the prohibition of extending a State's jurisdiction beyond its physical borders. Other jurisdictional principles merely function as exceptions to the territoriality principle'. More explicit is Rosalyn Higgins, *Problems and Process: International Law and how we use it* (OUP 1995) 77: 'In the great debate on extraterritorial jurisdiction those who believe it lawful [...] have invoked the *Lotus Case* as authority for the proposition that, unless conduct is *prohibited* by international law, it is permitted. [...] I do feel that one cannot read too much into a mere dictum of the Permanent Court. This is, for me, another example of the futility of deciding law by reference to an unclear dictum of a court made long years ago in the face of utterly different factual circumstances. We have better ways of determining contemporary international law.'

495 Ringbom, *The EU Maritime Safety Policy and International Law* (n 20) 360–61.

first. Attempting to find a reliable definition of extraterritoriality is not straightforward. Rather, one must quickly concede that '"[t]erritoriality" and "extra-territoriality" are [...] just container terms that are semantically unstable. What one protagonist considers territorial, another protagonist with different underlying interests might consider as extra-territorial.'[496] In other words: 'They are claims of authority, or of resistance to authority, that are made by particular actors with particular substantive interests to promote.'[497] Since the terms are mutually contradictory, and both are subject to uncertainty, a definition of extraterritoriality through exclusion in the sense that '[l]ogically, all exercises of jurisdiction that are not based on the territoriality principle are exercises of extraterritorial jurisdiction' cannot be helpful.[498] The ILC has found that

> [t]he assertion of extraterritorial jurisdiction by a State is an attempt to regulate by means of national legislation, adjudication or enforcement the conduct of persons, property or acts beyond its borders which affect the interests of the State in the absence of such regulation under international law. [...] The notion of extraterritorial jurisdiction may be understood as referring to the exercise of sovereign power or authority by a State outside of its territory.[499]

Hence, the terms *extraterritoriality* and *extraterritorial jurisdiction* refer to the competence of a State to make, apply and enforce rules of conduct in respect of persons, property or events beyond its territory.[500] This under-

496 Ryngaert and Ringbom (n 486) 381; see also Menno T Kamminga, 'Extraterritoriality' (last updated September 2020) in Peters and Wolfrum (eds) *MPEPIL* (n 31) <https://opil-1ouplaw-1com-100b98fpw031a.emedien3.sub.uni-hamburg.de/display/10.1093/law:epil/9780199231690/law-9780199231690-e1040?rskey=9A6no9&result=1&prd=OPIL> accessed 12 May 2023, para 2, calling extraterritoriality 'an elusive concept that may include a wide variety of practices'; Natalie L Dobson and Cedric Ryngaert, 'Provocative Climate Protection: EU Extraterritorial Regulation of Maritime Emission' (2017) 66 Int'l & Comp LQ 295 (2017) 295, 306 speak of 'considerable disagreement as to precisely when such a jurisdictional assertion should be characterized as "extraterritorial"'. Ryngaert (n 488) 8, prefers that the use of the term *extraterritorial* be avoided altogether due to its implied bias that has resulted from the term often being used to describe assertions of jurisdiction deemed 'illegitimate or outrageous'.

497 Hannah L Buxbaum, 'Territory, Territoriality, and the Resolution of Jurisdictional Conflict' (2009) 57 Am J Comp L 631, 635.

498 Higgins (n 494) 73.

499 UNGA, 'Report of the International Law Commission: Fifty-eighth session' (n 487) Annex E, paras 2 and 4.

500 Kamminga (n 496) para 1.

standing also neatly fits with the more general idea of *extraterritorial* 'as shorthand for "not exclusively territorial"'.[501]

Among the three possible forms of jurisdiction, namely prescriptive, adjudicative and enforcement jurisdiction, it is the prescriptive type of jurisdiction that is relevant in the context of the MRV-Regulation.[502] This follows-up on the argument in the previous chapter that there exists from the point of view of the port State the authority to determine norms of conduct, as well as the authority to sanction violations of those rules. However, instead of a strict distinction, one could also see a quasi-hierarchical, interdependent relationship between the notion of prescriptive and enforcement jurisdiction since 'the scope of a state's (territorial) enforcement jurisdiction cannot be wider than the scope of its prescriptive jurisdiction. Put differently, a state can only enforce norms which it had the authority to prescribe in the first place.'[503]

The exercise of prescriptive jurisdiction is naturally given where the State regulates conduct that takes place in its territory. Based on this most basic assumption, there seems to be some agreement that a State can also determine so-called CDEM standards of ships—that is, standards on construction, design, equipment or manning of ships—as a port-entry requirement.[504] This has been argued, due to CDEM standards being static, meaning that the breach of regulatory standards of CDEM necessarily also occurs in port, ie 'since standards of a continuous nature "follow" the ship,

501 Ryngaert (n 488) 8.

502 In brief: 'Prescriptive jurisdiction refers to a State's authority to lay down legal norms. Adjudicative jurisdiction refers to a State's authority to decide competing claims. Enforcement jurisdiction refers to a State's authority to ensure compliance with its laws', Kamminga (n 496) para 1.

503 Ryngaert and Ringbom (n 486) 382–83; see also Ringbom, *The EU Maritime Safety Policy and International Law* (n 20) 357; Kathleen Hixson, 'Extraterritorial Jurisdiction Under the Third Restatement of Foreign Relations Law of the United States' (1988) 12 Fordham Int'l L J 127, 130; see also the ILC along the same lines clarifying that '[t]he potential interference resulting from the extraterritorial exercise of prescriptive jurisdiction is less than that resulting from either adjudicative or enforcement jurisdiction', UNGA, 'Report of the International Law Commission: Fifty-eighth session' (n 487) Annex E, para 5.

504 Ryngaert and Ringbom (n 486) 383; Robin Churchill, 'Port State Jurisdiction Relating to the Safety of Shipping and Pollution from Ships—What Degree of Extra-territoriality' (2016) 31 Int'l J Marine & Coastal L 442, 447, 467; Molenaar, 'Port State Jurisdiction: Toward Comprehensive, Mandatory and Global Coverage' (n 80) 230.

[...] violations of those standards are continuous'.[505] Therefore, while the actual and initial relevant conduct does not take place in the port State's territory, the consequences of that conduct persist and are thought to be a (sufficient) basis to assert a violation of CDEM standards in port. With that, the consequences of a conduct extending into the port State's territory effectively compensate for the fact that the relevant conduct—whether intentionally or by chance—did not occur in the territory of the port State. Furthermore, in favour of CDEM standards as port-entry requirements, it has been argued that the NMFT principles contained in IMO Conventions 'assume that port States have the legislative jurisdiction to apply CDEM standards [...] to foreign ships calling at their ports.'[506] To sum it up: 'Given the static nature of such standards, such assertions of territorial jurisdiction will almost [sic] as a matter of course produce extra-territorial *effects*, but this need not detract from their principled legality'.[507]

Consequently, the situation must look different where the norms in question seek to regulate conduct outside of the State's territory.[508] In the

505 Ringbom, *The EU Maritime Safety Policy and International Law* (n 20) 337; Molenaar, 'Port State Jurisdiction: Toward Comprehensive, Mandatory and Global Coverage' (n 80) 230; Kopela (n 494) 95.

506 Churchill (n 504) 450. See also, Ringbom, *The EU Maritime Safety Policy and International Law* (n 20) 243, who points out that 'the mere inclusion of an NMFT clause in a convention can hardly in itself justify the application of the standards of the convention with respect to third parties. The alternative interpretation would render meaningless the pacta tertiis principle as laid down in Article 34 of the Vienna Convention on the Law of Treaties.'

507 Ryngaert and Ringbom (n 486) 383. See also Dobson and Ryngaert (n 496) 314, who argue that 'as vessels will have to comply with construction standards before arrival at port, there remains an "extraterritorial element" to be considered in light of customary law'.

508 See, however, Kopela (n 494) 98, who considers it more relevant that even in the case of an obligation to collect and report information, the actual 'breach, however, arises in the port when the vessel is found to have provided either false or no information.' At the same time, it is ascertained that '[d]espite the extraterritorial element, state practice indicated that there is a jurisdictional link with the port state.' See further Bevan Marten, 'Port State Jurisdiction over Vessel Information: Territoriality, Extra-territoriality and the Future of Shipping Regulation' (2016) 31 Int'l J Marine & Coastal L 470, 488–89, who distinguishes between a rule on how to operate the vessel outside the port State's territory and its request to provide information on the vessel's operation upon port entry. The author thereby disregards the level of detail in the MRV-Regulation on how exactly the information to be presented has to be generated as well as the coercive power of the consequences where a vessel fails to do so. The author, nonetheless, admits an 'extra-territorial element' of the MRV-Regulation.

case of the MRV-Regulation, ships are required to monitor their CO_2-relevant data to be able to present them upon entry into an EU port. Therefore,

> [p]rovisions formally framed as territorial requests for information, may, de facto, operate as extraterritorial conduct requirements. [...] in the context of the present MRV, companies will only be able to prove compliance if they have abided by EU information collection *methods* when abroad. This constitutes a relevant extraterritorial element, triggering the need for the EU to demonstrate a 'substantial and genuine connection' to the regulated subject matter.[509]

The same must then hold true—even more so in fact—for a possible ETS, which is exactly not just a 'purely financial obligation for the ship operator without direct implications for the operation of the ship itself.'[510] Rather,

> [i]t seems [...] that the fact that the extraterritorially collected information in the case of the ETS will be used as basis for calculating financial obligations, is suited to make this a more concrete extraterritorial rule than the MRV regulation. It can thus be concluded that the new EU ETS would in fact regulate conduct extraterritorially [...].[511]

c. The Notion of a Jurisdictional Link

The notion that a measure with an extraterritorial element for its permissibility requires a jurisdictional link has many names. Apart from the 'substantial and genuine connection' just mentioned, this notion has also been

509 Dobson and Ryngaert (n 496) 311.

510 See Henrik Ringbom, 'Global Problem—Regional Solution? International Law Reflections on an EU CO_2 Emissions Trading Scheme for Ships' (2011) 26 Int'l J Marine & Coastal L 613, 638. The financial obligation within an ETS is usually calculated based on the actual carbon dioxide emissions and the MRV-Regulation was designed specifically with a future market-based measure in mind (see its Recital 13). The objective of the ETS is to incentivise a reduction in emission that is given a price tag through the ETS. In the context of shipping and the MRV-Regulation in place, this dynamic must have a direct effect on the operation of a ship.

511 Anne Fougner Helseth, 'Rocking the Boat: The Question of Jurisdiction for Applying the European Emissions Trading System to International Shipping' (2017) 2017 Scandinavian Inst Mar L YB 1, 38, with reference to a previous legislative proposal to include shipping in the EU ETS.

called a 'sufficient nexus'[512], 'territorial link'[513], 'territorial connection'[514] or 'close relation [...] between a state exercising jurisdiction [...] and the actual state of affairs it is to be applied to'[515] or more broadly 'a sufficiently close or substantial connection with the person, fact or event and the state exercising jurisdiction.'[516] While it does appear that the terms represent different levels of intensity in the relationship between the measure and the State in question,[517] the underlying notion is more or less the same: the matter being regulated has to be in some kind of a relationship with the regulating State.[518] It is also noteworthy that there are differing opinions as to whether the jurisdictional link renders legal an otherwise illegal extraterritorial measure, ie rectifies a legal wrong,[519] or whether the jurisdictional link by and all precludes a possible extraterritorial element.[520] The latter view is the position taken by the Advocate General (AG) in the ECJ case *Air Transport Association of America and others (*hereafter *ATA)*[521] that challenged Directive 2008/101/EC[522] which included the aviation sector

512 See Dobson and Ryngaert (n 496) 307.
513 ibid 307; Kopela (n 494) 94.
514 Joanne Scott, 'Extraterritoriality and Territorial Extension in EU Law' (2014) 62 Am J Comp L 87, 90.
515 Krzysztof Zalucki, 'Extraterritorial Jurisdiction in International Law' (2015) 17 Int'l Comm L Rev 403, 410.
516 Molenaar, 'Port State Jurisdiction: Toward Comprehensive, Mandatory and Global Coverage' (n 80) 228.
517 See Dobson and Ryngaert (n 496) 307.
518 Apart from the *effects principle* discussed in more detail below, possible other concepts to resort to in cases of measures with an extraterritorial element are the *active nationality principle*, the rather controversial *passive nationality principle*, the *protective principle*, the *universality principle*, all of which refer to criminal jurisdiction; Kamminga, (n 496) paras 11–14.
519 Dobson and Ryngaert (n 496) 308.
520 Apparently arguing both, see Kopela (n 494) 92 referring to jurisdictional links that 'justify' the exercise of extraterritorial jurisdiction; at 94 asserting that 'territorial jurisdiction, which is based on the concept of sovereignty, requires a territorial link for its exercise'; at 103 (discussing Directive 2008/101/EC (n 210)) arguing that '[t]he question is whether this extraterritorial element negates the territorial link necessary to substantiate territorial jurisdiction'); at 112 referring to 'extraterritorial elements which need to be validated by the existence of a reasonable jurisdictional link'. See also Ryngaert (n 488) 7: '"Extraterritorial jurisdiction" ought to imply that a State exercises its jurisdiction without any territorial link ("*extra*-territorial"), although the expression is typically used in a context of States asserting jurisdiction on the basis of some, admittedly non-exclusive, territorial link.'
521 *Air Transport Association of America* (n 207).
522 n 210.

into the EU ETS. Famously, more instructive than the judgment itself,[523] the AG's opinion is apparently supposed to give testimony to the EU's stance on the question of extraterritorial measures and presumably can be considered valid with regard to other similar legislative acts as well. In brief, the AG asserts that there are no extraterritorial provisions in the Directive in question, since its provisions only relate to aircraft that arrive or depart from an EU aerodrome and it is only upon this presence in an EU aerodrome that sovereignty is exercised over the respective airlines.[524] The AG does concede that the Directive takes into account events that take place outside of EU territory when calculating emission allowances based on the full route of a flight. Nonetheless, extraterritoriality is denied because the Directive does not prescribe a specific conduct:

> This might indirectly give airlines an incentive to conduct themselves in a particular way when flying over the high seas or on the territory of third countries, in particular to consume as little fuel as possible and expel as few greenhouse gases as possible. However, there is no concrete *rule* regarding their conduct within airspace outside of the European Union.[525]

It is further asserted that the concept that events that take place outside of a State's territory can be made subject to that State's sovereignty is exemplified in the concepts of income tax that is applied to income generated outside of a State's territory, or antitrust law and merger control, where the agreement has been concluded outside of the State's jurisdiction.[526] This comparison, however, falls short as neither income tax laws nor competition laws intend to generate a specific, predetermined conduct before the event that triggers a legal obligation has taken place.[527] The considerations on extraterritoriality conclude inter alia with a reference to 'an adequate territorial link' that is given for flights that take-off or land in EU territory

---

523 See Churchill (n 504) 455 calling the AG's opinion 'much clearer and more cogent tha[n] the Court's judgment'; Kopela (n 494) 103, calling it 'more nuanced'.

524 Case C-366/10 *Air Transport Association of America and Others v Secretary of State for Energy and Climate Change*, Opinion of AG Kokott ECLI:EU:2011:637, paras 145–46.

525 *Air Transport Association of America*, Opinion of AG Kokott (n 524) para 147.

526 ibid para 148.

527 See similarly Dobson and Ryngaert (n 496) 308, who find that 'even where a measure has been framed around territorial conduct or presence (ie "territorialized"), such as presence in an aerodrome, the actual requirements to be met at that point relate to extraterritorial events.'

and the territoriality principle that is not violated only because the ETS also applies to parts of those flights that occur outside of EU territory.[528]

The ECJ follows this reasoning by briefly referring to the principle of territoriality and the EU's unlimited jurisdiction; it then rather bluntly states that the application of EU law in its territory with regard to an event that takes place partly outside of its territory is not in violation of customary international law.[529] The word *extraterritorial* is not used once in the text of the judgment. What can be found though, is a reference to the status of flag States:

> As regards [...] the principle that aircraft overflying the high seas are subject to the exclusive jurisdiction of the State in which they are registered, it must be found by contrast that [...] insufficient evidence exists to establish that the principle of customary international law, recognized as such, that a vessel on the high seas is in principle governed only by the law of its flag [...] would apply by analogy to aircraft overflying the high seas.[530]

One can safely assume the Court never intended to make a point against the permissibility of an ETS for the shipping sector (or an MRV-Regulation for that matter). Nonetheless, the question remains, to what extent the elaborations of the AG and the ECJ can be used to argue for or against the permissibility of the MRV-Regulation or the Shipping ETS.

One thing to keep in mind is that the monitoring requirements provided for in Annex II of the MRV-Regulation are more complex than those required by the Aviation ETS (see Annex IV Part B of Directive 2003/87/EC[531]). The monitoring within the framework of the MRV-Regulation does require specific conduct to be carried out on board a ship during its voyage, since the data to be reported has to be generated in accordance with one of the specific methods given. Arguing that there is no 'concrete rule of conduct' is rather difficult in this context. Nonetheless, it seems unlikely that a legal challenge of the MRV-Regulation or the Shipping ETS would yield a result different than the ruling the *ATA* case. This is not least because the EU has been observed to practice a policy of what

528 *Air Transport Association of America*, Opinion of AG Kokott (n 524) paras 152, 154.

529 *Air Transport Association of America* (n 207) paras 125, 129.

530 ibid para 106; see also the Opinion of the AG in this case (n 524) para 128, referring to the existence of a principle of exclusive flag State jurisdiction for vessels on the high seas.

531 n 476.

has been named *territorial extension.* According to this theory, 'a measure will be regarded as giving rise to territorial extension when its application depends upon the existence of a relevant territorial connection, but where the relevant regulatory determination will be shaped as a matter of law, by conduct or circumstances abroad.'[532]

By contrast, in accordance with the notion of *extraterritorial extension,* a measure has only been deemed to be extraterritorial 'when it imposes obligations on persons who do not enjoy a relevant territorial connection with the regulating state.'[533] Hence, for the measure to qualify as a mere *territorial extension,* the territorial connection has to be between the regulated person and the regulating State. The connection between a person and the State, on the other hand, can easily be established when the person enters the State's territory. When applied to the inclusion of aviation into the EU ETS this means 'it actually rests upon a territorial trigger as it only applies to flights arriving or departing from an EU airport.'[534] More generally, it is argued that

> territorial extension is used by the EU to incentivize a high level of performance on the part of third country actors, with their performance being judged by reference to an individual transaction or by reference to a group of transactions, aggregated at the level of a third country or firm. The "bundling together" of transactions, only some of which are centered on the territory of the EU, is a key characteristic of territorial extension in EU law. It serves to create legal interdependence between transactions, some of which the EU would find [...] difficult to "touch" if it were to seek to regulate these transactions alone.[535]

Here again, it is argued that the EU's intention is to exercise and strengthen its role as a normative power[536]:

> [t]he EU [...] uses territorial extension both to prompt the emergence of international (bilateral or multilateral) agreements, and to encourage states to sign up to and comply with existing international norms.[537] [...] It is then clear that one of the most striking features of territorial

532 Scott (n 514) 90.
533 ibid 89–90.
534 ibid 97.
535 ibid 107.
536 On the concept of *normative power,* see n 24.
537 ibid 108.

> extension in EU law is the manner in which the EU uses the existence of a territorial connection to leverage legal or behavioral change in spheres that are so widely drawn that they can encompass activities that have only a weak and indirect territorial connection with the EU. [...] An international orientation is inherent in the EU's very preference for territorial extension. This preference reflects the EU's often repeated conviction that prescriptive jurisdiction must be exercised in a manner that is consistent with public international law, and its belief that territorial extension complies with this standard.[538]

The last sentence interestingly and ironically suggests that it is the EU's desire to comply with international law standards that drives it to stretch concepts of international law to fit its needs. This reinforces the picture that the EU is torn between its own ambitions and its adherence to international law, with a tendency to sacrifice the latter for the former.

d. The Prerogative of the Port State and 'Territorialising' Extraterritorial Conduct

It is thought that the reasoning of the AG in the *ATA* case, namely the extending of jurisdictional power over aircrafts because they choose to visit an EU aerodrome, is very similar to the notion of the port State's freedom to impose port-entry conditions.[539] It can safely be assumed that the AG and the ECJ would argue along those lines if they were to justify the MRV Regulation or the Shipping ETS. The following considerations, therefore, imply that the ECJ would deny an extraterritorial element of the MRV or Shipping ETS and would invoke the port State prerogative to impose port-entry condition. On the other hand, those who believe—eg based on the judgment in the *Lotus* case discussed above—that an express legal basis is required for the exercise of extraterritorial jurisdiction, have often resorted to Art 211 (3) UNCLOS.[540] In light of the discussions in the previous chapter (B.V.3.a.), in particular the scope of Art 211 (3) UNCLOS, this is

538 ibid 111, 114, 115.

539 See Helseth (n 511) 36–37; see also Kopela (n 494) 103–04.

540 Ringbom, 'Global Problem—Regional Solution?' (n 510) 625; Dobson and Ryngaert (n 496) 312, 313, arguing against the requirement of an explicit legal basis is UNCLOS.

a plausible choice.[541] To make this argument work, carbon dioxide would have to qualify as a source of *pollution of the marine environment* under UNCLOS, which can reasonably be argued—considering the definition in Art 1 (4) UNCLOS and the acidification of oceans that result from CO_2 emissions.[542] Nonetheless, it has been argued that even the possibility for port-entry conditions given in Art 211 (3) UNCLOS, does not provide for prescriptive jurisdiction over operational measures.[543] Rather,

> [t]he broad geographical jurisdiction of port States to regulate and enforce violations of discharges under Article 218 suggests *a contrario* that a corresponding extra-territorial jurisdiction does *not* exist with respect to other types of (operational) requirements or to discharge standards that exceed those which are internationally applicable.[544]

It is with an easy move though, that Art 211 (3) UNCLOS can be used to '"territorialise" extraterritorial conduct by means of reformulating the offence, for example, by making the entry into the port [...] without having complied with a given type of conduct the offence against which enforcement action is being taken'.[545]

541 For an extensive investigation on UNCLOS provisions on port state jurisdiction, see Ringbom, *The EU Maritime Safety Policy and International Law* (n 20) 211 ff.

542 See Helseth (n 511) 17–18, who bases this on 'a good faith interpretation in line with the Vienna Convention of the Law of the Treaties Art. 31 (1), codifying customary law'; see also Tim Stephens, 'Warming Waters and Souring Seas: Climate Change and Ocean Acidification' in Donald Rothwell and others (eds), *The Oxford Handbook of the Law of the Sea* (OUP 2015) 783; Alexander Proelss, 'Article 1: Use of terms and scope' in Proelss and others (eds), *United Nations Convention on the Law of the Sea* (n 55) paras 12–13, who argues for an open and flexible interpretation of the term 'pollution of the marine environment'. This question seems to be implied in the request for an Advisory Opinion by a group of small island States to the International Tribunal for the Law of the Sea that inter alia asks for the specific obligations resulting from UNCLOS 'to prevent, reduce and control pollution of the marine environment in relation to the deleterious effects that result or are likely to result from climate change', ITLOS, 'Request for an Advisory Opinion submitted by the Commission of Small Island States on Climate Change and International Law (Request for Advisory Opinion submitted to the Tribunal) <https://www.itlos.org/en/main/cases/list-of-cases/request-for-an-advisory-opinion-submitted-by-the-commission-of-small-island-states-on-climate-change-and-international-law-request-for-advisory-opinion-submitted-to-the-tribunal/> accessed 15 December 2023.

543 Ringbom, *The EU Maritime Safety Policy and International Law* (n 20) 361.

544 Ringbom, 'Global Problem—Regional Solution?' (n 510) 624–25.

545 Ringbom, *The EU Maritime Safety Policy and International Law* (n 20) 359. Enforcement of a port-entry requirement can be in the form of denying benefits, such as future access to the port to which a foreign ship has no legal claim, or

On the other hand, if one refused to accept the *territorialising* of extraterritorial conduct as a legitimate manoeuvre, recourse to Art 211 (3) UNCLOS would not be possible. Additionally, Art 218 UNCLOS would preclude the legality of the rules of conduct associated with the MRV-Regulation or ETS outside of EU territory, as arguably a contrario it does not apply to port State enforcement related to discharges that are only in violation of national standards.[546] At the same time, the principle of flag State jurisdiction (Art 92 UNCLOS) and the prohibition of States to subject the high seas to their sovereignty (Art 89 UNCLOS) would at least pose serious legal obstacles.[547] For those who believe that UNCLOS provisions are non-exhaustive, however, there is always the possibility to invoke the port State's prerogative under customary international law to determine who gets to enter their port.[548] Recourse to this principle has often been accompanied by the reminder that there is no given right of a ship to enter a port[549] and that any ship is free not to enter the port of a State if it is not willing to abide by the port State's entry requirements.[550]. While this argument may seem very similar to territorialising extraterritorial conduct, it differs in that the simple reference to the prerogative of the port State needs no further

---

they can be punitive (see the distinction in Molenaar, 'Port State Jurisdiction: Toward Comprehensive, Mandatory and Global Coverage' (n 80) 229). From that a 'somewhat paradoxical situation seems to result, in which it is easier for a State to defend its right to refuse entry to its ports for non-complying ships than to find a legal basis for enforcing those conditions by means of other sanctions once the ship has actually entered. […] In the context of a regional ETS for shipping, the foregoing suggests that it would be easier to justify the extra-territorial reach of the requirements if the measure chosen to enforce the rules were based on denying (future) access to ports by non-complying ships, rather than issuing fines', Ringbom, 'Global Problem—Regional Solution?' (n 510) 627. This then means that 'no question of enforcement jurisdiction arises, if […] refusing entry of a foreign ship to a port is better seen as an exercise of sovereignty rather than an exercise in enforcement jurisdiction', Churchill (n 504) 466.

546 Kopela (n 494) 93.

547 ibid. For the opposing view that Art 92 UNCLOS only addresses enforcement jurisdiction and, therefore, does not pose a restriction to port State prescriptive jurisdiction, see Arron N Honniball, 'The Exclusive Jurisdiction of Flag States: A Limitation on Pro-active Port States?' (2016) 31 Int'l J Marine & Coastal L 499, 508; Ryngaert and Ringbom (n 486) 386.

548 Ringbom, 'Global Problem—Regional Solution?' (n 510) 625.

549 Dobson and Ryngaert (n 496) 313.

550 Ringbom, 'Global Problem—Regional Solution?' (n 510) 625; the same author points out that a measure put in place in such a manner must take into account the 'criteria of reasonableness that follow[s] from general international law', there at 641.

explanation or bridging a logical gap. Whether one invokes Art 211 (3) UNCLOS or customary international law, it has been argued that both sources additionally require an actual jurisdictional basis to render actions of a State lawful.[551]

e. The EU's Relationship with the Effects Doctrine

The need for such a jurisdictional basis may be found in the so-called *Effects Doctrine.*

> The *effects doctrine* may be understood as referring to jurisdiction asserted with regard to the conduct of a foreign national occurring outside the territory [of] a State which has a substantial effect within that territory. This basis, while closely related to the objective territoriality principle, does not require that an element of the conduct take place in the territory of the regulating State.[552]

Rooted in a United States of America court decision from 1945[553], the Effects Doctrine, as its name suggests, exists on the assumption that a conduct carried out outside of a State's territory produces a 'substantial effect' within the territory of a state.[554] Based on this notion, it is thought, the Effects Doctrine provides justification for the exercise of extra-territorial

---

551 Molenaar, 'Port State Jurisdiction: Toward Comprehensive, Mandatory and Global Coverage' (n 80) 229; Ryngaert and Ringbom (n 486) 383; Kopela (n 494) 94.

552 UNGA, 'Report of the International Law Commission: Fifty-eighth session' (n 487) Annex E, para 12.

553 For an extensive discussion of the *Alcoa* decision, including its context within US antitrust law and the political and economic background and implications, see James J Friedberg, 'The convergence of Law in an Era of Political Integration: The *Wood Pulp* Case and the *Alcoa* Effects Doctrine' (1991) 52 U Pitt L Rev 289, 298–304.

554 UNGA, 'Report of the International Law Commission: Fifty-eighth session' (n 487) Annex E, para 21; Kopela (n 494) 92. Because the effects of the conduct in question materialise within the territory of a State, it is at times assumed that the effects principle is a subcategory of objective territorial jurisdiction, see Kopela (n 494) 92, who also points out that there is actually 'no physical act taking place within the territory', with further references on both opinions; see also UNGA, 'Report of the International Law Commission: Fifty-eighth session' (n 487) Annex E, para 42, where the Effects Doctrine is listed as part of the territoriality principle but distinct from the objective territoriality principle—this is consequential as the ILC defines the objective territoriality principle as 'referring to the jurisdiction that a State may exercise with respect to persons, property or acts outside its territory when a

jurisdiction.[555] This section explores the Effects Doctrine and how it could serve to justify the basis for the obligations under the MRV-Regulation.

The Effects Doctrine is not a universally agreed concept for justifying the exercise of extraterritorial jurisdiction[556]—the more significant it is that the AG in the *ATA* case, while denying an element of extraterritoriality, seems to invoke the Effects Doctrine when she points to the effects of air pollution and greenhouse gases on the environment and climate of the EU.[557] Also, the ECJ itself, in this context, invokes two cases (*Ahlström Osakeyhtiö and Others v Commission*[558] and *Commune des Mesquer*[559]) that prompt the assumption that it, too, tries to allude to the Effects Doctrine.[560] However, the reference stands on somewhat shaky grounds. In the *Ahlström Osakeyhtiö* case, the Court did not focus on the effect of a conduct but rather argued that the implementation of an illegal pricing agreement in the common market qualified as a conduct in the territory of the EU and triggered EU jurisdiction to apply its competition laws based on the territoriality principle.[561] In the *Commune des Mesquer* case, the Court skipped to the conclusion that hydrocarbons spilled outside of EU territory that drifted along the coast of an EU MS and ultimately washed up on that coast, are hydrocarbons that actually have been 'discharged on the Member State's land territory'.[562] In the first instance, the Court made a point to argue that the conduct actually took place in its territory in which case no additional jurisdictional basis would be needed. In the second case the Court argued that the discharge outside EU territory amounted to a discharge actually into an EU territory. With that it made a case for equalling an event that took place outside of its territory to an event that took place inside its territory when the consequences of that event become manifest inside its territory. While the argumentation of the court seems to be missing a link,

---

constitutive element of the conduct sought to be regulated occurred in the territory of the State', there at para 11.

555 UNGA, 'Report of the International Law Commission: Fifty-eighth session' (n 487) Annex E, para 43.

556 Kamminga, (n 496) 16.

557 *Air Transport Association of America*, Opinion of AG Kokott (n 524) 154.

558 Joined Cases 89, 104, 114, 116, 117 and 125 to 129/85 *Ahlström Osakeyhtiö and Others v Commission* [1988] ECLI:EU:C:1988:447.

559 Case C-188/07 *Commune des Mesquer v Total France SA and Total International Ltd* ECLI:EU:C:2008:359.

560 Kopela (n 494) 104.

561 *Ahlström Osakeyhtiö* (n 558) paras 16–18.

562 *Commune des Mesquer* (n 559) paras 60–61.

however, it comes very close to the notion of the Effects Doctrine. Be it as it may, the ECJ citing these two decisions in the *ATA* case emphasised the place of the occurrence of the event rather than its effects: 'the fact that [...] certain matters contributing to the pollution of the air, sea or land territory of the Member States originate in an event which occurs partly outside that territory is not such as to call into question [...] the full applicability of European Union law in that territory'.[563] Hence, it is far from clear whether the EU, in general, has taken a stance in favour of the Effects Doctrine[564] or whether it has merely resorted to its notion where it has been convenient. What may be read as an allusion to the Effects Doctrine might just be a side effect of it trying to dodge the question of a jurisdictional basis while asserting it at the same time.[565] Remarkably, '[t]he EU is using the

563 *Air Transport Association of America* (n 207) para 129.

564 Answering this in the negative, see M Jeffrey, 'The Implications of the Wood Pulp Case for the European Communities (1991) 4 LJIL 75, 104. On the other hand, answering this questions in the positive, see Higgins (n 494) 75: 'The effects doctrine has now been accepted in all but name', referring to *Ahlström Osakeyhtiö* (n 558); Friedberg (n 553) 320–21; Kopela (n 494) 92: 'The European Union, despite its initial reluctance, appears to have accepted the doctrine in both cases where there is an intraterritorial element, such as the existence of an agent of a subsidiary company within the framework of the concept of "economic utility", but also in cases with no apparent intraterritorial activity without, however, clearly recognizing the effects doctrine as its jurisdictional basis.' The attribution of actions of a subsidiary to its parent company based on the idea that they form an 'economic unit' can eg be found in Case C-48/69 *Imperial Chemical Industries Ltd v Commission* ECLI:EU:C:1972:70, 661–63.

565 Friedberg in his comprehensive historic account of the EC's approach to the Effects Doctrine lays out how, until its judgment in the *Ahlström Osakeyhtiö* case (n 558), the ECJ had relied on the argument of the 'economic unit' for the application of EU competition law on the grounds that the conduct in question had occurred within the territory of the common market, usually through a subsidiary within a MS, Friedberg (n 553) 308ff. This approach is considered to be a disguised version of the effects principle, see David Edward, 'The Practice of the Community Institutions in Relation to the Extraterritorial Application of EEC Competition Law' in Roland Bieber and Georg Ress (eds), *The Dynamics of EC-Law* (Nomos 1987) 369: 'The economic entity doctrine dresses up the wolf of the effects doctrine in other, though not (in the eyes of some) less objectionable, clothing.' The practice of the Court to apply the notion of 'economic unit' could, however, not have worked for the *Ahlström Osakeyhtiö* case as they were no actions taken by subsidiaries, hence the shift in argumentation, see for further elaboration on this, Friedberg (n 553) 319–20. For a summary of the events and developments at EC/EU level surrounding the Effects Doctrine, see also Steven T Gubner, 'Wood Pulp—The European Economic Community and Effects Doctrine Jurisdiction: The Community's New Weapon' (1990) 3 Transnat'l Law 759 (also published by (1990) 3 Glob Bus and Dev L J

mechanism of territorial extension, in circumstances of inescapable interdependence, to gain regulatory traction in respect of activities that take place abroad but that also impact negatively upon the EU or upon globally shared resources.'[566] This idea of *globally shared resources* the EU is thought to want to protect offers a possible alternative basis for justification. It would make it redundant to invoke the Effects Doctrine, which has only been asserted rather ambiguously in the AG's opinion and has seemingly not been accepted by the EU as a whole.[567] After all, where an evasive concept such as climate protection is at stake, a direct effect on the actual territory of an individual State may be difficult to argue.[568]

f. Climate Change as a Common Concern of Humankind

The idea that shared resources are universally deserving of protection is found in the concept of the *Common Concern*. The concept of Common Concern is thought to be the result of the

---

<https://scholarlycommons.pacific.edu/cgi/viewcontent.cgi?article=1213&context=globe> accessed 26 May 2023).

566 Scott (n 514) 124.

567 As Friedberg (n 553) 308–09 points out, the Commission and the AG accepted the Effects Doctrine early on. Therefore, here reference to the EU as an entity that recognises the Effects Doctrine would have to mean the universal acceptance of the Effects Doctrine by all institutions of the EU followed by an unambiguous reliance on this principle, in particular by the ECJ. This would ultimately mean a clear message that the Effects Doctrine is recognised, similar to the Commission professing it explicitly in Commission, *Fourteenth Report on Competition Policy* (Office for the Publications of the European Communities 1984) <https://op.europa.eu/en/publication-detail/-/publication/3c93e6fa-934b-4fb9-b927-dc9fed71ccfe/language-en> accessed 26 May 2023, 59. For an example of an AG recognising the 'location of the effects' as a valid jurisdictional basis and confirming the Commission's stance taken in this particular case, see Joined Cases 89, 104, 114, 116, 117 and 125 to 129/85 *Ahlström Osakeyhtiö and Others v Commission*, Opinion of AG Darmon ECLI:EU:C:1988:258, para 3.

568 See Manolis Kotzampasakis, 'Intercontinental Shipping on the European Union Emissions Trading System: A "fifty-fifty" Alignment with the Law of the Sea and International Climate Law?' (2023) 32 Rev Eur Comp & Int'l Envtl L 29, 39: 'A strict application of the [effects] doctrine would require the EU to showcase a direct causal link between the maritime emissions to be covered [by an ETS] and the damage inflicted upon its territory, which is scientifically difficult to establish due to the cumulative manner in which GHGs impact the Earth's climate system.'

> 'challenges facing humankind today [that] could hardly be faced on the basis of the traditional postulates of reciprocity or mutual interests on a strictly inter-State dimension. The protection of present and future generations and the very survival of humankind, require proper responses with the mobilization of all subjects of international law.'[569]

Therefore, it is suggested that

> 'issues of common concern are those that inevitably transcend the boundaries of a single state and require collective action in response; no single state can resolve the problems they pose or receive all the benefits they provide. Harm to a matter of common concern is often widespread and diffuse in origin, making it difficult if not impossible to rely on traditional bilateral notions of state responsibility to enforce international norms. When that harm is mitigated, all or at least large parts of the community benefit.'[570]

In 1988, the UN General Assembly, recognising the threat it poses to 'present and future generations with potentially severe economic and social consequences', declared climate change a 'common concern of mankind, since climate is an essential condition which sustains life on earth'.[571] The UNFCCC's first preambular paragraph reiterates this notion, '[a]cknowledging that change in the Earth's climate and its adverse effects are a common concern of humankind', and so does the Paris Agreement's pream-

569 Antônio Augusto Cançado Trindade, *International Law for Humankind: Towards a New Jus Gentium* (3rd ed, Brill 2020) 327.

570 Dinah Shelton, 'Common Concern of Humanity' (2009) 39 Envtl Policy and Law 83, discussing this in the context of the concept of *Common Concern of Humanity*, viewing the UNFCCC's reference to the *Common Concern of Humankind* as one expression of it (see at 85). For more on the rationale of the notion of Common Concern and a brief history of its evolution, see Alexandre Kiss, 'International Trade and the Common Concern of Humankind' in Klaus Bosselmann and Benjamin J Richardson (eds), *Environmental Justice and Market Mechanisms: Key Challenges for Environmental Law and Policy* (Kluwer Law International 1999) 145–51. For a more detailed account of the history, evolution and discussions of the principle of Common Concern, see Thomas Cottier, 'The Principle of Common Concern of Humankind' in Thomas Cottier and Zaker Ahmad (eds) *The Prospect of Common Concern of Humankind in International Law* (Cambridge University Press 2021), 11–24.

571 UNGA Res 43/53 (6 December 1988) UN Doc A/RES/43/53, preambular para 2 and para 1.

bular paragraph 11.[572] It is thought that the term *Common Concern* in a treaty 'implies an agreement to recognise the very existence of a shared problem'[573], and as expressed in the UNFCCC, 'is premised on a common responsibility to protect and a legal interest in not harming'[574].

The concept of the *Common Concern of (Hu)mankind* is different from the concepts of the *Global Commons* and the *Common Heritage of (Hu)Mankind* (most prominently found in preambular para 6 and Art 136 UNCLOS, and most recently adopted in the draft treaty on biodiversity beyond national jurisdiction[575]). The Global Commons 'consist of those areas which are not subject to the sovereignty of any state'.[576] The Global

---

572 Other treaties that include the term *Common Concern* are: the Convention on Biological Diversity (adopted 5 June 1992, entered into force 29 December 1993) 1760 UNTS 79, preambular para 3 ('common concern of humankind); the International Treaty on Plant Genetic Resources for Food and Agriculture (adopted 3 November 2001, entered into force 29 June 2004) 2400 UNTS 303, preambular para 3 ('common concern of all countries'); and the Convention for the Safeguarding of the Intangible Cultural Heritage (adopted 17 October 2003, entered into force 20 April 2006) 2368 UNTS 3, preambular para 5 ('common concern to safeguard the intangible cultural heritage of humanity'). See also Alexandre Kiss, 'The Common Concern of Mankind' (1997) 27 Envtl Policy and Law 244, 246, who points to preambular paragraphs 2 through 4 of the Convention on International Trade in Endangered species of Wild Fauna and Flora (adopted 3 March 1973, entered into force 1 July 1975) 993 UNTS 243 and finds that '[t]he logic of this text follows exactly that of the common concern.' Similarly, in a Note of the Executive Director of UNEP, Mostafa K Tolba, 'The Implications of the "Common Concern of Mankind" Concept on Global Environmental Issues' (1991) 13 Revista IIDH 237, 239, also places the latter treaty in the context of the concept of common concern. Boyle and Redgwell (n 56) 142 find that '[a]lthough the ozone layer is nowhere referred to as a "common concern", it is in substance treated by the 1985 Ozone Convention and the 1987 Montreal Protocol in essentially the same way.'

573 Thomas Cottier and others, 'The Principle of Common Concern and Climate Change' (2014) 52 Archiv des Völkerrechts 293, 301.

574 ibid 308.

575 Agreement under the United Nations Convention on the Law of the Sea on the Conservation and Sustainable Use of Marine Biological Diversity of Areas beyond National Jurisdiction (adopted 19 June 2023, not yet in force) A/CONF.232/2023/4, Art 7 (b).

576 Malgosia Fitzmaurice, 'Liability for Environmental Damage Caused to the Global Commons' (1996) 5 Rev Eur Comp & Int'l Envtl L 305. See also Marianne Riddervold and Akasemi Newsome, 'Introduction: Cooperation, Conflict, and Interaction in the Global Commons' (2021) 35 International Relations 365, referring to the Global Commons as 'resource domains outside the authority of states'; Susan J Buck, *The Global Commons: An Introduction* (Island Press 1998), 5–6, who additionally distinguishes between Global Commons and International Commons, the

Commons are understood to consist (more or less) of the High Seas, the Seabed, the Atmosphere, Antarctica and Outer Space.[577] They are considered 'domains that have an inherent value for humankind and the planet, and therefore have assumed a non-national status in international relations.'[578] The concept of Common Heritage of (Hu)Mankind, on the other hand, is less clear and subject to debate as to its elements and scope.[579] However, for one, there seems to be some agreement that the notion of Common Concern of (Hu)Mankind was introduced for political reasons to avoid the use of the term Common Heritage of (Hu)Mankind.[580] Secondly, there seems to be an understanding that the former is directed towards environmental protection and equitable burden-sharing, while the latter is directed towards the beneficial exploitation of natural resources.[581]

---

former being considered resource domains 'to which all nations have legal access', while the latter being considered shared resources that are exclusive.

577 Denise Garcia, 'Global Commons Law: Norms to Safeguard the Planet and Humanity's Heritage' (2021) 35 International Relations 422; Susan J Buck (n 576) 1. See also Fitzmaurice (n 576) 305, referring only to the atmosphere above the high seas and Antarctic as 'possibly' part of the Global commons, due its disputed status; Riddervold and Newsome (n 576) 365, on the other hand, do not mention the Seabed.

578 Garcia (n 577) 423.

579 Pointing to the insecurities surrounding Common Heritage principle, John E Noyes, 'The Common Heritage of Mankind: Past. Present, and Future' (2012) 40 Denv J Int'l L & Policy 447, 454; Rüdiger Wolfrum, 'Common Heritage of Mankind' (last updated November 2009) in Peters and Wolfrum (eds) *MPEPIL* (n 31) <https://opil-1ouplaw-1com-100b98ffu0256.emedien3.sub.uni-hamburg.de/display/10.1093/law:epil/9780199231690/law-9780199231690-e1149?rskey=VknBeE&result=1&prd=MPIL> accessed 2 June 2023, para 3.

580 Cançado Trindade (n 569) 344; Tolba, 238–39. Both, therefore, consider the notion of Common Concern of (Hu)Mankind a derivative of the concept of Common Heritage of (Hu)Mankind; Boyle and Redgwell (n 56) 144; Cottier (n 570) 18. See also Jimena Murillo, 'Common Concern of Humankind and Its Implications in International Environmental Law' (2008) 5 Macquarie J Int'l & Comp Envtl L 133, 138, considers the concept of Common Concern to be a 'more ambiguous concept'.

581 Cançado Trindade (n 569) 344; Cottier and others (n 573) 308; Tolba (n 572) 239; Lakshman Guruswamy, 'International Environmental Law: Boundaries, Landmarks, and Realities' (1995) 10 (2) Natural Resources & Environment 43, 48; Murillo (n 580) 138; see Edith Brown Weiss, 'The Coming Water Crisis: A Common Concern of Mankind' (2012) 1 Transnational Envtl Law 153, 163, who less pointedly asserts that the Common Heritage of (Hu)Mankind has '[t]raditionally [...] been associated with elements of property in the sense that all may have a property interest in the resource designated as common heritage of mankind.' See also Wolfrum, 'Common Heritage of Mankind' (n 579) para 9, who finds that 'the term "common concern of mankind" [...] seems to call predominantly for co-operation and equi-

While a thorough discussion of these three concepts is beyond the scope of this analysis, it is worth considering that climate change being recognised by the international community as a Common Concern of Humankind could provide a viable legal basis for climate protection measures of the EU outside of its own jurisdiction. It has been suggested that 'a principle of Common Concern forms the normative foundation and the limits for States to take lawful unilateral action with extraterritorial effects within the bounds of international law where international cooperation and joint action remains absent.'[582] This said, a measure invoking to protect a

table burden sharing, and does not cover the full spectrum of the common heritage principle'. With regard to the relationship between the Common Heritage principle and the Global Commons, it is asserted that the former provides 'an appropriate foundation for the governance of the global commons', Karin Mickelson, 'Common Heritage of Mankind as a Limit to Exploitation of the Global Commons' (2019) 30 EJIL 635, 636. Similarly, Garcia (n 577) 429, who suggests that the notion of Common Heritage is one of the 'foundational principles [that] underpin the legal scope of global commons law'.

582 Cottier and others (n 573) 296, see there also at 323 referring even to an 'obligation to take action at home and the right to address climate change mitigation even by measures having extraterritorial effect.' Boyle and Redgwell (n 56) discussing the concept of Common Concern in the context of Global Environmental Responsibility also argue in favour of the permissibility of extraterritorial action when—with regard to the implications of the concept of Common Concern—they assert that 'it is no longer possible to characterize international environmental law as no more than a system governing transboundary relations among neighbouring states', rather '[t]he characterization of issues such as climate change and biological diversity as the "common concern of humankind" [...] places them on the international agenda and declares them to be a legitimate object of international regulation and supervision, thereby overriding the reserved domain of domestic jurisdiction or the possible contention that they relate to economic activities and resources which fall mainly within the exclusive territorial sovereignty of individual states', 143 and 146, respectively. See also Kiss (n 572) 247: 'In principle, the proclamation that safeguarding the global environment or one of its components is a matter of common concern for the whole of mankind would mean that it can no longer be considered as solely within the domestic jurisdiction of States'; Frank Biermann, '"Common Concern of Humankind": The Emergence of a New Concept of International Environmental Law' (1996) Archiv des Völkerrechts 426, 449, 464, 480, who argues that UNGA Res 43/53 (n 571) implies States' obligation to address climate change beyond their own jurisdiction. Taking a different path and combining the Effects Doctrine and the principle of Global Commons in favour of port-entry requirements with extraterritorial effect, Kopela (n 494) 107, who asserts a 'legitimate and reasonable jurisdictional link based on the concept of global commons as an issue of common concern and the effect the regulated activities have upon them. [...] these concepts legitimize the exercise of extraterritorial jurisdiction by the port state'. It is noteworthy, that in a different approach Fanø, *Enforcing International Maritime*

common concern still has to adhere to general principles of law, eg not be arbitrary or protectionist.[583]

This option seems more suitable to justify an ETS, however—a system which actually aims to reduce emissions by making it financially attractive to do so. With regard to the MRV-Regulation, it is difficult to conceive how the prescribed conduct, ie the monitoring and reporting of emissions alone, would reduce emissions or mitigate their effects, even though its Recital 13 does claim that.[584] One could argue, that the MRV-Regulation is an intended preparatory step towards an ETS and, therefore, logically can be justified as a measure to mitigate climate change as a Common Concern of Humankind, if the stricter ETS measure can be too. This would follow the logic of 'who can do more can also do less'.[585]

Either way, such a readily available justification may be considered by some to provide a much needed legal instrument, but may be concerning to others as it can be (viewed as) an invitation for unilateral measures.[586] On the other hand, the argument that the lack of a consensus in unilateral action may violate the principle of *pacta tertiis nec nocent nec prosunt* does not hold.[587] The principle that a third party cannot be bound by a treaty

---

Legislation on Air Pollution through UNCLOS (n 40) 368 finds that '[i]nternational rules (norms) regulating GHG emissions could [...] in principle be considered peremptory norms of a jus cogens character. This would match the assumption that '[t]he doctrine of *jus cogens* and peremptory norms [...] can be conceptualised as an expression of the principle of CCH [Common Concern of Humankind]', Cottier (n 570) 71.

583 Ryngaert and Ringbom (n 486) 394. In general, '[port] entry requirements have to comply with the principle of good faith and nonabuse of rights, which also relate to issues of jurisdictional reasonableness, proportionality, and nonencroachment upon the rights of other states', Kopela (n 494) 105.

584 The claim that the introduction of the MRV-Regulation will bring 'emissions reductions of up to 2%', however, is considered unsubstantiated, Nelissen and Faber, 'Economic Impacts of MRV of fuel and emissions in maritime transport' (n 451) 6; see also there at 30–31 and 36 for further explanations why the MRV-Regulation will not likely result in significant emission reductions. Even if this was the case, it has to be taken into account that in its very structure the MRV-Regulation is not directed towards emission reductions and any actual reductions would be incidental.

585 See Molenaar, 'Port State Jurisdiction: Toward Comprehensive, Mandatory and Global Coverage' (n 80) 228, albeit using this figure to refer to the right of the State to deny access to its port vs to regulate entry into port.

586 On giving up consensual practices in international law in favour of more effectiveness and 'global public goods', see Nico Krisch, 'The Decay of Consent: International Law in an age of global public goods' (2014) 108 Am J Int'l L 1.

587 See Kopela (n 494) 110.

without its consent is codified as Art 34 of the VCLT[588] and expression of the sovereignty and equality of States. Therefore, a person linked to a State—be it as a citizen or, as may be the case here, as a person under the authority of a flag State—and affected by unilateral regulatory restrictions of another State does not qualify as being protected by the pacta tertiis principle.

5. Brief Considerations of WTO Law

To fully appreciate the MRV-Regulation as a basis for the Shipping ETS and its relationship with international law, one last aspect has to be touched upon in this chapter. It is the question of possible conflicts with WTO law, which becomes most significant with regard to a Shipping ETS, rather than the MRV-Regulation itself, due to its direct financial implications. The relevant regulatory framework of WTO law has been extensively discussed in the previous chapter on Ship Recycling. Some of those considerations apply here, too.

In a rather unconvincing approach, it has been argued that 'companies transporting "like" products from further away will be faced with higher compliance costs than those from closer-by', resulting in differentiated treatment that violates Art III:2 and the MFN principle of Art I:1 GATT.[589] This is asserting that of two ships carrying 'like' products, the one with the shorter journey is enjoying some kind of 'advantage, favour, privilege or immunity' pursuant to Art I:1 GATT. It is at the same time asserting that the yielding of emission certificates is an internal tax or other internal charge in the sense of Article III:2 GATT. This argument barely holds, because ships do not always carry products to import or export, and also since the products themselves are not actually 'subjected' to any particular treatments (see Art III:2 GATT), just as any financial obligation that could be regarded as a duty or charge is not 'imposed on or in connection with importation or exportation' (see Art I:1 GATT). Rather, the data requirements or financial obligation imposed on ships upon entry into port are modalities imposed on the movement of the ship as such, independent of its cargo. Any products affected are affected incidentally. More apparent, however, a Shipping

588 Art 34 VCLT reads: 'A treaty does not create either obligations or rights for a third State without its consent.'

589 Dobson and Ryngaert (n 496) 316.

ETS could potentially violate the Freedom of Transit enshrined in Art V:3 GATT that prohibits 'unnecessary delays or restrictions' or Art XI GATT that bans quantitative import restrictions.[590] Especially, with regard to the MRV-Regulation the application of Art V:3 is debatable, as the requirement to collect and submit data would need to be regarded to cause an 'unnecessary delay or restrictions' of the traffic itself.

Be it as it may, it can safely be assumed that with regard to the Shipping ETS a violation of WTO law could be justified through Art XX (b) GATT that allows exceptions where they serve to protect 'human, animal or plant life or health'.[591] For the MRV-Regulation, once again, an actual benefit for climate or the environment would have to be argued, which could prove difficult as seen above. Unlike the potential Ship Recycling Fund discussed in the previous chapter, the MRV-Regulation applies indiscriminately to EU-flagged and non-EU-flagged ships calling at an EU port, as does the ETS. Therefore, both measures would stand a good chance of passing the test of the chapeau of Art XX GATT. The interaction of these measures with WTO law, therefore, can be considered not too problematic. However, what once again strikes as strange in this context, is that a discussion on WTO principles in the context of a Shipping ETS did not and does not seem to take place at EU level in any way. This reinforces the impression that the EU prefers to avoid discussions on potential problems or conflicts that are relevant in the realm of international law with regard to EU measures.

590 See Ryngaert and Ringbom (n 486), who refer to port State measures in general, see there also at 387. Churchill (n 504) 451, who discusses these GATT violations in the context of CDEM measures.

591 Churchill (n 504) 452, 458; for a more elaborate discussion on the applicability of Arts XX (g) and (b) to climate mitigation measures, see Christina Voigt, 'WTO Law and International Emissions Trading: Is There Potential for Conflict?' (2008) 2 Carbon & Climate L Rev 54, 61–63 who suggests that 'the capacity of the Earth's atmosphere to accumulate GHGs at a level that does not lead to changes in the average surface temperature has to be regarded as a natural resource' and concludes that recourse to both provisions would generally be possible. See also Kotzampasakis (n 568) 32, with further references, who asserts with regard to the proposed Shipping ETS that it is 'widely accepted in the literature' that conflicts with WTO law are 'unlikely', alternatively 'could likely be justified under Article XX(b) or (g) [GATT].' See also Lorand Bartels, 'The WTO Legality of the Application of the EU's Emission Trading System to Aviation' (2012) 23 EJIL 429, 466, who in the context of the EU's Aviation ETS similarly finds that 'any discriminatory effects of the measure are likely to be justified on environmental grounds.'

V. Conclusion

This chapter has shown that the EU's MRV-Regulation followed an extensive time of unfruitful discussions on potential measures and MBMs at the IMO. The MRV-Regulation accelerated discussions at the IMO towards the DCS and with the adoption of the Shipping ETS has created a scenario that the international shipping community cannot ignore. The Initial GHG Strategy reminded its Parties that they should take into account 'the need to avoid regional or unilateral measures'.[592] At the same time, however, the expectation that the MRV-Regulation would be matched with an international carbon dioxide monitoring system of the same calibre was disappointed.[593] The EU, refusing to tone down the MRV-Regulation to fully align with the IMO's DCS has left the shipping industry with two instruments running in parallel, with only some congruency. No doubt, the EU's initiative in this context served a purpose and accelerated much needed IMO action. The IMO has so far only followed up on its GHG Strategy with short-term measures that rely on the well-known energy-efficiency measures—reducing fuel consumption and carbon dioxide emissions in individual ships, rather than the overall emissions of the international shipping sector. It remains to be seen, whether the EU's Shipping ETS requiring sector-wide emission reduction becomes a role model for an IMO MBM.

The MRV-Regulation has an extraterritorial element, however. It, therefore, begs the question of a jurisdictional basis. The safest way would be to invoke the prerogative of the port State and to claim that all obligations resulting from the MRV are nothing more nor less than port-entry requirements. While such an approach is viewed technically acceptable[594], it is thought of as a tactical manoeuvre that 'twist[s] the scope of territoriality under international law'[595] and 'works a strain on the logic of those prin-

592 Res MEPC.304 (72) (n 374) para 4.7.6.

593 The International Chamber of Shipping proclaimed that 'nothing less than full alignment with the IMO DCS would be regarded as acceptable and that partial alignment would be seen as "bad faith" by those non-EU States which had been encouraged to agree to the IMO system on the understanding that the EU would then fully align its unilateral regulation', ICS, 'Reducing CO_2 Emissions to Zero' (n 377) 14–15.

594 See Ringbom, *The EU Maritime Safety Policy and International Law* (n 20) 367, 369.

595 Nelson F Coelho, 'Extraterritoriality from the Port: EU's Approach to Jurisdiction over Ship-Source Pollution' (2015) 19 SYbIL 269, 284, who nonetheless concludes: 'This twisting highlights the insufficiency of the jurisdiction principles to tackle global issues such as marine environmental governance.'

ciples [of jurisdiction]' while undermining jurisdictional principles[596]. It should not be the preferred line of argumentation; however, it is the safest line of argumentation with regard to the MRV-Regulation which does not actually aim at reducing emissions. With regard to the Shipping ETS, a second and third option the EU could resort to as a legitimate basis for jurisdiction are the Effects Doctrine and/or the notion of climate protection as a Common Concern of Humankind. Based on the judicial precedents discussed above, it is most likely that the AG and the ECJ would opt for the first line of argumentation, staying on the safe side of arguing in favour of port State privileges. Continuing to circle around the question of the role of the Effects Doctrine would be a step back.[597] It would also be at odds with the Commission which has openly accepted the Effects Doctrine[598]. Invoking the concept of Common Concern of Humankind, on the other hand, would be a clear signal of commitment to international law principles and a more convincing approach.

This case study has shown a lack of awareness of the EU on the matter of available jurisdiction or a reluctance to address it. The following third case study demonstrates the EU's outright avoidance to address possible conflicts of EU legislation with existing MARPOL provisions and UNCLOS even when explicitly confronted with them. These questions become relevant when discussing the effects of more stringent implementation of MARPOL standards within the EU—once again a different approach of the EU—and the right to regulate within the EEZ, a maritime zone that has not yet been touched upon in this study.

596 Brian D Smith, *State Responsibility and the Marine Environment: The Rules of Decision* (Clarendon Press 1988) 176.

597 See Case C-48/69 *Imperial Chemical Industries Ltd. v Commission of the European Communities*, Opinion of AG Mayras ECLI:EU:C:1972:32, 694, basing his opinion on the Effects Doctrine while even laying out three conditions, namely that the effects must be 'direct and immediate', 'reasonably foreseeable' and 'substantial'.

598 See n 567.

D. Case Study III: Reducing Sulphur Oxide Emissions from Marine Fuel

So far EU action has been analysed within two sets of circumstances: the EU acting upon an existing (draft) international instrument, namely the HKC, to expedite its entry into force, and, also EU action in an attempt to provide a blueprint and—at the very least—increase pressure for action on the international plane, as seen with regard to the MRV-Regulation. This chapter looks at a third type of situation, namely where the EU builds on agreed upon international standards and modifies them, while also, in one case, overriding their entry into force.

This chapter first looks at the effects of sulphur oxide emissions from shipping (I.), and subsequently at the evolution of MARPOL Annex VI and its regulations on sulphur oxide emissions (II.) before it discusses the parallel developments at EU level (III.). The last section analyses the EU's provisions on the sulphur content of ship fuel with regard to their compatibility with UNCLOS (IV.1.) and MARPOL (IV.2.). Lastly, this chapter discusses to what extent MSs can invoke Art 351 (1) TFEU to protect them from the consequences of conflicting treaty obligations (V.).

I. The Effects of Shipping's Sulphur Oxide Emissions

Sulphur oxides (SO_x)[599] resulting from the combustion of fossil fuels (the main anthropogenic source of SO_x[600]) contribute to acidification on land and sea and affect human health through respiratory diseases and premature deaths from cardiopulmonary diseases.[601] SO_x emissions are related

599 'The abbreviation SO_x is often used for sulphur dioxide (SO_2) and sulphur trioxide (SO_3), although nearly all sulphur is emitted as SO_2', Salo and others (n 2) 169, 186. For better readability, this chapter sometimes refers to *sulphur emissions* to mean *sulphur oxides emissions*.

600 V Vestreng and others, 'Twenty-Five Years of Continuous Sulphur Dioxide Emission Reduction in Europe' (2007) 7 *Atmospheric Chemistry and Physics* 3663, 3664.

601 Salo and others (n 2) 169–70.

to the high sulphur content of fossil fuels.[602] Therefore, the dominant use of high-sulphur HFO[603] makes international shipping a potent contributor to SO_x emissions.[604] The most recent tightening of the sulphur content in ship fuel that became effective as of 1 January 2020 (discussed below) was, therefore, considered 'the most ambitious and life-saving environmental maritime regulation in recent years.'[605] It was projected that the further sulphur reduction in global shipping would reduce the number of related premature deaths by ca 34% (that is by 137,000 to ca 266,300) and the cases of childhood asthma by 54% (that is by 7.6 million to 6.4 million) in 2020.[606] Enforcement, however, is crucial and is more difficult as the violation on-board happens not only outside the port, but possibly outside of national territory.[607] At the same time, violating the sulphur limit requirements is highly lucrative: in the run-up to the latest global sulphur limit that came into force in 2020, it was estimated that the branch of container shipping was going to experience an additional expense of USD 10 billion in fuel costs.[608] The world's largest container shipping company, Maersk, alone was expecting an annual increase in fuel costs by USD 2 billion or more.[609] This could mean that a large container vessel travelling from Asia

602 ibid 187. The authors also explain that '[t]he sulphur contents are even higher in the heavy fuel oils (HFOs or residual fuels) used by ships than in the original crude oil because the sulphur is enriched in the heaviest fractions during the refining process'.

603 See n 1.

604 It is estimated that shipping contributes to 4–9% of global SO_2 emissions, Salo and others (n 2) 171.

605 Jesper Jarl Fanø, 'Enforcement of the 2020 Sulphur Limit for Marine Fuels: Restrictions and Possibilities for Port States to Impose Fines under UNCLOS' (2019) 28 Rev Eur Comp & Int'l Envtl L 278.

606 Mikhail Sofiev and others, 'Cleaner Fuels for Ships provide Public Health Benefits with Climate Tradeoff' (2018) 9:406 Nature Communication (2018) <https://doi.org/10.1038/s41467-017-02774-9> accessed 2 June 2023, 4, 5.

607 'A violation on the high seas prior to going into port could for example be proven by a sniffer attached to a drone used in combination with fuel sampling during a PSC, especially recalling the effect of the carriage ban which enters into force in March 2020', Fanø, 'Enforcement of the 2020 sulphur limit for marine fuels' (n 605) 284 (footnote 81).

608 Compared to fuel prices in 2018; AlixPartners, '2019 Global Container Shipping Outlook: IMO 2020 Weighs on an Industry Struggling to Generate Sustained Profitability' (February 2019) <https://www.alixpartners.com/media/14481/ap_global_container_shipping_outlook_feb_2019.pdf> accessed 2 June 2023, 3.

609 Jack Wittels, 'Maersk sees Fuel Bill Soaring by $2 Billion from 2020 Rules' (Bloomberg 2018) <https://www.bloomberg.com/news/articles/2018-08-29/maersk-sees-fuel-bill-soaring-by-2-billion-from-2020-rules> accessed 2 June 2023.

to Europe can save around USD 700,000 by disregarding the low-sulphur fuel requirements.[610] This substantial financial incentive makes violation the more attractive.

> Lack of effective enforcement [...] could therefore quickly create a vicious circle, where compliant shipowners are faced with the bleak outlook of either being strong-armed out of the shipping market by non-compliant competitors, or becoming non-compliant themselves in an attempt at self-preservation and survival in an uneven competitive market. As most international shipowners in such a scenario steadily become non-compliant, or disappear, the environmental and human health benefits from using maximum 0.5% instead of maximum 3.5% marine fuels are consequently also lost.[611]

Interestingly, it is expected that the latest sulphur cap will increase maritime transport costs so much so (20–85%) that it can be deemed an 'implicit carbon price', making low-carbon ships (such LNG-powered ships) more attractive: International Transport Forum, 'Decarbonising Maritime Transport: Pathways to zero-carbon shipping by 2035' (2008) <https://www.itf-oecd.org/sites/default/files/docs/decarbonising-maritime-transport-2035.pdf> last accessed 2 June 2023, 19. On the trade-off between carbon dioxide reduction and methane increase through LNG, see n 4.

610 Wittels (n 609). Similarly, the Danish Shipowner's Association asserts that a 'container ship (10,000 TEU) can save almost 1,200,000 USD on a return trip from Europe to Japan by illegally operating non-compliant fuel', Danish Shipping, 'Sulphur in Marine Fuels' (Policy Paper, January 2019) <https://www.danishshipping.dk/politik/miljoe/svovl/download/Basic_Model_Linkarea_Link/964/191213_dre_policypaper_sulphur.pdf> accessed 6 April 2023.

611 Fanø, *Enforcing International Maritime Legislation on Air Pollution through UNCLOS* (n 40) 17. See also, Henrik Ringbom, 'Enforcement of the Sulphur in Fuel Requirements: The Same, Only Different' in (2017) 1 Scandinavian Inst Mar L YB 45, 50–51, who refers to a USD 150,000 in fuel savings for a non-compliant, medium-sized container ship operating on heavy fuel on a return trip through the North European SECA: 'As opposed to oil spills, air emissions do not happen as a result of isolated events or incidents of a one-off nature, but are of a continuous operational nature. Compliance with the rules entails significant costs for ship operators. Conversely, there are important gains to be made by rule avoidance and it is technically relatively easy to switch between compliant and non-compliant fuel. This starting point would call for a robust monitoring and enforcement system, including at sea, and sizeable penalties for identified instances of non-compliance.'

II. The IMO's Journey to Reduce Sulphur Oxide Emissions

This section summarises the long process of IMO negotiations that led to the IMO's sulphur regulations that are in place today. It dates back to the 1980s when air emissions were first addressed by the IMO and experienced a milestone and a revision process. However, MEPC session documents and reports are digitally available only for the time starting at the end of the 1990s. One author has already thoroughly reviewed the relevant documents previous to this time.[612] This author gives a comprehensive and clear account of the developments that led to the adoption of Annex VI to MARPOL and the evolution of the sulphur regulations therein. This section, therefore, relies on this secondary source and gives a brief summary of the account for the following reason: The summary on the work of the IMO in this case study (and in the previous case studies) is given to demonstrate how the lengthy processes at IMO level have compelled the EU to assume the role of an accelerator and take action to further the cause of environmental protection. In that, the history and evolution of the relevant IMO regulations provide background information to make EU action in that particular field more fathomable. This background information provides context but is not inherently relevant for the hypothesis or the conclusion of this analysis. That is, the circumstances surrounding the adoption of IMO provisions do not directly feed into the core question of this analysis, namely how EU action in each of the presented fields fares from a legal and political stance. Therefore, it can safely be assumed that consulting and reviewing the primary sources would not yield any additional insights or benefits. For the time periods for which IMO/MEPC session documents are digitalised and publicly available, the primary sources have been consulted and relied upon. This is generally the case for documents generated and/or submitted ca the end of the 1990s and for texts of IMO Resolutions[613]. This said, the following two sections lay out the efforts of the IMO to draft and bring into effect the Annex VI of MARPOL to address air pollution.

612 Erik Svensson, *The Regulation of Global SOx Emissions from Ships: IMO proceedings 1998–2008* (Chalmers University of Technology 2011) <https://publications.lib.chalmers.se/records/fulltext/140528.pdf> accessed 19 May 2023.

613 Resolutions adopted by the key organs and committees are available directly through the Knowledge Centre of the IMO, 'Index of Resolutions' <https://www.imo.org/en/KnowledgeCentre/IndexofIMOResolutions/Pages/Default.aspx> accessed 2 June 2023.

1. The Road to Annex VI MARPOL

In the 1980s, air pollution from ships and its contribution to acid rain shifted into public focus. This section outlines the developments at IMO level that culminated in the adoption of an entirely new Annex to MARPOL addressing air pollution, as well as the following review procedure that was initiated in parallel.

a. Drafting the Text of a New Annex VI

The problem of sulphur emissions was first addressed by the MEPC in the mid-1980s. However, it was addressed with regard to the quality of fuel oil and possible oil discharges that would fall within the purview of MARPOL Annex I (Regulations for the Prevention of Pollution by Oil).[614] The topic gained momentum through the 1987 Second International Conference on the Protection of the North Sea. In a Ministerial Declaration (the London Declaration 1987), the North Sea States decided to

> initiate actions, within the appropriate international bodies concerned such as the International Maritime Organization and the International Standards Organization as may be appropriate, leading to improved quality standards of heavy fuels, and actively support this work aimed at reducing marine and atmospheric pollution; [...].[615]

As a direct consequence, the subject of air pollution made its way into the deliberations of the 26th session of the MEPC in 1988 that then agreed to add the prevention of air pollution to its future work programme. At that time, one submission to MEPC 26 contended that ships were responsible for 10% of the total global emission of SO_2. Possible options to address sulphur emission were presented and discussed, namely a limit of 1% of sulphur content in ship fuels or lowering the sulphur content in fuels through on-board technology. In 1990, air pollution made it onto the agenda of the MEPC for the first time (MEPC 29).[616] The cause of reducing sulphur emissions from shipping had been strongly supported by Norway, the Baltic

614 See Svensson (n 612) 27.

615 'Second International Conference on the Protection of the North Sea, London, 24-25 November 1987' <https://www.ospar.org/site/assets/files/1239/2nsc-1987_london_declaration.pdf> accessed 2 June 2023, para 31 of Ministerial Declaration.

616 See Svensson (n 612) 28.

Sea States and the Baltic Marine Environment Protection Commission (HELCOM), and they continued to play an active role in the deliberations. One Norwegian submission to MEPC 29 summarised two studies that estimated international shipping's SO_x emissions to be between 4.5 and 6.5 million tonnes about 4–5% of total global emissions, with the likelihood of further increase. Both, Norway and the Baltic States pushed for discussions on reduction measures, with HELCOM (a Baltic Sea States club) suggesting a sulphur limit of ca 0.8% for ships that run on the standard HFO. A counter proposal to maintain the status quo suggested that a 1% sulphur limit would possibly lead to a price increase of 20% for HFO.[617] At the end of MEPC 29 nothing more than the most basic groundwork had been set: 'The Committee recognized that air pollution from ships "*constitutes a significant problem of global nature which requires international action by the Organization*"'.[618]

For the following MEPC session in 1990, the North Sea States honoured their pledge 'to take concerted action within the International Maritime Organization [...] to establish effective measures to minimize air pollution from ships' and '[submit] proposals containing reduction objectives and target dates', inter alia regarding the sulphur content of HFO and sulphur dioxide emissions.[619] Supported in their general approach by the EC and the Baltic States, they proposed a reduction of SO_2 emissions by 50% by the year 2000 at the latest. This was to be accomplished by a maximum permitted sulphur content in HFO of 1.5% and 1% for areas that were prone to be particularly affected by SO_2 emissions (such as eg ports and other coastal areas).[620]

With this, extensive discussions were triggered. While an actual agreement on reduction rates and limits on sulphur content was still not within reach, IMO Parties in 1991 did agree on Assembly Resolution A.719(17) that appreciated 'the urgent necessity of establishment of a policy on prevention of air pollution from ships, and development of reduction objectives and measures to achieve the objectives for control of emissions of all the ele-

617 See ibid 29.

618 See ibid 30.

619 Ministerial Declaration of the Third International Conference on the Protection of the North Sea, The Hague, 8 March 1990 <https://www.ospar.org/site/assets/files/1239/3nsc-1990-hague_declaration.pdf> accessed 2 June 2023, para. 25.1 (iii), Annex 2, D.

620 See Svensson (n 612) 30.

ments of air pollution' (Recital 5).[621] For this, the Assembly tasked MEPC in cooperation with the IMO's Maritime Safety Committee 'to prepare a draft new annex to MARPOL 73/78 which could be considered for adoption'.[622]

The drafting process was going to be an arduous one, with a first text for a new Annex VI to MARPOL being adopted only in 1997. The contentious points were essentially the following:

- what would be the appropriate measure to take, ie limiting the sulphur content of bunker fuels (and if so, to what level) and/or the mandatory operation of exhaust gas cleaning systems (EGCS)[623];
- the economic implications of a sulphur reduction measure (including cost-benefit considerations);[624]

---

621 IMO Assembly Res A. 719(17) adopted on 6 November 1991, A17/Res.719.

622 IMO Assembly Res A. 719(17) (n 621) para 1 (g).

623 Put simply, an EGCS (also called *scrubber*) is a device that 'removes[s] sulphur oxides from ship's engine and boiler exhaust gases', Exhaust Gas Cleaning Systems Association, 'What is an exhaust cleaning system' <https://www.egcsa.com/technical-reference/what-is-an-exhaust-gas-cleaning-system/> accessed 2 June 2023. For a brief overview on the types of EGCSs and their functioning, see Oil Companies International Marine Forum (OCIMF), 'Guide for Implementation of Sulphur Oxide Exhaust Gas Cleaning Systems' (First Edition 2016) <https://ocimf.org/document-libary/98-guide-for-implementation-of-sulphur-oxide-exhaust-gas-cleaning-systems-final/file> accessed 2 June 2023, 6–7. For a more detailed presentation, see American Bureau of Shipping 'ABS Advisory on Exhaust Gas Scrubber Systems' (July 2018) <https://ww2.eagle.org/content/dam/eagle/advisories-and-debriefs/exhaust-gas-scrubber-systems-advisory.pdf> accessed 2 June 2023, 18–25.

624 For some context as to the course and nature of the discussions on sulphur limits in bunker fuels, the estimated environmental benefits and economic costs of such a sulphur cap and the reason for the intense controversy: a study submitted by Japan in 1991 on the effects of low-sulphur fuel requirements estimated that a 2% sulphur cap would increase bunker fuel prices by USD 30 per tonne and a 1% cap would do so by double that (Svensson (n 612) 32, referring to IMO document BCH 21/11/6—BCH being the *Sub-committee on Bulk Chemicals Handling* that was supporting MEPC work on this matter). The OCIMF in 1993 submitted a study that indicated that a global limit of 3.5% on the sulphur content in fuel would reduce SOx emission from ships by 5%, but would result in estimated global investment costs of between USD 1.4 billion and 2 billion (see Svensson (n 612) 37, referring to IMO document MEPC 34/3/1). A Correspondence Group report, on the other hand, noted (also in 1993) that a 3.5% sulphur cap would result in an increase in fuel price of USD 14 per tonne, while achieving negligible reductions in sulphur oxides emissions; the report, however, clarified that the objective of a sulphur cap would be to avoid an increase of sulphur levels in fuels (see Svensson (n 612) 38, referring to a Correspondence Group report submitted to BCH 23). In contrast to this, the World Watch Institute estimated that sulphur depositions result in forest damage

- with regard to sulphur limits in bunker fuels, the question of availability of low-sulphur bunker fuels, ie possible shortages in supply;
- and finally, the question of a global vs a regional regulation, ie applying reduction measures globally or only for traffic in specific geographical areas.

During the deliberations, different varieties and sets of solutions to these questions were discussed.[625] Eventually, a Protocol to the MARPOL Convention containing the text for an additional Annex VI was adopted at the Third Conference on Marine Pollution in 1997.[626] The Conference adopted Resolution 1, urging IMO Members to work towards expressing their consent to be bound by latest 31 December 2002.[627]

This first version of MARPOL Annex VI consisted of 19 Regulations and 5 Appendices.[628] Apart from regulations on SO_x emissions, it also contained regulations addressing nitrogen oxide emissions (Reg 13) and Volatile Organic Compounds (Reg 15).[629] Reg 14 of the Annex combined a globally applicable restriction with stricter rules for specific geographical

---

at an annual cost of USD 30.4 billion (see Svensson (n 612) 39, referring to IMO document BCH 24/7/7). One State submitted findings of a study that showed the average sulphur content in the North-Eastern Atlantic in 1990 to be at 2.7% and that 'the target level of a 50% reduction of SOx emissions in 2000 could not be achieved with a sulphur content of 1.5%, "even if it were to be applied on a global basis"', while admitting that the North Atlantic was an area of unusually high frequency traffic, Svensson (n 612) 44, referring to IMO document MEPC 36/22. Similarly, other delegations stated that even a 1.5% global cap 'would only reduce the sulphur deposition in Northern Europe by about 1% and at "prohibitive" costs' or that a 'compromised cap of 4% would have "*essentially no global environmental benefit*" but "*severe burden on some Member States*"', Svensson (n 612) 45, referring to IMO document MEPC 37/22/Add.1, Annex 15, 1).

625 For a detailed account of the discussions up to the adoption of the final text for an Annex VI to MARPOL, see Svensson (n 612) 31–49. For a brief summary of the negotiations and the stances taken by the relevant actors, see Tan (n 16) 155–60.

626 IMO, Conference of Parties to the International Convention for the Prevention of Pollution from ships 1973, modified by the Protocol of 1978 relating thereto, 'Text of the Protocol of 1997 to amend the International convention for the prevention of Pollution from Ships, 1973, as modified by the Protocol 1978 relating thereto as adopted by the Conference' (28 October 1997) MP/CONF.3/34.

627 Conference of Parties to MARPOL, 'Text of Conference Resolutions 1 to 8 and the Technical Code on Control of Emission of Nitrogen Oxides from Marine Diesel Engines' (n 349).

628 It is noteworthy that the text also contained regulations to limit nitrogen oxides (NO_x) emissions and emissions of volatile organic compounds.

629 For the sake of readability, the then adopted text version of Annex VI is referred to fully in the past tense, regardless of whether parts of it were later revised or are still

areas designated as so-called SO_x Emission Control Areas (SECAs). It provided for a maximum sulphur content of any fuel used on board ships of 4.5% m/m[630] and 1.5% in SECAs (Reg 14.1 and .4 (a)). The first SECA was the Baltic Sea Area (Reg 14.3 (a)). As a feature of the SECA, the sulphur limits could be achieved through the operation of EGCS or other approved technology (Reg 14.4 (b) and (c)). Furthermore, Reg 14.2 required that the 'worldwide average sulphur content of residual fuel oil[631] supplied for use on board ships shall be monitored taking into account guidelines to be developed' by the IMO. MARPOL's new Annex VI was going to enter into force 12 months after at least 15 States had become party to the Protocol, representing at least 50% of the world's merchant fleet's GT.[632] This was not going to be until eight years later.

b. The Coming into Effect of Annex VI

The adoption of a text for a new MARPOL Annex VI was a painstaking seven-year process leading to the fulfilment of the entry-into-force requirements only in 2004 and the eventual entry into force in mid-2005. The most obvious reason for this delay could have been the lack of universal acceptance, simply the possibility that the agreed-on text of Annex VI was too much or too little of a compromise for too many States. Indeed, many States believed that the Annex VI Protocol was not ambitious enough.[633] Presumably to rectify the wrong that the North Sea had not achieved SECA status during the deliberations, a group of North Sea States and their sup-

part of the current text. The current text version will be referred to in the present tense later in this chapter once the revision process of Annex VI has been discussed.

630 *% m/m* representing *mass percent* which is calculated as *mass percent = component's mass/total mass *100%*. For simplicity, hereafter the sulphur content measured in % m/m is only referred to in %.

631 Para 3 (1) of the IMO Guidelines for Monitoring the World-Wide Average Sulphur Content of Residual Fuel Oils Supplied for Use on Board Ships adopted later in 1999 and discussed below (n 643) defines *Residual fuel* as 'Fuel oil for combustion purposes delivered to and used on board ships with a kinematic viscosity at 100°C greater than or equal to 10.0 centistoke.'

632 Art 6 of the Protocol.

633 See Tan (n 16) 160–61 asserting that 'many developed state governments [...] found it politically difficult to accept the Protocol simply because the 4.5 per cent cap was meaningless for them.' See Boyle and Redgwell (n 56) 528, who point to the difficulty of reaching the 50% tonnage requirement due to the flagging out of ships to open ship registries of so-called developing states.

porters submitted the proposal to also designate the North Sea a SECA.[634] While receiving 'considerable support', it was clear that the amendment was thought to only take effect once the Protocol had actually entered into force.[635]

By the end of 2001, only four States had expressed their consent to be bound by the Protocol.[636] The IMO Assembly reacted by adopting a Resolution stressing the urgency for States to accept the Protocol and calling on the MEPC to 'review the situation concerning entry into force' of the Protocol and 'consider necessary measures to alleviate any impediments'.[637] While the MEPC during its following session in January 2002 merely took note of the Assembly Resolution,[638] an NGO (albeit unsuccessfully)[639] proposed a revision of Reg 14 and the sulphur limits therein, claiming that 'the inadequacy of the Annex VI provisions is an impediment to its adoption and ratification by member states.'[640] It proposed to lower the sulphur limit for all ship fuels to 1.5% as 'it is with great difficulty that Member States can garner the necessary political support at the national level to convince decision makers to endorse the backward looking provisions on sulphur content of bunkers as they currently exist in Annex VI.'[641] Shortly after, the claim of the ineffectiveness of the agreed-on sulphur limit was supported by one Party's presentation of the outcome of a trial project on the monitoring of sulphur contents of fuel. The trial run had been welcomed by the MEPC[642] and the proposed guidelines for such a monitoring had

634 IMO, MEPC, 'Designation of the North Sea area as a SO_x Emission Control Area': Submitted by Austria and others (3 December 1999) MEPC 44/11/4.

635 IMO, MEPC, 'Report of the Marine Environment Protection Committee on its Forty-Fourth Session' (12 April 2000) MEPC 44/20, paras 11.26 and 11.25.

636 For a full account, history and chronology of accessions of treaties overseen by the IMO, see the continuously updated 'Status of IMO Treaties' (n 44).

637 IMO Assembly Res A.929(22) adopted on 29 November 2001, A22/Res.929, 2.

638 IMO, MEPC, 'Progress report on follow-up activities: Note by the Secretariat' (17 January 2002) MEPC 47/4.

639 See IMO, MEPC, 'Report of the Marine Environment Protection Committee on its Forty-Seventh Session' (18 March 2002) MEPC 47/20, para 4.24, where the Committees finding that the proposal found no support and need not be considered further.

640 IMO, MEPC, 'SO_x Emissions: Submitted by Friends of the Earth International' (28 December 2001) MEPC 47/4/4, 1.

641 ibid 3, 4.

642 IMO, MEPC 'Report of the Marine Environment Protection Committee on its Forty-Second Session' (16 November 1998) MEPC 42/22, paras 9.25–9.31.

previously been adopted[643]. Based on the Guidelines, it was determined that the three-year rolling average of the worldwide sulphur content of residual fuel oils supplied for the use on board ships was 2.7%.[644]

Thus, when the MEPC announced in October 2004 that the entry-into-force conditions for the Protocol had finally been met a few months before and entry into force was imminent on 19 May 2005[645], the MEPC had three major topics to deal with: the outstanding proposal for the designation of the North Sea as a SECA,[646] the resubmitted request of an NGO to lower the global sulphur limit to 1.5%,[647] and the submission by one State Party invoking 'technical limitations' and limited availability of low-sulphur bunker fuels (for operations in SECAs)[648]. With this, the MEPC invited proposals for amendments to Annex VI and initiated a revision process before the Protocol had even entered into force.[649]

2. Revising MARPOL Annex VI

When MEPC 53 convened in July 2005, Annex VI of MARPOL had entered into force roughly two months before—nonetheless, numerous proposals for amendments had been submitted over time,[650] and Annex VI was going to undergo a three-year long revision process.

643 IMO, Res MEPC.82(43) adopted on 1 July 1999, MEPC 43/21, Annex 15.

644 IMO, MEPC, 'Sulphur monitoring 2001: Submitted by the Netherlands' (13 June 2002) MEPC 48/INF.4, 2.

645 IMO, MEPC, 'Report of the Marine Environment Protection Committee on its Fifty-Second Session' (18 October 2004) MEPC 52/24, para 4.1.

646 Report of the Marine Environment Protection Committee on its fifty-second session, 18 October 2004, MEPC 52/24, para. 4.19, 4.21.

647 IMO, MEPC, 'Comments on Annex VI: Submitted by Friends of the Earth (FOEI)' (9 July 2004) MEPC 52/4/4; MEPC, 'Report of the Marine Environment Protection Committee on its Fifty-Second Session' (n 645) para 4.24.

648 IMO, MEPC, 'Comments on Regulation 14 of MARPOL Annex VI: Submitted by the Islamic Republic of Iran' (20 August 2004) MEPC 52/4/12; MEPC, 'Report of the Marine Environment Protection Committee on its Fifty-Second Session' (n 645) para 4.22.

649 MEPC, 'Report of the Marine Environment Protection Committee on its Fifty-Second Session' (n 645) para 4.23.

650 Including on Reg 13 and 15 on Nitrogen Oxides and the NO_x Technical Code and volatile organic compounds, respectively. For a list of previously proposed amendments to Annex VI, see IMO, MEPC, 'Amendments to MARPOL Annex VI and the NO_x Technical Code: Note by the Secretariat' (17 January 2005) MEPC 53/5/1.

From the numerous amendment proposals that had already been submitted, the proposal to designate the North Sea area as a SECA specifically related to Reg 14, ie the actual regulation on sulphur.[651] The designation of the North Sea as a SECA was adopted at this very 53rd session[652] to enter into force on 22 November 2006[653] and to become fully effective 12 months later[654].

At the same time, some countries recommended that the Committee initiate 'a process to investigate how Annex VI could be updated to better respond to the present and future environmental challenges and technology developments.'[655] To this end, they noted that the 'primary technique for reducing SO_x emissions is to reduce the sulphur content of fuel.'[656] Ultimately, the Committee 'agreed to initiate a general review of MARPOL Annex VI'.[657] With regard to sulphur emissions, the revision of the sulphur caps, including discussions on the role of distillate fuels,[658] was going to be the centre of the deliberations surrounding the Annex VI review.[659]

Following these extensive debates, the MEPC adopted a revised Annex VI to MARPOL in October 2008.[660] Amended Reg 14 now provided for a gradual reduction of fuel oil's sulphur content: the 4.5% limit would

651 MEPC 53/5/1, Annex para 10. All other proposals did not relate to sulphur oxide emission.

652 See IMO, Res MEPC.132 (53) adopted on 22 July 2005, MEPC 53/24/Add.2, para 10.

653 ibid, see Recitals 2 and 3.

654 Reg 14 para 7 MARPOL Annex VI allows a 12-month grace period during which ships are exempt from the requirements related to newly designated ECAs.

655 IMO, MEPC, 'MARPOL Annex VI—Proposal to initiate a revision process': Submitted by Finland and others (15 April 2005) MEPC 53/4/4, para 11.

656 ibid para 33; the same proposal was tabled by the NGO Friends of the Earth based on a paper produced by a coalition of NGOs, see IMO, MEPC, 'Reducing Shipping Emissions of Air Pollution—Feasible and Cost-effective Options: Submitted by Friends of the Earth International' (7 April 2005) MEPC 53/4/1, Annex, 16.

657 MEPC, 'Report of the Marine Environment Protection Committee on its Fifty-Third Session' (n 127) para 4.50.

658 See eg the IMO, MEPC, 'Report on the outcome of the Informal Cross Government/Industry Scientific Group of Experts established to evaluate the effects of the different fuel options proposed under the revision of MARPOL Annex VI' (20 December 2007) MEPC 57/4; especially Annex 3 providing a 'Fuel and Refining Glossary' and Annex 4 containing a table comparing the different 'Options for reduction of sulphur oxides and particulate matter emission'.

659 For a detailed account of the discussions, positions, session outcomes and developments, see Svensson (n 612) 59–77.

660 IMO, Res MEPC.176(58) adopted on 10 October 2008, MEPC 58/23/Add.1, Annex 13.

expire in 2011, with a 3.5% limit becoming applicable as of 1 January 2012 and a further reduction to 0.50% as of 1 January 2020. The latter date, however, came with the requirement to conduct a review on the availability of compliant fuel by 2018 and the possibility to postpone the 0.5% limit to become effective as of 1 January 2025 (Reg 14.8–.10). The following discussion on fuel availability was a controversial one with strong objections from the industry and some State Parties.[661] The MEPC ultimately decided to retain the global 0.5% limit as of 1 January 2020[662]. Also, a so-called carriage ban was adopted to become effective as of 1 March 2020, prohibiting ships from carrying on-board any fuel oil for combustion purposes or operation exceeding the sulphur content of 0.5.%.[663] For the Baltic Sea SECA[664] and the North Sea SECAs,[665] the 1.5% was replaced by a 1.0% limit as of 1 July 2010 and a 0.1% limit as of 1 January 2015. Later, a North American[666] and United States Caribbean Sea[667] SECA were added to Reg 14 of Annex VI MARPOL.[668] A consolidated and revised version of MARPOL Annex VI was adopted in 2021 by Resolution MEPC.328(76).[669] With the

661 See eg on the final report of the Steering Committee and the ensuing discussions: MEPC, 'Report of Marine Environment Protection Committee on its Seventieth Session' (n 373) paras 5.48–5.54.

662 MEPC, Report of Marine Environment Protection Committee on its Seventieth Session' (n 373) para 5.56; and IMO, Res MEPC.280(70) adopted on 28 October 2016, MEPC 70/18/Add.1, implemented into the text of Annex VI by IMO, Res MEPC.305(73) adopted on 26 October 2018, MEPC 73/19/Add.1, para 1 of the Annex. It is noteworthy that the 2008 version of MARPOL Annex VI already contained Reg 18 which allowed individual ships to invoke non-availability of compliant fuel if found by a Party to be non-compliant with the fuel requirements.

663 Res MEPC.305(73) (n 662) para 1 of the Annex.

664 As defined in Reg 1.11.2 of Annex I MARPOL.

665 For a definition, Reg 14.3.2 MARPOL VI refers to Reg 1.14.6 of Annex V MARPOL. The list of delimitations of all Emission Control Areas of MARPOL Annex VI can also be found at IMO, 'Emission Control Areas (ECAs) designated under MARPOL Annex VI' <https://www.imo.org/en/OurWork/Environment/Pages/Emission-Control-Areas-(ECAs)-designated-under-regulation-13-of-MARPOL-Annex-VI-(NOx-emission-control).aspx> accessed 2 June 2023.

666 See IMO, Res MEPC.190(60) adopted on 26 March 2010, MEPC 60/22, para 2 of the Annex.

667 See IMO, Res MEPC.202(62) adopted on 15 July 2011, MEPC 62/24, para 3 of the Annex (corrected by Corrigendum MEPC 62/24/Corr. 4 of 7 September 2012).

668 The possibility to comply with the sulphur limits through operation of an EGCS is now included in Reg 4 Annex VI MARPOL.

669 n (413). MARPOL Annex VI is supplemented by a number of documents. For a list, see IMO, 'Index of MEPC Resolutions and Guidelines related to MARPOL Annex VI' <https://www.imo.org/en/OurWork/Environment/Pages/Index-of-M

global sulphur limit of 0.5% becoming effective as of 1 January 2020, the IMO's journey to tackle international shipping's sulphur oxide emissions has reached its height. A little over one year after the last step in the sulphur regulations had become effective, the IMO reported a '70% cut in total sulphur oxide emissions from shipping, ushering in a new era of cleaner air in ports and coastal areas'.[670]

III. The Evolution of EU Legislation to Address Sulphur Emissions in Ship Fuel

Throughout the process, while the international community struggled to find common ground on the question of sulphur reductions in international shipping, a possible single-handed approach of the EU was looming. References for that can be found on both sides: namely, those that speak of the EU's impatience (specifically the Commission itself) and those that attest to the international community's fear of a unilateral EU approach. As early as 1994, there was talk of a possible EU Directive should there be no 'acceptable sulphur limits [...] in place by 1995'.[671] The Commission, while expressing its 'strong preference for global solutions' upheld its threat during the review process of MARPOL Annex VI with regard to the agreed timeline it deemed necessary to maintain.[672] On the other hand, matching the EU's reminders of its rule-making powers, there were

EPC-Resolutions-and-Guidelines-related-to-MARPOL-Annex-VI.aspx> accessed 2 June 2023.

670 IMO, 'Reduced limit on sulphur in marine fuel implemented smoothly through 2020' (28 January 2021) <https://www.imo.org/en/MediaCentre/PressBriefings/pages/02-IMO-2020.aspx> accessed 2 June 2023.

671 See Svensson (n 612) 40–41, referring to IMO document BCH 24/7/6.

672 It is worth looking at the full summary statement here as taken from the MEPC Report: 'The observer of the European Commission reiterated the Commission's strong preference for global solutions, as may be agreed by IMO, with the objective of reducing air pollution and greenhouse gas emissions from ships. On both issues the Commission had always clearly indicated that it would await IMO action, in accordance with the timelines already established by the Organization, for the necessary global mandatory measures to be developed and adopted. The European Commission was, therefore, fully in line with IMO on the work being carried out and, while significant progress needed to be made during 2008, its position had not changed. However, should it not be possible for the Organization to maintain the established timelines, the Commission retained the right to initiate appropriate action to protect the environment', MEPC, 'Report of the Marine Environment Protection Committee on its Fifty-Seventh Session' (n 433) para 4.9.

repeated concerns of the international community about unilateral/regional initiatives.[673] Upon adoption of the revised Annex VI MARPOL, the IMO Secretary-General asserted that

> [t]he successful outcome of the efforts undertaken proved, once again, that IMO was focused, united and determined to reach decisions by consensus, thereby underlining IMO's relevance as an international body capable of dealing with all items on its agenda, an Organization with the mandate and competence to set global standards in a global environment.[674]

Against the backdrop of the EU's presence throughout the deliberations, these words could be read as a reaffirmation of the IMO's status and a defiant response to regional ambitions. Ultimately, the EU did pass its own piece of legislation. The next section gives an account of the legislative initiatives.

673 In 1994 Norway—supported by Denmark, Germany, the Netherlands, Poland and Sweden—was 'gravely concerned that there would be a real possibility that steps leading to unilateral legislations might now be taken. [...] Such an approach might greatly affect the role of IMO in this particular area', Svensson (n 612) 44, referring to IMO document BCH 24/15, para 7.57. During the 1997 Third Conference on Marine Pollution, BIMCO—a service provider to the industry—expressed its preference 'to see an internationally agreed solution instead of a development with more regional standards that would cause difficult operational problems', Svensson (n 612) 49, referring to IMO document MP/CONF.3/10. In 2007, the IMO Secretary-General opened the sub-committee discussing the Annex VI review by 'empasiz[ing] that in order to avoid unilateral or regional action, and to maintain, even enhance, the globally-acknowledged status of MARPOL and the primacy of the IMO as shipping's global regulator and the custodian of the Convention, the Organization should [...] pursue a long-term strategy on the prevention and minimization of harmful emissions from ships', IMO, Sub-Committee on Bulk Liquids and Gases, 'Report to the Maritime Safety Committee and the Marine Environment Protection Committee' (11 May 2007) BLG 11/16, para 1.3.

674 See MEPC 'Report of the Marine Environment Protection Committee on its Fifty-Eighth Session' (n 433) para 5.46. In a more patronising way and still with a subtle reference to unilateral action, the Commission gave the following statement at the 1997 Third Conference on Marine Pollution: 'The European Commission appreciated the well established IMO spirit and the use thereof during this Conference, the outcome of which will be taken note of and assessed in view of possible initiatives', Svensson (n 612) 52, referring to IMO document MP/CONF.3/RD/8, 2.

1. Directive 1999/32/EC—Leaving Ship Fuels Aside

With discussions picking up at the international level, the topic of sulphur oxides in ship fuel became prominent on the EU's agenda in 1997. The Commission's 'Community strategy to combat acidification'[675], inter alia acknowledged the developments at IMO level on sulphur reductions in bunker fuels. Recognizing the Baltic Sea and the North Sea as sensitive areas requiring special protection, it called on MSs to support the efforts at IMO level to establish these areas as SECAs.[676] The strategy was accompanied by the *Proposal for a Council Directive relating to a reduction of the sulphur content of certain liquid fuels and amending 93/12/EEC.*[677]

Directive 93/12/EEC of 23 March 1993 already established a sulphur limit of 0.2% by weight (as of 1 October 1994) and 0.05% by weight (as of 1 October 1996) for gas oils and diesel fuels, however, not for fuels used onboard ships.[678] While the Commission's amendment proposal included HFO in the list of fuels generally to be addressed, the Commission deliberately left bunker fuels unaddressed. In its strategy paper it acknowledged bunker fuels to be 'a significant source of acidifying emissions'. It, however, referred to the ongoing discussions surrounding the amendment of MARPOL to address the sulphur content of bunker fuels and concluded:

> Rather than introduce unilateral EC wide measures to limit the concentration of sulphur in bunker fuels, the Commission considers that it would be more effective for the Community countries to pursue a common position in the current negotiations for the revision of the MARPOL Convention whereby the Baltic Sea and parts or all of the North Sea/English Channel would be designated as SO_x sensitive areas under the Convention. Following the conclusion of the revision to the

675 Commission, 'Communication to the Council and the European Parliament on a Community strategy to combat acidification—Proposal for a Council Directive relating to a reduction of the sulphur content of certain liquid fuels and amending Directive 93/12/EEC—Proposal for a Council Decision on the conclusion by the European Community of the Protocol to the 1979 Convention on long-range transboundary air pollution on further reductions of sulphur emissions' COM (97) 88 final.

676 ibid 16.

677 ibid 63ff.

678 Art 1 of Council Directive 93/12/EEC of 23 March 1993 relating to the sulphur content of certain liquid fuels.

MARPOL Convention the Commission will review its position as to the need to include provisions for bunker oils in this Directive.[679]

On the other hand, the record shows that during the legislative process, the EP tried to introduce bunker fuels into the Directive by means of a ban on the use or marketing of bunker fuels that exceed a sulphur content of 1.5% by weight.[680] The Commission rejected this proposal considering discussions at IMO[681], while the Council mainly pointed to the pending international process.[682] What remained in the final legislative text of Directive 1999/32/EC[683] was the obligation of the Commission to investigate the possibility to address sulphur limits for bunker fuels on the basis of cost effectiveness studies (Art 7 (3) and Recital 12). Also, the Community committed itself to continue advocating 'more effective protection of areas sensitive to SO_x emissions and a reduction in the normal limit value for bunker fuel oil (from the present 4,5%)' in the IMO's MARPOL negotiations as well as upholding efforts 'to have the North Sea/English Channel declared a special low SO_x emissions control area' (Recital 21).

679 Commission, 'Communication on a Community strategy to combat acidification' (n 675) 49.

680 See the EP, Committee on the Environment, Public Health and Consumer Protection, 'Report on the proposal for a Council Directive relating to a reduction of the sulphur content of certain liquid fuels and amending Directive 93/12/EEC (COM(97)0088)' (4 May 1998) <https://www.europarl.europa.eu/doceo/document/A-4-1998-0174_EN.html?redirect> accessed 2 June 2023, Amendments 8 and 22; in its Explanatory Statement the Committee states: 'It is now clear that the International Maritime Organisation (IMO) has failed to limit the sulphur content of this type of fuel' (para 2). Amendments 8 and 22 were adopted by the EP in its sitting of 13 May 1998: EP, 'Minutes of the sitting of Wednesday 13 May 1998' [1998] OJ C167/73, 79, 112, 116.

681 Commission, 'Amended proposal for a Council Directive relating to a reduction of the sulphur content of certain liquid fuels and amending Directive 93/12/EEC' [1998] OJ C259/5, document COM (1998) 385 final additionally contains an Explanatory Memorandum.

682 Council, '2106th Council meeting – Environment –: Luxembourg, 16-17 June 1998' <https://ec.europa.eu/commission/presscorner/detail/en/PRES_98_205> accessed 2 June 2023.

683 Council Directive 1999/32/EC of 26 April 1999 relating to a reduction in the sulphur content of certain liquid fuels and amending Directive 93/12/EEC [1999] OJ L121/13; Council, 'Common Position (EC) No 61/98 of 6 October 1998 adopted by the Council, acting in accordance with the procedure referred to in Article 189c of the Treaty establishing the European Community, with a view to adopting a Council Directive relating to a reduction in the sulphur reduction content of certain liquid fuels and amending Directive 93/12/EEC' [1998] OJ C364/20, 26.

The fact that HFO as the most relevant bunker fuel was eventually exempted from the purview of Directive 1999/32/EC and the reasons given for this decision speak of an early hesitation of the Commission and the MSs to interrupt international negotiations with unilateral measures. It seems to show that in those times there was sufficient trust within the Community that satisfactory solutions could be found through the IMO processes. This is particularly interesting as it stands in stark contrast to the rather strong and uncompromising stance the EU has taken in the context of the more recent MRV- and Ship Recycling Regulation discussed in the previous chapters.

2. Amending Directive 2005/33/EC—The EU's First Sulphur Limits

A little later in 2002, the tone started to change. Apparently, sobered by the slow process surrounding the new Annex VI MARPOL,[684] the Commission presented a proposal for amendment of Directive 1999/32/EC[685] along with the first calls within the IMO for a revision of Annex VI. The initial proposal would designate the Baltic Sea, the North Sea and the English Channel as SECAs and impose a sulphur limit on all marine fuels (ie including HFO) of 1.5%[686] in those zones, regardless of a ship's flag or its starting point of journey. The same limit would apply to passenger ships regularly operating to or from EC ports.[687] Additionally, marine fuel used by ships travelling inland waterways or at berth in an EC port, would not exceed a sulphur limit of 0.2%, and 0.1% as of 1 January 2008. Interestingly, the Commission submitted this proposal

> [a]nticipating that EU Member States and accession candidate countries will soon ratify MARPOL Annex VI, and that other major flag states will follow, this will mean that the internationally-agreed sulphur limit

684 See Commission, 'Proposal for a Directive of the European Parliament and of the Council amending Directive 1999/32/EC as regards the sulphur content of marine fuels' [2003] OJ C45E/277, 279.

685 ibid 292.

686 This time the percentage would be given in % by mass, opposed to weight as was the case in Directive 1999/32/EC.

687 'in order to improve air quality around ports and coasts, and create sufficient demand to ensure an EU-wide supply of low sulphur fuel', Commission, 'Proposal for a Directive amending Directive 1999/32/EC as regards the sulphur content of marine fuels' (n 684) 280.

is implemented 12 months after entry into force of this directive, or one year after entry into force of Annex VI, whichever is the earlier.[688]

Accordingly, the requirements would become applicable 12 months after the Directive had entered into force.[689] With this, the Commission demonstrated its willingness to consider the prospective coming into force of an international agreement. However, at the same time, it demonstrated its willingness to sidestep an international process to accelerate sulphur limits in its territory where it deemed necessary—even if it meant misaligning with the internationally agreed standards, both, in terms of timeline and rigour of its regulations.

The proposal was welcomed by the Council generally, but also specifically regarding its promotion of stricter sulphur limits for Annex VI MARPOL.[690] The EP, however, did not find the draft far-reaching enough. It proposed a two-step approach that would lower the initial sulphur limit of 1.5% in the designated SECAs and for passenger ships on regular service to 0.5% as of 31 December 2008. At the same time, it would introduce a 1.5% sulphur limit on marine fuel in MSs' territorial seas and EEZs outside of SECAs from 31 December 2010 that would be lowered to 0.5% from 31 December 2012.[691] Furthermore, the EP amendments provided that the sulphur limits become applicable six months after the entry into force of the Directive,[692] thereby decoupling the effects of the Directive from the ongoing process around MARPOL Annex VI. In contrast to the Commission's careful considerations, this could be seen as an attempt of the EC to emancipate from the parallel international process. The EP also very confidently at this point suggested the following addition to the Recital: 'Given the global nature of shipping, every effort should be made to find international solutions. The Commission and the Member States should campaign more forcefully for the provisions of this Directive to be incorporated into the IMO framework.'[693] This would have been followed up with an obligation

688 ibid 280.

689 ibid 294–95.

690 Council, 'Council conclusions of 22 December 2003 — A European Union strategy to reduce atmospheric emissions from seagoing ships' [2004] OJ C8/3, paras 12, 20.

691 EP, 'Position of the European Parliament adopted at first reading on 4 June 2003 with a view to the adoption of European Parliament and Council Directive 2003/.../EC amending Directive 1999/32/EC as regards the sulphur content of marine fuels' (P5_TC1-COD(2002)0259) [2004] OJ C68E/311, 316-17.

692 ibid.

693 ibid 313.

of the Commission to 'submit to the European Parliament and the Council a report on the measures taken to anchor the provisions of this Directive in the MARPOL Convention.'[694]

The Council, while encouraging MSs to push for stricter sulphur limits during the IMO revision process of MARPOL Annex VI,[695] rejected the stepwise approach by the EP[696] (as did the Commission[697]). It also maintained the applicability within 12 months of entry into force of the Directive and additionally proposed the alignment of SECAs with MARPOL Annex VI,[698] rather than single-handed SECAs designations. In the compromise legislative act of Directive 2005/33/EC[699], the more conciliatory spirit of the Commission and the Council prevailed over the EP's more vigorous tone. The Council's call for MSs' involvement in IMO negotiations on MARPOL Annex VI remained in the final text (Recital 15), while the EP's proposal was watered down. It only required MSs to 'endeavour to secure within the IMO a worldwide reduction in the maximum authorised sulphur content of marine fuels' and lacking the mission statement of incorporating the Directive into the IMO framework (Recital 11).

Directive 2005/33/EC of 6 July 2005 ultimately amended Directive 1999/32/EC by introducing a 1.5% sulphur limit in SECAs and for passenger ships operating on regular services within MSs' territorial seas, EEZs and pollution control zones outside SECAs (Art 4a (1) and (4)). To remain faithful to the IMO process, the SECA's were regulated in Art 4a (2) to apply as follows:

(a) for the Baltic Sea area referred to in regulation 14(3) (a) of Annex VI to MARPOL, 11 August 2006;
(b) for the North Sea:

694 ibid 319.

695 Council, 'Common Position (EC) No 13/2005 adopted by the Council on 9 December 2004 with a view to adopting Directive 2005/…/EC of the European Parliament and of the Council of … amending Directive 1999/32/EC as regards sulphur content of marine fuels' [2005] OJ C63E/26, 27 (Recital 12).

696 ibid 30.

697 Commission, 'Amended proposal for a Directive of the European Parliament and of the Council amending Directive 1999/32/EC as regards the sulphur content of marine fuels' COM(2003) 476 final, 7.

698 Council, Common Position (EC) No 13/2005 (n 695) 30.

699 Directive 2005/33/EC of the European Parliament and of the Council of 6 July 2005 amending Directive 1999/32/EC [2005] OJ L191/59.

- 12 months after entry into force of the IMO designation, according to established procedures, or
- 11 August 2007,

whichever is the earlier;

(c) for any other sea areas, including ports, that the IMO subsequently designates as SOx Emission Control Areas in accordance with regulation 14(3) (b) of Annex VI to MARPOL: 12 months after the date of entry into force of the designation.[700]

Additionally, Directive 2005/33/EC provided for a 0.1% sulphur limit in inland waterways and ships in port as of 1 January 2010.[701]

To put this into IMO context: Annex VI MARPOL entered into force on 19 May 2005 with the Baltic Sea SECA becoming effective 12 months later and a few months before the EU Baltic Sea SECA. The North Sea SECA, however, was adopted by MEPC on 22 July 2005 to become applicable as of 22 November 2007,[702] meaning that the EU North Sea SECA ended up being effective a little over three months before the MARPOL Annex VI SECA. What might seem like a trivial misalignment raises some questions that will extensively be dealt with below (IV.1.c.).

700 11 August 2007 as one possible application date for the North Sea SECA corresponds to the application date 12 months from the entry into force of Directive 2005/33/EC, as the Directive entered into force on 11 August 2005, 20 days following its publication on 22 July 2005, see Art 3 Directive 2005/33/EC. The initial 'whichever is later' adopted by the Council's 'Common Position No 13/2005' (n 695) was changed to 'whichever is the earlier' through EP 'Position of the European Parliament adopted at second reading on 13 April 2005 with a view to the adoption of Directive 2005/.../EC of the European Parliament and of the council amending Directive 1999/32/EC as regards the sulphur content of marine fuels' (P6_TC2_COD(2002)0259) [2006] OJ C33E/469, 474.

701 Exceptions applied as provided for in Art 4b (2) Dir 2005/33. Also, however, not quite as relevant as the regulations including HFO, Directive 2005/33/EC additionally provided for a marketing ban on MGO exceeding a sulphur content of 0.1% as of 1 January 2010 (Art 4b para 3) and on MDO exceeding 1.5% as of 11 August 2006 (Art 4a para 7). The use of 'emission abatement technologies' (basically EGCS) was regulated in Art 4c.

702 See section D.II.2.

3. Amending Directive 2012/33/EU—Aligning with MARPOL Regulations

In July 2011, the Commission tabled a proposal to further amend Directive 1999/32/EC to take into account the ongoing developments at IMO level.[703] When the Commission filed its proposal, the new global 3.5% sulphur limit was going to become effective on 1 January 2012 with the next step expected to be the global 0.5% limit as of 1 January 2020. The stricter 1.0% in SECAs had become effective as of 1 July 2010 and was going to be replaced by a 0.1% limit as of 1 January 2015. Accordingly, the Commission proposed limits in line with the MARPOL global limits to apply in MSs' territorial seas, EEZ and pollution control zones, and an immediately effective SECA limit of 1.0% with the tightening to 0.1% scheduled in line with MARPOL. Additionally, it proposed a more stringent 0.1% limit as of 1 January 2020 for passenger ships on regular service in MS's territorial sea, EEZs and pollution control zones outside SECAs.[704] Furthermore, the draft proposal included a marketing ban on marine fuels with a sulphur content higher than 3.5% that did not prevail during the legislative process.[705] This propos-

703 It is asserted that 'a planned revision of Dir. 2005/33/EC in 2008 had been postponed to deliberately wait for the completion of a Revised MARPOL 73/78 Annex VI 2008. Nevertheless, the Commission had made it clear before the adoption of the revised Annex VI that it would not postpone the directive's revision much longer. This "threat" of EU unilateral measures was thus used as a pressure to reach a round up of the MARPOL 73/78 Annex VI 1997 revision process at IMO', Philip Almestrand Lineé, *Regulating Vessel-Source Air Pollution: Standard-Setting in the Regulation of SO_x Emissions* (University of Gothenburg 2017) 164, with a reference to document MEPC, 'Report of the Marine Environment Protection Committee on its Fifty-Seventh Session' (n 433) para 4.9, that contains the account of a statement of the Commission in which it expressed its 'strong preference for global solutions'. This preference for global solutions with regard to sulphur dioxide and nitrogen oxides from ships had previously been expressed in Commission Staff Working Paper 'Annex to: The Communication on Thematic Strategy on Air Pollution and The Directive on "Ambient Air Quality and Cleaner Air for Europe": Impact Assessment', SEC (2005) 1133, 98.

704 Commission, 'Proposal for a Directive amending Directive 1999/32/EC as regards the sulphur content of marine fuels' (n 16) 13–14.

705 ibid 13; the Commission's rationale for this, was 'the risk that the possibility to use heavy fuel oil in combination with emission abatement m[e]thods instead of low sulphur distillate fuels could result in use and placing on the market of poor quality fuel. Abatement methods would allow desulphurisation of high sulphur fuel and reduction of sulphur dioxide emissions to air. However, if poor quality fuel with high sulphur content is used for abatement, it could result in discharge of high density waste water and have negative effects on [the] marine environment', there at 5.

al initiated a comparably smooth legislative procedure. It is noteworthy, though, that both, the EP Committee on Environment and the Committee on Transport, suggested to extend the 0.1% limit to MSs' territory.[706] This suggestion, however, did not make it into the final text. This was also the case for the EP Environment Committee's suggestion to amend one of the Recitals to read, that the Directive should 'as a minimum' be aligned with Annex VI MARPOL, suggesting that the EU generally reserves its right to introduce stricter standards than agreed at IMO level.[707]

The final Directive 2012/33/EU[708] was adopted on 21 November 2012 with the limits and time frames suggested by the Commission, with the exception that the initial effective date for the 3.5% limit, 1 January 2012, had passed and was set for 18 June 2014. The Sulphur Directive was later consolidated as *Directive (EU) 2016/802 of the European Parliament and of the Council of 11 May 2016 relating to a reduction in the sulphur content of certain liquid fuels.*[709] In the following analysis, any articles cited refer to this Sulphur Directive unless there is explicit reference to a previous

706 Albeit for different reasons and on a different schedule: EP, Committee on the Environment, Public Health and Food Safety, 'Report on the proposal for a directive of the European Parliament and of the Council amending Directive 1999/32/EC as regards the sulphur content of marine fuels' (27 February 2012) A7-0038/2012, 23, 41. The Committee on the Environment argued that this 'would make it possible to achieve significant health and environmental benefits and would also create a level playing field as regards the cost impacts for reform', there at 37. The Committee on Transport reasoned that '[e]xtending the geographical scope of the 0.1% limit would also address concerns about different limits applying in different European coastal waters. It can be argued that this places shipping firms operating in SECAs at a competitive disadvantage both relative to those in other areas and relative to land transport', there at 65.

707 EP, 'Report on the proposal for a directive amending Directive 1999/32/EC as regards the sulphur content of marine fuels' (n 706) 10.

708 Directive 2012/33/EU of the European Parliament and of the Council of 21 November 2012 amending Council Directive 1999/32/EC as regards the sulphur content of marine fuels [2012] OJ L327/1. The Directive was later supplemented by Commission Implementing Decision (EU) 2015/253 of 16 February 2015 laying down the rules concerning the sampling and reporting under Council Directive 1999/32/EC as regards the sulphur content of marine fuels [2015] OJ L41/55.

709 Directive (EU) 2016/802 of the European Parliament and of the Council of 11 May 2016 relating to a reduction in the sulphur content of certain liquid fuels [2016] OJ L132/58.

version of the Directive.[710] The term *Sulphur Directive* is used to mean the instrument in general, without regard for a specific version of it.

IV. Diverging Sulphur Emission Standards and its Consequences

The previous section, while laying out the history and evolution of the EU provisions on marine fuel's sulphur limits, also carves out where the EU's provisions at one time deviated or still deviate from MARPOL provisions. This inevitably raises the question how these deviations are to be legally assessed against the backdrop of and the intersection between MARPOL and UNCLOS where they apply to foreign-flagged[711] ships. Therefore, the second part of this chapter first examines the following three deviations of the Sulphur Directive: the sulphur limit for ships in transit in EU ports, the regulation for passenger ships on regular service, and the pre-empted coming into effect of the North Sea SECA (1.a.-c.).

As the EU is not a party to MARPOL, the legality of EU action can only be assessed against UNCLOS provisions. Nonetheless, whether the provisions of the Sulphur Directive conflict with MARPOL Annex VI and whether MARPOL allows for such exceeding standards is still a relevant question discussed in the second part of this section (IV.2.). While it can safely be assumed that MARPOL does allow for more stringent measures, a regulatory conflict would place MSs that are parties to MARPOL Annex VI potentially in breach of their MARPOL obligations when transposing the Sulphur Directive into national law. In this case, Art 351 (1) TFEU could become relevant, which is briefly discussed in the last section of this chapter (V.).

1. The Sulphur Directive and Potential Conflicts with UNCLOS

This section analyses whether the Sulphur Directive is in breach of UNCLOS where it deviates from MARPOL requirements in the three instances just mentioned. For the discussions to come, it is helpful to keep in mind that unlike the SRR and the MRV-Regulation, the requirements of the Sul-

710 Where there is reference to a previous version, for simplicity, the Amending Directive is referred to by its number, to be understood as Directive 1999/32/EC as amended by that Directive.

711 ie non-EU flagged ships, which are also referred to as *foreign ships*.

phur Directive are not designed as port-entry requirements—ie compliance with those requirements is not considered a precondition for entry into port. The sulphur limit applicable to ships transiting in EU ports is a rule of conduct for the duration of a ship's presence in an EU port. Entering the port triggers the requirement to only use on board fuel with a maximum sulphur content of 0.1%. Similar to the case of port-entry requirements, however, port State rights can be invoked to reprimand a detected violation. This can be different in the case of SECA requirements or the rules applicable to passenger ships in regular service. In both cases, violations can occur in territorial waters or the EEZ, without the ship necessarily entering the respective State's port. In this case, therefore, the MS may only invoke its rights as a coastal State. Therefore, the distinction between the authority of the coastal State and the port State granted through UNCLOS does become relevant in the case of the sulphur limits and their compatibility with UNCLOS provisions.

a. The Sulphur Limit for Transit in EU Ports

The first provision investigated in this section is the requirement of Art 7 (1) Sulphur Directive that requires MS 'to ensure that ships at berth in Union ports do not use marine fuels with a sulphur content exceeding 0[.]10% by mass'[712]. It may be intuitive at first sight to assume that it is a State's prerogative to regulate within its territory emissions of ships that voluntarily enter its port and choose to remain there. UNCLOS, however, does address the prescriptive jurisdiction of States within their territory—that is because a State's right to regulate in its territory in the context of UNCLOS is bound to conflict with the right of innocent passage granted by Art 17 UNCLOS.

One such norm regulating prescriptive jurisdiction is Art 211 (4) UNCLOS. It affirms the coastal State's right to 'adopt laws and regulations for the prevention, reduction and control of marine pollution from foreign vessels.' Art 211 (4) emphasises this right to be the expression of State sovereignty and reminds of and refers to the right of innocent passage. Therefore, to be able to consider Art 211 (4) UNCLOS as a valid basis for Art 7 (1) of

712 With two exceptions in para 2 for ships 'due to be at berth for less than two hours' and those that 'switch off all engines and use shore-side electricity while at berth in ports.'

the Sulphur Directive two criteria have to be checked off. Firstly, sulphur emissions would have to be considered *marine pollution*, which can be established rather easily considering the wide interpretation of the term 'pollution of the marine environment' (Art 1 (4) UNCLOS)[713] and the ocean acidification that sulphur oxide emissions cause. Secondly, it must be ensured that Art 7 (1) Sulphur Directive does not hamper the right of foreign vessels to innocent passage through EU territorial waters. Here, the EU could rely on Art 21 (1) (f) UNCLOS that allows a costal State to regulate innocent passage through its territory for the purpose of preserving its environment and pollution prevention, reduction and control.

The limitation of Art 21 (2) UNCLOS to 'generally accepted international rules or standards' where requirements pertain to the CDEM of ships does not apply here.[714] As elaborated above, the requirements of the Sulphur Directive are designed as rules of conduct pertaining to the operation of the ship. The fact that certain compliant fuel or a specific treatment system would need to be available on board to fulfil the emission standards, does not render the low-sulphur fuel requirement a matter of design or equipment of the ship.[715] This is especially so, as there is not one piece or type of equipment that allows the ship to meet the emission standard.[716]

713 See also sections B.V.3.a. and C.IV.4.d.

714 See also Doris König, 'The EU Directive on Ship-Source Pollution and on the Introduction of Penalties for Infringements: Development or Breach of International Law' in Tafsir Malik Ndiaye and Rüdiger Wolfrum (eds) *Law of the Sea, Environmental Law and Settlement of Disputes: Liber Amoricum Thomas A. Mensah* (Martinus Nijhoff Publishers 2007) 772, who with regard to Art 21 (2) UNCLOS concludes that '[b]y means of an argumentum e contrario, coastal States retain the competence based on their sovereignty over their territorial sea to regulate the activities of foreign ships'.

715 In favour of qualifying the limit on the sulphur content in marine fuel as an emission standard 'which has merely consequential (and often minor) effects on CDEM matters', while rejecting the 'intellectually unsatisfying' possibility of regarding the sulphur limit as an emission standard within territorial waters and as a CDEM standard beyond territorial waters, see BMT Murray Fenton Edon Liddiard Vince Limited, 'Study on the Economic, Legal, Environmental and Practical Implications of a European Union System to Reduce Ship Emissions of SO_x and NO_x' (2000) <https://ec.europa.eu/environment/enveco/taxation/ship_emissions/pdf/app4final.pdf> accessed 18 June 2022, Appendix 4, para 72.

716 Disagreeing with this is Molenaar, *Coastal State Jurisdiction over Vessel-Source Pollution* (Kluwer Law International 1998) 67: 'The regulation of the sulphur content in fuel oil and fuel oil quality must be regarded as an equipment standard, as it concerns a requirement to ensure that an emission standard is met.' Rejecting this very assumption, see BMT (n 715) Appendix 4, para 70: 'Implicit in this is the

Since a breach of Art 24 (1) (a) UNCLOS as a restraint to the abuse of rights[717] could hardly be established here either, it must be assumed that the right of innocent passage is not unlawfully restricted. Based on this argumentation, Art 211 (4) UNCLOS can be deemed as a valid legal basis for the at-berth requirement of Art 7 (1) Sulphur Directive.

However, it is also possible to take a different angle on the justification for the at-berth-requirement of the Sulphur Directive. This is possible because UNCLOS is not considered to have been drafted with ships' air emissions specifically in mind.[718] Rather, UNCLOS dedicates one set of norms (Arts 212 and 222) to *pollution from or through the atmosphere* while also specifically regulating *pollution from vessels* (Art 211, 217–221). This, together with the position of Art 212 UNCLOS as the last source of pollution addressed in Part XII Section 5 of UNLCOS, can lead to the conclusion that Art 212 UNCLOS should be regarded as lex specialis over Art 211 UNCLOS where airborne pollution through vessels is concerned.[719] At a closer look, however, this is debatable. The regulations designed to address ship-source pollution and the corresponding rules for enforcement distinguish between the flag, port and coastal State. They, thereby, accom-

argument that a sulphur content regulation is not a standard directly controlling emissions at the point of release, but merely a method by which to achieve this. [...] It would be strange [...] to treat as a 'design' or 'equipment' standard, a requirement that does not necessarily require a particular engine or exhaust system design or involve the fitting or use of any additional equipment [...] In fact, no particular construction, design, equipment or manning changes at all need to be made, and this is arguably a pre-requisite to classification as a CDEM standard.' For a discussion on this (in the context of the requirement for passenger ships in regular service that will discussed in the next section), see Ringbom, *The EU Maritime Safety Policy and International Law* (n 20) 433–35, who concludes that 'it is probably safer to consider fuel quality requirements as being analogous to CDEM standards for the purpose of establishing the jurisdictional limits of coastal State laws in the territorial sea.' The reference to an application through analogy, however, seems to contradict the assumption that Art 21 (f) UNCLOS as 'an exception to the main rule [...] should be interpreted in a restrictive manner [...]', there at 434.

717 Richard A Barnes, 'Article 24: Duties of the coastal State' in Proelss and others (eds), *United Nations Convention on the Law of the Sea* (n 55) para 6.

718 Ringbom, 'Enforcement of the Sulphur in Fuel Requirements' (n 611) 59–60.

719 Bartenstein (n 195) para 2, read in conjunction with Frank Wacht, 'Article 212: Pollution from or through the atmosphere' in Proelss and others (eds), *United Nations Convention on the Law of the Sea* (n 55) para 2; BMT (n 715) Appendix 4, para 35. See also Fanø, *Enforcing International Maritime Legislation on Air Pollution through UNCLOS* (n 40) 168, who asserts that 'article 222 is in principle the primary *lex specialis* provision for a coastal State's enforcement of rules on air pollution', pointing out that Art 222 only applies to internal and territorial waters.

modate the very specific circumstances of shipping and seem most suitable to apply to all *pollution of the marine environment from vessels.*[720] This notion is supported by Reg 11.6 MARPOL Annex VI that stipulates that 'international law concerning the prevention, reduction and control of pollution of the marine environment from ships' applies to MARPOL's Annex VI mutatis mutandis.[721] Therefore, if anything, it could safely be argued that UNCLOS norms tailored to ship-source pollution are lex specialis norms over the general norms that regulate air pollution. It is precisely the proclaimed 'right balance between navigational rights [...] and environmental protection'[722] established through Art 211 UNCLOS and '[t]he sophisticated balance'[723] of flag, coastal and port State rights that would speak in favour of Art 211 UNCLOS being lex specialis over Art 212 UNCLOS.

Another possible approach would be to look at Art 211 (4) and 212 (1) UNCLOS as coexisting norms that need not be placed in a relationship of hierarchy. That is because the very characteristic of a lex specialis relationship between two norms seems to be missing here—namely, some congruency in the scope of two provisions that in the lex specialis norm then occurs in a supplemented, more enhanced, elaborated, ie specialised form[724]. Incompatibility, conflict or concurrence of norms[725] can after all only exist where each norm would be applicable in the given situation if it were not for the existence of the other one. This, however, does not seem to be the case when closely comparing the wordings of Arts 211 (4) and 212 (1). Rather, Art 212 (1) contrasts with Art 211 (4), which exclusively refers to foreign-flagged ships. The contrast becomes even clearer when noticing the resemblance of the wording of Art 212 (1) with Art 211 (2) that provides for the obligation of the State Party to regulate ships flying its flag. In short, Art 211 (4) and Art 212 (1), both, by wording apply to sulphur emissions and ships in general—one as an obligation to regulate the State's own ships, the other as a right to regulate foreign ships. Otherwise, however, they do not show an overlapping scope of application; in fact, they may

720 Ringbom, 'Enforcement of the Sulphur in Fuel Requirements' (n 611) 60.

721 See ibid 61.

722 Bartenstein (n 195) para 2.

723 ibid para 3.

724 See Dorota Marianna Banaszewska, 'Lex specialis' (last updated November 2015) in Peters and Wolfrum (eds) *MPEPIL* (n 31) <https://opil-1ouplaw-1com-100b98f6m07b3.emedien3.sub.uni-hamburg.de/display/10.1093/law:epil/9780199231690/law-9780199231690-e2171?rskey=q34qqH&result=1&prd=MPIL> accessed 7 June 2023, para 8.

725 See ibid para 5.

be considered mutually exclusive. At the same time, there is no indication that one of the provisions is meant to be exclusive, in that it is supposed to be the only norm to regulate sulphur emissions from ships, barring the application of the other provision. For one, Art 212 (1) could be read to lay down cumulative elements, in that it applies to the airspace under the sovereignty of the respective State with regard to the vessel flying its flag or the aircraft registered with it.[726] Considering it the only norm granting prescriptive jurisdiction to regulate sulphur emissions from ships would also mean denying coastal States this authority with regard to their EEZ (Art 211 (5) UNCLOS).[727] This would appear curiously restrictive, eg in the light of Art 56 (1) (b) (iii) UNCLOS that by and all affords coastal States jurisdiction in their EEZ to adopt provisions to protect and preserve the marine environment.[728] Secondly, while UNCLOS might have been drafted at a time that did not consider air pollution a problem to the environment, the definition of Art 1 (4) UNCLOS was purposefully drafted to also include indirect introduction of harmful substance into the marine environment. The wording is clear and, therefore, must apply where the indirect pollution is the result of air pollution through sulphur emissions. Therefore, there is a good case to argue that Art 212 (1) and Art 211 (4) UNCLOS are meant to coexist, each being applicable independently of the other.

In conclusion, the at-berth requirement of Art 7 (1) Sulphur Directive could arguably be justified based on Art 211 (4) UNCLOS. Some insights have been given here on the question of the possible applicability of Art 212 UNCLOS. However, a complete and in-depth analysis of the question presented here lies outside of the scope of this analysis. It suffices here to

726 Ringbom, *The EU Maritime Safety Policy and International Law* (n 20) 432. Wacht (n 719) para 7, refers to Ringbom and seems to be supporting this notion: 'Within this context, it needs to be highlighted that this part of the wording does not provide States with the power to establish rules and regulations that are binding on foreign-flagged/-registered vessels/aircraft.'

727 See Ringbom, *The EU Maritime Safety Policy and International Law* (n 20) 432–33, who, therefore, brings Reg 11.6 MARPOL Annex VI into play that would allow the coastal State recourse to Art 211 (5) UNCLOS to regulate within its EEZ.

728 See Molenaar, *Coastal State Jurisdiction over Vessel-Source Pollution* (n 716) 502, who solves this predicament by declaring Art 212 lex specialis to Art 56 (1) (b) (iii) UNCLOS. This claim, however, seems to contradict the decision in Art 211 (5) UNCLOS to generally grant coastal States prescriptive jurisdiction to regulate vessels in their EEZ, and begs the question what justifies such a significant restriction in coastal States' rights in the case of atmospheric pollution that is also harmful to the marine environment.

conclude that Art 211 (4) UNCLOS would be a reasonable provision for the EU to invoke as a basis for Art 7 (1) Sulphur Directive.[729]

b. Regulating Passenger Ships Operating on Regular Services

Art 6 (5) Sulphur Directive reads:

> Member States shall take all necessary measures to ensure that marine fuels are not used in their territorial seas, exclusive economic zones and pollution control zones falling outside SOx Emission Control Areas by passenger ships operating on regular services to or from any Union port if the sulphur content of those fuels exceeds 1[.]50 % by mass until 1 January 2020.

As far as this provision regulates passenger ships operating on regular services in the territorial sea, the discussion in the previous section applies equally here. In line with the conclusions above, Art 211 (4) UNCLOS could reasonably be invoked as a legal basis for that part of Art 6 (5) Sulphur Directive that addresses the territorial sea.[730]

As far as the application of Art 6 (5) Sulphur Directive in the EEZ is concerned, however, UNCLOS does not offer a legal basis for the EU to justify this provision. The coastal State's prescriptive jurisdiction for the EEZ derives from Art 211 (5) UNCLOS. It allows the coastal State to 'adopt laws and regulations for the prevention, reduction and control of pollution from vessels', however, only when they are 'conforming to and giving effect to generally accepted international rules and standards established through the competent international organization [ie the IMO][731] or general diplo-

729 This is specially so as Art 212 UNCLOS and its corresponding enforcement provision, Art 222 UNCLOS, 'seem to have been largely ignored in practice when the jurisdictional limits on the regulation of ship emissions have been discussed'. Also '[d]uring the drafting of the two articles at UNCLOS III, very little reference was made to ship-source pollution, the focus being mostly on pollution caused by air traffic', Ringbom, *The EU Maritime Safety Policy and International Law* (n 20) 431 with further references.

730 As far as this provision regulates activity in the territorial sea, it can safely be assumed that Art 21 (1) (f) UNCLOS allows this regulation of innocent passage. See also n 714.

731 Bartenstein (n 195) para 14. See also Ringbom, *The EU Maritime Safety Policy and International Law* (n 20) 398, who discusses other bodies that could qualify as a 'competent international organization', albeit not in the present context.

matic conference.'[732] As a mere stand-alone measure of the EU with no precedence or example in MARPOL or anywhere else, Art 6 (5) Sulphur Directive addressing passenger ships in regular service in the EEZ clearly falls outside of the scope of Art 211 (5) UNCLOS. It, thereby, cannot be considered in conformity with the law of the sea. This rationale has indirectly also been confirmed by the AG in the context of the ECJ's *Intertanko* case discussed in more detail below.[733]

While its time limit[734] has rendered Art 6 (5) Sulphur Directive obsolete, it is, nonetheless, worth noting its incompatibility with UNCLOS as an example of the constellation it represents: a regulatory measure of the EU as a coastal State pertaining to emissions of foreign ships travelling through its EEZ that has no precedent in MARPOL. The conclusions that UNCLOS does not provide for a basis for such action should be kept in mind for the future, as there is every reason to believe that the EU will not hold back with similar measures in the future where it deems IMO processes too slow or its standards too weak. For the same reason, it is worthwhile analysing the legality of the early entry into force of the North Sea SECA for EU MSs in 2007, even though it has now long been aligned with MARPOL's North Sea SECA.

c. Pre-empting the MARPOL Annex VI North Sea SECA

To recall, Art 4a (2) (b) of Directive 2005/33/EC provided the basis for a North Sea SECA becoming effective as of 11 August 2007. While the amendment procedure within the IMO was completed, however, it did not provide for an applicable MARPOL Annex VI North Sea SECA until 22 November 2007. This means, there was a short period of time in which the EU had a designated North Sea SECA without an equivalent MARPOL provision. With the knowledge of the EU legislator that the MARPOL Annex VI North Sea SECA was imminent, the pre-empted coming into

732 The term *generally accepted international rules and standards* is discussed in more detail in the next section.

733 Case C-308/06 *The Queen, on the application of International Association of Independent Tanker Owners (Intertanko)and Others v Secretary of State for Transport*, Opinion of AG Kokott, ECLI:EU:C:2007:689, para 68, who finds that 'under the Convention on the Law of the Sea, only rules on discharges which implement Marpol 73/78 are permitted outside the territorial sea'.

734 The date of 1 January 2020 is aligned with Art 6 (1) (b) Sulphur Directive and the global 0.5% sulphur cap of Reg 14.1 Annex VI MARPOL.

effect at EU level may not be considered a unilateral approach.[735] It is indeed striking that Directive 2005/33 fully relies on the text of MARPOL Annex VI for a definition of the North Sea SECA (see Art 2 (3e)), not offering a delimitation of the area itself. This may prompt the conclusion, that until the text of MARPOL Annex VI introducing the North Sea SECA was adopted (on 22 July 2005), Directive 2005/33/EC (adopted on 6 July 2005) was missing a crucial element. Consequently, if the Annex VI amendment procedure had failed, the Directive's North Sea SECA regulation would have failed, too.[736] While this is true from a strictly legalistic point of view, the record shows that this is by no means the interpretation of the EU.[737] In

735 See Ringbom, *The EU Maritime Safety Policy and International Law* (n 20) 429, who points out that while 'it was evident by the time of adoption of the EU Directive [...] that the international designation of the North Sea as a SECA could not be made in time for the cut-off date imposed by the EU [...] it was quite clear at the time of adoption of Directive 2005/33 that the North Sea *would* be adopted as a SECA. [...] the political decision to amend Annex VI had already been "agreed in principle" several years before its entry into force. [...] The wording chosen in Article 4a (1) of Directive 2005/33 could be taken as signifying that the formal adoption by the IMO of the North Sea as a SECA is a condition precedent for the application of the EU rules. Read in this way, the Directive only authorises the early implementation of a rule which has already been agreed at international level [...] and cannot be used as an example of, or precedent for, purely unilateral coastal measures without the presence of a corresponding decision by the IMO.' It is noteworthy that Ringbom still sees the need to legally justify this early implementation.

736 Ringbom, *The EU Maritime Safety Policy and International Law* (n 20) 429 (footnotes 185 and 186).

737 See eg Commission Staff Working Paper, 'Impact Assessment – Accompanying the document Proposal for a Directive of the European Parliament and of the Council amending Directive 1999/32/EC as regards the sulphur content of marine fuels' (SEC(2011) 918 final, 6 (footnote 8), 39, 54, 75; see also EP, 'Report on the proposal for a Directive of the European Parliament and of the Council amending Directive 1999/32/EC as regards the sulphur content of marine fuels' (n 706) 36 and 40, which refers inter alia to 'Europe's SECAs' in their own right rather than the North Sea SECA being an adoption or an implementation of an international standard. Similarly, it was widely understood in the industry that a somewhat independent North Sea SECA had entered into force on 11 August 2007, see eg Olav Tveit, 'MARPOL Annex VI – Solving the low sulphur issue' <https://www.gard.no/web/updates/content/53096/marpol-annex-vi-solving-the-low-sulphur-issue> accessed 7 June 2023; EGCSA, 'Regulations and Guidelines: The International Maritime Organization – MARPOL Annex VI' <https://www.egcsa.com/regulatory/> accessed 7 June 2023; riviera, '"Complexity and confusion" rule in SECA land' <https://www.rivieramm.com/news-content-hub/news-content-hub/complexity-and-confusion-rule-in-seca-land-51949> accessed 7 June 2023; The London P&I Club, 'North Sea SECA in force – 11 August 2007' <https://www.londonpandi.com/knowledge/news-alerts/north-sea-seca-in-force-11-august-2007/> accessed 7 June 2023.

fact, the alternative entry-into-force date of 11 August 2007 in Art 4a (2) (b) Directive 2005/33/EC itself demonstrates the general willingness of the EU to misalign with IMO procedures if necessary, if the IMO designation of the SECA does not happen earlier. The question, therefore, remains whether the EU declaring a North Sea SECA before the corresponding MARPOL Annex VI provision had been formally applicable, complied with the EU's commitments under UNCLOS.

The EU could rely on Art 211 (5) UNCLOS as the legal basis for such action.[738] The crux in the application of Art 211 (5) UNCLOS to coastal States' regulation of foreign ships in their EEZ, however, is the requirement of any action to be in line with 'generally accepted international rules and standards' (GAIRS),[739] as briefly mentioned in the previous section. The applicability of Art 211 (5) UNCLOS, therefore, depends on the question whether the North Sea SECA—formally adopted by IMO Parties, established in Reg 14 MARPOL Annex VI, but not yet applicable as to its requirements—could be considered to have been a GAIRS at the time the EU North SECA became effective.[740]

The concept of GAIRS that is found in other instances throughout UNCLOS is far from clear. It is understood that the concept of GAIRS serves

---

738 To the knowledge of the author, there is no information available on how the North Sea SECA exactly relates to the maritime zones as determined by UNCLOS (ie calculated based on geographic coordinates). Comparing the graphics of the North Sea SECA area with graphics that show the EEZs of the North Sea States allows the assumption that the North Sea SECA lies within the EEZ of the North Sea States, see eg the maps of EMSA, 'Sulphur Inspection Guidance: Directive (EU) 2016/802' (December 2019) <https://www.emsa.europa.eu/publications/reports/download/5910/2407/23.html> accessed 7 June 2023, 5; and Arctic Portal Library, 'Arctic EEZ-map in the European Union' <http://library.arcticportal.org/1504/1/eu_eez.jpg> accessed 7 June 2023. Therefore, the following assessment assumes that the UNCLOS provisions on regulations within the EEZ apply. This is, however, not to assert that parts of the North Sea SECA could not also be overlapping with other maritime zones, albeit presumably minimally. See also Ringbom, *The EU Maritime Safety Policy and International Law* (n 20) 428 (footnote 183), who similarly assumes that the legality of the North Sea SECA has to be based on the coastal State's right to legislate within its EEZ.

739 For easier readability, the abbreviation GAIRS is used in the following to refer to the plural as the legal requirement as well as to the singular relating to the North Sea SECA, which potentially qualifies as one *international rule or standard* rather than a set of *international rules and standards*.

740 This question, therefore, is about the regional application/implementation of GAIRS, to be distinguished from 'regional standard-setting' as discussed by Molenaar, *Coastal State Jurisdiction over Vessel-Source Pollution* (n 716) 158ff.

as a corrective or restraint on national unilateral action to 'secur[e] the pre-eminence of [...] international rules and standards over national laws and regulations'.[741] In that GAIRS must be different from what constitutes customary international law, or else reference to it would be redundant.[742] That said, there are different interpretations as to when exactly it is that rules and standards become *generally accepted*. The spectrum of possible decisive moments ranges from when norms are codified in a treaty that has not yet entered into force to the notion that GAIRS equal the set of norms provided by general and customary international law.[743] The underlying question is what constitutes a sufficient level of consent within the international community. It seems reasonable to use State practice as an indicator here, as the manifestation of States' will to be bound or their belief that they are bound by an existing norm. Therefore:

> The central element [...] to determine the generally accepted character of a specific rule or standard appears to be the practice of states, no matter in what form the rule or standard might have been expressed. This may

741 Erik Franckx (ed), *Vessel-source Pollution and Coastal State Jurisdiction: The Work of the ILA Committee on Coastal State Jurisdiction Relating to Marine Pollution (1991–2000)* (Kluwer Law International 2001), 107. See also Molenaar, *Coastal State Jurisdiction over Vessel-Source Pollution* (n 716) 152. The latter in this context addresses the underlying '[t]raditional conflict between coastal States' interests in environmental protection and flag States' interests in maintaining freedom of navigation' in line with the ILA, Franckx, 11; see also, there at 12 where the ILA refers to the 'umbrella' structure of Part XII of UNCLOS 'providing general rules primarily apportioning competence and leaving technicalities to the relevant conventions, already existing or still to be created.' A similar argument is made by Molenaar, *Coastal State Jurisdiction over Vessel-Source Pollution* (n 716) 140, regarding the evolution of UNCLOS and the decision not to incorporate ever changing technical details into the text of UNCLOS. For a slightly more detailed account of the inclusion of the concept of GAIRS in UNCLOS, see Bernard H. Oxman, 'The Duty to Respect Generally Accepted International Standards' (1991) 24 NYU J Int'l L & Pol 109, 155–56.

742 Franckx (n 741) 110. See Oxman (n 741) 146; Barnes, 'Article 21' (n 200) para 22. Molenaar, *Coastal State Jurisdiction over Vessel-Source Pollution* (n 716) 152, 156, 157 (who also concludes that '[c]onsequently, the level of acceptance for GAIRAS must be somewhat lower than that for customary international law' (there at 157)). For an extensive discussion on the relationship between *International Rules and Standards* and customary law, see there at 143ff. The latter also notably points out that while GAIRS do not have customary law status, the rules of reference (of UNCLOS) in which they are incorporated seem to, there at 181.

743 Molenaar, *Coastal State Jurisdiction over Vessel-Source Pollution* (n 716) 153–55. For an overview of interpretations to be found in scholarly works, see Franckx (n 741) 108–09.

well be by means of a non-binding document, [...] a resolution of an international organization [...].[744]

Thus, based on the notion that the mention of GAIRS must have an added value and evades traditional legal categories, it seems most reasonable to translate GAIRS to equal 'a significantly widespread acceptance of the rules or standards – by whatever form of international consent'[745].

The notion that acceptance of the rule or standard in question must be *significantly widespread* is similar, if not congruent, with the notion that 'the required level of acceptance is determined by quantitative and qualitative criterion, the latter of which takes the relative importance of states into account.'[746] More concretely, and lending from the ICJ's *North Sea Continental Shelf Cases* where the court discussed the emergence of a customary international law, it is argued that an international rule or standard qualifies as *generally accepted*, where it has generated 'very widespread and representative participation [...] included that of States whose interests were specially affected'[747].[748] It is clarified, however, that the use of this

744 Franckx (n 741) 111–12; see also at 107, where the concise conclusion is that GAIRS 'are primarily based on state practice, attaching only secondary importance to the nature and status of the instrument containing the respective rule or standard.'

745 Bartenstein (n 195) para 35, where this is presented as part of an overview of interpretations and based on the elaborations of Gregorios J. Timagenis, *International Control of Marine Pollution: Volume 2* (Oceana Publications 1980), 606 (who uses the term 'wider acceptance') and Tan (n 16) 196–97, who finds it relevant whether 'it can be established that a specific rule or standard enjoys sufficiently general state practice in a particular field of regulation'. It is important here to keep in mind that making these GAIRS binding on those States that have not accepted them otherwise, but are party to UNCLOS, does not violate the pacta tertiis principle of Art 34 VCLT. Those States have agreed to be bound by these GAIRS in the context of and through UNCLOS by virtue of their declaration of consent to be bound by UNCLOS provisions. See Molenaar, *Coastal State Jurisdiction over Vessel-Source Pollution* (n 716) 157 (with further references), who nonetheless attaches importance to the level of acceptance since a 'lower level of acceptance renders it more likely that a flag State Party to the LOSC will be bound by a larger body of norms which it has otherwise not consented to.'

746 Molenaar, *Coastal State Jurisdiction over Vessel-Source Pollution* (n 716) 152, who identifies this to be the common feature of the different views he outlines. The ILA seems to mean the same, when it speaks of 'quantitative as well as functional majorities', Franckx (n 741) 112–13.

747 ICJ, *North Sea Continental Shelf Cases (Federal Republic of Germany v Denmark; Federal Republic of Germany v Netherlands)* <https://www.icj-cij.org/sites/default/files/case-related/51/051-19690220-JUD-01-00-EN.pdf> accessed 7 June 2023, para 73.

748 Oxman (n 741) 157; see also Molenaar, *Coastal State Jurisdiction over Vessel-Source Pollution* (n 716) 156–57.

standard does not equal GAIRS with customary international law. Rather, to uphold the notion of GAIRS being distinct from customary international law, the 'level of acceptance' required must be lower than that for customary international law.[749] In line with these considerations, it seems safe to assert that the MARPOL treaty itself contains GAIRS.[750] Consequently, the North Sea SECA established in MARPOL Annex VI would have to be regarded as a GAIRS—strictly speaking, however, so would the 12-month grace period of Reg 14.7 MARPOL Annex VI during which the EU North Sea SECA became effective.

Following the analysis above though, it would appear too formalistic and an oversimplification of the concept of GAIRS to deny the EU the authority of Art 211 (5) UNCLOS to regulate within its territory a North Sea SECA as it did: a North Sea SECA that was geographically identical with the North Sea SECA fully and formally adopted, codified in MARPOL Annex VI and with its official applicability imminent within a little more than three-month's reach. This assertion also aligns with the notion that discussions on the interpretation of GAIRS are rather theoretical in nature and State practice indicates a rather 'liberal practice'.[751]

In conclusion, there is a very good case to argue that pre-empting the coming into effect of the MARPOL Annex VI North Sea SECA by means of Directive 2005/33/EC could be based on the EU's right as a coastal State to regulate within its EEZ in line with Art 211 (5) UNCLOS. Considering the difficulties in determining what GAIRS means and the favourable position of the EU in this constellation, it seems rather unfortunate that there is no indication to be found that the applicability of Art 211 (5) UNCLOS or UNCLOS in general were ever investigated at any stage in the legislative process. Clear communication on this matter would have confirmed the EU's commitment as a party to UNCLOS and would have attested to a prudent approach of EU legislative action where it potentially could come into conflict with existing international law.

---

749 Molenaar, *Coastal State Jurisdiction over Vessel-Source Pollution* (n 716) 157.

750 Boyle and Redgwell (n 56) 525; see Franckx (n 741) 112–13; see also Ringbom, *The EU Maritime Safety Policy and International Law* (n 20) 435 (implying that for MARPOL Annex VI).

751 Bartenstein (n 195) para 38.

2. The Relationship between the Sulphur Directive and MARPOL

The previous section discussed the compatibility of three of the Sulphur Directive's specific measures with UNCLOS. All three measures are or were a deviation from existing MARPOL standards and in one way or the other exceeding them. At first sight, the EU (as Party to UNCLOS but not to MARPOL) does not have to worry about its legislation being in line with MARPOL standards—unless, as seen above, they have found their way into UNCLOS through reference. This is different for its MSs that may find themselves in the position to have to nationally transpose or implement EU legislation that will bring them into conflict with their obligations under MARPOL. With almost all EU MSs being Party to MARPOL Annex VI,[752] there is a real possibility that EU legislation which exceeds MARPOL standards results in conflicting treaty obligations. Therefore, this section explores the relationship between the Sulphur Directive and MARPOL and their potential conflict of norms, as well as the ECJ's stance on it. To this end, this section first explores whether MARPOL Parties can even legally adopt stricter measures than those they agreed to in MARPOL, ie exceed the standards laid down therein (a.). Secondly, it looks at how the ECJ views the relationship between MARPOL rules and EU legislation (b.). This paves the way for the last section of this chapter (V.) that explores Art 351 TFEU as a norm that addresses treaty conflicts of MSs.

a. The Right of MARPOL Parties to Adopt More Stringent Measures

To assume a conflict of norms of the Sulphur Directive with MARPOL, it first has to be established whether MARPOL actually bars its State Parties from adopting more stringent measures—in the case of the EU MSs through transposition of the Sulphur Directive into national law. A conflict between MSs' treaty obligations can only occur if MARPOL norms are to be regarded as exclusive, either in the selection of their measures or as to the scope of their measures. This has often been discussed in the context of Directive 2005/35/EC[753] that introduced penalties for infringements of

752 At time of writing in 2023 only two EU MSs—Austria and Hungary—are not Party to MARPOL Annex VI.

753 Directive 2005/35/EC of the European Parliament and of the Council of 7 September 2005 on ship-source pollution and on the introduction of penalties for infringements [2005] OJ L 255/11.

some ship-source pollution provisions (often and hereafter referred to as the Sanctions Directive). Therefore, a number of the sources consulted for and cited in this section, discuss this question in the context of Directive 2005/35/EC and its compatibility with MARPOL. The latter, generally speaking deviated from MARPOL's system of criminal liability and with that prompted quite some controversy. The arguments on the central question of whether MARPOL allows for stricter measures are, however, equally valid here.

While MARPOL is the main treaty on ship-source pollution, it is hard to imagine that State Parties to it intend(ed) to waive their rights to adopt further measures otherwise compatible with UNCLOS. While the historical course of negotiations is rather uninstructive[754], Art 9 (2) MARPOL reads: 'Nothing in the present Convention shall prejudice [...] the present or future claims and legal views of any State concerning the law of the sea and the nature and extent of coastal and flag State jurisdiction.' On the one hand, it may be desirable to have uniform international law governing ship-source pollution to avoid fragmentation and potentially resulting conflicts of norms. It, nonetheless, would be a long stretch to argue that the preamble to MARPOL, which speaks of the 'complete elimination of intentional pollution' and its rules having 'universal purport', implies its provisions to be exhaustive. In fact, there is no convincing argument that MARPOL is an expression or exercise of UNCLOS in the sense of a (quasi-) lex specialis that would bar Parties to MARPOL from invoking other rights granted to them by UNCLOS with regard to ship-source pollution. Rather, the reference norms (such as the reference to GAIRS discussed above) are UNCLOS' in-built safeguards to avoid unfettered national regulation. Consequently, where MARPOL does not regulate a specific matter, there is a 'regulatory gap' that allows coastal States to fill the gap through national or, in this case, EU legislation.[755] One such instance is the Sulphur Directive's provision on passenger ships in regular service discussed above. It is, consequently, compatible with UNCLOS as far as it pertains to traffic within EU territory (as seen above, D.IV.1.b.) and MARPOL.

A different situation occurs where MARPOL has a measure in place and the State Party decides to apply this measure in a more stringent way,

754 See König, 'The EU Directive on Ship-Source Pollution and on the Introduction of Penalties for Infringements' (n 714) 777–78, whose conclusions, however, as to what constitutes such a 'regulatory gap' in consequence differ from the conclusions below.

755 ibid 782.

thereby altering its scope. A more stringent approach could—in the present context—be eg the application of a stricter sulphur limit or the early, ie pre-empted, application of a measure (as in the case of the North Sea SECA) In this case, MARPOL is not silent on the matter and there seems to be no *regulatory gap* to be filled.[756] Rather, the measure in question regulated by MARPOL could be seen to represent the outcome of negotiations among the relevant IMO States, ie Parties to MARPOL—it is the common ground negotiators eventually found, subject to the fundamental notion of pacta sunt servanda that implies a good faith execution of treaty obligations (Art 26 VCLT). In that, '[t]he principle of good faith obliges the Parties to apply [the treaty] in a reasonable way and in such a manner that its purpose can be realized.'[757] One purpose of MARPOL, inherent to it as a global treaty, is to provide a concerted approach of States to tackle pollution from international shipping, which—on the other hand, even if reflexively—benefits from a uniform approach opposed to fragmented regulation.[758] Therefore, introducing a different, preferred outcome of negotiations through the national backdoor could fairly be seen as an act of bad faith. After all, parties to MARPOL have also agreed to its amendment procedure (Art 16 MARPOL) that does not require a unanimous vote, and also retain their freedom to not commit themselves to MARPOL or its Optional Annexes or to remove themselves from those (Art 18 MARPOL and Art VII of the 1978 Protocol). This could be one way to look at it. However, this is not the view generally taken.[759] The following sections nonetheless assume, for the sake of argumentation, that there is a way in

---

756 Arguing eg that the designation of the North Sea SECA to become effective on a specific later date leaves a regulatory gap as to it being adopted earlier, would be stretching the rules of logic and legal argumentation.

757 ICJ, *Case concerning the Gabčíkovo-Nagymaros Project (Hungary v Slovakia)* <https://www.icj-cij.org/sites/default/files/case-related/92/092-19970925-JUD-01-00-EN.pdf> accessed 7 June 2023, para 142.

758 The EP's Committee commenting on the Draft Sanctions Directive pointed out that the derogations from the MARPOL rules 'are undesirable in terms of content but also contribute to a proliferation of divergent global, European and national rules', calling it a 'mistaken approach', EP, Committee on Regional Policy, Transport and Tourism 'Report on the proposal for a European Parliament and Council directive on ship-source pollution and on the introduction of sanctions, including criminal sanctions, for pollution offences (5 November 2003) A5-0388/2003, 18.

759 König, The EU Directive on Ship-Source Pollution and on the Introduction of Penalties for Infringements' (n 714) 785–86, assumes a regulatory gap is also being filled where the scope of an existing treaty regulation is rendered more stringent. This is a controversial stance, as is the debate surrounding the Sanction Directive's liability standards and their deviation from MARPOL standards. See Ringbom, *The*

which MSs' obligations from MARPOL could come into conflict with EU legislation. It allows insight into how the ECJ has been navigating this question (b.) and how the TFEU caters for the possibility of MSs' treaty conflicts (V.). It thereby helps create a broader, more complete picture of the questions discussed in this chapter and this analysis as a whole.

b. The Relationship between EU Law and MARPOL according to the ECJ

Assuming that Parties to MARPOL could fall short of their treaty obligations, where they adopt stricter standards for a specific measure that has already been regulated by MARPOL, this would effectively mean that adoption of EU legislation that deviates from MARPOL standards in such a way would create conflicting treaty obligations for MSs. This is, unless EU legislation would (have to) take into account internationally agreed rules such as those contained in MARPOL, regardless of whether the EU is actually a party to that treaty. This, on the other hand, depends on whether the EU can be viewed—most importantly views itself—and its legislative actions in the light of the international legal order it is a part of.

EU Maritime Safety Policy and International Law (n 20) 415–16, who takes a simple and indiscriminate approach: 'Marpol does not affect the right of its parties to exercise jurisdiction to the extent they have such jurisdiction under UNCLOS', but takes a more differentiated view on early implementation of already agreed rules and standards: 'to the extent the early regional implementation of the rules only reiterates what has been agreed at a global level, the measures may still be argued to be in line with the global rules and 'in the spirit of' the international community [...]. Presumably, the degree to which such early implementation will be controversial will also depend on the extra-legal factors, such as the likelihood and proximity of international entry into force', there at 245. See similarly Michael Höltmann, *Schiffssicherheit und Meeresumweltschutz in der EU nach Erika und Prestige* (Nomos 2012) 182, who declares all MARPOL Annex VI standards to constitute mere minimum standards for coastal states allowing EU MSs to adopt more stringent sulphur limits. Proelss, 'The "Erika III" Package: Progress or Breach of International Law?' (n 74) 143, asserts that it cannot be 'generally said' that MARPOL lays down 'more than mere minimum standards'. See also ECJ, Case 537/11 *Mattia Manzi and Compagnia Naviera Orchestra v Capitaneria di Porto di Genova* ECLI:EU:C:2014:19, para 53, where the court asserts with regard to Art 4a (4) Directive 1999/32/EC that 'in the light of the objective pursued by that annex and set out in the title thereof, namely to protect the atmosphere by a reduction in harmful emissions produced by marine transport, that provision, in so far as it fixes a maximum limit on the sulphur content of marine fuel lower than that provided for by that annex, does not appear to be incompatible with such an objective.'

aa. The ECJ Decisions *Intertanko*, *Manzi* and *Bosphorus Queen*

The ECJ's often-cited decision on this problem is its 2008 judgment in the *Intertanko* case[760], the findings of which serve as a starting point here. The claimants in the *Intertanko* case, referred to the ECJ for a preliminary ruling by a British Court, challenged the EU's Sanctions Directive. This section discusses the ECJ's ruling with regard to the specific question of whether it was permissible for the EU to regulate criminal responsibility for ship-source pollution in the Sanctions Directive more stringently compared to the existent MARPOL standards. In essence, the Court had to clarify the relationship between EU legislation and MARPOL as a treaty it is not a party to. The conclusion of the Court on this question was rather simple and sober: since the EU is not a party to MARPOL it is not bound by it, unless MARPOL rules can be considered customary international law, in which case the Court would have to take them into account when interpreting the provisions of the Sanctions Directive. At second glance, there is a little more to the Court's argumentation, even though it does not get much more intricate.

The very basic notion the Court departs from is that the EU cannot be bound by a treaty it has not agreed to. For that, it refers to Art 300 (7) of the Treaty establishing the European Community (TEC)[761] (the equivalent now being Art 216 (2) TFEU) that provided that treaties concluded between the EC and on or more States or international organisations are 'binding on the institutions of the Community and on Member States'.[762] Furthermore, the Court held:

> It is true that all the Member States of the Community are parties to Marpol 73/78. Nevertheless, in the absence of a full transfer of the pow-

760 Case C-308/06 *The Queen, on the application of International Association of Independent Tanker Owners (Intertanko)and Others v Secretary of State for Transport* ECLI:EU:C:2008:312.

761 The consolidated version of the TEC is published as part of the 'Consolidated Versions of the Treaty on European Union and of the Treaty Establishing the European Community (2002)' [2002] OJ C325/1, 33.

762 See *Intertanko* (n 760) para 47. The AG (n 733) in her opinion simply refers to the principle expressed in *Netherlands v Parliament and Council*, namely, that 'as a rule, the lawfulness of a Community instrument does not depend on its conformity with an international agreement to which the Community is not a party' (Case C-377/98 *Kingdom of the Netherlands v European Parliament and Council of the European Union* ECLI:EU:C:2001:523, para 52); see *Intertanko*, Opinion of AG (n 733) para 38.

> ers previously exercised by the Member States to the Community, the latter cannot, simply because all those States are parties to Marpol 73/78, be bound by the rules set out therein, which it has not itself approved.
> Since the Community is not bound by Marpol 73/78, the mere fact that Directive 2005/35 has the objective of incorporating certain rules set out in that Convention into Community law is likewise not sufficient for it to be incumbent upon the Court to review the directive's legality in the light of the Convention.[763]

In this, the Court relies on the idea that the Community may have 'assumed [...] the powers previously exercised by the Member States in the field to which that convention applies' expressed in the *Peralta* case[764] that rejects a binding effect of MARPOL on the EU.[765] In *Peralta*, on the other hand, the Court borrows its argumentation from its *International Fruit Company* case that affirms a binding effect of GATT based on the same rationale[766].

The Court in a further step, however, does profess to be bound by treaty rules 'in so far as they codify customary rules of general international law' which it denies for the specific MARPOL provisions of Annex I and II in question.[767] The Court, therefore, concludes:

> In those circumstances, it is clear that the validity of Directive 2005/35 cannot be assessed in the light of Marpol 73/78, even though it binds the Member States. The latter fact is, however, liable to have consequences for the interpretation of, first, UNCLOS and, second, the provisions of secondary law which fall within the field of application of Marpol 73/78. In view of the customary principle of good faith, which forms part of general international law, and of Article 10 EC, it is incumbent upon the Court to interpret those provisions taking account of Marpol 73/78.[768]

Unfortunately, the Court's deliberations stop here, providing no further insight as to how interpretation of secondary EC law *taking into account*

763 *Intertanko* (n 760) paras 49–50.
764 ECJ, Case 379/92 *Criminal proceedings against Matteo Peralta* ECLI:EU:C:1994:296.
765 ibid para 16; see to the same effect also *Intertanko*, Opinion of AG (n 733) para 45.
766 ECJ, Joined Cases 21/72 to 24/72 *International Fruit Company and Others v Produktschap voor Groenten en Fruit* ECLI:EU:C:1972:115, para 18.
767 *Intertanko* (n 760) para 51, with further references to case law.
768 ibid para 52. Art 10 TEC is the predecessor norm to Art 4 (3) subparas 2–3 Treaty on European Union (TEU). The consolidated version of the Treaty on European Union is published as part of the 'Consolidated Versions of the Treaty on European Union and of the Treaty Establishing the European Community (2002)' (n 761) 5.

MARPOL provisions its MSs are bound to could look like. The AG on the *Intertanko* case seems to be taking an attempt at a similar idea:

> [P]rovisions of secondary Community law must, so far as possible, be interpreted in a manner that is consistent with the international agreements concluded by the Community. Under Article 300 (7) EC, those agreements are binding on the institutions. Secondary law may not infringe them. They have primacy over secondary law.
> Accordingly, interpretation in conformity with international law must be given priority over other methods of interpretation. This requirement is limited only by rules and principles which take precedence over the Community's obligations under international law. Such rules and principles include, for example, general legal principles and in particular the principle of legal certainty. Therefore, an interpretation contra legem is not possible.[769]

Based on this assumption, the AG continues to argue that one of the contentious phrases of the Sanctions Directive (the 'serious negligence' standard) '[i]n this sense [...] can be interpreted restrictively as not going beyond Marpol 73/78.'[770] In this, however, the AG seems to have missed the essence of the case, namely that MARPOL is precisely not an agreement concluded by the Community.[771]

The Court further develops the notion that EU legislation would have to be interpreted in the light of MARPOL provisions in its 2014 preliminary ruling on the *Manzi* case[772]. In this, the Court rules on the compatibility of the sulphur limits imposed on ships in EU ports and on passenger ship operating on regular services provided by Sulphur Directive 2005/33/EC

769 *Intertanko*, Opinion of AG (n 733) para 107–08.

770 ibid para 109.

771 This confusion is even more surprising, since the AG previous to that clearly states along the lines of the subsequent deliberations of the Court that 'the lawfulness of a Community instrument cannot depend on its conformity with an international agreement to which the Community is not a party', while pointing to the exception in case of customary international law which, the AG establishes, MARPOL is not (*Intertanko*, Opinion of AG (n 733) paras 38–39). The AG takes this assumption even one small step further: '[T]here is no discernible legal basis for examining secondary law on the basis of international-law obligations of the Member States which the Community has not itself assumed. Rather, such an examination would run counter to the finding made in the judgment in *Netherlands v Parliament and Council* that the Community is not bound by the Member States' obligations under international law.'

772 n 759.

(see D.IV.1.b.) with MARPOL Annex VI. The submitting Italian court's request contained just the right question, namely, whether those sulphur limits are

> invalid on the basis that it is contrary to the general principle of international law *pacta sunt servanda* and to the principle of cooperation in good faith as between the Community and its Member States, in that it requires Member States which have agreed to and ratified Annex VI to act in breach of the obligations entered into towards the other States which are party to (Annex VI)?[773]

The circumstances in *Manzi* are, therefore, different in one important point. In *Intertanko* the court had to rule on the compatibility of EU provisions with MARPOL Regulations of the non-Optional Annexes I and II to which all EU MSs were a party at that time[774]. The *Manzi* case brought up the question of compatibility of Sulphur Directive provisions with MARPOL Annex VI to which—even at time of writing in 2023—not all EU MSs are party to[775]. This prompted the Court to further elaborate and restrict the *Intertanko* premise.

The Court first echoes the test of *Intertanko* in stressing that the EU is not bound by MARPOL and that MARPOL Annex VI does not represent customary international law.[776] The Court then finds that the principle that the validity of the Sulphur Directive cannot be tested against MARPOL Annex VI cannot be circumvented through recourse to the principle of sincere cooperation of Art 4 (3) subpara 1 TEU.[777] It thereby manifests the rationale in *Intertanko* and refuses to open a backdoor through which to challenge the validity of the Sulphur Directive, even where a breach of the principle of sincere cooperation is invoked. Subsequently, the Court partly rejects the premise of *Intertanko*, that EU legislation would have to be interpreted taking account of MARPOL with regard to its Annex VI; the Court finds it not to be applicable to international agreements to which only some, not all, MSs are a party to:

> To interpret the provisions of secondary law in the light of an obligation imposed by an international agreement which does not bind all the

773 *Manzi* (n 759) para 16.
774 See IMO, 'Status of IMO Treaties' (n 44) 120ff.
775 In addition to Austria and Hungary, the Czech Republic was not party to Annex VI at time of judgment.
776 *Manzi* (n 759) paras 37–39.
777 ibid 40–41.

> Member States would amount to extending the scope of that obligation to those Member States which are not contracting parties to such an agreement. The latter Member States must however be regarded as 'third countries' for the purposes of that agreement. Such an extension would be incompatible with the general international law principle of the relative effect of treaties, according to which treaties must neither harm nor benefit third countries ('pacta tertiis nec nocent nec prosunt').
> It is clear from the case-law of the Court that the latter is required to observe that principle since it constitutes a customary rule of international law which, as such, is binding upon the European Union institutions and forms part of its legal order [...].[778]

This principle—while not challenged or weakened—is put into perspective in the ECJ's 2018 judgment on *Bosphorus Queen*[779]. There, a Finnish court submitted questions on the interpretation of the Sanctions Directive with regard to definitions of the relevant terminology provided for in UNCLOS and the International Convention Relating to Intervention on the High Seas 1969[780]. The ECJ briefly repeats the rule of interpretation from *Intertanko* adding a reference to the principle of sincere cooperation to its reasoning.[781] Leaving MARPOL aside, the Court then asserts that while neither the EU nor all MSs are party to it[782], the 1969 High Seas Convention must be taken into account to interpret UNLCOS 'since the latter convention is part of the relevant rules for the interpretation' of UNCLOS.[783] It may be considered of relevance that the Court initially mentions that Finland (the punitive mea-

778 ibid paras 47–48. The obiter dictum of the ECJ in this case already referred to at n 759 is also noteworthy here. It holds that even if the Sulphur Directive in question were to be interpreted taking account of MARPOL, 'in the light of the objective pursued by that annex and set out in the title thereof, [...] that provision, in so far as it fixes a maximum limit on the sulphur content of marine fuel lower than that provided for by that annex, does not appear to be incompatible with such an objective.'

779 ECJ, Case 15/17 *Bosphorus Queen Shipping Ltd Corp. v Rajavartiolaitos* ECLI:EU:C:2018:557.

780 The International Convention Relating to Intervention on the High Seas in Cases of Oil Pollution Casualties (adopted 29 November 1969, entered into force 6 May 1975) 970 UNTS 211.

781 'In view of the customary principle of good faith, which forms part of general international law, and of Article 4(3) TEU, the Court is to interpret the provisions by taking account of the Marpol Convention 73/78', *Bosphorus Queen* (n 779) para 45.

782 At time of writing in 2023, 17 of 27 MSs were party to the International Convention Relating to Intervention on the High Seas 1969.

783 *Bosphorus Queen* (n 779) para 47.

sures of which were challenged) and Panama (where the vessel in question was registered) are both party to the 1969 High Seas Convention.[784] While the Court's main elaborations are on the interpretation of the Sanctions Directive in the light of this treaty and UNCLOS, it does offer a glimpse on how interpretation of secondary EU law in the light of MARPOL could look like, in that interpretations are aligned to make for a coherent legal argumentation. This last aspect is emphasised and illustrated by the AG who first refers to *Manzi* and 'the Court's interpretative jurisdiction [that] extends only to rules that form part of the EU legal order'[785], to then conclude:

> While that might have been, in practice, the outcome in the circumstances underlying Manzi, the Court's statement cannot in my view be taken to mean that the Court may not take into consideration, in interpreting provisions of EU law, rules of international law that do not bind the European Union, or all of its Member States.
> As is commonly accepted, judicial interpretation does not take place in a vacuum. While it is clear that the Court lacks jurisdiction to interpret authoritatively rules that do not form part of the EU legal order, I find it difficult to accept that lessons could not — where relevant — be drawn from such rules for the purposes of interpreting provisions of EU law. That is so, in particular, where the legislative history of an international agreement that binds the European Union, or its Member States, suggests a close nexus to an agreement that does not.
> Put differently, it does not follow from the clear lack of jurisdiction to interpret the Intervention Convention that inspiration could not be drawn from that convention in interpreting similar notions that can be found in UNCLOS. In other words, it is not impossible that the Court may interpret UNCLOS in a manner that coincides with the terminology employed in the Intervention Convention (Relating to Intervention on the High Seas).[786]

These assertions differ slightly from the Court's argumentation that solely relied on the 1969 High Seas Convention playing directly into UNCLOS itself. The AG, therefore, offers a clearer perspective on how eg MARPOL

784 ibid para 3.

785 ECJ, Case 15/17 *Bosphorus Queen Shipping Ltd Corp. v* Rajavartiolaitos, Opinion of the AG Wahl ECLI:EU:C:2018:123, paras 45–46.

786 ibid paras 47–49. It is this argumentation that fits the conclusion of *Intertanko*, Opinion of AG (n 733) para 109.

Annex VI could affect the interpretation of the Sulphur Directive. It has to be acknowledged though that the Court decided not to reiterate or build on the more extensive argumentation of the AG.

Ultimately, the main takeaways of the judgments discussed above are that in the ECJ's view the legality of secondary EU law cannot be tested against MARPOL provisions as long as those rules do not represent customary international law (which it does not deem to be the case for Annex I, II or VI provisions). However, good-faith interpretation of secondary EU law requires that MARPOL provisions be taken into account where all Member States have committed to those provisions (which does not hold true for MARPOL's Annex VI). Nonetheless, and despite the exercise of the Court in *Bosphorus Queen,* the question remains how exactly interpretation of EU legislation taking into account MARPOL provisions would look like—other than, of course, that basic rules of legal interpretation have to be respected in the course of it. More importantly, while this rule of interpretation appears to be a small concession to the MSs, the Court does not provide remedy for the dilemma articulated by the AG in *Intertanko* that 'the Community can in principle require the Member States to take measures which run counter to their obligations under international law.'[787] While this assertion is further discussed in the next section (V.), it is worth taking a closer look at the *Intertanko* decision and its implications first.

bb. *Intertanko*—A Missed Opportunity

It is difficult to argue against the legal reasoning of the ECJ in the decisions discussed above as there is no inherent fallacy in the legal argumentation. Yet, the approach of the ECJ leaves the aftertaste of an argumentation left incomplete, the feeling that the matter at hand has not been seen through. It is no surprise then that some discussion emerged in the aftermath of the *Intertanko* decision. Apart from the unsolved deadlock of MSs' conflicting treaty obligations, an EU institution missed yet another chance to test the legality of EU legislation against UNCLOS. Despite the clear request of the national court to assess two provisions of the Sanctions Directive as to their

787 *Intertanko*, Opinion of AG (n 733) para 77.

compatibility with the right of innocent passage,[788] the ECJ managed to avoid that exercise. It found that

> UNCLOS does not establish rules intended to apply directly or immediately to individuals and to confer upon them rights or freedoms capable of being relied upon against States [...] It follows that the nature and broad logic of UNCLOS prevent the Court from being able to assess the validity of a Community measure in the light of that Convention.[789]

It, thereby, essentially denies the claimants legal standing. Two of the claimants were INTERTANKO and INTERCARGO—that is, two major associations representing independent tanker owners and dry cargo shipowners, respectively, whose members are directly affected by the Sanctions Directive. The Court's legal assessment on the direct applicability of UNCLOS norms cannot be dismissed outright.[790] However, it leaves the impression that the ECJ escaped a thorough and satisfying analysis through the backdoor by conveniently replacing the national court's deliberations of what clarifications are relevant to reach a decision with its own.[791]

---

788 *Intertanko* (n 760) para 29. The claimant's assertion of a breach of UNCLOS was supported by the Greek, Cypriot and Maltese governments as MSs with a maritime interest, there at para 37.

789 *Intertanko* (n 760) paras 64–65.

790 Agreeing with the court's finding, Eileen Denza, 'A note on Intertanko' (2008) 33 E L Rev 33, 870, 875. Proelss, 'The "Erika III" Package: Progress or Breach of International Law?' (n 74) 139, points out that 'it can in fact be assumed that many UNCLOS norms are self-executing—at least to the extent that they indirectly reference MARPOL by using the term "generally accepted international rules and standards"'. It is also asserted that 'a lack of direct effect in a particular instance does not relieve European courts from the obligation of taking into account the external rule that is being invoked', Jan Willem van Rossem, 'Interaction between EU Law and International Law in the Light of *Intertanko* and *Kadi*: The Dilemma of Norms Binding the Member States but not the Community' (2009) NYIL 183, 196.

791 According to (then applicable) Art 234 (2) TEC (now Art 267 (2) TFEU) a MS court can request a preliminary ruling on the validity of acts of the institutions 'if it considers that a decision on the question is necessary to enable it to give judgment'. In line with the express wording, therefore, '[i]t is for the national court to decide whether the questions of interpretation or validity raised by the case are relevant', Markus Kotzur, 'Article 267 TFEU [Preliminary rulings]' in Rudolf Geiger, Daniel-Erasmus Khan, Markus Kotzur (eds), *European Union Treaties* (CH BECK Hart 2015), para 15—referring to ECJ, Case C-348/89 *Mecanarte - Mealúrgica da Lagoa Ld v Chefe do Serviço da Conferência Final da Alfândega do Porto* ECLI: EU:C:1991:278, that granted MSs' national courts 'the widest possible powers to refer questions to the Court of Justice if they consider that a case pending before them raises issues requiring an interpretation or an appraisal of the validity of

Thus, the ECJ has been scolded for reviving an abandoned 'judicial avoidance technique' 'of calling for rejection of a relevant treaty as a review criterion for Community action' to avoid the likely undesired outcome of having to find EU legislation in violation of that treaty, in this case UNCLOS.[792]

> The thin reasoning advanced in *Intertanko* therefore constitutes a thoroughly unsatisfactory basis for not engaging with the specific UNCLOS provisions at issue. Given its own recent case law, it is unconvincing for the ECJ to invoke formalistic reasoning which seeks to paint a picture of an inter-state treaty which is not concerned with the protection of individual rights.[793]

In fact, in its *Poulsen and Diva Navigation* case, the ECJ has relied on UNCLOS, even before its entry into force as an expression of customary law, to determine the applicability of a Regulation on fishing to a specific vessel and its crew.[794] The AG's opinion on *Intertanko* explicitly refers to this judgment and reinforces the notion that individuals can rely on UNCLOS norms, asserting that 'the claimants correctly pointed out that it would be completely incomprehensible if they were to be deprived of this opportunity after the Convention on the Law of the Sea had entered into force.'[795] It also puts the notion of direct applicability of norms into perspective:

> Whether or not the provisions in question are directly applicable and – correlatively – whether they confer rights on individuals is not conclusive for the purpose of responding to the request for a preliminary ruling. Even the legal bases of the Treaties are in principle not directly applicable in the sense that individuals can derive from them rights or legal

provisions of Community law whose determination is necessary for the resolution of the dispute brought before them' (there at para 44). For reflections on the relationship between the Preliminary ruling procedure of Art 267 and the legal protection awarded to individuals by Art 263 (4) TFEU in this context, see Proelss, 'The "Erika III" Package: Progress or Breach of International Law?' (n 74) 138–40.

792 Mendez (n 790) 100, 103.

793 ibid 102. Similarly, Proelss, 'The "Erika III" Package: Progress or Breach of International Law?' (n 74) 141 and 145, stressing that 'in *Intertanko* the ECJ unjustifiably evaded making a decision on the matter' and criticising the 'far too formalistic tone of the entire judgment'.

794 ECJ, Case C-286/90 *Anklagemyndigheden v Peter Michael Poulsen and Diva Navigation Corp.* ECLI:EU:C:1992:453, paras 10, 13, 15, 25.

795 *Intertanko*, Opinion of AG (n 733) para 50.

consequences to their benefit. Nevertheless, individuals may question the legality of rules of secondary law by contesting the legal basis thereof.[796]

The reluctance of the ECJ to take a stance on the compatibility of EU law with UNCLOS is yet another missed opportunity by an EU institution to demonstrate its awareness of possible conflicts of secondary law and UNCLOS. From a more elevated perspective, it is argued that 'the Court's habitual insistence on the autonomous nature of the Community legal order [...] entails that the legality of EU measures can only be judged against its own legal framework.'[797]

It is debatable whether '[i]t is [...] entirely proper for the Community to take advantage of its superiority in adopting, applying and enforcing legislation to tighten the application within the Union of international conventions to which all or even some of the Member States are parties.'[798] It is clear though that exercising its powers in this way comes at a cost. It is argued that where the EU 'seems to use its autonomy to fence itself off from the international legal order [...] [t]his gnaws at the legitimacy of EU law.'[799] Where the EU derogates from other treaty law, however, this must also have consequences for the legitimacy and credibility of its MSs. This, therefore, begs the question whether the EU has a responsibility to protect its MSs from such conflicting treaty obligations—in this specific case conflicts arising from MSs' obligations under EU treaty law, on one hand, and its MARPOL obligations, on the other hand.

V. EU Member States' Conflicting Treaty Obligations and Art 351 (1) TFEU

The case-law of the ECJ demonstrates the Court's reluctance to test EU legislation against MARPOL norms. The very practical consequence at

796 ibid para 66.

797 van Rossem (n 790) 185. On how the notion of an independent EU legal order came into being and the ECJ's judgments that paved the way, see there at 192–97. See also Proelss, 'The "Erika III" Package: Progress or Breach of International Law?' (n 74) 141, who asserts that 'the judgment is arguably based on an exaggerated and one-sided understanding of the autonomy of the EU legal order.'

798 Denza (n 790) 878.

799 van Rossem (n 790) 212; or to put it mildly: 'the Court's autonomy conception sits uncomfortably within the broader international legal configuration', there at 185. The same author also offers an argumentative pathway for the ECJ to exercise such a judicial review based on its decision *Netherlands v Parliament and Council* (n 762), there at 217.

this point is, therefore, that there is no possibility for MSs to challenge EU legislation and obtain legal remedy where EU legislation places them in conflict with their MARPOL obligations—as not all conflict in norms can be solved by means of interpretation. This is even the case, where all MSs are party to a MARPOL Annex before the coming into being of the legal act containing the conflicting norms. Legal remedy should only be available, though, where there is an actual right that needs to be defended. Therefore, taking the discussion on the ECJ's decisions one step further, one could ask whether and to what extent Art 351 TFEU protects MSs from the consequences of conflicting treaty obligations and whether the Court should have addressed this possibility in its decisions discussed above.

Art 351 (1) TFEU provides that MSs' rights and obligations[800] from agreements with third countries and committed to before 1 January 1958 or before the MS's date of accession shall remain unaffected by the Treaties' provisions.[801] It is asserted that this provision is also applicable by analogy to instances where MSs have become party to a treaty before the EU has assumed legislative competence in that area of shared competence[802].[803] This is a viable claim in so far as Art 351 (1) TFEU is, without the possibility of further interpretation, limited to prior agreements; thereby a normative gap exists for the comparable situation that a MS commits to a treaty

800 It is noteworthy that obligations from agreements can only arise for MSs from treaties in force and to which they are Party, 'whereas no rights and obligations arise from agreements merely signed', Manzini (n 811) 786.

801 van Rossem (n 790) 198 notes that '[t]he clause reflects the international law principle of *res inter alios acta*, meaning that a treaty cannot adversely affect the rights of one that is not a party.' See also Höltmann (n 759) 59; and Proelss, 'The "Erika III" Package: Progress or Breach of International Law?' (n 74) 143, who more specifically views Art 351 (1) TFEU to be an expression of the principle of pacta sunt servanda.

802 Both, the area of Environment and Transport are areas of shared competence (Art 4 (2) (e) and (g) TFEU, respectively). While the Sulphur Directive was adopted as a measure in the area of environment (Title XX TFEU), the Sanctions Directive was adopted as a measure in the area of Transport (Title VI TFEU).

803 Proelss, 'The "Erika III" Package: Progress or Breach of International Law?' (n 74) 141, who points to this 'majority view' with further references; Höltmann (n 759) 59, considers this to be generally accepted; Robin R Churchill and Nigel G Foster, 'European Community Law and Prior Treaty Obligations of Member States: The Spanish Fishermen's Cases' (1987) 36 ICLQ 504, 520, 523 (discussing ex Art 234 TEC). Rudolf Geiger, 'Article 351 TFEU [Former Agreements of Member States]' in Geiger, Khan, Kotzur (n 791) para 2, assumes application by analogy 'to later unforeseeable new competences of the EU.' See on the other hand, van Rossem (n 790) 199 (on ex Art 307 TEC), who asserts that such an analogy is 'generally rejected'.

prior to EU legislative competence in an area of shared competence being established and, therefore, before it can foresee the possibility that it may enter into obligations that may conflict with its future EU obligations.[804] In the following discussion that considers MSs' commitments to MARPOL, Art 351 (1) TFEU is potentially applicable either in favour of the acceded MSs or by analogy with regard to the subsequent exercise of EU legislative competence in the area of shares competence.

In this, it is understood that the application of Art 351 (1) TFEU can only take effect with regard to MARPOL where the standards laid down therein are considered maximum standards, ie where MARPOL does not allow for the adoption of stricter provisions, or—usually not the case with regard to EU legislation—the regulatory measures falls short of binding minimum standards set by MARPOL.[805] The consequence would then be 'a duty on the part of the institutions of the Community not to impede the performance of the obligations of Member States which stem from a prior agreement.'[806] This brings the focus back to the question discussed in the previous section (IV.2.a.), namely whether MARPOL is only setting minimum standards and allows for more stringent ones. Clearly, if MAR-

---

804 This is in line with the criteria that legal analogies are justified 'to close normative gaps if a rule is seen as just and/or useful for a number of cases which are similar', given that an analogy can only be subsidiary to the means of interpretation and that the similarities of the regulated and unregulated case can be considered relevant, see Silja Vöneky 'Analogy in International Law' (last updated February 2008) in Peters and Wolfrum (eds) *MPEPIL* (n 31) <https://opil-1ouplaw-1com-100b98ftx087f.emedien3.sub.uni-hamburg.de/display/10.1093/law:epil/9780199231690/law-9780199231690-e1375?rskey=R2a1UF&result=1&prd=MPIL> accessed 4 December 2023, para 2, 16, 17.

805 Proelss, 'The "Erika III" Package: Progress or Breach of International Law?' (n 74) 142–43; König, The EU Directive on Ship-Source Pollution and on the Introduction of Penalties for Infringements' (n 714) 775; Höltmann (n 759) 60–61, who admits this to be a rather theoretical assumption.

806 ECJ, Case C-812/79 *Attorney General v Juan C. Burgoa* ECLI:EU:C:1980:231, para 9 (regarding ex Art 234 TEC). In Case C-62/98 *Commission of the European Communities v Portuguese Republic* ECLI:EU:C:2000:358, para 44, the Court refers to *Burgoa* and holds that the 'application of the EC Treaty does not affect the duty of the Member State concerned to respect the rights of third countries under a prior agreement and to perform obligations thereunder.' Similarly, see Case C-84/98 *Commission of the European Communities v Portuguese Republic* ECLI: EU:C:2000:359, para 53. See this premise also confirmed in *Levy* (n 808) para 12; ECJ Case C-466/98 *Commission of the European Communities v United Kingdom of Great Britain and Northern Ireland* ECLI:EU:C:2002:624, para 24; *Budějovický Budvar* (n 808) para 145.

POL is understood to not bar MSs from more stringent measures—and this is widely assumed[807]—then recourse to Art 351 (1) TFEU would be unnecessary as there would be no conflict to speak of.

In any way, Art 351 (1) TFEU only offers a temporary solution to MSs' conflicting treaty obligations.[808] That is, because Art 351 (2) TFEU provides that where agreements entered into by MSs are not compatible with the Treaties, MSs 'shall take all appropriate steps to eliminate the incompatibilities established.' With that, it contains a corresponding duty of MSs to rectify the conflict situation.[809] Therefore,

> Article 351 para. 2 TFEU lays down a duty of Member States to reconcile their treaty obligations towards third States with Union law. The Member States must endeavour to resolve possible collisions in favour of Union law in a way that is in conformity with international law [...].[810]

In the view of the ECJ, this can mean (in the worst case), the obligation of the MS to withdraw from the agreement.[811]

---

807 See n 759.

808 Proelss, 'The "Erika III" Package: Progress or Breach of International Law?' (n 74) 142, with further references, discusses whether a breach of Art 351 (1) TFEU renders the legislative act in question invalid due to the provision's 'competence-limiting effects' or 'merely unlawful'. A third option is offered by the ECJ, that in the context of this provision discusses the possibility that 'a Community rule may be deprived of effect by an earlier international agreement', ECJ, Case C-158/91 *Ministère public and Direction du travail and de l'emploi v Levy* ECLI:EU:C:1993:332, para 13. This notion is repeated in ECJ, Case C-216/01 *Budějovický Budvar, národní podnik v Rudolf Ammersin GmbH* ECLI:EU:C:2003:618, para 146. This discussion is of a rather theoretical nature in this context and, therefore, not pursued here.

809 Allan Rosas, 'The Status in EU Law of International Agreements Concluded by EU Member States' (2011) 34 Fordham Int'l L J 1304, 1323.

810 Geiger, 'Article 351' (n 803) para 6.

811 See C-62/98 *Commission v Portuguese Republic* (n 806) para 43, 49; C-84/98 *Commission v Portuguese Republic* (n 806) para 40. It is noteworthy that in both cases the Court refers to its findings in Case C-170/98 *Commission of the European Communities v Kingdom of Belgium* [1999] ECLI:EU:C:1999:441, para 40, which is found not to be a suitable precedent by Pietro Manzini, 'The Priority of Pre-Existing Treaties of EC Member States within the Framework of International Law (2001) 12 EJIL 781, 788–92, including a discussion on the 'Obligation of Denunciation'. See also 'Act concerning the conditions of accession of the Czech Republic, the Republic of Estonia, the Republic of Cyprus, the Republic of Latvia, the Republic of Lithuania, the Republic of Hungary, the Republic of Malta, the Republic of Poland, the Republic of Slovenia, and the Slovak Republic and the adjustments to the Treaties on which the European Union is founded' [2003] OJ L236/33, Article 6 (10) subpara 2: 'To the extent that agreements between one or more of the new Member

This possible application of Art 351 (1) TFEU and the related duty of MSs in Art 351 (2) TEFU to solve existing conflicts, however, were not addressed at all by the ECJ in *Intertanko*.[812] The Court's failure to address the possible application and effect of then Art 307 (1) TEC, now Art 351 (1) TFEU, confirms the impression that it was avoiding a clear stance. It could have shown its legal sensitivity by assessing the applicability of this provision. This would have meant at least discussing MARPOL as a treaty providing only for minimum standards to ultimately reject a treaty conflict.

The Court, however, instead invokes the 'customary principle of good faith, which forms part of general international law' and ex Art 10 TEC to assert that it is to interpret the provisions of the Sanctions Directive taking into account MARPOL.[813] This argument today would translate into invoking Art 4 (3) TEU, including its subpara 1 defining the principle of sincere cooperation that is worded as a reciprocal duty of the MSs and the Union.[814] This makes for an incomplete argument since Art 351 (1) TFEU (ex Art 307 (1) TEC) must be considered at least the primary norm to regulate MSs' conflicting obligations resulting from other treaties.[815] The

---

States on the one hand, and one or more third countries on the other, are not compatible with the obligations arising from this Act, the new Member State shall take all appropriate steps to eliminate the incompatibilities established. If a new Member State encounters difficulties in adjusting an agreement concluded with one or more third countries before accession, it shall, according to the terms of the agreement, withdraw from that agreement.'

812 Also criticised by Proelss, 'The "Erika III" Package: Progress or Breach of International Law?' (n 74) 141. The AG in *Intertanko* briefly mentions ex Art 307 EC only to conclude, however, that its existence proves that 'the Community can in principle require Member States to take measures which run counter to their obligations under international law', and at the same time points to MSs obligation under its paragraph 2 'to put an end to such conflicts', *Intertanko*, Opinion of AG (n 733) para 77.

813 *Intertanko* (n 760) para 52.

814 See Rudolf Geiger, 'Article 4 TEU: [Union competences]' in Geiger, Khan, Kotzur (n 791) para 5, asserting that '[i]n the period before the Lisbon Treaty (2007) only the corresponding duty of the Member State was explicitly provided for [...] it was considered self-evident that this duty also applied to the Union in regard to the Member States.'

815 It is generally asserted that the principle of sincere cooperation is only applicable directly where there do not 'exist independently in primary law positive or negative obligations to act or not to act', ie where 'situations [...] are not regulated exhaustively by a specific provision (*lex specialis*) of the Treaties', Hermann-Josef Blanke, 'Article 4 [The Relations Between the EU and the Member States] in Hermann-Josef Blanke and Stelio Mangiameli, *The Treaty on European Union (TEU): A Commentary* (Springer 2013) paras 82 and 93. AG Tizzano in his opinion in case C-466/98

Court could have easily mentioned and dismissed the applicability of ex Art 307 (1) TEC, on the basis that MARPOL does allow for more stringent measures, and thereby maintained that no conflict exists. The failure to address this provision is the more striking since at the time of the *Intertanko* judgment in mid-2008 an overall of 16 MSs had been party to MARPOL including its non-Optional Annexes I and II before they had become MSs of the EU.[816]

In the *Manzi* case the ECJ again missed its chance to correct its neglect of Art 351 (1) TFEU. It would have been a legally insightful exercise but, here too, it could have been a source of great trouble for the Court. Only the assertion that there is, in fact, no treaty conflict because MARPOL does allow for stricter provisions could have saved the Court from having to admit the applicability of Art 351 (1) TFEU in favour of one MS.[817] For all other MSs the analogous application of Art 351 (1) TFEU could arguably have applied. This would crucially depend on the legislative competence of the EU in a matter of shared competence (environmental policy being one, Art 4 (2) subpara (e) TFEU) exercised after a MS's commitment to an agreement with a third country. MARPOL Annex VI entered into force on 19 May 2005; the Sulphur Directive 2005/33/EC entered into force a little

refers to the Commission's argument that 'the second paragraph of Article 234 [now Art 351 (2) TFEU] is no more than a specific enunciation of the duty to cooperate in good faith laid down in Article 5 of the Treaty [now slightly modified in Art 4 (3) subparas 2 and 3 TEU]', Case C-466/98 *Commission of the European Communities v United Kingdom of Great Britain and Northern Ireland*, Opinion of AG Tizzano ECLI:EU:C:2002:63, para 36. Panos Koutrakos, 'International Agreements Concluded by Member States Prior to Their EU Accession: Burgoa' in Graham Butler and Ramses A Wessel (eds), *EU External Relations Law: The Cases in Context* (Hart Publishing/Bloomsbury 2022) 137, asserts that 'the reference to the duty of the EU institutions not to impede the performance of the obligations of Member States flowing from prior international treaties [ie Art 351 (1) TFEU] [...] follows from the duty of sincere cooperation'. Marcus Klamert, 'Article 3 TEU', paras 33 and 35, as well as Marcus Klamert and Manuel Kellerbauer, 'Article 351 TFEU', para 1, both in Manuel Kellerbauer, Marcus Klamert and Jonathan Tomkin (eds), *The EU Treaties and the Charter of Fundamental Rights: A Commentary* (Oxford University Press 2019) suggesting Art 351 TFEU being a 'specific' and 'concrete' expression, respectively, of the general principle of sincere cooperation to be lex specialis.

816 Those MSs are Austria, Bulgaria, Cyprus, Czech Republic, Estonia, Finland, Hungary, Latvia, Lithuania, Malta, Poland, Romania, Slovakia, Slovenia, Spain and Sweden.

817 Croatia acceded to MARPOL Annex VI in 2005 but did not become an EU MS until 2013.

less than three months later on 11 August 2005.[818] By then, 9 of 25 MSs had become party to Annex VI.[819] Art 351 (1) TFEU could have potentially applied to these nine MSs, releasing them—at least temporarily—from their secondary obligations, while all other MSs could have been held accountable in the case of non-transposition of the Sulphur Directive 2005/33/EC into national law. To avoid this conundrum, the Court would have had to argue that the Union had established the respective legislative competence before the Sulphur Directive 2005/33/EC and MARPOL Annex VI had come into force. Therefore, it is understandable, nonetheless unsatisfactory, that the Court again chose to ignore Art 351 (1) TFEU altogether.

In conclusion, Art 351 (1) TFEU is well worth a discussion. However, even if applicable, it only offers a temporary solution for the dilemma of MSs finding themselves in conflicting treaty obligations. The ECJ, on the other hand, does little to support MSs where mere interpretation cannot solve the conflict between its obligation under Union law and third-party treaty it has committed to. Hence, the overall conclusion is rather simple:

> The ECJ is of the opinion that avoiding conflict is largely the responsibility of the Member States, which, in their capacity as members of the Council of the EU, should think twice before adopting a measure that implements international rules to which the Union is not committed.[820]

In the case of the Sanctions Directive—from the MSs most affected by maritime legislation—Greece and Malta opposed its adoption, while Cyprus abstained.[821] Similarly, and equally unsuccessfully, Italy and Malta voted against the adoption of the Sulphur Directive 2005/33/EC.[822] All these four countries together by far lack a blocking minority to prevent the adoption of a legislative act.[823] At the same time, maritime legislation mostly affects

---

818 That is 20 days after its publication in the Official Journal (22 July 2005), see its Art 3.

819 Seven of those nine MSs became party to MARPOL Annex VI on the day it entered into force on 19 May 2005.

820 van Rossem (n 790) 199.

821 See Council, '2672nd meeting of the Council of the European Union (Economic and Financial Affairs), held in Brussels on 12 July 2005, Addendum to Draft Minutes, 11128/05 Add 1 Rev 1, 7–10; all three MSs pointed to the Directive being incompatible with international law/MARPOL in their statements.

822 See Council, '2661st meeting of the Council of the European Union (Education, Youth and Culture), held in Brussels on 23 and 24 May 2005, Addendum to Draft Minutes, 9252/05 Add 1, 3.

823 See the Council's Voting Calculator <https://www.consilium.europa.eu/en/council-eu/voting-system/voting-calculator/> accessed 7 June 2023.

private parties (with limited possibilities to challenge legislation). Therefore, (other) governments' interest to interfere may be limited.

> This not only means that well-founded grievances may go without remedy; it can also lead governments taking measures which are guided less by international law than by the precedent of other states acquiescing in departures from it. At best this engenders uncertainty as to where people stand; at worst it undermines respect for international legal order.[824]

For MSs this could mean tolerating their conflicting treaty obligations, where they have not exercised sufficient caution during the legislative process. This can be the case where they are not invested in avoiding treaty conflicts (for themselves or other MSs), eg where they are not affected in a particular case or have no stakes in maritime matters or matters of environmental protection from shipping in general.

Therefore, while an expectation that the ECJ somehow rectify this dilemma would seem unjustified, the Court's disregard for the problem is not well-received. The criticism that the *Intertanko* decision, in particular, has generated seems to add to the overall impression that treaty conflict is generally ignored by the ECJ and 'any possible conflict is eradicated by simply assuming the supremacy of community law, even in circumstances where an appeal to international law might lead to a different result.'[825] It has been suggested that one option

> would be for the Community to consider itself materially bound by the international commitments of its Member States as a matter of EU law; that is, without succeeding to the immediate corresponding responsibilities of the latter. While not piercing through any direct normative relationship internationally, the advantage of such self-binding would lie in ruling out the eventuality of conflict between obligations of the Member States to the EU and at the international level. Crucially, legal substitution under Community law does not have to limit itself to a de facto commitment of the EU – meaning only seeking interpretative

824 de la Rue (n 17) para 2.44.

825 Jan Klabbers, *Treaty Conflict and the European Union* (Cambridge University Press 2009), 219, who, therefore, pointedly concludes that 'the Court's policy is that of an ostrich, aiming to avoid problems by sticking its head in the sand and pretending they do not exist.'

> harmony – but should amount to treating these obligations as an integral part of the European legal order.[826]

The downside of this approach, it is also understood, would be nothing less than the potential threat to 'the uniformity and integrity of that legal order.'[827] If nothing else,

> [if] international agreements entered into by one or more Member States outside the EC framework were to be accorded a position in the hierarchy of this legal order similar to treaties concluded by the Community, then the Member States could feel invited to circumvent the supremacy of Community (secondary) law by imposing their will through the backdoor.[828]

Ultimately, where secondary law places a MS in a conflict with its MARPOL obligations, it is up to the MS alone to solve its dilemma. While there is some help that could be generated through the Union's treaty law, the ECJ refuses to address it, while it also refuses to try too hard to find a stance that can be considered satisfactory. It is all up to the MSs to either prevent a piece of legislation that conflicts with their third-country treaty obligations (which they only can with considerable support from other MSs), to revoke their conflicting obligations or to remain in conflict, especially, where this brings no tangible consequences.

VI. Conclusion

This final case study analysed a setting different from the two previous case studies. Here, the EU passed legislation that put in place measures more

826 van Rossem (n 790) 214.

827 See van Rossem (n 790) 218, at the same time somewhat weakening this idea; see there at 219ff for a full discussion, including a situation where the international commitments of a MS cannot be incorporated into EU law.

828 van Rossem (n 790) 200. Proelss, 'The "Erika III" Package: Progress or Breach of International Law?' (n 74) 143, in a more moderate approach argues in favour of interpreting EU law 'in a manner friendly toward the international rights and obligations of the Member States deriving from treaties in terms of Art 351 (1) TFEU. In light of the principle of uniform application of EU law as well as the wording of Art 351 TFEU, this premise should also apply where only some (and not all) Member States are contractually bound.' This, however, does not provide a solution for instances where the conflict of commitments that MSs find themselves in cannot be solved through interpretation alone.

stringent than the measures that were provided for in MARPOL (the sulphur limit in EU ports and pre-empting the North Sea SECA). Additionally, it specifically regulated passenger ships on regular services—an altogether single-handed measure unprecedented in MARPOL. All three measures were assessed against UNCLOS, with the latter measure clearly having no basis in the law of the sea as far as it relates to ship's activities in the EEZ. The fact that this chapter has dealt with a Directive rather than a Regulation (as was the case in the previous two chapters) is not relevant for the discussion. The Directive equally affects the MSs, albeit through the duty of national transposition. This chapter has also found that there is no compelling case that MARPOL would prevent parties from implementing more stringent measures. Nonetheless, the MSs' conflicting treaty obligations were discussed for the sake of offering a full picture, first against the backdrop of existing ECJ jurisdiction, then with regard to a possible obligation of the EU to protect its MSs from such conflicting treaty commitments. The ECJ's rulings on the relationship between MARPOL and EU law show a lack (or arguably an unwillingness) to fully and satisfactorily appraise the matter, and with that a lack of legal and political sensitivity that would be desirable when acting at the intersection of international law. It must be concluded, on the other hand, that it is the EU MSs' sole responsibility to ensure that they do not manoeuvre themselves into a situation of conflicting treaty commitments.

As a recurring theme here, too, the EU felt the need to interfere being confronted with the slow pace and strenuous nature of international decision-making, on the one hand, and regulations it considered not ambitious enough, on the other.[829] If nothing else, it demonstrated its willingness and ability to choose a path different from the course of the IMO, without necessarily taking into account potential legal and political concerns. At the same time, the ECJ has shown to be unreliable in addressing concerns of possible conflicts with MARPOL and UNCLOS in the context of the Sulphur Directive (and also in the similar context of the Sanctions Directive). The Court, unfortunately, exercised a very careful evasion of important aspects presumably for political reasons. Especially in the controversial *Intertanko* ruling, this has reflected poorly on the Court. Such a strategy can undermine the Court's credibility and leave an aftertaste of it being a political accomplice rather than a legal authority that faces the legal

829 On the EU as a catalyst for international decision-making, see section A. with references.

challenges at hand and is willing to offer a full account. This would offer insights into legal relationships and concepts for future instances, more specifically help clarify the EU's role as a normative power[830] and actor on the international plane and evolve the relationship between EU and international law.

830 On the EU as a normative power, see n 24.

E. Final Conclusions

EU legislation on ship-source pollution fosters environmental and climate protection and can even save lives—this much is clear. Despite the recent UN Assembly Resolution declaring a clean, healthy and sustainable environment a human right,[831] some may, nonetheless, find it premature to claim that the EU engages in human rights protection where it regulates pollution from international shipping. Be it as it may, this analysis has confirmed the role of the EU as a catalyst and an important counterpart to the IMO. The threat of unilateral action alone seems sufficient at times to strengthen the resolve and accelerate decision-making within the IMO. At best, it can help push stricter regulations and standards where the international community wishes to avoid regulatory fragmentation. However, while quicker action on the international level can be desirable, such an approach risks stifling necessary political discussions that can produce results more readily accepted by all parties involved. There may be merit in parties feeling like decisions have been made freely, rather than having been taken hostage by the threat of an uncoordinated approach of a regional power. In fact, this analysis has shown that the EU itself seems ambiguous about its approach. It often expresses its preference for global solutions but somehow seems to feel compelled to act as a driving force in the face of what it seems to perceive as a failure of the international community.

The end result of EU legislation may be desirable from an environmental protectionist point of view. From a legal and policy point of view, the ends alone cannot justify the means, where the EU places itself in between the decision-making processes of the international community and international law. The EU's unilateral approach has not only been questioned by the shipping industry and the IMO as has been demonstrated in the course of this analysis. Academic discourse, too, has been critical about the EU making such use of its political and economic power. Its approach has been called potentially 'green imperialism [...] and an infringement upon sovereignty and state equality'[832]. Also, pointing to the so-called *Brus-*

831 UNGA Res 76/300 (28 July 2022) UN Doc A/RES/76/300.

832 See Kopela (n 494) 110, qualifying this statement by pointing out that 'international standards enforced vis-à-vis third states may not truly be unilateral where they are in line with objectives and obligations derived from international instruments.'

sels Effect, the result of 'unilateral regulatory globalization'[833], it has been observed that '[t]he picture that is beginning to emerge is of an EU that is unilateralist, hegemonic and where the direction of regulatory travel is all one way, namely from the EU to the rest of the world.'[834]

One reason for the unfavourable view on EU initiatives may be the impression that the EU does not always seem to act with an understanding that its legislation should harmonise with international law and integrate into the international legal system—an understanding that, ultimately, the EU is an actor in the realm of international law. How it manages the interplay between its institutions and the EU as a whole with international law directly reflects on it as an actor in the international community. At the same time, the international community and international law can either be strengthened or weakened, depending on how the EU approaches potential difficulties and conflicts. Nonetheless, in the area of this analysis the EU fails to display the necessary amount of legal and political sensitivity—may be sometimes even purposefully as thorough legal and political consideration would possibly force it to bring a desired project to a halt.

In the given context, this analysis allows the conclusion, however, that the EU does have potential to shift how it is perceived. As a reminder, the three criteria that led the analysis were: 1. potential conflicts of EU norms with international law; 2. transparency as to how EU institutions have considered arising questions of international law; 3. the implications for and disruptions of existing systems and dynamics, in particular the obstacles being created for the actors traditionally involved. The EU does not fare very well in either of these criteria. The following paragraphs will guide through the conclusions of the three case studies with these three criteria in mind, while also pointing to possibilities and ideas for further research.

---

833 Anu Bradford, 'The Brussels Effect' (2013) 107 North Western University Law Review 1, 3.

834 Scott (n 514) 88. Taking a more differentiated stance, Georg Shaffer, 'International Law and Public Goods in a Legal Pluralist World' (2012) 23 EJIL 669, 691–92: 'Unilateral action is problematic because it can be self-serving and fail to take account of the values and perspectives of affected others. Yet unilateral action may also be an important part of a broader transnational process leading to the production of a global public good over time. In a world of interacting legal orders, certain actors will have to act, sometimes unilaterally, to catalyse international and global action. These actors most likely will exercise some form of power, such as market power wielded by the US and EU. [...] In practice, unilateralism may help to produce a global public good where common action fails.'

The first case study analysed the SRR, an example of how the EU has gotten ahead of itself with its ambitions. Almost 10 years in, the SRR is still missing the financial mechanism provided for in the regulation and an essential tool for ensuring compliance. With that, the EU has undermined its own efforts and at the same time has clearly drawn attention to its own legal limits. The impression remains that the regulation was not thought through from the outset and potential conflicts with WTO law were not considered. The assessment of WTO law was complex enough that several studies on the compatibility of potential measures with WTO law were not able to give a satisfactory answer. A comprehensive assessment of the WTO law in this context would have been outside the scope of this analysis. However, the question how WTO law limits the EU's capacity to regulate financial instruments (fees, charges, taxes etc) as a port-entry requirement is an important one, well worth further investigation. For this, a thorough investigation into how shipping places itself in the context of GATT and GATS would be helpful, specifically taking into account the evolution of the treaties. Further research would then ideally involve a distinction between financial obligations imposed non-discriminately on EU- and non-EU-flagged ships, as well as discriminatory ones only imposed on non-EU-flagged ships. It would also address the exceptions of Art XX GATT and Art XIV GATS and how any of these exceptions could apply in a given situation, especially with regard to specific ship-source pollutions in mind. In the case of the SRR, ultimately, there is no conflict with WTO law as the EU has refrained from putting into place a financial mechanism as part of the SRR. In this case, the EU commissioning studies and making them publicly available was also a rather open and transparent approach to the problems surrounding the financial mechanism, especially when compared to its handling in the second and third case studies.

Ultimately, with no significant practical benefit to speak of—other than committing its MSs, not party to the HKC to standards of ship recycling, albeit with the option for their ships to simply re-flag—the SRR has nonetheless sparked discussions as to its relationship with the BC and, more specifically, the BC's Ban Amendment. In the latter case, it has taken steps to rectify the situation through a current legislative proposal to clarify the relationship between the EU's WSR and the SRR, applying the stricter Ban Amendment in the former instrument to ships that have become waste under EU jurisdiction. This and the few deviations of the SRR from the HKC can be considered rather minor disruptions, not least in comparison to the disruptions caused by the MRV-Regulation and the Sulphur Directive. Again, those disruptions could have been considered acceptable, if the SRR would have actually had a significant impact on accelerating the entry-into-force of the HKC, and most importantly, if it were actually able to ensure compliance of non-EU-flagged ships beyond the documentary requirements with its recycling standards. It is noteworthy in this context that the reason the SRR needs a separate compliance mechanism to begin with, is that the EU cannot rely on the NMFT principle included in IMO treaties. The NMFT clause is the established answer of the international community and IMO treaties to the dilemma the EU is facing here: applying rules to ships where their flag States are not bound by those rules, not least to prevent re-flagging of EU-flagged ships to bypass the Regulation. In this setting, the IMO has one major advantage when regulating shipping internationally and within an established system in that it can address all ships. EU Legislation on ship-source pollution addressing EU-flagged ships, however, is easy to circumvent through re-flagging in the absence of a complementing mechanism. Such a mechanism would be most sensible and effective where it addresses non-EU-flagged ships, too. This, one the other hand, brings with it other challenges, as has been demonstrated in the second case study in relation to the MRV-Regulation.

The MRV-Regulation opposed to the SRR was thought of as a blueprint for the IMO, but more importantly, it regulates conduct outside of EU territory. Arguing that the MRV-Regulation's reporting requirements are nothing more than a port-entry requirement is stretching the concept. Therefore, a discussion on the permissibility of regulations with an extraterritorial element is warranted here. Based on the scope of research for this study, the legislative bodies remained silent on the matter, ie did not see it or chose to ignore it. The stance the EU would presumably take have been deducted from the arguments and elaborations on the permissibility of the EU ETS for aviation and the corresponding ECJ judgment. The discussion could benefit from further research into extraterritoriality and the conditions under which it is deemed permissible.

Similarly, further investigation into the Effects Doctrine and the principle of Common Concern of Humankind, specifically with regard to justifying climate protection measures in international shipping that have extraterritorial effects, would provide important insight for the future. As the EU does not seem to want to unambiguously rely on the Effects Doctrine and an immediate effect of GHG emissions on any one single country is difficult to argue[835], there is indeed a justification gap that the concept of the Common Concern of Humankind could fill. While more relevant in the context of the EU Shipping ETS (as an actual reduction measure) than for the MRV-Regulation, an argument in favour of the applicability of these concepts could provide a sound basis for future legislative projects. It would suit the EU well to invoke recognised concepts to justify jurisdiction for its legislative endeavours. Even more desirable would have been for the EU to contribute to the establishment of these concepts. With environmental and climate protection being a major topic on the international scene, the EU could have taken a stance for the Effects Doctrine and/or for climate change as a Common Concern of Humankind to further the cause of these instruments in international law and help them gain further recognition. After all, these are concepts that can help vest States with the jurisdictional basis to take measures that involve an extraterritorial element to combat pollution that affects them indirectly. With that, the EU would have demonstrated awareness for its legislation being passed in the larger context of international law—rather than an EU-centric vacuum—and its role as an actor in its own right within the international community. It is conceded that for this the EU would have had to make the difficult argument that the MRV-Regulation actually reduces emissions. Similarly, it could have benefitted from the Effects Doctrine and/or the notion of the Common Concern of Humankind in the context of its Shipping ETS. It could have gone through the effort of laying the groundwork for the application of these concepts and created a precedent for them in EU law.

Apart from the overarching question of extraterritorial jurisdiction, the MRV-Regulation also comes with some non-negligible disruption on the basic level of implementation—the unaligned reporting parameters, the publication of data and the verification system. With all this, it is safe to say that the MRV-Regulation contributed to keeping the discussions on a DCS and an MBM at IMO level alive. As a next step, the EU Shipping ETS itself would also benefit from further investigation. There is academic literature on the general permissibility of the measure[836], and there will continue to be. In this context, however, it would be also interesting to see how a

835 See n 568.

836 See eg Tim Bäuerle, 'Integrating Shipping into the EU Emission Trading Scheme?' in Hans-Joachim Koch and others, *Climate Change and Environmental Hazards Related to Shipping* (Martinus Nijhoff Publishers 2013) 109; Bäuerle and others, *Integration of Marine Transport into the European Emissions Trading System* (n 322); Helseth (n 511); Claudia Hermeling and others, 'Sailing into a Dilemma: An Economic and Legal Analysis of an EU Trading Scheme for Maritime Emissions' (Centre

possible IMO MBM compares with the Shipping ETS, as well as whether, and if so, how the Shipping ETS will ultimately affect discussions within the IMO. Furthermore, it would be worthwhile to take a closer look at how the Shipping ETS and a potential MBM could coexist and what additional burden and disruptions these two parallel systems would create.

The third case study has discussed the Sulphur Directive, which other than the SRR and the MRV-Regulation, is an implementation of existing MARPOL standards already in force, however, with some regulatory deviations, all of which raise questions of compatibility with UNCLOS. For the first of these, the sulphur limit for transiting ships in EU ports, a basis can arguably be found in Art 211 (4) UNCLOS. In this context, an exhaustive investigation of the relationship between Art 211 (4) and Art 212 (1) UNCLOS would have been beyond the scope of this analysis. Further research on how these two norms relate to each other would provide further insight as to the regulatory authority of the coastal State as provided for in UNCLOS and with regard to atmospheric pollution. The second regulatory deviation, the regulation of passenger ships in regular services, is found to only be compatible with UNCLOS as far as it pertains to the territorial sea. For regulating within the EEZ Art 211 (5) UNCLOS would require it to be an expression of GAIRS, which it is not. Art 211 (5) UNCLOS and the GAIRS criteria have also been relevant when assessing the third deviation, the pre-empted designation of the North Sea SECA. Here, the compatibility of this measure with UNCLOS boils down to the question, whether the North Sea SECA, formally adopted by IMO Parties and codified in MARPOL Annex VI, but not yet applicable, constituted a GAIRS when the Sulphur Directive referred to it. As has been elaborated, there is a good case for a not too formalistic approach in determining what constitutes GAIRS. Here again, a full appraisal of the extent and limits of the concept of GAIRS would have been outside the scope of this study. A thorough investigation of the term GAIRS, however, could improve understanding of Art 211 (5) UNCLOS and the coastal State's authority to regulate within its EEZ.

Even though these three regulatory measures of the Sulphur Directive raise questions of UNCLOS compatibility, the research for this study has not shown that potential conflicts with international law were addressed at any point in the legislative process. This also holds true for the very general question of whether MARPOL allows its Parties to adopt stricter

for European Economic Research, Discussion Paper No. 14-021) <https://ftp.zew.de/pub/zew-docs/dp/dp14021.pdf> accessed 27 October 2023; Kotzampasakis (n 568); Ringbom, 'Global Problem—Regional Solution?' (n 510).

measures. As can be inferred from the ECJ decisions on *Intertanko*, *Manzi* and *Bosphorus Queen*, the EU does not see itself restricted by MSs' MARPOL obligations. In its *Intertanko* decision, the Court even avoided taking a stance on the compatibility of the Sanctions Directive with UNCLOS, to which the EU is a Party. While there is a good case to argue that Parties are free to adopt more stringent measures than provided for in MARPOL, the further discussion in the third case study shows that it is the MSs' responsibility to ensure (especially and foremost through their intervention in the legislative process) that EU legislation does not drive them into conflicting treaty obligations.

Ultimately, with regard to the Sulphur Directive, the EU fares rather poorly when it comes to potential conflicts with international law and transparency as to how EU institutions deal with them. For one, when it comes to the three additional measures of the Sulphur Directive, UNCLOS considerations did not seem to have played a role for the EU, even though regulating in the EEZ, for example, would clearly suggest an assessment against UNCLOS. Furthermore, while the *Intertanko* and *Bosphorus Queen* cases dealt with the Sanctions Directive, the court did have a chance in the *Manzi* case to fully clarify the relationship between the Sulphur Directive and MARPOL. Rather than insisting on the independence of EU legislation from MARPOL norms, it could have conducted an admittedly perhaps more extensive examination into whether MSs actually violate MARPOL norms when transposing the Sulphur Directive. This would have actually offered clarity on a wider scale and for the future.

To sum up, EU legislation that promotes and enacts environmental standards in international shipping comes at a cost. The largest problem appears to be how the EU does not see or chooses to ignore conflicts with international law and avoids taking a clear stance on them, rather than actually offering conceptual solutions that create legal certainty and would prove helpful in other instances and in future legislative endeavours. This creates the impression of the EU being inconsiderate or ignorant at best, and reckless and EU-centric at worst.[837] What has been observed with regard to SRR, the MRV-Regulation and the Sulphur Directive is that the EU consistently fails to seize the opportunity to elaborate on how its legislation relates to international law, specifically how and why international law

837 *EU-centric* meaning essentially 'an exaggerated understanding of the autonomy of the European Union's legal system' as expressed by Proelss, 'The "Erika III" Package: Progress or Breach of International Law?' (n 74) 156; a similar argument was made in relation to *Intertanko*, n 797.

permits these regulations. With this, it risks losing credibility as an actor in international law, much less one that has committed itself to 'the strict observance and the development of international law' (Art 3 para 5 TEU), and it misses the chance to create for itself a more stable, less objectionable position as a global player. With this, it also misses the opportunity to help shape international law, which would further its role on the international plane and allow for it to be perceived more as an integrated actor in addressing ship-source pollution rather than a disruptor of the existing international legal system. Even if its positions on international law sparked debate, an honest and open legal strategy would be preferable to avoiding the necessary legal debates altogether and appearing to rely on its political and economic power instead.

To be clear, this is not making a case against EU action in this field. Quite the opposite, this conclusion is making a case for EU action as a complementary force to international efforts, however, more prudent and credible than the approach the EU has taken in the areas investigated in this study. Most importantly, there is a strong argument for the EU to act with heightened awareness and regard for international law, for the sake of its own integrity, and more practically, for the sake of the integrity and increased acceptance of its legislation and policies. If all its organs involved contributed to this cause, the EU could achieve this by openly addressing legal concerns and ensuring that they are transparently solved in the legislative process or even before. Where measures are challenged, the ECJ could contribute by offering more thorough analysis and help paint a full picture rather than carefully keeping their assessments to a minimum. Such an approach would also involve refraining from legislative action where international law would be breached, even if it hurts the environmental cause, and the ECJ deciding against the legality of a measure where need be. All this would help create a major shift in the cost-benefit-analysis in favour of EU legislation that regulates international shipping to further environmental and climate protection (standards). After all, avoiding or minimising incompatibilities with international law or the international community's accepted policies, and openly addressing possible conflicts, would strengthen the EU's standing as an international player and a normative force. At the same time, it would contribute to evolving and advancing international law to match the present and future legal challenges the EU or other regional actors face when drafting environmental and climate protection regulations for international shipping.

Bibliography

Books

Abbott F M, Breining-Kaufmann C and Cottier T, *International Trade and Human Rights: Foundations and Conceptual Issues* (The University of Michigan Press 2006)

Boyle A and Redgwell C, *Birnie, Boyle & Redgwell's International Law and the Environment* (4th ed, Oxford University Press 2021)

Buck S J, *The Global Commons: An Introduction* (Island Press 1998)

Cançado Trindade A A, *International Law for Humankind: Towards a New Jus Gentium* (3rd ed, Brill 2020)

Churchill R and Lowe A, *The Law of the Sea* (3rd ed, Manchester University Press 1999)

Churchill R, Lowe V and Sander A, *The Law of the Sea* (4th ed, Manchester University Press 2022)

Chrysostomou A and Vågslid E S, 'Climate Change: A challenge for IMO too' in Asariotis R and Benamara H (eds) *Maritime Transport and the Climate Change Challenge* (Routledge 2012)

Engels U D, *European Ship Recycling Regulation: Entry-Into-Force Implications of the Hong Kong Convention* (Springer 2013)

Fanø J J, *Enforcing International Maritime Legislation on Air Pollution through UNCLOS* (Hart 2019)

Franckx E (ed), *Vessel-source Pollution and Coastal State Jurisdiction: The Work of the ILA Committee on Coastal State Jurisdiction Relating to Marine Pollution (1991–2000)* (Kluwer Law International 2001)

Frank V, *The European Community and Marine Environmental Protection in the International Law of the Sea: Implementing Global Obligations at the Regional Level* (Martinus Nijhoff Publishers 2007)

Galley M, *Shipbreaking: Hazards and Liabilities* (Springer 2014)

Higgins R, *Problems and Process: International Law and how we use it* (OUP 1995)

Höltmann M, *Schiffssicherheit und Meeresumweltschutz in der EU nach Erika und Prestige* (Nomos 2012)

Klabbers J, *Treaty Conflict and the European Union* (Cambridge University Press 2009)

Lineé P A, *Regulating Vessel-Source Air Pollution: Standard-Setting in the Regulation of SO_x Emissions* (University of Gothenburg 2017)

Molenaar E J, *Coastal State Jurisdiction over Vessel-Source Pollution* (Kluwer Law International 1998)

Puthucherril T G, From Shipbreaking to Sustainable Ship Recycling: Evolution of a Legal Regime (Martinus Nijhoff Publishers 2010)

Ringbom H, *The EU Maritime Safety Policy and International Law* (Martinus Nijhoff Publishers 2008)

Ryngaert C, *Jurisdiction in International Law*, (2nd edn, OUP 2015)

Smith B D, *State Responsibility and the Marine Environment: The Rules of Decision* (Clarendon Press 1988)

Svensson E, *The Regulation of Global SOx Emissions from Ships: IMO proceedings 1998–2008* (Chalmers University of Technology 2011) <https://publications.lib.chalmers.se/records/fulltext/140528.pdf> accessed 19 May 2023

Tan A K-J, *Vessel-Source Marine Pollution: The Law and Politics of International Regulation* (Cambridge University Press 2006)

Timagenis G J, *International Control of Marine Pollution: Volume 2* (Oceana Publications 1980)

Van den Bossche P and Prévost D, *Essentials of WTO Law* (2nd edn, Cambridge University Press 2021)

Wolfrum R and Matz N , *Conflicts in International Environmental Law* (Springer 2003)

Articles, Contributions and Papers

AlixPartners, '2019 Global Container Shipping Outlook: IMO 2020 Weighs on an Industry Struggling to Generate Sustained Profitability' (February 2019) <https://www.alixpartners.com/media/14481/ap_global_container_shipping_outlook_feb_2019.pdf> accessed 2 June 2023

American Bureau of Shipping 'ABS Advisory on Exhaust Gas Scrubber Systems' (July 2018) <https://ww2.eagle.org/content/dam/eagle/advisories-and-debriefs/exhaust-gas-scrubber-systems-advisory.pdf> accessed 2 June 2023

Andersson K and others, 'Shipping and the Environment', in Andersson K and others (eds), *Shipping and the Environment: Improving Environmental Performance in Marine Transportation* (Springer 2016)

Anthony O G, 'Criminalization of Seafarers for Accidental Discharge of Oil: Is there Justification in International Law for Criminal Sanction for Negligent or Accidental Pollution of the Sea?' (2006) 37 J Mar L & Com 219

Banaszewska D M, 'Lex specialis' (last updated November 2015) in Peters A and Wolfrum R (eds), *The Max Planck Encyclopedia of Public International Law* (Oxford University Press 2008) <https://opil-1ouplaw-1com-100b98f6m07b3.emedien3.sub.uni-hamburg.de/display/10.1093/law:epil/9780199231690/law-9780199231690-e2171?rskey=q34qqH&result=1&prd=MPIL> accessed 7 June 2023

Barnes R A, 'Article 21: Laws and regulations of the coastal State relating to innocent passage' in Proelss A and others (eds), *United Nations Convention on the Law of the Sea: A Commentary* (CH BECK, Hart, Nomos 2017)

—— 'Article 24: Duties of the coastal State' in Proelss A and others (eds), *United Nations Convention on the Law of the Sea: A Commentary* (CH BECK, Hart, Nomos 2017)

Bartels L, 'The WTO Legality of the Application of the EU's Emission Trading System to Aviation' (2012) 23 EJIL 429

Bartenstein K, 'Article 211: Pollution from vessels' in Proelss A and others (eds), *United Nations Convention on the Law of the Sea: A Commentary* (CH BECK, Hart, Nomos 2017)

Bäuerle T, 'Integrating Shipping into the EU Emission Trading Scheme?' in Hans-Joachim Koch and others, *Climate Change and Environmental Hazards Related to Shipping* (Martinus Nijhoff Publishers 2013)

Biermann F, '"Common Concern of Humankind": The Emergence of a New Concept of International Environmental Law' (1996) Archiv des Völkerrechts 426

Blanke H-J, 'Article 4 [The Relations Between the EU and the Member States] in Blanke H-J and Mangiameli S, *The Treaty on European Union (TEU): A Commentary* (Springer 2013)

Bradford A, 'The Brussels Effect' (2013) 107 North Western University Law Review 1

Bodansky D, 'What's So Bad about Unilateral Action to Protect the Environment?' (2000) 11 EJIL 339

Boyle A, 'EU Unilateralism and the Law of the Sea' (2006) 21 Int'l J Marine & Coastal L 15

Buxbaum H L, 'Territory, Territoriality, and the Resolution of Jurisdictional Conflict' (2009) 57 Am J Comp L 631

Carpenter A, 'The EU and Marine Environmental Policy: A Leader in Protecting the Marine Environment' (2012) 8 JCER 248

Churchill R, 'Port State Jurisdiction Relating to the Safety of Shipping and Pollution from Ships —What Degree of Extra-territoriality' (2016) 31 Int'l J Marine & Coastal L 442

Churchill R R and Foster N G, 'European Community Law and Prior Treaty Obligations of Member States: The Spanish Fishermen's Cases' (1987) 36 ICLQ 504

CIEL, 'Legality of the EU Commission Proposal on Ship Recycling', <https://www.shipbreakingplatform.org/wp-content/uploads/2018/11/CIEL-legal-opinion-on-EU-Ships-Proposed-Regulation-12-Dec-2012.pdf> accessed 10 March 2023

—— 'Legality of EU Proposals on Ship Recycling: Updated Legal Opinion of the Center for International Environmental Law (CIEL)' <https://www.shipbreakingplatform.org/wp-content/uploads/2020/09/CIEL-Legality-EU-Proposals-on-Ship-Recycling-2020.pdf> accessed 18 May 2023

—— 'Shipbreaking and the Basel Convention: Analysis of the Level of Control established under the Hong Kong Convention' <https://www.ciel.org/Publications/Shipbreaking_22Apr11.pdf> accessed 10 March 2023

Coelho N F, 'Extraterritoriality from the Port: EU's Approach to Jurisdiction over Ship-Source Pollution' (2015) 19 SYbIL 269

Cottier T, 'The Principle of Common Concern of Humankind' in Cottier T and Ahmad. Z (eds) *The Prospect of Common Concern of Humankind in International Law* (Cambridge University Press 2021)

Cottier T and others, 'The Principle of Common Concern and Climate Change' (2014) 52 Archiv des Völkerrechts 293

Danish Shipping, 'Sulphur in Marine Fuels' (Policy Paper, January 2019) <https://www.danishshipping.dk/politik/miljoe/svovl/download/Basic_Model_Linkarea_Link/964/191213_dre_policypaper_sulphur.pdf> accessed 6 April 2023

de Búrca G, 'The European Court of Justice and the International Legal Order after *Kadi*' (2010) 51 Harv Int'l LJ 1

de la Rue C, 'Pollution from Ships: EU Directive on Criminal Sanctions for Ship-source Pollution' in Thomas D R (ed) *Liability Regimes in Contemporary Maritime Law* (Informa Law from Routledge 2007)

Denza E, 'A note on Intertanko' (2008) 33 E L Rev 33, 870

de Vries R F, 'European Union, Membership in International Organization or Institutions' (last updated July 2019) in Peters A and Wolfrum R (eds), *The Max Planck Encyclopedia of Public International Law* (Oxford University Press 2008) <https://opil-1ouplaw-1com-100b98fpw031a.emedien3.sub.uni-hamburg.de/display/10.1093/law:epil/9780199231690/law-9780199231690-e627?rskey=tT9jfr&result=1&prd=OPIL> accessed 12 May 2023

Dobson N L and Ryngaert C, 'Provocative Climate Protection: EU Extraterritorial Regulation of Maritime Emission' (2017) 66 Int'l & Comp LQ 295 (2017) 295

Edward D, 'The Practice of the Community Institutions in Relation to the Extraterritorial Application of EEC Competition Law' in Roland Bieber and Georg Ress (eds), *The Dynamics of EC-Law* (Nomos 1987)

European Community Shipowners' Association, 'Proposal for a Regulation of the European Parliament and of the Council on the monitoring, reporting and verification of carbon dioxide emission from maritime transport and amending Regulation (EU) No 525/2013: ECSA Position Paper (11 October 2013)' <https://www.ecsa.eu/sites/default/files/publications/EU%20MRV%20Regulation%20proposal_ECSA%20Position%20paper_Final_11.10.2013.pdf> accessed 26 May 2023

European Federation for Transport and Environment, 'Bunker Fuels and the Kyoto Protocol: How ICAO and the IMO Failed the Climate Change Test' (2009) <https://www.transportenvironment.org/wp-content/uploads/2021/05/2009_06_aviation_shipping_icao_imo_history.pdf> accessed 19 May 2023

Fanø J J, 'Enforcement of the 2020 Sulphur Limit for Marine Fuels: Restrictions and Possibilities for Port States to Impose Fines under UNCLOS' (2019) 28 Rev Eur Comp & Int'l Envtl L 278

Fedi L, 'The Monitoring, Reporting and Verification of Ships' Carbon Dioxide Emissions: A European Substantial Policy Measure towards Accurate and Transparent Carbon Dioxide Quantification' (2017) 31 Ocean YB 381

Fitzmaurice M, 'Liability for Environmental Damage Caused to the Global Commons' (1996) 5 Rev Eur Comp & Int'l Envtl L 305

Forsberg T, 'Normative Power Europe, Once Again: A Conceptual Analysis of an Ideal Type' (2011) 49 J Common Mkt Stud 1183

Frank V, 'Consequences of the Prestige Sinking for European and International Law' (2005) 20 Int'l J Marine & Coastal L 1

Friedberg J J, 'The convergence of Law in an Era of Political Integration: The *Wood Pulp* Case and the *Alcoa* Effects Doctrine' (1991) 52 U Pitt L Rev 289

Garcia D, 'Global Commons Law: Norms to Safeguard the Planet and Humanity's Heritage' (2021) 35 International Relations 422

Geiger R, 'Article 4 TEU: [Union competences]' in Geiger R, Khan D-H, Kotzur M (eds), *European Union Treaties* (CH BECK Hart 2015)

—— 'Article 351 TFEU [Former Agreements of Member States]' in Geiger R, Khan D-H, Kotzur M (eds), *European Union Treaties* (CH BECK Hart 2015)

Gubner S T, 'Wood Pulp—The European Economic Community and Effects Doctrine Jurisdiction: The Community's New Weapon' (1990) 3 Transnat'l Law 759 (also published by (1990) 3 Glob Bus and Dev L J <https://scholarlycommons.pacific.edu/cgi/viewcontent.cgi?article=1213&context=globe> accessed 26 May 2023)

Guilfoyle D, 'Article 92: Status of ships' in Proelss A and others (eds), *United Nations Convention on the Law of the Sea: A Commentary* (CH BECK, Hart, Nomos 2017)

Guruswamy L, 'International Environmental Law: Boundaries, Landmarks, and Realities' (1995) 10 (2) Natural Resources & Environment 43

Halvorssen A M, 'Common but Differentiated Commitments in the Future Climate Change Regime—Amending the Kyoto Protocol to Include Annex C and the Annex C Mitigation Fund' (2007) 18 Colo J Int'l Envtl L & Pol'y 247

Handeyside H, 'The Lotus Principle in ICJ Jurisprudence: Was the Ship ever Afloat?' (2007) 29 Mich J Int'l L 71

Helseth A F, 'Rocking the Boat: The Question of Jurisdiction for Applying the European Emissions Trading System to International Shipping' (2017) 2017 Scandinavian Inst Mar L YB 1

Hermeling C and others, 'Sailing into a Dilemma: An Economic and Legal Analysis of an EU Trading Scheme for Maritime Emissions' (Centre for European Economic Research, Discussion Paper No. 14-021) <https://ftp.zew.de/pub/zew-docs/dp/dp14021.pdf > accessed 27 October 2023.

Hey E and Paulini S, 'Common but Differentiated Responsibilities' (last updated October 2021) in Peters A and Wolfrum R (eds), *The Max Planck Encyclopedia of Public International Law* (Oxford University Press 2008) <https://opil-1ouplaw-1com-100b98fdz01e3.emedien3.sub.uni-hamburg.de/display/10.1093/law:epil/9780199231690/law-9780199231690-e1568?rskey=nmstZ2&result=1& prd=MPIL> accessed 19 May 2023

Hixson K, 'Extraterritorial Jurisdiction Under the Third Restatement of Foreign Relations Law of the United States' (1988) 12 Fordham Int'l L J 127

Honkonen T, 'The principle of Common But Differentiated Responsibility in Post-2012 Climate Negotiations' (2009) 18 Rev Eur Comp & Int'l Envtl L 257

Honniball A N, 'The Exclusive Jurisdiction of Flag States: A Limitation on Pro-active Port States?' (2016) 31 Int'l J Marine & Coastal L 499

Hui W, 'The EU Marine Oil Pollution Prevention Regime – Recent Developments' (2004) 13 EELR 292

International Association of Classification Societies, 'Classification societies – what, why and how?' (2020) <https://iacs.org.uk/media/8871/classification-what-why-how.pdf> accessed 19 May 2023

—— 'Classification societies – their key role' <https://iacs.org.uk/media/8875/classification-societies-key-role.pdf> accessed 26 May 2023

International Chamber of Shipping, 'Reducing CO_2 Emissions to Zero: The "Paris Agreement for Shipping"' (Marisec Publication 2018) <https://www.ics-shipping.org/wp-content/uploads/2020/08/reducing-co2-emissions-to-zero-the-paris-agreement-for-shipping.pdf> accessed 30 March 2023

International Council on Clean Transportation, 'The International Maritime Organization's initial greenhouse gas strategy' (2018) <https://theicct.org/wp-content/uploads/2021/06/IMO_GHG_StrategyFInalPolicyUpdate042318.pdf> accessed 17 April 2023

Jeffrey M, 'The Implications of the Wood Pulp Case for the European Communities (1991) 4 LJIL 75

Kamminga M T, 'Extraterritoriality' (last updated September 2020) in Peters A and Wolfrum R (eds), *The Max Planck Encyclopedia of Public International Law* (Oxford University Press 2008) <https://opil-1ouplaw-1com-100b98fpw031a.emedien3.sub.uni-hamburg.de/display/10.1093/law:epil/9780199231690/law-9780199231690-e1040?rskey=9A6no9&result=1&prd =OPIL> accessed 12 May 2023

Karim M S and Alam S, 'Climate Change and Reduction of Emissions of Greenhouse Gases from Ships: An Appraisal' (2011) 1 AsianJIL 131, 147

Keen M, Parry I and Strand J, 'Market-Based Instruments for International Aviation and Shipping as a Source of Climate Finance' (World Bank 2012) <http://documents1.worldbank.org/curated/en/678661468155734989/pdf/WPS5950.pdf> accessed 19 May 2023

Kirchner A, 'Law of the Sea, History of', (last updated September 2007) in Peters A and Wolfrum R (eds), *The Max Planck Encyclopedia of Public International Law* (Oxford University Press 2008) <https://opil-1ouplaw-1com-100b98fld03b0.emedien3.sub.uni-hamburg.de/display/10.1093/law:epil/9780199231690/law-9780199231690-e1187?rskey=RTBGY5&result=1&prd=MPIL> accessed 2 October 2023

Kiss A, 'The Common Concern of Mankind' (1997) 27 Envtl Policy and Law 244

—— 'International Trade and the Common Concern of Humankind' in Bosselmann K and Richardson B J (eds) *Environmental Justice and Market Mechanisms: Key Challenges for Environmental Law and Policy* (Kluwer Law International 1999)

Klamert M, 'Article 3 TEU' in Kellerbauer M, Klamert M and Tomkin J (eds), *The EU Treaties and the Charter of Fundamental Rights: A Commentary* (Oxford University Press 2019)

Klamert M and Kellerbauer M, 'Article 351 TFEU' in Kellerbauer M, Klamert M and Tomkin J (eds), *The EU Treaties and the Charter of Fundamental Rights: A Commentary* (Oxford University Press 2019)

König D, 'Article 218: Enforcement by port States' in Proelss A and others (eds), *United Nations Convention on the Law of the Sea: A Commentary* (CH BECK, Hart, Nomos 2017)

—— 'The EU Directive on Ship-Source Pollution and on the Introduction of Penalties for Infringements: Development or Breach of International Law' in Ndiaye T M and Wolfrum R (eds) *Law of the Sea, Environmental Law and Settlement of Disputes: Liber Amoricum Thomas A. Mensah* (Martinus Nijhoff Publishers 2007)

König D and Salomon T R, 'Flags of Convenience' (last updated February 2022) in Peters A and Wolfrum R (eds), *The Max Planck Encyclopedia of Public International Law* (Oxford University Press 2008) <https://opil-1ouplaw-1com-100b98fpw031a.emedien3.sub.uni-hamburg.de/display/10.1093/law:epil/9780199231690/law-9780199231690-e1167?rskey=tgUikl&result=1&prd= OPIL> accessed 12 May 2023

Kopela S, 'Port-State Jurisdiction, Extraterritoriality, and the Protection of the Global Commons' (2016) 47 Ocean Dev Int'l L 89

Kotzampasakis M, 'Intercontinental Shipping on the European Union Emissions Trading System: A "fifty-fifty" Alignment with the Law of the Sea and International Climate Law?'(2023) 32 Rev Eur Comp & Int'l Envtl L 29

Kotzur M, 'Article 267 TFEU [Preliminary rulings]' in Geiger R, Khan D-H, Kotzur M (eds), *European Union Treaties* (CH BECK Hart 2015)

Koutrakos P, 'International Agreements Concluded by Member States Prior to Their EU Accession: Burgoa' in Graham Butler and Ramses A Wessel (eds), *EU External Relations Law: The Cases in Context* (Hart Publishing/Bloomsbury 2022)

Krämer L, 'The Commission proposal for a Regulation on ship recycling, the Basel Convention and the protection of the environment' <https://www.shipbreakingplatform.org/wp-content/uploads/2018/11/Legal-Analysis-of-EC-proposal_Ludwig-Kramer_FINAL-1.pdf> accessed 18 May 2023

Krisch N, 'The Decay of Consent: International Law in an age of global public goods' (2014) 108 Am J Int'l L 1

Lerch M and Schwellnus G, 'Normative by Nature? The role of coherence in justifying the EU's external human rights policy' (2006) 13 J Eur Public Policy 304

Lindgren J F, Karin Andersson K and Landquist H, 'Infrastructure, Marine Spatial Planning and Shipwrecks' in Andersson K and others (eds), *Shipping and the Environment: Improving Environmental Performance in Marine Transportation* (Springer 2016)

Liu N and Maes F, 'The European Union's Role in the Prevention of Vessel-Source Pollution and its Internal Influence' (2009) 15 JIML 411

Manners I, 'Normative Power Europe: A Contradiction in Terms?'(2002) 40 J Common Mkt Stud 235

Manzini P, 'The Priority of Pre-Existing Treaties of EC Member States within the Framework of International Law (2001) 12 EJIL 781

Marten B, 'Port State Jurisdiction over Vessel Information: Territoriality, Extra-territoriality and the Future of Shipping Regulation' (2016) 31 Int'l J Marine & Coastal L 470

McDorman T L, 'Port State Control: A comment on the Tokyo MoU and issues of international law' (1997) 7 Asian Yearbook of International Law 229

Mendez M, 'The Legal Effect of Community Agreements: Maximalist Treaty Enforcement and Judicial Avoidance Techniques'(2010) 21 EJIL 83

Mickelson K, 'Common Heritage of Mankind as a Limit to Exploitation of the Global Commons' (2019) 30 EJIL 635

Moen A E, 'Breaking Basel: The Elements of the Basel Convention and its Application to Toxic Ships' (2008) 32 Mar Policy 1053

Moffat J, 'Arranging Deckchairs on the Titanic: Climate Change, Greenhouse Gas Emissions and International Shipping' (2010) 24 Austl & NZ Mar LJ 104

Molenaar E J, 'Port State Jurisdiction' (last updated January 2021) in Peters A and Wolfrum R (eds), *The Max Planck Encyclopedia of Public International Law* (Oxford University Press 2008) <https://opil-1ouplaw-1com-100b98fpw031a.emedien3.sub.uni-hamburg.de/display/10.1093/law:epil/9780199231690/law-9780199231690-e2052?rskey=YdRpQs&result=1&prd=OPIL> accessed 12 May 2023

—— 'Port State Jurisdiction: Towards Comprehensive, Mandatory and Global Coverage' (2007) 38 Ocean Dev Int Law 225

Murillo J, 'Common Concern of Humankind and Its Implications in International Environmental Law' (2008) 5 Macquarie J Int'l & Comp Envtl L 133

Nollkaemper A, 'Unilateralism/Multilateralism' (last updated March 2011) in Peters A and Wolfrum R (eds), *The Max Planck Encyclopedia of Public International Law* (Oxford University Press 2008) <https://opil-1ouplaw-1com-100b98fpw031a.emedien3.sub.uni-hamburg.de/display/10.1093/law:epil/9780199231690/law-9780199231690-e1682?rskey=cndLTN&result=1&prd=OPIL> accessed 12 May 2023

Nollkaemper A and Hey E, 'Implementation of the LOS Convention at Regional Level: European Community Competence in Regulating Safety and Environmental Aspects of Shipping' (1995) 10 Int'l J Marine & Coastal L 281

Oberthur S and Groen L, 'The Effectiveness Dimension of the EU's Performance in International Institutions: Toward a More Comprehensive Assessment Framework' (2015) 53 J Common Mkt Stud 1319

Oil Companies International Marine Forum (OCIMF), 'Guide for Implementation of Sulphur Oxide Exhaust Gas Cleaning Systems' (First Edition 2016) <https://ocimf.org/document-libary/98-guide-for-implementation-of-sulphur-oxide-exhaust-gas-cleaning-systems-final/file> accessed 2 June 2023

Oxman B H, 'The Duty to Respect Generally Accepted International Standards' (1991) 24 NYU J Int'l L & Pol 109

Proelss A, 'Article 1: Use of terms and scope' in Proelss A and others (eds), *United Nations Convention on the Law of the Sea: A Commentary* (CH BECK, Hart, Nomos 2017)

—— 'Article 56: Rights, jurisdiction and duties of the coastal State in the exclusive economic zone' in Proelss A and others (eds), *United Nations Convention on the Law of the Sea: A Commentary* (CH BECK, Hart, Nomos 2017)

—— 'The "Erika III" Package: Progress or Breach of International Law?' in Koch H-J and others (eds), *Climate Change and Environmental Hazards Related to Shipping: An International Legal Framework* (Martinus Nijhoff Publishers 2013)

Psaraftis H N and Kontovas C A, 'Influence and Transparency at the IMO: The Name of the Game' (2020) 22 Maritime Economics & Logistics 151

Rajamani L, 'The Principle of Common but Differentiated Responsibility and the Balance of Commitments under the Climate Regime' (2000) 9 Rev Eur Comp & Int'l Envtl L 120

Rehmatulla N and Smith T, 'The Impact of Split Incentives on Energy Efficiency Technology Investments in Maritime Transport' (2020) 147 Energy Policy 111721

Riddervold M and Newsome A, 'Introduction: Cooperation, Conflict, and Interaction in the Global Commons' (2021) 35 International Relations 365

Ringbom H, 'Global Problem—Regional Solution? International Law Reflections on an EU CO_2 Emissions Trading Scheme for Ships' (2011) 26 Int'l J Marine & Coastal L 613

Romera B M, 'The Paris Agreement and the Regulation of International Bunker Fuels' (2016) 25 Rev Eur Comp & Int'l Envtl L 215

Rosas A, 'The Status in EU Law of International Agreements Concluded by EU Member States' (2011) 34 Fordham Int'l L J 1304

Ryngaert C and Ringbom H, 'Introduction: Port State Jurisdiction: Challenges and Potential' (2016) 31 Int'l J Marine & Coastal L 379

Salo K and others, 'Emissions to the Air' in Andersson K and others (eds), *Shipping and the Environment: Improving Environmental Performance in Marine Transportation* (Springer 2016)

Scott J, 'Extraterritoriality and Territorial Extension in EU Law' (2014) 62 Am J Comp L 87

Scott J and Rajamani L, 'EU Climate Change Unilateralism' (2012) 23 EJIL 2012, 469

Shaffer G, 'International Law and Public Goods in a Legal Pluralist World' (2012) 23 EJIL 669

Shelton D, 'Common Concern of Humanity' (2009) 39 Envtl Policy and Law 83

Smith T, 'The IMO's 2018 climate agreement explained' <https://gmn.imo.org/wp-content/uploads/2018/05/IMOs-2018-climate-agreement-explained-a-UCL-document.pdf> accessed 30 March 2023

Sofiev M and others, 'Cleaner Fuels for Ships provide Public Health Benefits with Climate Tradeoff' (2018) 9:406 Nature Communication (2018) <https://doi.org/10.1038/s41467-017-02774-9> accessed 2 June 2023

Staker C, 'Jurisdiction' in Evans M D (ed), *International Law* (5th edn, OUP 2018)

Stephens T, 'Warming Waters and Souring Seas: Climate Change and Ocean Acidification' in Donald Rothwell and others (eds), *The Oxford Handbook of the Law of the Sea* (OUP 2015)

Stone C D, 'Common but Differentiated Responsibilities in International Law' (2004) 98 Am J Int'l L 276

Treves T, 'Regional Approaches to the Protection of the Marine Environment' in Nordquist M H, Moore J N and Mahmoudi S (eds) *The Stockholm Declaration and Law of the Marine Environment* (Martinus Nijhoff Publishers 2003)

Tveit O, 'MARPOL Annex VI – Solving the low sulphur issue' <https://www.gard.no/web/updates/content/53096/marpol-annex-vi-solving-the-low-sulphur-issue> accessed 7 June 2023

Ulfstein G, 'Legal aspects of Scrapping of Vessels', Annex I to UNEP, 'Legal Aspects of the Full and Partial Dismantling of Ships' (4 December 2001) UNEP/CHW/LWG/4/4 van Leeuwen J and Kern K, 'The External Dimension of European Union Marine Governance: Institutional Interplay between the EU and the International Maritime Organization' (2013) 13 Global Environmental Politics 69

van Rossem J W, 'Interaction between EU Law and International Law in the Light of *Intertanko* and *Kadi*: The Dilemma of Norms Binding the Member States but not the Community' (2009) NYIL 183

Vestreng V and others, 'Twenty-Five Years of Continuous Sulphur Dioxide Emission Reduction in Europe' (2007) 7 *Atmospheric Chemistry and Physics* 3663

Voigt C, 'WTO Law and International Emissions Trading: Is There Potential for Conflict?' (2008) 2 Carbon & Climate L Rev 54

Vöneky S 'Analogy in International Law' (last updated February 2008) in Peters A and Wolfrum R (eds), *The Max Planck Encyclopedia of Public International Law* (Oxford University Press 2008) <https://opil-1ouplaw-1com-100b98ftx087f.emedien3.sub.uni-hamburg.de/display/10.1093/law:epil/9780199231690/law-9780199231690-e1375?rskey=R2a1UF&result=1&prd=MPIL> accessed 4 December 2023

Wacht F, 'Article 212: Pollution from or through the atmosphere' in Proelss A and others (eds), *United Nations Convention on the Law of the Sea: A Commentary* (CH BECK, Hart, Nomos 2017)

Weiss E B, 'The Coming Water Crisis: A Common Concern of Mankind' (2012) 1 Transnational Envtl Law 153

Wittels J, 'Maersk sees Fuel Bill Soaring by $2 Billion from 2020 Rules' (Bloomberg 2018) <https://www.bloomberg.com/news/articles/2018-08-29/maersk-sees-fuel-bill-soaring-by-2-billion-from-2020-rules> accessed 2 June 2023

Wolfrum R, 'Common Heritage of Mankind' (last updated November 2009) in Peters A and Wolfrum R (eds), *The Max Planck Encyclopedia of Public International Law* (Oxford University Press 2008) <https://opil-1ouplaw-1com-100b98ffu0256.emedien3.sub.uni-hamburg.de/display/10.1093/law:epil/9780199231690/law-9780199231690-e1149?rskey=VknBeE&result=1&prd=MPIL> accessed 2 June 2023

Zalucki K, 'Extraterritorial Jurisdiction in International Law' (2015) 17 Int'l Comm L Rev 403

Studies and Reports

Anger A and others, 'International Shipping and Market Based Instruments 2009: Final Report' (2009) MEPC 60/INF.21 (15 January 2010)

Bäuerle T and others, *Integration of Marine Transport into the European Emissions Trading System: Environmental, Economic and Legal Analysis of Different Options* (Umweltbundesamt 2010) <https://www.umweltbundesamt.de/sites/default/files/medien/461/publikationen/3942.pdf> accessed 27 October 2023

Bazari Z and Longva T, 'Assessment of IMO Mandated Energy Efficiency Measures for International Shipping', IMO, MEPC, 'Estimated CO_2 emissions reduction from the introduction of mandatory technical and operational energy efficiency measures for ships: Executive summary: Note by the Secretariat' (31 October 2011) MEPC 63/4/1

Bio Intelligence Service, 'The Feasibility of a List of "Green and Safe" Ship Dismantling Facilities and of a List of Ships likely to go for Dismantling' (2010) [To the knowledge of the author, this document is not publicly accessible anymore at time of finalization of this study, but can be viewed here: <https://dokumen.tips/documents/2004-06-scrapping-study-en.html?page=1> accessed 18 May 2023. A digital copy can also be made available upon request.]

BMT Murray Fenton Edon Liddiard Vince Limited, 'Study on the Economic, Legal, Environmental and Practical Implications of a European Union System to Reduce Ship Emissions of SO_x and NO_x' (2000) <https://ec.europa.eu/environment/enveco/taxation/ship_emissions/pdf/app4final.pdf> accessed 18 June 2022

Buhaug Ø and others, *Second IMO GHG Study 2009* (IMO 2009) <https://wwwcdn.imo.org/localresources/en/OurWork/Environment/Documents/SecondIMOGHGStudy2009.pdf> accessed 6 February 2023

Commission, Directorate-General Energy and Transport, 'Oil tanker phase out and the Ship Scrapping Industry: A Study on the Implications of the Accelerated Phase out Scheme of Single Hull Tankers proposed by the EU for the World Ship Scrapping and Recycling Industry' (2004) [To the knowledge of the author, this study is not publicly accessible anymore, however can be viewed here: <https://dokumen.tips/documents/2004-06-scrapping-study-en.html?page=1> accessed 18 May 2023. Also, a digital copy of the document is available upon request.]

Crippa M and others, *CO_2 Emissions of all World Countries* (Publications Office of the European Union 2022) <https://edgar.jrc.ec.europa.eu/booklet/CO2_emissions_of_all_world_countries_2022_report.pdf> accessed 20 March 2023

Ecorys, 'The Ship Recycling Fund: Financing Environmentally Sound Scrapping and Recycling of Sea-Going Ships' (2005) <https://www.shipbreakingplatform.org/wp-content/uploads/2019/01/ECORYS-survey-on-a-ship-recycling-fund.pdf> accessed 3 October 2017 [To the knowledge of the author, this document is not publicly accessible anymore at time of finalization of this study. A digital copy can, however, be made available upon request.]

Ecorys, DNV GL and Erasmus School of Law, 'Financial Instrument to Facilitate Safe and Sound Ship Recycling: Final Report (Commission 2016) < https://op.europa.eu/de/publication-detail/-/publication/68d273df-433c-11e6-9c64-01aa75ed71a1> accessed 19 May 2023

EEA/EMSA, *European Maritime Transport Environmental Report 2021* (Publications Office of the European Union 2021) <https://www.emsa.europa.eu/publications/download/6733/4513/23.html> accessed 18 May 2023

EMSA, 'Study on the certification of ship recycling facilities' <https://www.emsa.europa.eu/damage-stability-study/download/1015/602/23.html> accessed 10 February 2023

EP, 'Financing the environmentally sound recycling and treatment of ships: Impact Assessment of a substantive amendment to the Proposal for a Regulation on ship recycling' (2013) <https://www.europarl.europa.eu/document/activities/cont/201303/20130305ATT62130/20130305ATT62130EN.pdf> accessed 19 May 2023

Faber J, 'Estimated Index Values of Ships 2009-2016: Analysis of the Design Efficiency of Ships that have Entered the Fleet since 2009' (2017) <https://cedelft.eu/wp-content/uploads/sites/2/2021/04/2017_07_CE_Delft_7L97_Estimated_Index_Values_of_Ships_2009-2016_def_2017.pdf> accessed 19 May 2023

Faber J and others, 'Aviation and Maritime Transport in a post 2012 Climate Policy Regime' (CE Delft 2006) <https://cedelft.eu/wp-content/uploads/sites/2/2021/03/06_7153_59.pdf> accessed 30 March 2023

—— *Fourth IMO GHG Study 2020* (IMO 2020) <https://wwwcdn.imo.org/localresources/en/OurWork/Environment/Documents/Fourth%20IMO%20GHG%20Study%202020%20-%20Full%20report%20and%20annexes.pdf> accessed 6 February 2023

—— *Fourth IMO GHG Study 2020: Executive Summary* (IMO 2020) <https://wwwcdn.imo.org/localresources/en/OurWork/Environment/Documents/Fourth%20IMO%20GHG%20Study%202020%20Executive-Summary.pdf> accessed 31 March 2023

—— Technical Support for European Action to Reducing Greenhouse Gas Emissions from International Transport' (CE Delft 2009) <https://cedelft.eu/wp-content/uploads/sites/2/2021/04/7731_finalreportJF.pdf> accessed 30 March 2023

Finska L and Ringbom H, *Regulation of GHGs from Ships: On the Available Discretion for Regulatory Solutions in a European and Finnish Perspective* <https://www.centrumbalticum.org/files/5185/Regulation_of_GHGs_from_ships_final.pdf> accessed 3 April 2023

IEA, *Energy Technology Perspectives 2017* <https://iea.blob.core.windows.net/assets/a6587f9f-e56c-4b1d-96e4-5a4da78f12fa/Energy_Technology_Perspectives_2017-PDF.pdf> accessed 5 May 2023

—— *Energy Technology Perspectives* 2020 (Revised version February 2021) <https://iea.blob.core.windows.net/assets/7f8aed40-89af-4348-be19-c8a67df0b9ea/Energy_Technology_Perspectives_2020_PDF.pdf> accessed 31 March 2023

IPCC, *Global warming of 1.5°: An IPCC Special Report on the impacts of global warming of 1.5°C above pre-industrial levels and related global greenhouse gas emission pathways, in the context of strengthening the global response to the threat of climate change, sustainable development, and efforts to eradicate poverty* <https://www.ipcc.ch/site/assets/uploads/sites/2/2022/06/SR15_Full_Report_HR.pdf> accessed 30 March 2023

Influence Map, 'Corporate Capture of the International Maritime Organization – How the Shipping Sector lobbies to stay out of the Paris Agreement' <https://influencemap.org/report/Corporate-capture-of-the-IMO-902bf81c05a0591c551f9650 20623fda> accessed 12 May 2023

ITF, 'Decarbonising Maritime Transport: Pathways to zero-carbon shipping by 2035' (2008) <https://www.itf-oecd.org/sites/default/files/docs/decarbonising-maritime-transport-2035.pdf> last accessed 2 June 2023

Kachi A, Mooldijk S, Warnecke C, 'Carbon pricing options for international maritime emissions' (NewClimate — Institute for Climate Policy and Global Sustainability gGmbH 2019) <https://newclimate.org/sites/default/files/2019/04/Carbon-pricing-options-for-international-maritime-emissions.pdf> accessed 19 May 2023

Milieu Ltd & COWI, 'Study in relation to options for new initiatives regarding dismantling of ships: Note on pros and cons of early transposition of the Ship Recycling Convention' (2009) <https://ec.europa.eu/environment/pdf/waste/ships/early_transposition_note.pdf> accessed 18 May 2023

—— Study in relation to options for new initiatives regarding dismantling of ships: Note on the ship dismantling fund: Pros and cons of the three options' (2009) <http://ec.europa.eu/environment/waste/ships/pdf/fund_note.pdf> accessed 18 May 2023

Nelissen D and Faber J, 'Economic impacts of MRV of fuel and emissions in maritime transport' (CE Delft 2014) <https://cedelft.eu/wp-content/uploads/sites/2/2021/04/CE_Delft_7B83_Economic_impacts_of_MRV_FINAL_1389349788.pdf> accessed 19 May 2023

Profundo, 'Financial mechanism to ensure responsible ship recycling: A research paper prepared for the NGO Shipbreaking Platform' (2013) <https://www.shipbreakingplatform.org/wp-content/uploads/2018/11/Financial-mechanisms-for-resonsible-ship-recycling-22_01_2013-FINAL.pdf> accessed 19 May 2023

Smith T and others, *Third IMO Greenhouse Gas Study 2014: Executive Summary and Final Report* (IMO 2015) <https://wwwcdn.imo.org/localresources/en/OurWork/Environment/Documents/Third%20Greenhouse%20Gas%20Study/GHG3%20Executive%20Summary%20and%20Report.pdf> accessed 19 May 2023

Transparency International, 'Governance at the International Maritime Organisation: The Case for Reform' <https://images.transparencycdn.org/images/2018_IMO_Governance_Report_EN.pdf> accessed 12 May 2023

UN, *The Second World Ocean Assessment, Volume I* <https://www.un.org/regularprocess/sites/www.un.org.regularprocess/files/2011859-e-woa-ii-vol-i.pdf> accessed 5 May 2023

UNCTAD, *Review of Maritime Transport 2023* <https://unctad.org/system/files/official-document/rmt2023_en.pdf> 27 October 2023

Treaties, Legislative Acts and Statutory Documents

– European Union

• Treaties

Act concerning the conditions of accession of the Czech Republic, the Republic of Estonia, the Republic of Cyprus, the Republic of Latvia, the Republic of Lithuania, the Republic of Hungary, the Republic of Malta, the Republic of Poland, the Republic of Slovenia, and the Slovak Republic and the adjustments to the Treaties on which the European Union is founded [2003] OJ L236/33

Consolidated Versions of the Treaty on European Union and of the Treaty Establishing the European Community (2002) [2002] OJ C325/1

Consolidated version of the Treaty on the Functioning of the European Union [2012] OJ C326/47

• *Secondary Law*

Commission Delegated Regulation (EU) 2016/2071 of 22 September 2016 amending Regulation (EU) 2015/757 of the European Parliament and of the Council as regards the methods for monitoring carbon dioxide emissions and the rules for monitoring other relevant information [2016] OJ L320/1

Commission Delegated Regulation (EU) 2016/2072 of 22 September 2016 on the verification activities and accreditation of verifiers pursuant to Regulation (EU) 2015/757 of the European Parliament and of the Council on the monitoring, reporting and verification of carbon dioxide emissions from maritime transport [2016] OJ L320/5

Commission Implementing Decision (EU) 2015/253 of 16 February 2015 laying down the rules concerning the sampling and reporting under Council Directive 1999/32/EC as regards the sulphur content of marine fuels [2015] OJ L41/55

Commission Implementing Decision (EU) 2015/2398 of 17 December 2015 on Information and Documentation related to an Application for a Facility located in a Third Country for inclusion in the European List of Ship Recycling Facilities [2015] OJ L332/145

Commission Implementing Regulation (EU) 2016/1927 of 4 November 2016 on templates for monitoring plans, emissions reports and documents of compliance pursuant Regulation (EU) 2015/757 of the European Parliament and of the Council on monitoring, reporting and verification of carbon dioxide emissions from maritime transport [2016] OJ L 299/1

Commission Implementing Regulation (EU) 2016/1928 of 4 November 2016 on determination of cargo carried for categories of ships other than passenger, ro-ro and container ships pursuant Regulation (EU) 2015/757 of the European Parliament and of the Council on monitoring, reporting and verification of carbon dioxide emissions from maritime transport [2016] OJ L 299/22

Commission Implementing Decision (EU) 2016/2321 of 19 December 2016 on the Format of the Ready for Recycling Certificate issued in accordance with Regulation (EU) No 1257/2013 of the European Parliament and of the Council on Ship Recycling [2016] OJ L345/112

Commission Implementing Decision (EU) 2016/2322 of 19 December 2016 on the Format of the Statement of Completion of Ship Recycling required under Regulation (EU) No 1257/2013 of the European Parliament and of the Council on Ship Recycling [2016] OJ L345/117

Commission Implementing Decision (EU) 2016/2323 of 19 December 2016 establishing the European List of Ship Recycling Facilities pursuant to Regulation (EU) No 1257/2013 of the European Parliament and of the Council on Ship Recycling [2016] OJ L345/119

Commission Implementing Decision (EU) 2016/2324 of 19 December 2016 on the Format of the Report of Planned Start of Ship Recycling required under Regulation (EU) No 1257/2013 of the European Parliament and of the Council on Ship Recycling [2016] OJ L345/129

Commission Implementing Decision (EU) 2016/2325 of 19 December 2016 on the Format of the Certification on the Inventory of Hazardous Materials issued in accordance with Regulation (EU) No 1257/2013 of the European Parliament and of the Council on Ship Recycling [2016] OJ L345/13

Commission Implementing Decision (EU) 2018/1906 of 30 November 2018 amending Implementing Decision (EU) 2016/2323 to update the European List of ship recycling facilities established pursuant to Regulation (EU) No 1257/2013 of the European Parliament and of the Council [2018] OJ L310/29

Commission Implementing Decision (EU) 2022/2462 of 14 December 2022 amending Commission Implementing Decision (EU) 2016/2323 establishing the European List of Ship Recycling Facilities pursuant to Regulation (EU) No 1257/2013 of the European Parliament and of the Council [2022] OJ L321/42

Commission Implementing Regulation (EU) 2023/2599 of 22 November 2023 laying down rules for the application of directive 2003/87/EC of the European Parliament and of the Council as regards the administration of shipping companies by administering authorities in respect of a shipping company [2023] OJ L 2023/2599, 23.11.2023

Council Directive 1999/32/EC of 26 April 1999 relating to a reduction in the sulphur content of certain liquid fuels and amending Directive 93/12/EEC [1999] OJ L121/13

Directive 2003/87/EC of the European Parliament and of the Council of 13 October 2003 establishing a system for greenhouse gas emission allowance trading within the Union and amending Council Directive 96/61/EC [2003] OJ L275/32

Directive 2005/33/EC of the European Parliament and of the Council of 6 July 2005 amending Directive 1999/32/EC [2005] OJ L191/59

Directive 2005/35/EC of the European Parliament and of the Council of 7 September 2005 on ship-source pollution and on the introduction of penalties for infringements [2005] OJ L 255/11

Directive 2006/12/EC of the European Parliament and of the Council of 5 April 2006 on Waste [2006] OJ L114/9

Directive 2008/98/EC of the European Parliament and of the Council of 19 November 2008 on Waste and repealing certain Directives [2008] OJ L312/3

Directive 2008/101/EC of the European Parliament and of the Council of 19 November 2008 amending Directive 2003/87/EC so as to include aviation activities in the scheme for greenhouse gas emission allowance trading within the Community [2009] OJ L8/3

Directive 2009/16/EC of the European Parliament and of the Council of 23 April 2009 on Port State Control [2009] OJ L131/57

Directive 2009/29/EC of the European Parliament and of the Council of 23 April 2009 amending Directive 2003/87/EC so as to improve and extend the greenhouse gas emissions allowance trading scheme of the Community [2009] OJ L140/63

Directive 2012/33/EU of the European Parliament and of the Council of 21 November 2012 amending Council Directive 1999/32/EC as regards the sulphur content of marine fuels [2012] OJ L327/1

Directive (EU) 2016/802 of the European Parliament and of the Council of 11 May 2016 relating to a reduction in the sulphur content of certain liquid fuels [2016] OJ L132/58

Directive (EU) 2023/959 of the European Parliament and of the Council of 10 May 2023 amending Directive 2003/87/EC establishing a system for greenhouse gas emission allowance trading within the Union and Decision (EU) 2015/1814 concerning the establishment and operation of a market stability reserve for the Union greenhouse gas emission trading system [2023] OJ L130/134

Regulation (EC) No 1013/2006 of the European Parliament and of the Council of 14 June 2006 on shipments of waste [2006] OJ L190/1

Regulation (EC) No 765/2008 of the European Parliament and of the Council of 9 July 2008 setting out the requirements for accreditation and market surveillance relating to the marketing of products and repealing Regulation (EEC) No 339/93 [2008] OJ L218/30

Regulation (EC) No 391/2009 of the European Parliament and of the Council of 23 April 2009 on common rules and standards for ship inspection and survey organisations [2009] OJ L131/11

Regulation (EU) No 1257/2013 of the European Parliament and of the Council of 20 November 2013 on Ship Recycling and Amending Regulation (EC) No 1013/2006 and Directive 2009/16/EC [2013] OJ L330/1

Regulation (EU) 2015/757 of the European Parliament and of the Council of 29 April 2015 on the monitoring, reporting and verification of carbon dioxide emissions from maritime transport, and amending Directive 2009/16/EC [2015] OJ L123/55

Regulation (EU) 2023/1805 of the European Parliament and of the Council of 13 September 2023 on the use of renewable and low-carbon fuels in maritime transport, and amending Directive 2009/16/EC [2023] OJ L234/48

Regulation (EU) 2023/957 of the European Parliament and of the Council of 10 May 2023 amending Regulation (EU) 2015/757 in order to provide for the inclusion of maritime transport activities in the EU Emission Trading System and for the monitoring, reporting and verification of emissions of additional greenhouse gases and emissions from additional ship types [2023] OJ L130/105

– *Multilateral*

Agreement under the United Nations Convention on the Law of the Sea on the Conservation and Sustainable Use of Marine Biological Diversity of Areas beyond National Jurisdiction (adopted 19 June 2023, not yet in force) A/CONF.232/2023/4

Basel Convention on the Control of Transboundary Movements of Hazardous Wastes and their Disposal (adopted 22 March 1989, entered into force 5 May 1992) 1673 UNTS 57

Amendment to the Basel Convention on the Control of Transboundary Movements of Hazardous Wastes and their Disposal (adopted on 22 September 1995, entered into force 5 December 2019) Registration No 28911 (no UNTS volume number determined yet)

Convention for the Safeguarding of the Intangible Cultural Heritage (adopted 17 October 2003, entered into force 20 April 2006) 2368 UNTS 3

Convention of the International Maritime Organization (adopted 6 March 1948, entered into force 17 March 1958) 289 UNTS 3

- *Amendments to the Convention of the International Maritime Organization*

Amendments to article 17 and 18 of the Convention on the International Maritime Organization (adopted 15 September 1964, entered into force 6 October 1967) 607 UNTS 276

Amendment to article 28 of the Convention on the International Maritime Organization (adopted 28 September 1965, entered into force 3 November 1968) 649 UNTS 335

Amendments to articles 10, 16, 17, 18, 20, 28, 31 and 32 of the Convention on the International Maritime Organization (adopted 17 October 1974, entered into force on 1 April 1978) 1080 UNTS 375

Amendments to the title and substantive provisions of the Convention on the International Maritime Organization (adopted 14 November 1975 and 9 November 1977, entered into force 22 May 1982, except for the amendment to article 51 which entered into force on 28 July 1982) 1276 UNTS 468 and 1285 UNTS 318

Amendments to the Convention on the International Maritime Organization relating to the institutionalization of the Committee on Technical Co-operation in the Convention (adopted 17 November 1977, entered into force 10 November 1984) 1380 UNTS 268

Amendments to articles 17, 18, 20 and 51 of the Convention on the International Maritime Organization (adopted 15 November 1979, entered into force 10 November 1984) 1380 UNTS 288

Amendments to the Convention on the International Maritime Organization (institutionalization of the Facilitation Committee) (adopted 7 November 1991, entered into force 7 December 2008)

Amendments to the Convention on the International Maritime Organization (adopted 4 November 1993, entered into force 7 November 2002) 2199 UNTS 113

Amendments to the Convention on the International Maritime Organization (London, 8 December 2021), adopted by Assembly Resolution A.1152 (32) of 8 December 2021 (not yet in force)

Convention on Biological Diversity (adopted 5 June 1992, entered into force 29 December 1993) 1760 UNTS 79

Convention on International Trade in Endangered species of Wild Fauna and Flora (adopted 3 March 1973, entered into force 1 July 1975) 993 UNTS 243

Convention on the Prevention of Marine Pollution by Dumping of Wastes and Other Matter (adopted 13 November 1972, entered into force 30 August 1975) 1046 UNTS 120

Protocol to the Convention on the Prevention of Marine Pollution by Dumping of Wastes and Other Matter, 1972 (adopted on 7 November 1996, entered into force 24 March 2006) (1997) 36 ILM 1

General Agreement on Tariffs and Trade 1947 (concluded 30 October 1947, provisionally entered into force 1 January 1948) 55 UNTS 187

General Agreement on Tariffs and Trade 1994, Annex 1A to the Marrakesh Agreement establishing the World Trade Organization (concluded 15 April 1994, entered into force 1 January 1995) 1867 UNTS 190

General Agreement on Trade in Services, Annex 1B to the Marrakesh Agreement establishing the World Trade Organization (concluded 15 April 1994, entered into force 1 January 1995) 1869 UNTS 183

International Convention for the Prevention of Pollution from Ships (adopted 2 November 1973) (1973) 12 ILM 1319

Protocol of 1978 relating to the International Convention for the Prevention of Pollution from Ships, 1973, (adopted 17 February 1978, entered into force 2 October 1983) 1340 UNTS 61

International Convention for the Prevention of Pollution of the Sea by Oil, 1954 (adopted 12 May 1954, entered into force 26 July 1958) 327 UNTS 3

International Convention on Tonnage Measurement of Ships, 1969 (adopted 23 June 1969, entered into force 18 July 1982) 1291 UNTS 3

International Convention Relating to Intervention on the High Seas in Cases of Oil Pollution Casualties (adopted 29 November 1969, entered into force 6 May 1975) 970 UNTS 211

International Treaty on Plant Genetic Resources for Food and Agriculture (adopted 3 November 2001, entered into force 29 June 2004) 2400 UNTS 303

Paris Agreement (adopted 12 December 2015, entered into force 4 November 2016) 3156 UNTS 79

Protocol of 2002 to the Athens Convention relating to the Carriage of Passengers and their Luggage by Sea, 1974 (adopted 1 November 2002, entered into force 23 April 2014) Registration No 24817, UNTS volume number determined 3283

Statute of the International Court of Justice, XV UNIO 355 (the UNIO volumes can be found at <https://digitallibrary.un.org/record/1300969> accessed 11 December 2023)

Statute of the International Court of Justice, XV UNIO 355 (the UNIO volumes can be found at <https://digitallibrary.un.org/record/1300969> accessed 11 December 2023

Vienna Convention on the Law of Treaties (adopted 23 May 1969, entered into force 27 January 1980), 1155 UNTS 331

United Nations Convention on the Law of the Sea (adopted 10 December 1982, entered into force 16 November 1994) 1833 UNTS 3

United Nations Framework Convention on Climate Change (adopted 9 May 1992, entered into force 21 March 1994) 1771 UNTS 107

Kyoto Protocol to the United Nations Framework Convention on Climate Change (adopted 11 December 1997, entered into force 16 February 2005) 2303 UNTS 162

European Commission Documents

'Amended proposal for a Council Directive relating to a reduction of the sulphur content of certain liquid fuels and amending Directive 93/12/EEC' [1998] OJ C259/5 (with document COM (1998) 385 final additionally containing an Explanatory Memorandum)

'Amended proposal for a Directive of the European Parliament and of the Council amending Directive 1999/32/EC as regards the sulphur content of marine fuels' COM(2003) 476 final

Commissioner for Transport Violeta Bulc at the Transport, Telecommunications and Energy Council on 8 June 2017 <https://video.consilium.europa.eu/event/en/22678?start_time=0> starting at 09:20:44, accessed 26 May 2023

'Communication to the Council and the European Parliament on a Community strategy to combat acidification—Proposal for a Council Directive relating to a reduction of the sulphur content of certain liquid fuels and amending Directive 93/12/EEC—Proposal for a Council Decision on the conclusion by the European Community of the Protocol to the 1979 Convention on long-range transboundary air pollution on further reductions of sulphur emissions' COM (97) 88 final

'Communication from the Commission to the European Parliament and the Council on the Safety of the Seaborne Oil Trade' COM (2000) 142 final

'Communication from the Commission to the European Parliament and the Council on a Second Set of Community Measures on Maritime Safety Following the Sinking of the Oil Tanker ERIKA' COM (2000) 802 final

'Communication to the Commission from the President in Agreement with Vice-President Ashton: Strategy for the progressive improvement of the EU status in international organisations and other for a in line with the objectives of the Treaty of Lisbon' C (2012) 9420 final

'EU strategy on better ship dismantling' COM (2008) 767 final

Fourteenth Report on Competition Policy (Office for the Publications of the European Communities 1984) <https://op.europa.eu/en/publication-detail/-/publication/3c93e6fa-934b-4fb9-b927-dc9fed71ccfe/language-en> accessed 26 May 2023

'Green paper on better ship dismantling' COM (2007) 269 final

'Integrating maritime transport emissions in the EU's greenhouse gas reduction policy', COM (2013) 479 final

'Proposal for a Directive of the European Parliament and of the Council amending Directive 1999/32/EC as regards the sulphur content of marine fuels' [2003] OJ C45E, 277

'Proposal for a Directive of the European Parliament and of the Council amending Directive 1999/32/EC as regards the sulphur content of marine fuels', COM (2011) 439 final

'Proposal for a regulation of the European Parliament and of the Council on the monitoring, reporting and verification of carbon dioxide emissions from maritime transport and amending Regulation (EU) No 525/2013' COM (2013) 480 final

'Proposal for a Regulation of the European Parliament and of the Council amending Regulation (EU) 2015/757 in order to take appropriate account of the global data collection system for ship fuel oil consumption data' COM (2019) 38 final

'Proposal for a Directive of the European Parliament and of the Council amending Directive 2003/87/EC establishing a system for greenhouse gas emission allowance trading within the Union, Decision (EU) 2015/1814 concerning the establishment and operation of a market stability reserve for the Union greenhouse gas emission trading scheme and Regulation (EU) 2015/757' COM (2021) 551 final

'Proposal for a Regulation of the European Parliament and of the Council on the use of renewable and low-carbon fuels in maritime transport and amending Directive 2009/16/EC' COM (2021) 562 final

'Proposal for a Council Directive restructuring the Union framework for the taxation of energy products and electricity (recast)' COM (2021) 563

'Proposal for a Regulation of the European Parliament and of the Council on Shipments of Waste and amending Regulations (EU) No 1257/2013 and (EU) No 2020/1056' COM (2021) 709 final

Public consultation, 'Including maritime transport emissions in the EU's greenhouse gas reduction commitment' <https://climate.ec.europa.eu/news-your-voice/consultations/including-maritime-transport-emissions-eus-greenhouse-gas-reduction-commitment_en> accessed 3 April 2023

'Public consultation on the options for new initiative regarding dismantling of ships' <http://ec.europa.eu/environment/waste/ships/pdf/Consultation_ship_dismantling.pdf> accessed 18 May 2023

'Recommendation from the Commission to the Council in order to open and conduct negotiations with the International Maritime Organization (IMO) on the condition and arrangements for accession by the European Community' SEC (2002) 381 final

'Ship recycling: reducing human and environmental impacts' <https://circabc.europa.eu/ui/group/636f928d-2669-41d3-83db-093e90ca93a2/library/2a971118-bfe1-4e4e-b6c9-53a8e6490a0e/details?download=true> accessed 18 May 2023

'Strategic Goals and Recommendations for the EU's Maritime Transport Policy until 2018' COM(2009) 8 final

Staff Working Document, 'Impact Assessment for an EU Strategy for Better Ship Dismantling' SEC (2008) 2846

Staff Working Paper, 'Annex to: The Communication on Thematic Strategy on Air Pollution and The Directive on "Ambient Air Quality and Cleaner Air for Europe": Impact Assessment', SEC (2005) 1133

Staff Working Paper, 'Impact Assessment – Accompanying the document Proposal for a Directive of the European Parliament and of the Council amending Directive 1999/32/EC as regards the sulphur content of marine fuels' (SEC(2011) 918 final

'White Paper: Roadmap to a Single European Transport Area – Towards a competitive and resource efficient transport system' (28 March 2011) COM (2011) 144 final

EU Parliament and Council documents

Council, 'Common Position (EC) No 13/2005 adopted by the Council on 9 December 2004 with a view to adopting Directive 2005/.../EC of the European Parliament and of the Council of ... amending Directive 1999/32/EC as regards sulphur content of marine fuels' [2005] OJ C63E/26

—— 'Common Position (EC) No 61/98 of 6 October 1998 adopted by the Council, acting in accordance with the procedure referred to in Article 189c of the Treaty establishing the European Community, with a view to adopting a Council Directive relating to a reduction in the sulphur reduction content of certain liquid fuels and amending Directive 93/12/EEC' [1998] OJ C364/20

—— 'Council conclusions of 22 December 2003 — A European Union strategy to reduce atmospheric emissions from seagoing ships' [2004] OJ C8/3

—— Council Decision of 14 April 2014 concerning the ratification of, or the accession to, the Hong Kong International Convention for the Safe and Environmentally Sound Recycling of Ships, 2009, by the Member States in the interest of the Union, 2014/241/EU [2014] OJ L128/45

—— 'EU position for the Copenhagen Climate Conference (7-18 December 2009)' (21 October 2009) 14790/09

—— Opinion of the Legal Service, 'Proposal for a Regulation of the European Parliament and of the Council on ship recycling - relationship between Regulation 1013/2006 on waste shipments, the Basel Convention, and the Hong Kong Convention' (28 November 2012) 16995/12

—— 2106th Council meeting - Environment -: Luxembourg, 16-17 June 1998' <https://ec.europa.eu/commission/presscorner/detail/en/PRES_98_205> accessed 2 June 2023

—— '2661st meeting of the Council of the European Union (Education, Youth and Culture), held in Brussels on 23 and 24 May 2005, Addendum to Draft Minutes, 9252/05 Add 1

—— '2671st meeting of the Council of the European Union (Transport/Telecommunications/ Energy), held in Luxembourg on 27-28 July 2005', 10566/05

—— '2672nd meeting of the Council of the European Union (Economic and Financial Affairs), held in Brussels on 12 July 2005, Addendum to Draft Minutes, 11128/05 Add 1 Rev 1

Decision No. 406/2009/EC of the European Parliament and of the Council of 23 April 2009 on the effort of Member States to reduce their greenhouse gas emissions to meet the Community's greenhouse gas emissions reduction commitments up to 2020 [2009] OJ L140/136

Decision (EU) 2018/853 of the European Parliament and of the Council of 30 May 2018 amending Regulation (EU) No 1257/2013 and Directives 94/63/EC and 2009/31/EC of the European Parliament and of the Council and Council Directives 86/278/EEC and 87/217/EEC as regards Procedural Rules in the Field of Environmental Reporting and repealing Council Directive 91/692/EEC, [2018] OJ L150/155

EP, 'Amendments adopted by the European Parliament on 18 April 2013 on the proposal for a regulation of the European Parliament and of the Council on ship recycling' (18 April 2013) P7_TA(2013)0182.

—— Committee on the Environment, Public Health and Consumer Protection, 'Report on the proposal for a Council Directive relating to a reduction of the sulphur content of certain liquid fuels and amending Directive 93/12/EEC (COM(97)0088)' (4 May 1998) <https://www.europarl.europa.eu/doceo/document/A-4-1998-0174_EN.html?redirect> accessed 2 June 2023

—— Committee on Regional Policy, Transport and Tourism 'Report on the proposal for a European Parliament and Council directive on ship-source pollution and on the introduction of sanctions, including criminal sanctions, for pollution offences (5 November 2003) A5-0388/2003

—— Committee on the Environment, Public Health and Food Safety, 'Report on the proposal for a directive of the European Parliament and of the Council amending Directive 1999/32/EC as regards the sulphur content of marine fuels' (27 February 2012) A7-0038/2012

—— Committee on the Environment, Public Health and Food Safety, 'Draft Report on the proposal for a regulation of the European Parliament and of the Council on ship recycling' (20 November 2012) 2012/0055(COD)

—— Committee on the Environment, Public Health and Food Safety, 'Report on the proposal for a regulation of the European Parliament and of the Council on ship recycling' (28 March 2013) A7-0132/2013

—— Committee on the Environment, Public Health and Food Safety, 'Report on the proposal for a regulation of the European Parliament and of the Council amending Regulation (EU) 2015/757 in order to take appropriate account of the global data collection system for ship fuel oil consumption data' (29 July 2020) A9-0144/2020

—— European Parliament resolution on improving safety at sea (2003/2235 (INI)) (adopted on 21 April 2004) P5_TA(2004)0350

—— 'Minutes of the sitting of Wednesday 13 May 1998' [1998] OJ C167/73

—— Statement of the Rapporteur of the Committee on the Environment, Public Health and Food Safety of the European Parliament, Carl Schlyter, during the final vote: <http://www.europarl.europa.eu/sides/getDoc.do?pubRef=-//EP//TEXT+CRE+20131022+ITEM-008-01+DOC+XML+V0//EN> accessed 18 May 2023

—— 'Position of the European Parliament adopted at first reading on 4 June 2003 with a view to the adoption of European Parliament and Council Directive 2003/.../EC amending Directive 1999/32/EC as regards the sulphur content of marine fuels' (P5_TC1-COD(2002)0259) [2004] OJ C68E/311

——'Position of the European Parliament adopted at second reading on 13 April 2005 with a view to the adoption of Directive 2005/.../EC of the European Parliament and of the council amending Directive 1999/32/EC as regards the sulphur content of marine fuels' (P6_TC2_COD(2002)0259) [2006] OJ C33E/469

EESC, 'Opinion of the European and Social Committee on "Proposal for a Regulation of the European Parliament and of the Council amending Regulation (EU) 2015/757 in order to take appropriate account of the global data collection system for ship fuel oil consumption data"' [2019] C240/41

ECJ Case Documents

Case C-48/69 *Imperial Chemical Industries Ltd v Commission* ECLI:EU:C:1972:70

Case C-48/69 *Imperial Chemical Industries Ltd. v Commission of the European Communities*, Opinion of AG Mayras ECLI:EU:C:1972:32,

Joined Cases 21/72 to 24/72 *International Fruit Company and Others v Produktschap voor Groenten en Fruit* ECLI:EU:C:1972:115

Case C-812/79 *Attorney General v Juan C. Burgoa* ECLI:EU:C:1980:231

Joined Cases 89, 104, 114, 116, 117 and 125 to 129/85 *Ahlström Osakeyhtiö and Others v Commission* ECLI:EU:C:1988:447

Joined Cases 89, 104, 114, 116, 117 and 125 to 129/85 *Ahlström Osakeyhtiö and Others v Commission*, Opinion of AG Darmon ECLI:EU:C:1988:258

Case C-348/89 *Mecanarte - Mealúrgica da Lagoa Ld v Chefe do Serviço da Conferência Final da Alfândega do Porto* ECLI:EU:C:1991:278

Case C-286/90 *Anklagemyndigheden v Peter Michael Poulsen and Diva Navigation Corp.* ECLI:EU:C:1992:453

Case C-158/91 *Ministère public and Direction du travail and de l'emploi v Levy* ECLI:EU:C:1993:332

Case 379/92 *Criminal proceedings against Matteo Peralta* ECLI:EU:C:1994:296

Case C-62/98 *Commission of the European Communities v Portuguese Republic* ECLI:EU:C:2000:358

Case C-84/98 *Commission of the European Communities v Portuguese Republic* ECLI:EU:C:2000:359

Case C-170/98 *Commission of the European Communities v Kingdom of Belgium* [1999] ECLI:EU:C:1999:441

Case C-377/98 *Kingdom of the Netherlands v European Parliament and Council of the European Union* ECLI:EU:C:2001:523

Case C-466/98 *Commission of the European Communities v United Kingdom of Great Britain and Northern Ireland* ECLI:EU:C:2002:624

Case C-466/98 *Commission of the European Communities v United Kingdom of Great Britain and Northern Ireland*, Opinion of AG Tizzano ECLI:EU:C:2002:63

Case C-216/01 *Budějovický Budvar, národní podnik v Rudolf Ammersin GmbH* ECLI:EU:C:2003:618

Case C-308/06 *The Queen, on the application of International Association of Independent Tanker Owners (Intertanko)and Others v Secretary of State for Transport* ECLI:EU:C:2008:312

Case C-308/06 *The Queen, on the application of International Association of Independent Tanker Owners (Intertanko)and Others v Secretary of State for Transport*, Opinion of AG Kokott, ECLI:EU:C:2007:689

Case C-188/07 Commune des Mesquer v Total France SA and Total International Ltd ECLI:EU:C:2008:359

Case C-366/10 *Air Transport Association of America and Others v Secretary of State for Energy and Climate Change* ECLI:EU:C:2011:864

Case C-366/10 *Air Transport Association of America and Others v Secretary of State for Energy and Climate Change*, Opinion of AG Kokott ECLI:EU:2011:637

Case 537/11 *Mattia Manzi and Compagnia Naviera Orchestra v Capitaneria di Porto di Genova* ECLI:EU:C:2014:19

Case C-399/12 *Federal Republic of Germany v Council of the European Union* ECLI:EU:C:2014:2258

Case C-600/14 *Federal Republic of Germany v Council of the European Union* ECLI:EU:C:2017:935

Case 15/17 *Bosphorus Queen Shipping Ltd Corp. v Rajavartiolaitos* ECLI:EU:C:2018:557

Case 15/17 *Bosphorus Queen Shipping Ltd Corp. v Rajavartiolaitos*, Opinion of the AG Wahl ECLI:EU:C:2018:123

ICJ, PCIJ and ITLOS case Documents

PCIJ, *The Case of the S.S. "Lotus" (France v Turkey)*, Series A No 10 <https://icj-cij.org/sites/default/files/permanent-court-of-international-justice/serie_A/A_10/30_Lotus_Arret.pdf> accessed 7 June 2023

ICJ, *North Sea Continental Shelf Cases (Federal Republic of Germany v Denmark; Federal Republic of Germany v Netherlands)* <https://www.icj-cij.org/sites/default/files/case-related/51/051-19690220-JUD-01-00-EN.pdf> accessed 7 June 2023

ICJ, *Legal Consequences for States of the Continued Presence of South Africa in Namibia (South West Africa) Notwithstanding Security Council Resolution 276 (1970)* (Advisory Opinion) 1971<https://www.icj-cij.org/sites/default/files/case-related/53/053-19710621-ADV-01-00-EN.pdf> accessed 19 May 2023

ICJ, *Case concerning the Gabčíkovo-Nagymaros Project (Hungary v Slovakia)* <https://www.icj-cij.org/sites/default/files/case-related/92/092-19970925-JUD-01-00-EN.pdf> accessed 7 June 2023

ITLOS, *The M/V Saiga (No. 2) Case (Saint Vincent and the Grenadines v Guinea)*, Judgment of 1 July 1999, ITLOS Reports 1999

ITLOS, 'Request for an Advisory Opinion submitted by the Commission of Small Island States on Climate Change and International Law (Request for Advisory Opinion submitted to the Tribunal) <https://www.itlos.org/en/main/cases/list-of-cases/request-for-an-advisory-opinion-submitted-by-the-commission-of-small-island-states-on-climate-change-and-international-law-request-for-advisory-opinion-submitted-to-the-tribunal/> accessed 15 December 2023

IMO Documents

– IMO Resolutions

Assembly Res A.719(17) adopted on 6 November 1991, A17/Res.719

Assembly Res A.929(22) adopted on 29 November 2001, A22/Res.929

Assembly Res A.962(23) adopted on 5 December 2003, A 23/Res.962

Assembly Res A.963(23) adopted on 5 December 2003, A 23/Res. 963

Assembly Res A.980(24) adopted on 1 December 2005, A 24/Res.980

Assembly Res A.981 (24) adopted 1 December 2005, A 24/Res.981

Assembly Res A.1070(2) adopted on 4 December 2013, A 28/Res.1070

Assembly Res A.1168(32) adopted on 15 December 2021, A 32/Res.1168

Res LDC.1(0) ('Designation of a Competent Organization to be Responsible for Secretariat Duties in Relation to the Convention') adopted on 18 December 1975, LDC (7) Rev 1

Res MEPC.82(43) adopted on 1 July 1999, MEPC 43/21

Res MEPC.132 (53) adopted on 22 July 2005, MEPC 53/24/Add. 2

Res MEPC.176(58) adopted on 10 October 2008, MEPC 58/23/Add.1

Res MEPC.190(60) adopted on 26 March 2010, MEPC 60/22

Res MEPC.202(62) adopted on 15 July 2011, MEPC 62/24 (corrected by Corrigendum MEPC 62/24/Corr. 4 of 7 September 2012)

Res MEPC.203(62) adopted on 15 July 2011, MEPC 62/24/Add.1

Res MEPC.210(63) adopted on 2 March 2012, MEPC 63/23

Res MEPC.227(64) 2012 adopted on 5 October, MEPC 64/23/Add.1

Res MEPC.237 (65) adopted on 17 May 2013, MEPC 65/22/Add.2

Res MEPC.278(70) adopted on 28 October 2016, MEPC 70/18/Add.1

Res MEPC.282 (70) adopted on 28 October 2016, MEPC 70/18/Add.1

Res MEPC.304 (72) adopted on 13 April 2018, MEPC 72/17/Add.1

Res MEPC.305(73) adopted on 26 October 2018, MEPC 73/19/Add.1

Res MEPC.323 (74) adopted on 17 May 2019, MEPC 74/18/Add.1

Res MEPC.324(75) adopted on 20 November 2020, MEPC 75/18/Add.1

Res MEPC.328(76) adopted on 24 August 2021, MEPC 76/15/Add.1

Res MEPC.338(76) adopted on 17 June 2021, MEPC 76/15/Add.2

Res MEPC.346(78) adopted on 10 June 2022, MEPC 78/17/Add.1

Res MEPC.348(78) adopted on 10 June 2022, MEPC 78/17/Add.1

Res MEPC.349(78) adopted on 10 June 2022, MEPC 78/17/Add.1

Res MEPC.377(80) adopted on 7 July 2023, MEPC 80/17/Add.1

– *MEPC Documents*

'Amendments to MARPOL Annex VI and the NO_x Technical Code: Note by the Secretariat' (17 January 2005) MEPC 53/5/1

'A rebate mechanism for a market-based instrument for international shipping: Submitted by International Union for Conservation of Nature (IUCN)' (29 January 2010) MEPC 60/4/55

'Calculation of recycling capacity for meeting the entry-into-force conditions of the Hong Kong Convention' (20 September 2022) MEPC 79/INF.3

Circular 'Guidance for Submission of Data to the IMO Data Collection System of Fuel Oil Consumption of Ships from a State Not Party to MARPOL Annex VI' (24 June 2022), MEPC.1/Circ.871/Rev. 1

Circular 'Sample Format for the Confirmation of Compliance, Early Submission of the SEEMP Part II on the Ship Fuel Oil Consumption Data Collection Plan and its Timely Verification Pursuant to Regulation 5.4.5 of MARPOL Annex VI' (16 April 2018), MEPC.1/Circ. 876

'Comments on Regulation 14 of MARPOL Annex VI: Submitted by the Islamic Republic of Iran' (20 August 2004) MEPC 52/4/12

'Comments on Annex VI: Submitted by Friends of the Earth (FOEI)'(9 July 2004) MEPC 52/4/4

'Designation of the North Sea area as a SO_x Emission Control Area': Submitted by Austria and others (3 December 1999) MEPC 44/11/4

'Ensuring no net incidence on developing countries from a global maritime Market-Based Mechanism: Submitted by World Wide Fund for Nature (WWF)' (22 December 2011) MEPC 63/5/6

'Full Report of the work undertaken by the Expert Group on Feasibility Study and Impact Assessment of possible Market-based Measures' (13 August 2010) MEPC 61/INF.2

'Legal aspects of the Organization's Work on Greenhouse Gas Emissions in the Context of the Kyoto Protocol: Note by the Secretariat' (1 August 2008) MEPC 58/4/20

'MARPOL Annex VI—Proposal to initiate a revision process': Submitted by Finland and others (15 April 2005) MEPC 53/4/4

'Proposal of the United States to enhance energy efficiency in international shipping: Submitted by the United States' (8 March 2013) MEPC 65/4/19

'Note by the International Maritime Organization to the thirty-fifth session of the Subsidiary Body of Scientific and Technical Advice (SBSTA 15)' <https://seors.unfccc.int/applications/seors/attachments/get_attachment?code=BK9JQY56QGYRELGCZJJR3XDTED1J4OUS> accessed 15 December 2023

'Progress report on follow-up activities: Note by the Secretariat' (17 January 2002) MEPC 47/4

'Reducing Shipping Emissions of Air Pollution – Feasible and Cost-effective Options: Submitted by Friends of the Earth International' (7 April 2005) MEPC 53/4/1

'Report of the Marine Environment Protection Committee on its Forty-Second Session' (16 November 1998) MEPC 42/22

'Report of the Marine Environment Protection Committee on its Forty-Fourth Session' (12 April 2000) MEPC 44/20

'Report of the Marine Environment Protection Committee on its Forty-Seventh Session' (18 March 2002) MEPC 47/20

'Report of the Marine Environment Protection Committee on its Forty-Ninth Session' (8 August 2003) MEPC 49/22

'Report of the Marine Environment Protection Committee on its Fifty-First Session' (22 April 2004) MEPC 51/22

'Report of the Marine Environment Protection Committee on its Fifty-Second Session' (18 October 2004) MEPC 52/24

'Report of the Marine Environment Protection Committee on its Fifty-Third session' (25 July 2005) MEPC 53/24

'Report of the Marine Environment Protection Committee on its Fifty-Fifth Session' (16 October 2006) MEPC 55/23

'Report of the Marine Environment Protection Committee on its Fifty-Seventh Session' (7 April 2008) MEPC 57/21

'Report of the third Intersessional Meeting of the working group on greenhouse gas emissions from ships' (8 April 2011) MEPC 62/5/1

'Report of the Marine Environment Protection Committee on its Fifty-Eighth Session' (16 October 2008) MEPC 58/23

'Report of the Marine Environment Protection Committee on its Fifty-Ninth Session' (27 July 2009) MEPC 59/24

'Report of the Marine Environment Protection Committee on its Sixtieth Session' (12 April 2010) MEPC 60/22

'Report of the Marine Environment Protection Committee on its Sixty-First Session' (6 October 2010) MEPC 61/24

'Report of the Marine Environment Protection Committee on its Sixty-Second Session' (26 July 2011) MEPC 62/24

'Report of the Marine Environment Protection Committee on its Sixty-Second Session' (26 July 2011) MEPC 62/24/Add.1

'Report of the Marine Environment Protection Committee on its Sixty-Third Session' (14 March 2012) MEPC 63/23

'Report of the Marine Environment Protection Committee on its Sixty-Fifth Session' (24 May 2013) MEPC 65/22

'Report of the Marine Environment Protection Committee on its Sixty-Sixth session' (25 April 2014) MEPC 66/21

'Report of the Marine Environment Protection Committee on its Sixty-Ninth session' (13 May 2016) MEPC 69/21

'Report of the Marine Environment Protection Committee on its Seventieth Session (11 November 2016) MEPC 70/18

'Report of the Marine Environment Protection Committee on its Seventieth Session (11 November 2016) Annex 11, MEPC 70/18/Add.1

'Report of the Marine Environment Protection Committee on its Seventy-First Session' (24 July 2017) MEPC 71/17/Add.1

'Report of the Marine Environment Protection Committee on its Seventy-Second Session' (3 May 2018) MEPC 72/17 and MEPC 72/17/Add.1

'Report of the Marine Environment Protection Committee on its Seventy-Third Session' (5 December 2018) MEPC73/19/Add.1

'Report on the outcome of the Informal Cross Government/Industry Scientific Group of Experts established to evaluate the effects of the different fuel options proposed under the revision of MARPOL Annex VI' (20 December 2007) MEPC 57/4

'SO_x Emissions: Submitted by Friends of the Earth International' (28 December 2001) MEPC 47/4/4

'Sulphur monitoring 2001: Submitted by the Netherlands' (13 Junc 2002) MEPC 48/INF.4

– *Other IMO Documents*

Conference of Parties to the International Convention for the Prevention of Pollution from ships 1973, modified by the Protocol of 1978 relating thereto, 'Text of the Protocol of 1997 to amend the International convention for the prevention of Pollution from Ships, 1973, as modified by the Protocol 1978 relating thereto as adopted by the Conference' (28 October 1997) MP/CONF.3/34

Conference of Parties to the International Convention for the Prevention of Pollution from Ships, 1973, as modified by the Protocol of 1978 relating thereto, 'Text of Conference Resolutions 1 to 8 and the Technical Code on Control of Emission of Nitrogen Oxides from Marine Diesel Engines' (22 October 1997) MP/CONF.3/35 [To the knowledge of the author, this document is not publicly available in full. The complete document was provided by the Dag Hammarskjöld Library of the UN. The author has a digital copy that can be made available upon request.]

'Convention on the Prevention of Marine Pollution by Dumping of Wastes and Other Matter', Consolidated version <https://wwwcdn.imo.org/localresources/en/OurWork/Environment/Documents/LC1972.pdf> accessed 12 May 2023

'Fifty years of ocean protection: Major milestones since adoption of the London Convention in 1972 regulating dumping at sea' <https://wwwcdn.imo.org/localresources/en/MediaCentre/HotTopics/Documents/London%20Convention%20timeline_FINAL_(16-9-22)_01.pdf> accessed 12 May 2023

'Guidelines for Voluntary use of the Ship Energy Efficiency Operational Indicator (EEOI)' (17 August 2009), MEPC.1/Circ.684

'IMO—What it is' <https://wwwcdn.imo.org/localresources/en/About/Documents/What%20it%20is%20Oct%202013_Web.pdf> accessed 12 May 2023

'International Conference on the Safe and Environmentally Sound Recycling of Ships, Adoption of the Final Act and any Instruments, Recommendations and Resolutions resulting from the Work of the Conference, Hong Kong International Convention on the Safe and Environmentally Sound Recycling of Ships, 2009,' (19 May 2009) SR/CONF/45

Intersessional Meeting of the Working Group on Reduction of GHG Emissions, 'Existing IMO activity related to reducing GHG emissions in the shipping sector' (21 February 2017) ISWG-GHG 1/2

Intersessional Meeting of the Working Group on Reduction of GHG Emissions from Ships, 'GHG emissions scenario to reach a temperature target of 1.75°C and candidate short-, mid- and long-term measures: Submitted by OECD' (22 September 2017) ISWG-GHG 2/2/14

'MARPOL – 25 years' <https://wwwcdn.imo.org/localresources/en/KnowledgeCentre/ConferencesMeetings/FocusOnIMOArchives/Focus%20on%20IMO%20-%20MARPOL%20-%2025%20years%20(October%201998).pdf> accessed 12 May 2023

'Status of IMO Treaties: Comprehensive information on the status of multilateral Conventions and instruments in respect of which the International Maritime Organization or its Secretary-General performs depository or other functions' (last updated 19 April 2023) <https://wwwcdn.imo.org/localresources/en/About/Conventions/StatusOfConventions/Status%202023.pdf> accessed 12 May 2023

'Status of Treaties' <https://wwwcdn.imo.org/localresources/en/About/Conventions/StatusOfConventions/Status%20of%20IMO%20Treaties.pdf> accessed 18 May 2023

Sub-Committee on Bulk Liquids and Gases, 'Report to the Maritime Safety Committee and the Marine Environment Protection Committee' (11 May 2007) BLG 11/16

'2011 Guidelines for the Development of the Ship Recycling Plan', MEPC.196(62)

'2012 Guidelines for Safe and Environmentally Sound Ship Recycling', MEPC.210(63)

'2012 Guidelines for the Authorization of the Ship Recycling Facilities', MEPC.211(63)

'2012 Guidelines for the survey and certification of ships under the Hong Kong Convention', MEPC.222(64)

'2012 Guidelines for the inspection of ships under the Hong Kong Convention', MEPC.223(64)

'2015 Guidelines for the development of the Inventory of the Hazardous Materials', MEPC.269(68)

WTO Body Decisions and Documents

– Decisions

Argentina: Measures Relating to Trade in Goods and Services—Report of the Appellate Body (14 April 2016) WT/DS453/AB/R

Brazil: Certain Measures Concerning Taxation and Charges—Report of the Panel (30 August 2017) WT/DS472/R, WT/DS497/R

Brazil: Measures Affecting Imports of Retreaded Tyres—Report of the Appellate Body (3 December 2007) WT/DS332/AB/R

China: Measures Affecting Trading Rights and Distribution Services for Certain Publications and Audiovisual Entertainment Products—Report of the Panel (12 August 2009) WT/DS363/R

China: Measures Affecting Trading Rights and Distribution Services for Certain Publications and Audiovisual Entertainment Products—Report of the Appellate Body (21 December 2009) WT/DS363/AB/R

China: Measures Related to the Exportation of Rare Earths, Tungsten, and Molybdenum—Report of the Appellate Body (7 August 2014) WT/DS431/AB/R, WT/DS432/AB/R, WT/DS433/AB/R

China: Measures Related to the Exportation of Various Raw Materials—Report of the Appellate Body (30 January 2012) WT/DS394/AB/R, WT/DS395/AB/R, WT/DS398/AB/R

Colombia: Measures relating to the Importation of Textiles, Apparel and Footwear—Report of the Appellate Body (7 June 2016) WT/DS461/AB/R

European Communities: Conditions for the Granting of Tariff Preferences to Developing Countries— Report of the Panel (1 December 2003) WT/DS246/R

European Communities: Measures Affecting Asbestos and Asbestos-Containing Products —Report of the Appellate Body (12 March 2001) WT/DS135/AB/R

European Communities: Measures Affecting Trade in Commercial Vessels—Report of the Panel (22 April 2005) WT/DS301/R

European Communities: Regime for the Importation, Sale and Distribution of Bananas—Report of the Appellate Body (9 September 1997) WT/DS27/AB/R

European Communities: Measure Prohibiting the Importation and Marketing of Seal Products—Report of the Appellate Body (22 May 2014) WT/DS400/AB/R, WT/DS401/AB/R

India: Certain Measures Relating to Solar Cells and Solar Products—Report of the Appellate Body (16 September 2016) WT/DS456/AB/R

Indonesia: Importation of Horticultural Products, Animals and Animal Products—*Report of the Appellate Body* (9 November 2017) WT/DS477/AB/R, WT/DS478/AB/R

Japan: Taxes on Alcoholic Beverages—Report of the Appellate Body (4 October 1996) WT/DS8/AB/R, WT/DS10/AB/R, WT/DS11/AB/R

Korea: Measures Affecting Imports of Fresh, Chilled and Frozen Beef—Report of the Appellate Body (11 December 2000) WT/DS161/AB/R, WT/DS169/AB/R

Mexico: Tax Measures on Soft Drinks and Other Beverages—Report of the Appellate Body (6 March 2006) WT/DS308/AB/R

United States: Import Prohibition of Certain Shrimp and Shrimp Products—Report of the Appellate Body (12 October 1998) WT/DS58/AB/R

United States: Measures Affecting the Cross-Border Supply of Gambling and Betting Services—Report of the Panel (10 November 2004) WT/DS285/R

United States: Measures Affecting the Cross-Border Supply of Gambling and Betting Services—Report of the Appellate Body (7 April 2005) WT/DS285/AB/R

United States: Measures Concerning the Importation, Marketing and Sale of Tuna and Tuna Products: *Recourse to Article 21.5 of the DSU by Mexico—Report of the Appellate Body* (20 November 2015) WT/DS381/AB/RW

United States: Measures Concerning the Importation, Marketing and Sale of Tuna and Tuna Products: Recourse to Article 21.5 of the DSU by the United States/Second Recourse to Article 21.5 of the DSU by Mexico (14 December 2014) WT/DS381/AB/RW/USA, WT/DS381/AB/RW2

United States: Standards for Reformulated and Conventional Gasoline—Report of the Appellate Body (29 April 1996) WT/DS2/AB

– Documents

Decision on Maritime Transport Services: Adopted by the Council for Trade in Services on 28 June 1996, S/L/24 (3 July 1996)

European Union: Schedule of Specific Commitments of the EU, GATS/SC/157 (7 May 2019)

WTO Members' GATS commitments, MFN exemptions, and preferences under the LDC Services Waiver as notified by Members <http://i-tip.wto.org/services/Search.aspx> accessed 27 March 2023

WTO Analytical Index GATS - Article II (Practice) <https://www.wto.org/english/res_e/publications_e/ai17_e/gats_art2_oth.pdf> accessed 19 May 2023

Other Documents of European or International Bodies

Andersen A B, 'Worker safety in the ship breaking industries' (International Labour Office, 2001) <http://www.ilo.org/wcmsp5/groups/public/---ed_protect/---protrav/---safework/documents/publication/wcms_110357.pdf> accessed 10 February 2023

BC, 'Conference of the Parties to the Basel Convention on the Control of Transboundary Movements of Hazardous Wastes and Their Disposal on its tenth meeting' (11 August 2011), 'Compilation of the completed tables and submissions received pursuant to decision OEWG VII/12', UNEP/CHW.10/INF/18

—— 'Technical Guidelines for the Environmentally Sound Management of the Full and Partial Dismantling of Ships' <http://www.basel.int/Portals/4/Basel%20Convention/docs/meetings/sbc/workdoc/techgships-e.pdf> accessed 18 May 2023

—— 'Report of the Conference of the Parties to the Basel Convention on the Control of Transboundary Movements of Hazardous Wastes and their Disposal' (25 January 2005) UNEP/CHW.7/33

—— 'Report of the Conference of the Parties to the Basel Convention on the Control of Transboundary Movements of Hazardous Wastes and Their Disposal on its tenth meeting' (1 November 2011) UNEP/CHW.10/28

EMSA, 'Sulphur Inspection Guidance: Directive (EU) 2016/802' (December 2019) <https://www.emsa.europa.eu/publications/reports/download/5910/2407/23.html> accessed 7 June 2023

ILO, 'Minutes of the 291st session' (November 2004) GB.291/PV, 36

—— 'Safety and health in shipbreaking: Guidelines for Asian countries and Turkey' (2004) <http://www.ilo.org/wcmsp5/groups/public/---ed_protect/---protrav/---safework/documents/normativeinstrument/wcms_107689.pdf> accessed 10 February 2023

Joint ILO/IMO/BC Group on Ship Scrapping (2nd session), 'Report of the Joint Working Group' (14 December 2005) ILO/IMO/BC WG 2/11

IPCC, *Revised 1996 IPCC Guidelines for National Greenhouse Gas Inventories* <https://www.ipcc-nggip.iges.or.jp/public/gl/invs4.html> accessed 19 May 2023

OECD, 'Decision of the Council Concerning the Revision of Decision C(92)39/Final on the Control of Transboundary Movements of Wastes destined for Recovery Operations' (15 March 2004) C(2001)107/Final

UNEP, 'Fourth Revised Draft Convention on the Control of Transboundary Movements of Hazardous Wastes' (14 September 1988) UNEP/WG.189/L.2Rev. 1

—— 'Legal Aspects of the Full and Partial Dismantling of Ships' (22 April 2002) UNEP/CHW/LWG/5/4

—— 'Note by the Executive Director on some Points of the Hazardous Wastes Convention which were not resolved at the Fourth Session of the Ad Hoc Working Group' (10 February 1989), UNEP/WG.191/2

UNFCCC, 'Communications from Parties included in Annex I to the Conventions: Guidelines, schedule and process for consideration, Addendum: Detailed Information on Electricity Trade and International Bunker Fuels' (26 June 1996) FCCC/SBSTA/1996/9/Add.2

—— 'Report of the Ad Hoc working Group on Long-term Cooperative Action under the Convention on its Seventh Session, held in Bangkok from 28 September to 9 October, and Barcelona from 2 to 6 November 2009' (20 November 2009) FCCC/AWGLCA/2009/14

——'Report of the Conference of the Parties on its First Session, held at Berlin from 28 March to 7 April 1995' (6 June 1995) FCCC/CP1995/7/Add.1

—— 'Report of the Conference of the Parties on its Third session, held at Kyoto from 1 to 11 December 1997, Addendum: Part Two: Action taken by the Conference of the Parties at its Third session (25 March 1998) FCCC/CP/1997/7/Add.1, Decision 2/CP.3

—— 'Report of the Subsidiary Body for Scientific and Technological Advice on the Work of its First Session held at Geneva from 28 August to 1 September 1995' (5 October 1995) FCCC/SBSTA/1995/3

—— 'Report of the Subsidiary Body for Scientific and Technological Advice on the Work of its Second Session, held at Geneva from 27 February to 4 March 1996' (25 April 1996) FCCC/SBSTA/1996/8

—— 'Report of the Subsidiary Body for Scientific and Technological Advice on the Work of its Fourth Session, Geneva, 16–18 December 1996' (27 January 1997) FCCC/SBSTA/1996/20

—— Subsidiary Body for Scientific and Technological Advice, 'Chronological development [of bunker fuels] under the SBSTA – archive' <https://unfccc.int/sites/default/files/resource/Chronological%20development%20bunkers%20under%20the%20SBSTA.pdf> accessed 19 May 2023

—— Subsidiary Body for Scientific and Technological Advice, 'Communications from Parties included in Annex I to the Conventions: Guidelines, schedule and process for consideration, Possible revisions to the guidelines for the preparation of national communications by Parties included in Annex I to the Convention, Addendum: Methodological Issues' (24 October 1996) FCCC/SBSTA/1996/9/Add.1

UNGA, 'Report of the International Law Commission: Fifty-eighth session' (2006) A/61/10

UNGA Res 43/53 (6 December 1988) UN Doc A/RES/43/53

UNGA Res 76/300 (28 July 2022) UN Doc A/RES/76/300

Diplomatic conferences documents

Final Act of the Intergovernmental Conference on the Convention on the Dumping of Wastes at Sea, see (1972) 11 ILM, 1291

Ministerial Declaration of the Third International Conference on the Protection of the North Sea, The Hague, 8 March 1990 <https://www.ospar.org/site/assets/files/1239/3nsc-1990-hague_declaration.pdf> accessed 2 June 2023

Report of the United Nations Conference on the Human Environment, Stockholm, 5-16 June 1972, A/CONF.48/14/Rev.1, Recommendations 86 (e) and 92 (a), 22-23

'Second International Conference on the Protection of the North Sea, London, 24-25 November 1987' <https://www.ospar.org/site/assets/files/1239/2nsc-1987_london_declaration.pdf> accessed 2 June 2023

United Nations Conference on Trade and Employment held at Havana, Cuba from 21 November 1947 to 24 March 1948, 'Reports of Committees and Principal Sub-Committees' <https://www.wto.org/gatt_docs/English/SULPDF/90180096.pdf> accessed 27 March 2023

Websites

Arctic Portal Library, 'Arctic EEZ-map in the European Union' <http://library.arcticportal.org/1504/1/eu_eez.jpg> accessed 7 June 2023

BIMCO, 'Position Statement on "Keep Shipping Regulation Global"' <https://www.bimco.org/about-us-and-our-members/bimco-statements/01-keep-regulation-global> accessed 18 May 2023

Carbon Pricing Leadership Coalition, 'What is Carbon Pricing' <https://www.carbonpricingleadership.org/what/> accessed 31 March 2023

Comer B, 'Zero-Emission Shipping and the Paris Agreement: Why the IMO Needs to Pick a Zero Date and Set Interim Targets in its Revised Strategy' (8 September 2021) <https://theicct.org/zero-emission-shipping-and-the-paris-agreement-why-the-imo-needs-to-pick-a-zero-date-and-set-interim-targets-in-its-revised-ghg-strategy/> accessed 6 April 2023

Comer B and Carvalho F, 'IMO's Newly Revised GHG Strategy: What it means for Shipping and the Paris Agreement <https://theicct.org/marine-imo-updated-ghg-strategy-jul23/> accessed 15 December 2023

Commission, 'Ships: EU rules on ship recycling aim to make it greener and safer, and to reduce the negative environmental and social impacts of ship recycling' <http://ec.europa.eu/environment/waste/ships/eu_policy.htm> accessed 18 May 2023

Council Voting Calculator <https://www.consilium.europa.eu/en/council-eu/voting-system/voting-calculator/> accessed 7 June 2023

EGCSA, 'Regulations and Guidelines: The International Maritime Organization – MARPOL Annex VI' <https://www.egcsa.com/regulatory/> accessed 7 June 2023

EMSA, 'The EU Maritime Profile—the maritime cluster in the EU' <https://emsa.europa.eu/eumaritimeprofile/section-2-the-eu-maritime-cluster.html> accessed 15 December 2023

—— THETIS-MRV <https://mrv.emsa.europa.eu/#public/emission-report> accessed 26 May 2023

Eurostat, 'International trade in goods by mode of transport' <https://ec.europa.eu/eurostat/statistics-explained/index.php?title=International_trade_in_goods_by_mode_of_transport> accessed 12 May 2023

—— 'Maritime freight and vessel statistics' <https://ec.europa.eu/eurostat/statistics-explained/index.php?title=Maritime_freight_and_vessels_statistics> accessed 12 May 2023

EGCSA, 'What is an exhaust cleaning system' <https://www.egcsa.com/technical-reference/what-is-an-exhaust-gas-cleaning-system/> accessed 2 June 2023

ICCT, 'New IMO Study Highlights Sharp Rise in Short-Lived Climate Pollution' (Press Release, 4 August 2020) <https://theicct.org/news/fourth-imo-ghg-study-finalreport-pr-20200804> accessed 6 February 2023

IEA, 'International Maritime Organization agreed to first long-term plan to curb emissions' <https://www.iea.org/commentaries/international-maritime-organization-agrees-to-first-long-term-plan-to-curb-emissions> accessed 19 May 2023

IMO, 'Address of the Secretary-General at the Opening of the Ninety-Fourth session of the Maritime Safety Committee (17 to 21 November 2014)' <https://www.imo.org/en/MediaCentre/SecretaryGeneral/Pages/MSC-94-opening.aspx> accessed 18 May 2023

——'Convention on the International Maritime Organization' <https://www.imo.org/en/About/Conventions/Pages/Convention-on-the-International-Maritime-Organization.aspx> accessed 12 May 2023

—— 'Convention on the Prevention of Marine Pollution by Dumping of Wastes and Other Matter' <https://www.imo.org/en/OurWork/Environment/Pages/London-Convention-Protocol.aspx> accessed 12 May 2023

—— 'Emission Control Areas (ECAs) designated under MARPOL Annex VI' <https://www.imo.org/en/OurWork/Environment/Pages/Emission-Control-Areas-(ECAs)-designated-under-regulation-13-of-MARPOL-Annex-VI-(NOx-emission-control).aspx> accessed 2 June 2023

—— 'Fourth Greenhouse Gas Study 2020: Key findings from the Fourth IMO GHG Study 2020 <https://www.imo.org/en/OurWork/Environment/Pages/Fourth-IMO-Greenhouse-Gas-Study-2020.aspx> accessed 31 March 2023

—— GISIS: Annex VI <https://gisis.imo.org/Public/MARPOL6/Notifications.aspx?Reg=19.6> accessed 19 May 2023

—— IMO, 'Hong Kong ship recycling Convention set to enter into force: Bangladesh and Liberia trigger entry into force of Convention for the Safe and Environmentally Sound Recycling of Ship' <https://www.imo.org/en/MediaCentre/PressBriefings/pages/Hong-Kong-Convention-set-to-enter-into-force-.aspx> accessed 8 December 2023

—— 'Improving the Energy Efficiency of Ships' <https://www.imo.org/en/OurWork/Environment/Pages/Improving%20the%20energy%20efficiency%20of%20ships.aspx> accessed 31 March 2023

—— 'Index of Resolutions' <https://www.imo.org/en/KnowledgeCentre/IndexofIMOResolutions/Pages/Default.aspx> accessed 2 June 2023

—— 'Index of MEPC Resolutions and Guidelines related to MARPOL Annex VI' <https://www.imo.org/en/OurWork/Environment/Pages/Index-of-MEPC-Resolutions-and-Guidelines-related-to-MARPOL-Annex-VI.aspx> accessed 2 June 2023

—— 'Index of MEPC Resolution and Guidelines related to MARPOL Annex VI: Guidelines related to Energy Efficiency of Ships <https://www.imo.org/en/OurWork/Environment/Pages/Index-of-MEPC-Resolutions-and-Guidelines-related-to-MARPOL-Annex-VI.aspx> accessed 19 May 2023

——'Integrated Technical Cooperation Programme (ITCP)' <https://www.imo.org/en/OurWork/TechnicalCooperation/ Pages/ITCP.aspx> accesses 19 May 2023

—— 'International Convention for the Prevention of Pollution from Ships (MARPOL)' <https://www.imo.org/en/About/Conventions/Pages/International-Convention-for-the-Prevention-of-Pollution-from-Ships-(MARPOL).aspx> accessed 12 May 2023

—— 'Joint ILO/IMO/BC Working Group on Ship Scrapping', see <https://www.imo.org/en/OurWork/Environment/Pages/JointILOIMOBCWorkingGroupOnShipScrapping.aspx> accessed 18 May 2023

—— 'London Convention (LDC, LC) and London Protocol (LP)' <https://www.imo.org/en/KnowledgeCentre/IndexofIMOResolutions/Pages/LDC-LC-LP.aspx> accessed 12 May 2023

—— 'Market-Based Measures' <https://www.imo.org/en/OurWork/Environment/Pages/Market-Based-Measures.aspx> accessed 19 May 2023

—— 'Member State Audit Scheme' <https://www.imo.org/en/ourwork/msas/pages/default.aspx> accessed 11 April 2023

—— 'Member States, IGOs and NGOs' <https://www.imo.org/en/About/Membership/Pages/Default.aspx> accessed 12 May 2023

—— 'Non-Governmental International Organizations which have been granted consultative status with IMO' <https://www.imo.org/en/OurWork/ERO/Pages/NGOsInConsultativeStatus.aspx> accessed 12 May 2023

—— 'Port State Control' <https://www.imo.org/en/OurWork/IIIS/Pages/Port%20State%20Control.aspx> accessed 12 May 2023

—— 'Reduced limit on sulphur in marine fuel implemented smoothly through 2020' (28 January 2021) <https://www.imo.org/en/MediaCentre/PressBriefings/pages/02-IMO-2020.aspx> accessed 2 June 2023

Mikelis N, 'The IMO Ship Recycling Regulations: A perspective' (Cambridge Academy of Transport, July 2009) <https://wwwcdn.imo.org/localresources/en/KnowledgeCentre/Docu ments/The%20IMO%20ship%20recycling%20regulations%20-%20N.%20Mikelis.pdf> accessed 10 February 2023

NGO Shipbreaking Platform, 'Annual Lists of Scrapped Ships' <https://shipbreakingplatform.org/annual-lists/> accessed 18 May 2023

—— 'Cash Buyers' <https://shipbreakingplatform.org/our-work/the-problem/cash-buyers/> accessed 16 October 2023

OECD, 'Tax' <https://www.oecd-ilibrary.org/taxation/tax/indicator-group/english_76e12892-en> accessed 15 December 2023

Oxford English Dictionary, 'marine, n & adj' (September 2023) <https://www.oed.com/search/dictionary/?q=marine> accessed 2 October 2023

—— 'maritime, adj & n' (September 2023) <https://www.oed.com/search/dictionary/?q=maritime> accessed 2 October 2023 riviera, ‘“Complexity and confusion” rule in SECA land’ <https://www.rivieramm.com/news-content-hub/news-content-hub/complexity-and-confusion-rule-in-seca-land-51949> accessed 7 June 2023

Safety4Sea, ‘The world’s first major oil tanker disaster’ <https://safety4sea.com/cm-torrey-canyon-the-worlds-first-major-oil-tanker-disaster/> accessed 12 May 2023

Secretariat of the Basel Convention, ‘Ship Dismantling’ <http://www.basel.int/Implementation/ShipDismantling/Overview/tabid/2762/Default.aspx> accessed 18 May 2023

—— Secretariat of the Basel Convention, ‘Legal Aspects’ <http://www.basel.int/Implementation/ShipDismantling/LegalAspects/Overview/tabid/2766/Default.aspx> accessed 3 March 2023

The London P&I Club, ‘North Sea SECA in force – 11 August 2007’ <https://www.londonpandi.com/knowledge/news-alerts/north-sea-seca-in-force-11-august-2007/> accessed 7 June 2023

Verifavia Shipping, ‘Verifavia inks as IMO DCS verifier for Liberian vessels’ <https://www.verifavia-shipping.com/shipping-carbon-emissions-verification/press-media-verifavia-inks-as-imo-dcs-verifier-for-liberian-vessels-273.php> accessed 3 April 2023

WTO, Guide to reading the GATS Schedules of Specific Commitments and the List of Article II (MFN) Exemptions’ <https://www.wto.org/english/tratop_e/serv_e/guide1_e.htm> accessed 28 March 2023

—— ‘Maritime Transport’ <https://www.wto.org/english/tratop_e/serv_e/transport_e/transport_maritime_e.htm> accessed 27 March 2023